GIVE US A KING

THE UNITED KINGDOM

SAUL, DAVID, SOLOMON
AND
THE WISDOM LITERATURE

by
Bob and Sandra Waldron

© Guardian of Truth Foundation 2005. All rights reserved. No part of this book may be reproduced in any form without written permission from the publisher. Printed in the United States of America.

ISBN 1-58427-110-8

Guardian of Truth Foundation
P.O. Box 9670
Bowling Green, Kentucky 42102

Table of Contents

The United Kingdom, Introduction 1

The Kingdom Begins:
    The Reign of Saul 4
    The Reign of David 48
    The Reign of Solomon 107

Appendix: The Wisdom Literature
    The Wisdom Literature, Introduction 135
    The Book of Job 138
    The Psalms 158
    Proverbs 176
    Ecclesiastes 194
    The Song of Solomon 213

The United Kingdom

Periods of Bible History:

   Creation Stories
   Flood
   Scattering of the People
   The Patriarchs
   The Exodus
   Wilderness Wandering
   Conquest of the Land
   Judges

   *United Kingdom

      *Saul
      *David
      *Solomon

   Divided Kingdom
   Judah Alone
   Captivity
   Return from Captivity
   Years of Silence
   Life of Christ
   Early Church
   Letters to Christians

At the close of the time of the judges, the people asked Samuel for an earthly king. By this choice the Israelites continued to show their tendency to reject God's plan and His order of things. God told Samuel to warn Israel how their king would treat them, but then to give them one. Beginning with Saul, there were three kings who ruled over the whole land: Saul, David, and Solomon. Thus, we call this period of history the United Kingdom. Review your periods of Bible history and look carefully at how this period fits with the overall outline of the Bible.

In much of the history of Israel, we have a contrast between obedience and disobedience, between men who loved and revered God and men who did not. Just such a contrast is made between Saul, David, and Solomon. Saul did what God said only if it were in keeping with plans he already had. David would not take a step without God's guidance; he loved God deeply and revered Him; God's commandments were his delight. Solomon is an example of a man who was given so many advantages and opportunities that they contributed to his downfall. How many times in history has a man been given gifts lavishly only to squander and waste them?

The stories of these men are fascinating narratives in themselves, but the lessons to be learned are valuable beyond measure. Without making sermons of every verse, we want to be sure that the lessons in contrasts are impressed upon the minds of our students.

Suggestions for teaching:

The value of God's warnings, and of His promises and prophecies, depends upon whether we notice them as they come true. Be sure to present the warnings God told Samuel to give the people concerning their king. Go back to Deuteronomy 17:14-20 and look at the warnings Moses gave concerning the days when Israel would have a king. Keep these warnings before the class through all the stories of Saul, David, and Solomon to observe how the kings prove that God's warnings were correct.

Many people play important roles in the story of the United Kingdom. The names can become confusing if there is not a special effort made to identify each one as a separate individual. Therefore, we suggest you post a blank chart in your room, and as you introduce a new character in your story, add his name to your chart. As each event unfolds, take time to notice exactly which characters are part of the story, and be sure you and your students know their identity. We identify best with these people in our own lives when we know them as individual people, with strengths and weaknesses just as we have. Review the names on your list frequently.

Books that tell this period of history:

First Samuel tells about the lives of three men: Samuel, Saul, and David. The first seven chapters are primarily about Samuel. Chapters 8 through 15 are primarily about Saul, and the rest of the book is primarily about David and his ascendancy over Saul. That means that the first seven chapters fit into the period of the Judges and we included that information in our book about that period of history (*In the Days of the Judges*). Information about the United Kingdom begins in chapter 8 when the people ask for a king.

The last chapter of 1 Samuel tells of the death of Saul. The book of 1 Chronicles tells that same story in chapter 10. From that point forward, the book of 1 Chronicles tells of the same period that 2 Samuel tells about. David's death and the appointing of Solomon as king are described in 1 Kings 1 and 2. The book of 2 Chronicles begins with Solomon as the new king. Therefore, the period of the United Kingdom covers 1 Samuel 8-31, the whole books of 2 Samuel and 1 Chronicles, the first 11 chapters of 1 Kings, and the first 9 chapters of 2 Chronicles.

It was also during the period of the United Kingdom that most of the wisdom literature was written. The book of Job tells of an event that happened very early in the history of mankind, but it seems to have been written down in its present form during the days of the kings. Psalms is a collection of songs and poetry written by different writers in different circumstances during the period of the Old Testament, but we include a look at the book in this period of history because David wrote about half of the Psalms. Proverbs is a collection of wise sayings that Solomon collected and included in the scriptures with the approval of the Holy Spirit. Solomon either wrote the book of Ecclesiastes himself, or the writer used his life as the example of one searching for the reason for life under the sun. Psalm 72 and the Song of Solomon are the only songs that Solomon wrote that we have recorded in the Bible. As we proceed with the history of the period, we include a look at some of David's psalms that can be fitted into the framework of the history itself. Then, in the appendix, we take a brief look at these and the other books of wisdom literature. It is beyond the scope of this study to go into a detailed study of the books.

Time sequence for this study:

If you are studying this book and its period of history in the sequence of study we have planned for in our series of books, allow two full quarters (Sunday morning and Wednesday night) to cover the material. It is a very full period of history, and the Bible devotes many chapters to the period. God must want us to know the period well since He included so many chapters in the Bible about it.

Map study:

It is necessary to know your map of the land of Israel in order to understand Bible history. Each place mentioned in the Bible text was a real place and it is possible to know the approximate location of most of the places mentioned. Therefore, we have included the maps that fit this period of Bible history. First, here in the front of the book, there is a map of the land as it was divided between the tribes in the days of Joshua. This is the land as God intended it to be. Compare the other maps to this one as we come to them in our study. As you make your comparison, look for the reasons why the maps are different. On the blank maps included for your use, add the names of places mentioned in the history as you come to them. Learn your maps well.

The Kingdom Begins
The Reign of Saul
1 Samuel 8 - 31

Creation Stories
The Flood
Scattering of the People
The Patriarchs
The Exodus
Wilderness Wandering
Conquest of the Land
Judges

*United Kingdom

　*Saul
　David
　Solomon

Divided Kingdom
Judah Alone
Captivity
Return from Captivity
Years of Silence
Life of Christ
Early Church
Letters to Christians

The people ask for a king (1 Sam. 8:1-22):
　Samuel was a righteous man who judged Israel faithfully during a long lifetime, but his sons were not like their father. Samuel made them judges in Beersheba, but they took bribes and were not good men. The people were very unhappy; the misbehavior of Samuel's sons, plus the encroachments of the enemies around them, created unrest in Israel.

　The elders of the people came to Samuel at Ramah and said, "Look, you are old, and your sons are not following in your ways. Make us a king to judge us so that we can be like the other nations." Samuel was very upset at their request because the thing that made Israel unique as a nation was their special relationship with God — He was their King. Samuel also felt that their request for a king was a personal rejection of him as their ruler as well as a rejection of God as their king.

　God told Samuel, "Do as the people have asked, because they are not rejecting you but me. They are acting as they have since I brought them up out of Egypt. Many times they have forsaken me. So do as they have asked, but first tell them plainly how their king will treat them."

　Samuel warned the people: "Instead of working for yourselves as you have done since you entered the land, you will soon be working for your king. Your sons will be his horsemen, and your daughters will be his cooks. Instead of paying no taxes, soon your king will take the best of your fields and of your vineyards to give to his officials and friends. Instead of having an army only when an enemy attacks, soon your sons will form a standing army. And when you are tired of oppression from your king, and ask God to remove him, God will not listen to your pleas."

　In spite of the warnings, the people insisted, "No, we want a king! We want to be like all the nations and have a king who will judge us and who will go out before us in battles."

God said, "Listen to them and give them a king." So Samuel sent the people home with the promise that God would select a man to be their king.

Saul is anointed king privately (1 Sam. 9:1-10:16):

A man named Kish, of the tribe of Benjamin, had lost some donkeys, and he sent his son Saul to look for them. Now Saul was an awesome young man, who stood head and shoulders above ordinary men. Kish told him, "Take one of the servants and go look for the donkeys which I have lost."

After searching a couple of days in southern Ephraim, Saul and his servant came to Zuph in Benjamin. They had had no luck. Saul said to his servant, "Come on; let's go back home, before my father becomes more worried about us than he is about his donkeys."

The servant answered, "Look, there is a man of God in this city. He is highly respected, and everything he says turns out as he foretells it. Let's go to him. Perhaps he can tell us where we should go to find the donkeys."

Saul asked, "But if we go, what gift shall we give the man? Our bread is gone; we have nothing to give him."

The servant replied, "I have here a fourth of a shekel of silver. I will give it to the man of God to tell us where we need to go."

In the early days of Israel, when a man went to ask God for information, he would say, "Come, let's go to the seer," because, in those days, a prophet *(one who tells forth)* was called a seer *(one who sees or observes)*.

Saul said, "Good enough. Come on and let us go."

As they approached the city, they found young girls going out to draw water, and they asked them, "Is the seer here?"

The girls answered, "Yes, he is. He has come because the people are having a sacrifice today at the high place. As soon as you go into the city, you should find him easily, because he will be going to the high place to eat, and the people will not eat until he comes to bless the sacrifice."

As they were going into the city, sure enough, they met Samuel on his way to the sacrifice. What Saul and his servant did not know was that the day before Jehovah had told Samuel, "Tomorrow about this time, I will send your way a man from the land of Benjamin. You will anoint him to be leader of my people, and he will save my people from the Philistines." Therefore, when Samuel saw Saul, the Lord said, "This is the man I told you about. This is the one I wish to bear authority over my people."

When they met, Saul asked Samuel, "Will you please tell me where the seer's house is?"

Samuel said, "I am the seer. Go before me to the high place because you two are going to eat with me today. In the morning I will send you on your way. As for the donkeys that were lost three days ago, don't worry about them, because they have been found. Besides, to whom do all the desirable things of Israel belong? Is it not to you and your father's house?" *(Samuel was hinting to Saul of the great honor about to be given to him.)*

Saul, perplexed by Samuel's words, said, "Am I not a Benjamite, of the smallest tribe in Israel, and isn't my family the least significant family in Benjamin? Why are you speaking to me like this?"

At the feast, Samuel took Saul and his servant to the guest room and seated them in the place of greatest prominence among the thirty people or so who were gathered together. Samuel told the cook, "Bring me the cut of meat which I told you to set aside."

The cook brought the leg or shoulder and set it before Saul, saying, "Here is the portion I saved for you. Eat, because it was kept for you for this occasion which Samuel arranged."

After they came down from the high place back into the city, Samuel talked with Saul upon the rooftop. The next morning, at early sunrise, Samuel called Saul to the rooftop again and said, "It is time for me to send you on your way."

Samuel walked with Saul out into the street and toward the city limits. As they approached the edge of the city, Samuel said to Saul, "Let the servant go on ahead" (and the servant quickly did so), "but you remain here so that I can tell you what God says." Samuel took out a small bottle of oil and poured it on Saul's head; then he kissed him and said:

> Is it not you that Jehovah has chosen to be prince over His inheritance? When you leave here, you will find two men by Rachel's sepulchre. They will say, "The donkeys you were hunting have been found, and your father has stopped worrying about the donkeys and is now worried about you." You will go from there till you come to the oak of Tabor where you will meet three men going up to God at Bethel. One will be carrying three kids, one will have three loaves of bread, and one will have a skin of wine. They will greet you and will give you two loaves of bread which you will accept from them.
>
> After that, you will come to Gibeah where the Philistines have a garrison. When you get near the city, you will meet a band of prophets coming down from the high place with a psaltery, a timbrel, a pipe, and a harp, and they will be prophesying. The Spirit of God will come upon you, and you will prophesy with them, and you will become a new man. When these signs happen, then take whatever actions seem appropriate, because God is with you. And if you go to Gilgal before me, I will come to offer burnt offerings and peace offerings. Wait seven days, till I come to you and show you what you are to do.

As Saul went on his way, all these signs came to pass. As a result of his prophesying, people began to say, "What has happened to the son of Kish? Is Saul also among the prophets?" So this expression became a proverb.

When Saul arrived home, his uncle asked him, "Where did you go?"

Saul said, "To hunt for the donkeys, and when we couldn't find them, we came to Samuel."

Saul's uncle asked, "What did he say?"

"He told us that the donkeys were found." But Saul said nothing about being anointed king.

Notice the humility of Saul at this point. When Samuel first hinted at God's plan for him, Saul discounted it because he was from the smallest of the tribes and from an insignificant family. (See Judges 19-21 to see why Benjamin was the smallest of the tribes by this time.) When he returned home, he did not even tell his family that he had been appointed king. Saul seems to have been a righteous young man at this time. Though an impressive young man, standing head and shoulders taller than the others, he was almost afraid to take his place of leadership. We will continue to see this humility for a time as we continue to follow his history, but it is not long before his attitude changed.

God appointed Saul "prince," or "captain" over the people. These people were still God's people, and God was still the One in ultimate control. Notice that it was God who chose Saul to be the leader, not Samuel. He was "God's anointed." This expression is used over and over in this period of history. He was the one God chose for this purpose. (See Deuteronomy 17:15.)

Samuel gave Saul specific signs so that he could know that what had been said was true. The first two signs were not of great significance within themselves — these were just things that Samuel knew would happen, and Saul saw that they took place just as Samuel foretold. The third sign was of more significance within itself. If Saul could prophesy with the prophets, then Saul had the Spirit from God. That is why Samuel told him that after these signs he could do as he thought best, because the Lord would be with him. In other words, God's Spirit came upon Saul that day to help him have the wisdom to lead the people as God wanted them led. Watch this feature about Saul also. The day will come in the story when that Spirit will leave Saul.

Saul is appointed king publicly (1 Sam. 10:17-27):

Samuel called the people together to Mizpah before the Lord, and told them the Lord's words: "I brought Israel up out of Egypt and I saved you from all the kingdoms that oppressed you, but today you have rejected your God who saved you from all your calamities and distresses. You have told Him, 'No, set a king over us.' Therefore, at this time, present yourselves by your tribes, and by your thousands."

As the tribes came by, the tribe of Benjamin was taken. From the tribe of Benjamin, the family of the Matrites was taken. Finally, the lot came out for Saul, son of Kish, but when they called for him, he was nowhere to be found. So they asked the Lord, "Has the man come here?"

The Lord said, "He is hiding among the baggage."

The people ran and brought him forward, and he stood taller than anyone else from his shoulders and up. Samuel said to all the people, "Do you see the one God has chosen, that there is none like him among all the people?"

All the people shouted, "Long live the king."

Samuel told the people how the kingdom should be regulated before God and wrote it in a book and laid it up before the Lord. Then Samuel sent all the people home. Saul also went home to Gibeah. Some of the brave men whom God inclined to receive him went to Gibeah with him, but there were certain worthless fellows who said, "How is this man going to save us?" And they scorned him, and showed him no respect at all.

There had never been a king in Israel, so there was no palace for the king to live in, nor any patterns to follow. Saul went back home to Gibeah and seemingly returned to his normal work of farming (see 11:5).

Begin your chart of names:
  Samuel
  Kish
  Saul

Label your blank map:
  Gibeah

Saul leads Israel to victory (1 Sam. 11:1-13):

Though Saul returned to his own home after he was anointed king, and continued farming, it was not long before his help was needed. Jabesh-Gilead, a city on the east side of the Jordan River, was attacked by the Ammonites.

The Ammonites lived on the edge of the desert, with their territory beginning about 25 or 30 miles east of the Jordan River. They wanted the rich lands of Gilead, so they fought many battles through the years, trying to take the area. This time they had ventured farther north than usual, and westward all the way to the edge of the Jordan Valley.

If a city name is hyphenated with the name Gilead, expect to find it on the east side of the Jordan because that was the name of the eastern plateau, particularly from north of the Arnon River to the Yarmuk River.

The men of Jabesh-Gilead felt helpless and said to the Ammonites, "Give us favorable terms, and we will surrender."

These were the terms Nahash the king of the Ammonites gave: "On this condition will I accept your surrender: all of you must have your right eyes put out; in this way, I will humiliate Israel."

The elders of the city said, "Give us seven days so that we can send messengers throughout all Israel. If there is no one to save us, then we will have no choice but to surrender." In arrogant confidence, Nahash let them have their week.

Messengers soon came to Gibeah where Saul lived and told everyone the bad news. Everyone in the city was grieving by the time Saul came with his oxen from the field. He said, "Why is everyone crying?" and they told him what had happened.

It seems the messengers had not come specifically for their new king Saul. Since the Israelites had never had an earthly king, they had not learned to rely upon him, just as Saul had not yet set up specific duties for himself. These messengers were just informing the Israelites in all the cities they came to.

The Spirit of God came mightily upon Saul when he heard the messengers' report, and he became very angry. He took a yoke of oxen and cut them in pieces and sent them throughout all Israel with this message: "Whoever does not come to follow Saul and Samuel will have his oxen slaughtered like these." The fear of Jehovah fell upon the people, and they came out as one: 330,000 of them. They gathered at Bezek which was across the river from Jabesh-gilead.

Obviously, all these things happened very quickly. The messengers were told to go back and tell the men of Jabesh-gilead, "Tomorrow, about this time, when the sun is hot, deliverance will come to you."

Hurrying back, the messengers told the men of Jabesh-gilead what they had learned — deliverance was on its way. The men of the city rejoiced and told Nahash, "Tomorrow, we will surrender, and you can do whatever you want with us."

The next day Saul divided his forces into three parts and attacked the Ammonites from early in the morning until the heat of the day. When they were through, the Ammonites were so scattered that two of them could not be found together.

Now the people were very enthusiastic in support of their new king, and said, "Who is it that said, 'Will Saul rule over us?' Bring them forth to be put to death."

But Saul said, "No one is going to be executed today, because this day Jehovah has delivered Israel from danger."

Remember that it is the men of Jabesh-Gilead who were the first to be rescued by Saul. This will play a part later in his story.

Look at your map of the land in Saul's day. See how the enemies are encroaching on all sides. On this particular occasion, the enemy is Nahash of the Ammonites. Compare this map with the map of the land divided among the tribes. Why is there such a difference? Could God not keep the enemies away, or had the people become lax in their service to God?

Label your map:
    Ammonite territory
    Gilead (the eastern plateau)
    Jabesh-Gilead

Names for your chart:
    Ammonites
    Nahash, king of the Ammonites

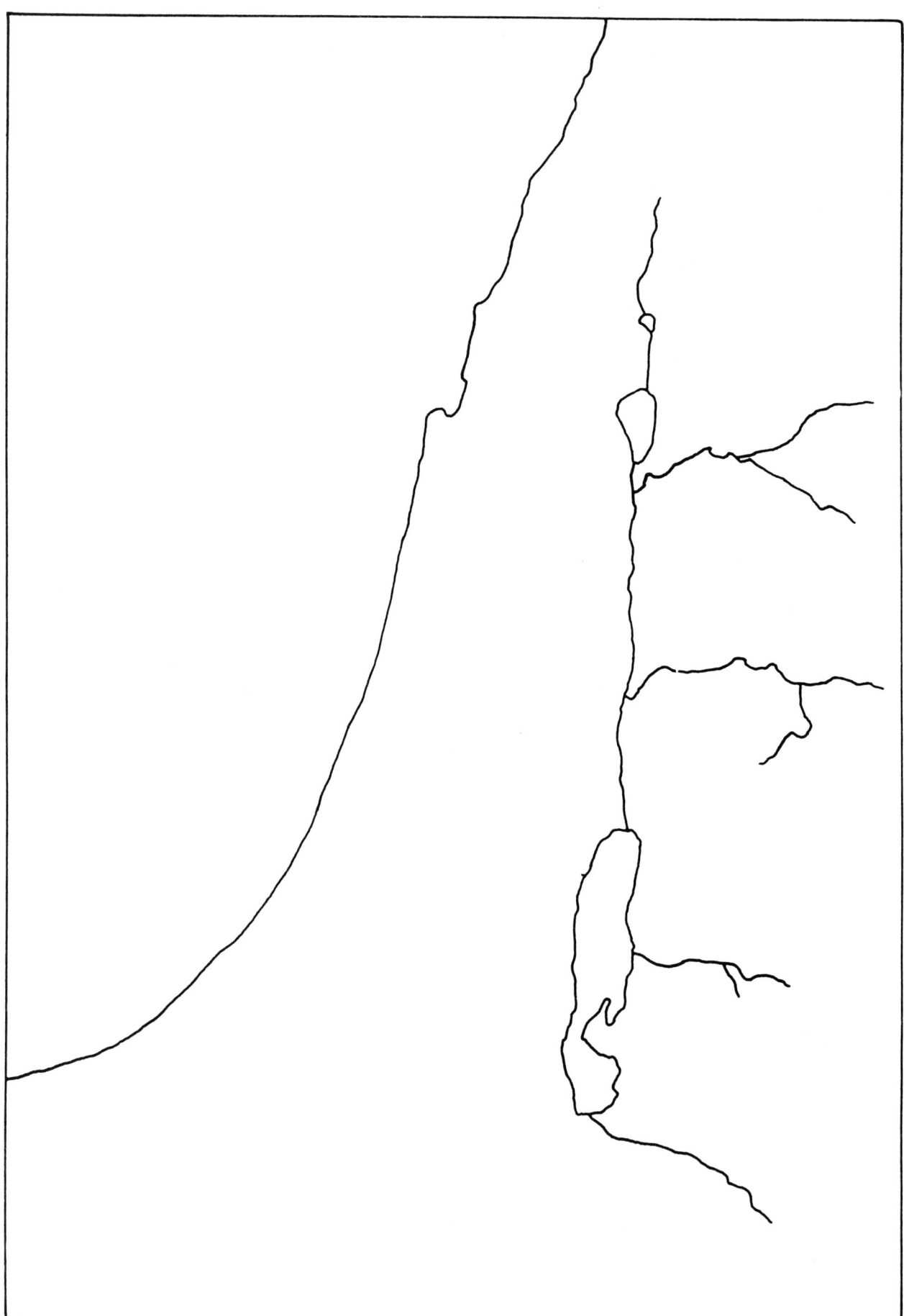

Samuel and the people renew the kingdom (1 Sam. 11:14-12:25):

After this great victory, while everyone was rejoicing over their new king, Samuel called the people to meet at Gilgal to renew the kingdom. So all the people went to Gilgal and made Saul king before Jehovah, and they offered peace offerings before Jehovah and rejoiced greatly.

Of course, Saul had already been appointed king, first privately, and then publicly. But there had been uncertainty about his qualifications at that time. Now, after this first victory, the people are ready to accept Saul wholeheartedly. This gathering was more a matter of celebrating over their new king and kingdom than it was an actual beginning of it. Samuel used the opportunity to talk earnestly to the people and their king about their responsibilities to each other and to their God. Samuel stressed that Saul was God's chosen one, he was God's anointed one.

Samuel spoke to the assembled people and publicly resigned as their leader. He said, "I have done what you asked: I have given you a king. Your king is before you, and I am old and gray-headed. I have been before you since my youth. Here I am. Testify against me before the Lord and before His anointed. Whose ox have I taken? Whom have I cheated? From whom have I taken a bribe?"

The people answered, "You haven't cheated anyone."

Samuel replied, "Jehovah is witness, and His chosen one is witness, that you have found no fault with me."

The people said, "We are witnesses."

Then Samuel spoke to the people:

It is Jehovah who appointed Moses and Aaron to be leaders, and who brought you up out of the land of Egypt. Please stand still and listen so that I can plead with you regarding all the righteous acts God has done for you and your ancestors.

When Jacob was in Egypt, and your fathers cried out, it was Jehovah who sent Moses and Aaron to bring them out of Egypt into this place. But they forgot the Lord, so He sold them into the hand of Sisera, and into the hand of the Philistines, and of the Moabites, and they fought against your ancestors. They cried out to Jehovah and said, "We have sinned because we have forsaken the Lord and have worshiped the Baalim and the Ashtaroth. Deliver us from our enemies, and we will serve you." So the Lord sent Jerubbaal, and Barak, and Jephthah, and Samuel, and delivered you from your enemies.

When, however, you saw that Nahash the king of the Ammonites came against you, you said to me, "No, but a king will rule over us," when the Lord was your King. So here is the king you have chosen, the one you asked for.

Now if you will fear the Lord, and serve Him, and listen to what He says, both you and your king, then things will be fine. But if you will not listen, but rebel against His commandment, then the Lord's hand will be against you.

Stand still and see the awesome thing the Lord is about to do before your eyes. Is it not wheat harvest today? I will call upon the Lord, and He will send thunder and rain so that you may know that you have done a very wicked thing in asking the Lord for a king.

So Samuel called upon Jehovah, and He sent thunder and rain, and all the people greatly feared the Lord and Samuel. (*The wheat harvest occurs from the middle of May to the middle of June, and it almost never rained in Israel during this period. Wet grain mildews, so it was very important that it be dry at the time of wheat harvest.*)

They said to Samuel, "Pray for us because we have added this sin to our other sins: we have asked for a king."

Samuel said, "Do not be afraid. You have indeed behaved wickedly, but be determined to serve God faithfully with all your heart, and do not turn aside after idols. The Lord will not forsake His people. Moreover, though I will no longer lead you as I have, far be it from me that I should stop praying for you; instead I will teach you the way that is good and right. Just be sure you fear the Lord and serve Him according to truth, because consider how great things He has done for you. But if you should continue to behave wickedly, you will be destroyed, both you and your king."

Label your map: Gilgal (in the central hill country)

Saul offers an ill-advised sacrifice (1 Sam. 13:1-22):

After the battle with the Ammonites, Saul began to act like a king. After two years of his rule he chose 3,000 soldiers, of which 2,000 were with him in Michmash, and 1,000 were with Jonathan his son in Gibeah of Benjamin. Saul sent all the rest of the people home. He made Gibeah, his old home, his capital (see 1 Sam. 15:34).

Before long, Jonathan took his men and attacked the Philistines at Geba. This attack angered the Philistines, and they quickly brought their army to challenge Israel.

A large contingency of Philistines had moved into the southern coastal plain during the early days of the judges. They were a threat over and over until God gave the Israelites victory over them in the early days of Samuel (see Judges 3:31; 10:7; 13-16; I Samuel 4-7). There had been peace in the land during the years that Samuel was the leader, but the enemies were not asleep. There had not been open warfare, but the Philistines had been inching their way farther and farther inland. They had a garrison in Gibeah before Saul was made king (1 Sam. 10:5), and, by chapter 13, we find they had set up an outpost at Geba — in the very midst of Israelite territory, only a few miles from Gibeah, Saul's capital.

Saul sounded the alarm and called the Israelites to battle. The people came to Gilgal in answer to the call, but they were frightened to learn that the Philistines were angry and were making a serious attack on Israel. The Philistines had indeed brought a strong army: 3,000 chariots, 6,000 cavalrymen, and soldiers without number.

The Israelites were very upset over these developments. Remember that God had promised He would be with His people — no matter how formidable the foe — *if* His people were faithful, but Saul let his fear of the enemy rob him of his faith in God. Soon his followers, taking their cue from him, were losing their courage also. The Israelite soldiers began slipping away from camp to hide in caves, in thickets, in pits, or even to cross over Jordan to escape having to fight.

Samuel had promised he would join the army camp on the seventh day in order to offer a sacrifice before time for the battle to begin. But the seventh day dawned and Samuel had not come. By now Saul was terribly frightened. He decided that he must offer the sacrifice. He said, "Bring the burnt offering here to me," and he offered it.

Just as Saul finished offering the sacrifice, Samuel arrived. "Why did you do such a thing?" he asked.

Saul tried to justify himself: "When I saw how the people were deserting me, and you had not come within the time appointed, and the Philistines were gathering at Michmash, I thought, 'The Philistines will descend upon me at Gilgal, and I have not sought the favor of Jehovah.' So I forced myself to go ahead and offer the burnt offering."

Samuel answered, "You have done foolishly. You have not kept the commandment of Jehovah which He commanded you. If you had, He would have established your kingdom over Israel forever, but now your kingdom will not continue. Instead Jehovah will seek for Himself a man after His own heart."

It is uncertain whether Saul personally offered this sacrifice. He may have given orders for it be to be done by some priest with the company of soldiers, but the wording of the text implies he offered it himself. The primary thing he is rebuked for is that he did not wait for Samuel to come to offer the sacrifice as he had been instructed. Samuel rebukes him for acting foolishly, "You have not kept the commandment of the Lord." This could mean Samuel was rebuking him for not waiting as he had been told, or it could be referring to a more specific reason why Saul should not have offered the sacrifice — that is, he was not a priest. Either way, Saul did not act in accordance with God's will and was rebuked for his actions. The penalty is that Saul's kingdom will not be established, that is, his family will not be established as the ruling dynasty.

Meanwhile, the Philistines were sending their men out in three different directions each day to raid the countryside. Saul was afraid to challenge them because of his own lack of faith — and because he had only 600 men left with him.

The Philistines had learned how to smelt iron and use it for their weapons and tools, but the Israelites did not have that skill. The Philistines were quick to use their advantage. If an Israelite had an iron tool, he had to go to a Philistine to have it sharpened, because there were no blacksmiths in the land of Israel. It seems the Philistines had removed any Israelite blacksmiths that might have been available, because they said, "Lest the Hebrews make swords or spears." The Philistines had used their skill to make iron swords and spears, but the Israelites were ill-equipped to do battle; only Saul and Jonathan had iron swords.

Label your map:
Philistine territory (on the southern coastal plain)
Geba

Jonathan leads Israel to victory (1 Sam. 14:1-46):

By this time, the two armies had shifted positions. A detachment of the Philistines were at Michmash (13:23), and Saul was on the outskirts of Gibeah. There were two cliffs between the camps with a narrow, steep ravine between them.

One day Jonathan proposed a plan to his young armor-bearer. He said, "Come, let us go up to these Philistines and see if God will give us the victory, because God does not care whether He has few or many."

The young armor-bearer was a man of faith, and he said, "I am with you heart and soul."

The two men started up the ravine separating the camps. Jonathan suggested a sign to let them know whether God was with them. If the first Philistines who saw them said, "You had better stay where you are," then Jonathan would know that God did not want him to go forward. But if they said, "Come up unto us," then Jonathan would know God was with him.

The first Philistines spotted the men and called out in mockery, "The Hebrews are coming out of hiding! Come up here and we will teach you a lesson."

The Philistines never dreamed that two Israelites would actually make the treacherous climb up the ravine to attack them. Also it was difficult to tell if anyone (or how many) were climbing up, due to the steepness of the cliff. It was therefore a shock when Jonathan and his armor-bearer came over the edge of the ravine, ran forward, attacked the first Philistine, killed him, and headed for the next one. God was with them, and they killed the first twenty men they found. Word began spreading, and the Philistines fled in panic, thinking the entire Israelite army had attacked. In their panic, they began killing and stabbing anyone in their path.

Meanwhile, Saul's watchmen brought him word that the Philistines seemed to be fleeing in panic. Saul said, "Count off to see who is missing," and they discovered that Jonathan and his armor-bearer were gone. Saul asked Ahijah the priest to inquire of God what they should do, but word continued to come that the Philistines were fleeing. Saul told the priest not to wait for an answer from God. He and his men fell into pursuit of the enemy. The Israelites who had been hiding now came out of their places and joined the battle. Even some Israelites who had joined the Philistines turned and began fighting for Israel. The Philistines fled toward home with the Israelites in pursuit for the rest of the day.

As the day wore on, Saul's men became weary and hungry. None stopped to eat, however, because Saul had given an order that no one was to eat until they had been avenged of their enemy. Jonathan did not hear that command because he was already fighting the enemy when the command was given. As he was going through the woods, he saw some wild honey. He dipped his staff into the honey, ate it, and was refreshed. Someone nearby told him, "Your father strictly commanded everyone with an oath, saying, 'Cursed be the man who eats food this day.'"

Jonathan said, "My father has brought trouble upon the country. Look at how refreshed I am from tasting just this little bit of honey. Think how much more would everyone be refreshed if they had been able to eat freely from the spoil of the Philistines. Then there would have been a much greater slaughter of the enemy."

By evening the people were so hungry that when they began killing their animals for meat, they did not wait to bleed them properly before cooking them. Saul made them bring the animals before him for slaying so that he could see that they were bled properly.

Saul wanted to continue chasing the Philistines that night. He asked God's advice, but God would not answer. Saul decided that there must be sin in the camp. He declared that the one who had sinned must die. He put himself and Jonathan on one side and the people on the other side. Lots were cast — and Saul and Jonathan were chosen. Lots were cast again — and Jonathan was chosen.

Saul said to Jonathan, "Tell me what you have done."

Jonathan answered, "Surely I tasted a little honey on the end of the rod that was in my hand, and it seems I must die."

When Saul agreed that Jonathan must surely die, the people said, "You think you are going to kill Jonathan who has brought us this great salvation today? No way! Not one hair of his head will be harmed, because he has worked with God today." Saul let the matter drop and also gave up his determination to continue chasing the Philistines.

Label your map: **Name for your chart:**
    Michmash   Jonathan

By Saul's fear of the enemy in this battle with the Philistines, he demonstrated his lack of faith in God's promises. His unbelief and fear are in vivid contrast with Jonathan's faith and courage. By offering the sacrifice he had no right to offer, Saul showed that he did not put God's law above all other considerations. And, he demonstrated a lack of wisdom as a leader of men by ordering his soldiers not to eat as they pursued the enemy. Therefore, in this one episode, he demonstrated he was not the kind of king God wanted. It is not surprising that we soon find God looking for a king after His own heart.

Ahijah was the high priest of Israel at this time in Shiloh (14:3), and the ark of the covenant was with the army (14:18). Ahijah was the son of Ahitub and the grandson of Eli. Ahitub was Ichabod's older brother (4:19-21). It is likely that Ahijah was another name for Ahimelech (21:1; 22:11, 20), although it is possible that Ahimelech was a brother of Ahijah. Notice that this is the line of Eli's family. Look back to 1 Samuel 2:27-36 and 3:11-14 and remind yourself and your students of the curse God placed upon the family of Eli. God predicted the day would come when the priesthood (that is, the position of high priest) would be taken from Eli's family, because of the wickedness of Eli's sons and because of Eli's failure to restrain them or to remove them from office. As we continue to follow the history of the kingdom of Israel let us watch and see how the prediction is fulfilled.

Though Samuel at least presided over sacrifices often (see 1 Sam. 7:9-10; 9:12-13; 13:8-13; 16:2-5), he was not the high priest. Samuel grew up at the tabernacle in the household of Eli, and he was a Levite according to his lineage in 1 Chronicles 6:22-28, but the only way he could have been in line to be a high priest would be for him to be the son of a high priest.

Victories for Saul (1 Sam. 14:47-52):

The battle with the Ammonites that is described in chapter 11 and the battle with the Philistines that is described in chapters 13 and 14 were the first of many battles in Saul's life. The last part of chapter 14 summarizes his various victories. Most of the stories of those battles are not told. He defeated the Moabites, the Ammonites, the Edomites, the kings of Zobah, the Philistines, and the Amalekites. The story of the battle with the Amalekites will be told in chapter 15. The Philistines were the only ones Saul did not always defeat — and on those occasions, Saul's inability to defeat them was due to a lack of faith on his part, not an inability on God's part to help. Saul reigned for many years, and many of these battles were probably fought in the early or middle part of his reign. As Saul reached the latter part of his reign, his problems with the Philistines grew severe, as he ignored God's wishes more and more.

Saul's family is named in chapter 14 also. His sons Jonathan, Ishvi (later called Ish-bosheth), and Malchi-Shua are named here. Another son, Abinadab, is named in 31:2. Saul's daughters were Merab and Michal. The captain of his army was Abner, Saul's first cousin. Some of these characters will play parts in later stories.

From this time forward, whenever Saul saw a valiant young man, he took him into his service.

Label these territories on your map:
  Moab
  Edom
  Zobah
  Amalek

Names to add:
  Ishvi (Ish-bosheth)
  Merab and Michal
  Abner

Do you see that Samuel's warnings are beginning to come true? By the first of chapter 13, we have a small standing army for the first time in Israelite history. Now Saul regularly takes any valiant young man he sees into his service. We are beginning to work for our king!

Saul's kingdom is rejected (1 Sam. 15:1-35):

Samuel told Saul, "Jehovah had me to anoint you as the king over His people. Listen therefore to what He says you are to do: 'I took note of how Amalek preyed upon Israel when he came up out of Egypt. Now go and attack Amalek and completely destroy everything they have. Do not spare them. Put to death every man, woman, and child, plus every cow, sheep, camel, or donkey. Do not leave anything alive.'" The instructions were clear. Saul went to do God's bidding.

It had been about 400 years since the Amalekites attacked the Israelites soon after they left Egypt. At that time, the Israelites were a group of newly released slaves, not trained soldiers. God gave them the victory that day, but He predicted that someday He would utterly destroy the Amalekites (see Exodus 17:8-16; Deut. 25:17-19). The time had come for God to bring about His punishment of the Amalekites.

Saul called the men of Israel together and assembled an army of 210,000 men at Telaim *(location unknown, probably somewhere in the south)*. He took his army to a valley near the city of Amalek and prepared for attack.

Saul warned the Kenites, who were living nearby or among the Amalekites, saying, "Get up and leave the Amalekites so that I will not destroy you with them, since you were kind to the children of Israel when they came up from Egypt." The Kenites did as they were told and promptly fled.

The attack was successful, and soon Saul had destroyed Amalekites all the way from Havilah to Shur, to the east of Egypt. It was a day of complete victory for Israel. They could have fully carried out God's decree with no problem, but they let human reasoning get in their way. They killed all the people — except King Agag. They killed all the weak, sickly, despised animals, but they let the best of the animals live. Saul and his army started home, happy over their victory.

Meanwhile, God spoke to Samuel. "I am sorry I made Saul king. He has *not* carried out my instructions." Samuel grieved all night long.

The next morning Samuel started out to meet Saul. At first he missed Saul because Saul had gone to Carmel to set up a monument to commemorate his victory and then had headed toward Gilgal. When Samuel finally caught up with him, Saul was delighted to see him. Saul said, "The Lord bless you. I have carried out all of God's instructions."

Samuel said, "If you have obeyed God, then why do I hear the bleating of sheep and the lowing of oxen?"

If the matter were not so serious, it would be almost amusing to watch as Saul tries to explain the presence of the animals he was supposed to have killed. "Oh, those? Well, the people brought those home. They spared the best of the animals so that we could sacrifice them to God. But we have destroyed all the rest."

Samuel said, "Wait! Let me tell you what God said to me last night. Although you were once small in your own sight, did you not become head of all the tribes of Israel? The Lord anointed you king over His people. Then He sent you on a special mission. He told you to go and completely destroy the wicked Amalekites. He said for you to make war on them until they were wiped out. Why did you not obey God? Why did you pounce on the plunder and do evil in the eyes of the Lord?"

"But I *did* obey God," Saul protested. "I went on the mission God assigned. I *did* destroy all the Amalekites — except for King Agag. The soldiers took the best of the sheep and cattle, but we were going to use those to offer a special sacrifice unto the Lord your God at Gilgal."

Samuel said, "Does God have as great a delight in sacrifices as He does in obedience?"

Think about it. Would God prefer that the Israelites obey Him, or disobey and then have to offer a sacrifice to ask His forgiveness? Today, had God rather we obey Him, or have to pray and ask His forgiveness for something we have done wrong?

Samuel continued, "To obey is better than sacrifice and to hearken than the fat of rams. Rebellion and arrogance are as bad as the sins of witchcraft or idolatry. Because you have rejected God's command, He has rejected you as king."

Now, at last, Saul said, "I have sinned. I did not do as God commanded. I was afraid of the people, and I gave in to them when they wanted to bring the animals back. Now please forgive me and come with us to worship the Lord."

But Samuel said, "I will not come with you. You have rejected God and He has rejected you as king over Israel." And Samuel turned to leave.

Saul reached out and grabbed his robe, trying to stop him. The robe tore, and Samuel said, "See, God has torn the kingdom of Israel from you today. He has taken it away from you and will give it to one of your neighbors, one who is better than you. The Glory of Israel does not lie or change His mind. He is not like a man."

Saul was very sad by now. He pled with Samuel, "I have sinned, but please honor me before the elders of my people and before Israel. Please come with us so that I may worship the Lord your God." So, Samuel turned back and went with them to worship God.

Samuel called for King Agag to be brought before him. King Agag was hoping that his life was going to be spared. He said, "Surely, the time for dying is past."

Samuel answered, "As you have made other mothers childless, so now your mother will be childless." Samuel himself then killed the king.

Samuel returned to Ramah and never again visited Saul. Samuel grieved for Saul as if he had died.

Names to add: **Label your map:**
  Amalekites   **Amalekite territory**
  King Agag   **Havilah to Shur**
  Kenites

Very little is known about the Amalekites as a people. Their exact origin is unknown. In Genesis 36:12, a man named Amalek is listed as the son of Eliphaz through a concubine, and the grandson of Esau. However, we read of Amalekites as early as Genesis 14:7, before Esau was even born, so the Amalekites were not descendants of Esau. In Exodus 17, when they attacked the Israelites, they were way down in the southern part of the Sinai Peninsula at Rephidim. In the book of Judges we find them on the east side of the Jordan joining with various ones of Israel's enemies (see Judg. 3:13; 6:3). In this story, it seems they had moved in on Israel's southern boundary, south of Beersheba, on the northern edge of the desert. They were, therefore, a wandering tribe. They made their living by raiding caravans on the trade routes, or by taking tribute (protection money) from them, as did so many of the other wandering tribes.

Even though Saul did not carry out God's command as he should have on this occasion, he did succeed in destroying this group of Amalekites. Naturally, all Amalekites were not in their city at that moment. Therefore, we read of Amalekites in later stories (see 1 Sam. 30; 2 Sam. 1; 1 Chron. 4:42, 43). Never again, however, do we read of them as a major enemy.

Saul told the Kenites to leave before he began the battle with the Amalekites. Who were the Kenites? They were the descendants of the family that Moses lived with near Mount Sinai when he was forced to flee from Egypt after he killed the Egyptian (Exod. 2:11-25). At that point, they were called Midianites. When the Israelites were ready to leave Mount Sinai after receiving their law, Moses asked Hobab, his brother-in-law, to go with them and share in the fortunes of the Israelites (Num. 10:29-32). At that point, Hobab is said to be the son of Reuel the "Midianite." After the Israelites conquered the land of Canaan and divided it among the tribes, the descendants of Moses' father-in-law, here called the "Kenites," moved from Jericho to the west side of the Dead Sea. There they lived inside Judah's territory, but seemingly as a distinct group (Judg. 1:16).

It is interesting to note in the story of Deborah the judge that one family of the Kenites had broken away from the rest and had moved north to Kedesh-Naphtali near the Sea of Galilee. That man's name was Heber. His wife Jael is the one who nailed Sisera's head to the floor with a tent-peg. Jael was a Kenite (Judg. 4:11-21).

Now, in this story, the Amalekites have moved in on Judah's southern boundary. Their exact location is uncertain. The location of the battle "from Havilah to Shur" sounds as if they were living west of the Kenites' territory, so we do not know how they had become mingled. Perhaps only a few Kenites were among the Amalekites. Saul wanted to protect the Kenites while he destroyed the Amalekites.

God's command to Saul was that he was to "put to death both man and woman, child and infant" among the Amalekites. Why did God command babies be killed? In the Old Testament, God's covenant was with a nation — not just with individuals as it is now. He dealt with individuals, in that each person was saved or lost on the basis of what he did or did not do, but He also dealt with the nation on matters such as fighting enemy nations. When it was to Israel's benefit as a nation for another people to be destroyed, God instructed them to utterly destroy that nation. For example, when the Israelites went into the land of Canaan in the days of Joshua, they were told to kill <u>all</u> the Canaanites. Now, on this occasion, Saul was told to kill all the Amalekites. In both instances, God had determined in His wisdom that the nation to be destroyed had become so wicked it was time for it to be blotted out as a nation. God was not "punishing" the babies as such, but He <u>was</u> punishing that nation for its wickedness. That nation was no longer "fit" to exist.

On a very practical level, which Amalekites and Canaanites will succeed in getting to Heaven? Will it not be the babies who died before they were old enough to worship the idols? As long as the Amalekites continued to live as they had for hundreds of years, what would happen to each new baby as it grew up? Would it not be taught to worship idols just as its parents did? Think about it. Were the babies who were killed actually harmed — or were they the ones blessed? Sometimes we get so caught up thinking of this physical life we forget there is a life beyond this.

Whatever reasons God had for giving such a commandment, it is up to us to accept His wisdom, and have enough faith in Him to know He made the right decision. Let us be careful when we begin to question God's motives. Let us have the attitude Abraham had when he said, "Shall not the Judge of all the earth do right?" (Gen. 18:25b).

Why did Saul and the soldiers bring back the best of the flocks and herds? The soldiers of that day were used to taking spoils from conquered people. That was their pay for their work. Sometimes the spoils were very valuable. That is why sometimes the men of a particular tribe protested when they were not called to battle (see Judges 8:1; 12:1). They wanted some of the wealth from the spoils. Therefore, the soldiers did not understand why Saul wanted to kill the animals.

This explanation helps us understand why Saul was under pressure to disobey God, but it does not take away his guilt. God had said for everything to be destroyed this time. Saul should have demanded it of his soldiers. When we take time to understand the pressures these Bible characters were under at the moment, it helps us identify with them and helps us see how we might have responded in the same circumstances. The better we understand their reactions the better we can apply the principles to our own lives.

Samuel anoints a new king (1 Sam. 16:1-13):

The Lord said to Samuel, "How long are you going to go on grieving over Saul, since I have rejected him as king of Israel? Fill your horn with oil and go, because I am sending you to Jesse of

Bethlehem. I have chosen my new king from his sons."

Samuel asked, "How can I succeed in going? If Saul hears of this, he will kill me."

The Lord replied, "Take a heifer with you and say, 'I have come to sacrifice to Jehovah.' Then call Jesse to the sacrifice, and I will show you what to do. You will anoint the one I tell you." Since Samuel often visited cities in order to offer special sacrifices, Saul would not know there had been an additional reason. Samuel's life would be safe.

Samuel did as he was commanded and went to Bethlehem. The elders of the city came to meet Samuel trembling. They asked, "Do you come peacefully?"

The question of these elders does not in any way imply that they knew of difficulties between Saul and Samuel. That the great judge and prophet of Israel had come to their little city was enough to create anxiety in their minds. Often such a coming would mean judgment, some problem to be dealt with. The question of the elders was really, "Is there some problem?" Samuel's answer assured them that he was not there to deal with some crisis.

Samuel answered, "Yes, peacefully. In fact I have come to offer a sacrifice to Jehovah. Prepare yourselves and come with me to the sacrifice." Samuel made sure that Jesse and his sons were invited to the sacrifice.

As Jesse introduced his sons, Samuel observed them, and when he saw Eliab, Jesse's oldest, he thought, "Surely the Lord's anointed is even now standing before me." But the Lord said, "Samuel, do not judge by how he looks, or by how tall he is. I have rejected him because I do not see as men see. Man looks at the outward appearance, but Jehovah looks upon the heart." The second son was brought before Samuel, and then the third. God did not choose either of these. Seven sons of Jesse passed before Samuel, but none of them was selected. Samuel asked Jesse, "Are all your children here?"

Jesse answered, "The youngest is not here; he is keeping the sheep."

Samuel said, "Send for him and bring him here, because we will not start till he arrives."

The young man who came in from the sheep was a ruddy, fine looking young man. His name was David. Samuel anointed David as the next king of Israel there before his family. The Spirit of the Lord came upon David, and God was with him from this time on.

Names to add: **Label your map:**
  Jesse   Bethlehem
  David

Saul's kingdom has been rejected, and a new king has been selected. Saul will continue as king as long as he lives, but his sons will not be allowed to reign after him. David has been anointed king, but only Samuel and David's family know it.

Psalm 23

This psalm is perhaps the best known and most beloved of all psalms. Several respected Bible students think that it was written during the rebellion of Absalom, but the evidence is scant. The background of the psalm, and its wonderful imagery, come from David's early life as a shepherd. Therefore, we choose to put it here, at the time when David was just a shepherd. Whether he wrote it at this early age, or later, looking back upon his love for shepherds and sheep, is not important. The content is what makes it beautiful.

The Lord is my shepherd; I shall not want. He maketh me to lie down in green pastures; He leadeth me beside the still waters. He restoreth my soul. He leadeth me in the paths of righteousness for His name's sake.

Yea, though I walk through the valley of the shadow of death, I will fear no evil, because you are with me. Your rod and your staff, they comfort me. You prepare a table before me in the presence of my enemies. You have anointed my head with oil; my cup is running over.

Surely goodness and mercy shall follow me all the days of my life, and I shall dwell in the house of the Lord forever.

David becomes Saul's servant (1 Sam. 16:14-23):
Do you remember that when Saul was made king he had no predecessor to follow? Therefore, he did not know how to act as a king. Now a new king has been anointed. Saul does not know that, and yet God's providence works so that Saul begins training the new king!

After Saul's kingdom was rejected by God, God's Spirit left Saul, and an "evil spirit from the Lord tormented him." There is not enough data given for us to know all that was involved in this "evil spirit," but it is obvious that Saul had periods of deep depression after this. Saul's servants suggested that one be found who could play music that might soothe the afflicted king. Saul agreed to the plan, and the young man David was suggested.

Saul sent word to Jesse asking that David be sent to him. Jesse agreed and sent him with gifts for the king. Saul liked the young man. Not only did he listen to his music, he soon made David one of his armor-bearers. It was not long before he sent word to Jesse asking that David be allowed to stay with him regularly. Permission was given, and David became part of Saul's regular staff, but he still went home often (see 17:15), and we find him back at home when chapter 17 begins.

David becomes a hero in Israel (1 Sam. 17:1-58):
The Philistines came again in battle. This time the Philistines encamped at Ephes Dammim (Field of blood) between Socoh and Azekah. The Israelites were in the Vale of Elah. The two camps faced each other across the valley. Each was in a strong position, but neither would attack.

The Philistines had come with a new strategy this time. They had brought a giant with them named Goliath. Each morning and each evening this giant came out in view and called to the Israelites: "Why do you line up for battle? I am a Philistine. You are servants of Saul. Choose a man and send him out to fight me. If he wins, then we will be your subjects. But, if I win, then all of you will be our servants." He would continue his challenge, "This day I defy the armies of Israel!"

Saul and his men were terrified. The idea of two men fighting instead of the whole armies engaging was not unheard of in that day — but this man was more than nine feet tall! The armor he wore weighed about 125 pounds. Just the iron point on his spear weighed about 15 pounds. How could any ordinary man hope to stand against such a man?!

Day after day passed. No one dared to go meet Goliath. Nearly six weeks (40 days) passed with the challenge being made twice a day.

Meanwhile, in Bethlehem, Jesse was concerned about his three older sons who were with Saul in the army. He wondered how they were faring and how the battle was going. He called for David and said, "Take six gallons of parched grain and these ten loaves and carry them to the camp where your brothers are, and deliver these ten cheeses to the captain of their thousand. See how they are, and bring me assurances that they are all right."

Early the next morning David started on his way with the supplies. Just as he arrived at the camp, the army was going out into battle position, shouting their war cry. David left his things with the keeper of the supplies and ran to greet his brothers. Just then Goliath stepped forward on the Philistine side and issued his usual challenge.

To David's astonishment, the Israelites began running back in great fear. He heard the soldiers talking about the rewards King Saul was offering to anyone who would volunteer to meet the giant. David turned to the men standing near him and asked, "What did you say the king would do for the one who kills this Philistine and removes this disgrace from Israel? Who is this uncircumcised Philistine that he should defy the armies of the living God?"

The men repeated all that had been said about the rewards: The king had promised great wealth to the one who would kill the giant; he would give his daughter in marriage to that man; and, that man's family would be exempt from taxes in Israel. These were great rewards.

Eliab, David's oldest brother, had heard the conversation and he rebuked David for speaking. "Why have you come down here? With whom did you leave those few sheep? I know how conceited you are and how wicked your heart is. You just wanted to come down here and watch the battle."

David protested, "Am I not allowed to speak?" He then turned to another and began inquiring more about going to fight Goliath. It was not long before someone took word to Saul that a young man had been found who was willing to fight the giant. Saul sent for him.

David told Saul, "Do not lose heart over this Philistine. I will go and fight him."

Saul was astonished. "You are not able to fight this man! You are only a youth; this man is a seasoned fighter, and has been since his youth."

David responded, "I have been keeping my father's sheep. When a bear or a lion came out against my sheep, I attacked it and rescued my sheep. When it turned on me I killed it. I have killed both the lion and the bear, and I can kill this uncircumcised Philistine because he has defied the armies of the living God. The same God who delivered me from the mouth of the lion and of the bear will deliver me from this man."

Saul desperately needed a man to break the impasse, even if he lost, so he said, "Go, and may God be with you." Saul offered David his own suit of armor. David tried it, but then rejected it, because he was not used to that kind of equipment. He went out with nothing more than his shepherd's staff, his shepherd's bag, and his sling. As he crossed the stream in the valley, he stooped and picked up five smooth stones.

Goliath saw David approaching and started to meet him with his armor-bearer in front of him. Goliath observed David and saw that he was young, fine-looking, and nearly unarmed. Goliath despised him, feeling almost insulted that such an unarmed man would approach him. He cursed David by his gods. "Am I a dog that you come to me with sticks and stones? Come, and I will feed your flesh to the birds of the air and to the beasts of the field!"

David replied, "You come against me with sword, spear, and javelin, but I come against you in the name of the Lord Almighty, the God of the armies of Israel, whom you have defied. This day God will hand you over to me, and I will strike you down and kill you. Today I will give the carcasses of all the Philistines to the birds and the beasts. Then all the world will know that there is a God in Israel. All who are gathered here will learn that God does not save by sword or spear, for the battle is the Lord's, and He will give all of you into our hands."

Then David placed one of his stones into his sling and ran to meet the giant. He slung his stone and hit Goliath in the forehead. The giant fell face down on the ground — dead (17:50). Since David had no sword, he ran forward, took out Goliath's sword, and cut off his head, and held it up for both armies to see.

The Philistines fled in terror, with Israel in hot pursuit. It was a day of great victory for Israel. David took the Philistine's head to Jerusalem, but he put his weapons in his own tent.

Saul asked Abner, his chief captain, "Whose son is this young man?"
Abner answered, "I have no idea."
Saul said, "Find out whose son the kid *[stripling]* is." David had been in Saul's service already, but he had been only one of many servants at that time. Now he had come into special notice, and Saul wanted to know more about him.

When David returned from the slaughter of the Philistines, Abner brought him before Saul. David had the head of Goliath with him. Saul said, "Whose son are you, young man?"
David answered, "I am the son of your servant Jesse the Bethlehemite."

New names: **Label your map:**
   Goliath   **Vale of Elah**
   Eliab   **Jerusalem**

This is one of the most beloved stories in the Bible. Almost everyone in America has heard of David and the giant. Ironically, we sometimes consider it harder to tell these old favorites than we do other stories because we consider it "old hat." But such stories are ever new. It is just as fascinating today as it was the day it happened. Tell it just that way! Do not try to think of some new "sermon" to preach about it. The story itself is the greatest sermon that could be preached.

The point of the story is not that David had more courage than the rest of the soldiers. He had more <u>faith</u> than they had. God had said He would help them fight their battles — no matter how big the foe. Now this foe had defied God. David marvelled that any Israelite would let that go unchallenged. That is the beauty of this story. "If God be for us, who can be against us?" (Romans 8:31b).

It is important to remember two things. The Spirit of the Lord was already upon David mightily (16:13). When David acted and spoke, the hand of the Lord was upon him. Therefore, his actions against Goliath were not foolish and impetuous. A second thing is that David was not calling upon God to work a miracle. If that is what he had been expecting, he would not have picked up <u>five</u> rocks! He was merely acting with the faith that God would give him victory.

David was not a mere child. He was young, not in the regular army with Saul against the Philistines, but he had already been serving as one of Saul's armor-bearers. Very soon, he will be given a high ranking position in the army and, as such, will soon be winning campaigns against the Philistines.

It was not until David ruled over all Israel that he took Jerusalem, the city of the Jebusites (see 2 Sam. 5). So how could David leave Goliath's head at Jerusalem at this point? Also, if he put Goliath's armor (weapons) in his own tent, then how did the sword of Goliath wind up among the priests at the city of Nob (see 1 Sam. 21:8-9)? No exact explanation is given, but there are several reasonable alternatives. The Israelites already possessed the environs of Jerusalem, although they did not possess the citadel of the Jebusites until David conquered it. On his way home after the battle, David may have put Goliath's head on display by the road that went by Jerusalem to Bethlehem. Or the historian may be speaking in view of what David did later when he took Jerusalem from the Jebusites. There is no problem with the statement that David took the equipment of Goliath to his own dwelling, since they were his by right of conquest. Then, at some point, he must have donated the sword of Goliath to the house of God, under the protection of the priests at Nob.

Jonathan admires David (1 Sam. 18:1-4):

Jonathan, Saul's son, took an instant liking for David and loved him dearly from this day forward. Jonathan made a covenant of friendship with David, and he took off his own princely robe and gave it to David along with his tunic, his sword, his bow, and his belt.

Jonathan was a remarkable man. In the story of chapter 14 we saw Jonathan as a young man of great faith, but even his faith faltered on this occasion against the challenge of the giant. Jonathan had not volunteered to fight Goliath during those forty days the two armies faced each other with the giant defying God's army twice a day. But now, instead of resenting the young man who showed the kind of faith needed when he himself had faltered, he greatly admired David.

Watch as time passes and it becomes more and more evident that this young man David is the one who will become king when Saul is dead. Saul's family has been rejected as the ruling dynasty, but David is not a threat to Saul's personal rule as king. God allows Saul to remain king until he is killed in battle. In reality, it would be Jonathan's place that David would take — yet Jonathan never let that knowledge create a problem between them. Jonathan knew what God was planning, and was willing to submit to His decision. He knew David was a better man than Saul.

David prospers in Saul's service (1 Sam. 18:5-9):

After this David remained at the court and did not go back and forth from home. He was successful with whatever task Saul gave him. It was not long before Saul gave him a high rank in the army. This pleased the people and the other officers.

The people in general held David as a hero. As he was returning from the battle with the giant, the women of the city came out to meet him with singing and dancing. Their song was:

> Saul has slain his thousands,
> but David his ten thousands.

As the days passed, David continued to prosper in all he did. The text says, "All Israel and Judah loved him."

All was not well, however. The growing popularity of this young man began to provoke the jealousy of Saul.

Saul's hatred for David grows (1 Sam. 18:10-30):

David is now deeply loved by the Israelites. But remember that Saul has been told that God will give the kingdom to a neighbor who is better than he is. Saul sees David's popularity growing. Where will his rise in power stop, short of taking over Saul's kingdom? And so, the stage is set for Saul's jealousy, fear, and resentment to grow.

When the young man David first entered Saul's service as the musician to soothe the afflicted king, Saul liked him. When David agreed to fight Goliath, Saul was appalled because he was untrained, but he was glad someone was willing to meet the giant and break the impasse. But when the women sang their song of praise to David as he entered the city after the victory, Saul was intensely angry. The song galled him. "They have credited David with killing his ten thousands and credited me with only thousands! What more can he have than the kingdom?" From that day he eyed David with jealousy.

On the very next day, the evil spirit came upon Saul again, and David went in before him to play his harp as he usually did. Instead of being soothed this time, however, Saul became very angry and threw his spear at David twice, hoping to pin him to the wall. David dodged and was unhurt.

Saul is a frightened, depressed man by now. Notice he has his spear by him on this occasion even though he was in his own house listening to music. Watch that spear. Nearly every time Saul is mentioned from here on, that spear is very near him.

Saul was afraid of David because it was obvious God was with him and not with Saul. He decided to send David away from him, so he put him in charge of 1,000 soldiers and sent him out on campaigns against the Philistines. But every time David fought, he came away in victory because the Lord was with him. The Israelites loved him — but Saul's fear and hatred of him only grew.

Saul thought of a way he might destroy David. He called David to him and said, "Here is my oldest daughter Merab. I will give her to you for a wife if you will be valiant and fight the Lord's battles." He thought David would fall in battle with the Philistines some day, and he would be rid of him.
David protested, saying, "Who am I, and what is my life or my father's family in Israel? I am not worthy to be the king's son-in-law." When the time came for Merab to be married, Saul gave her to a man named Adriel.

Time passed, and David was still safe. Saul learned some news that gave him hope again. He learned that his daughter Michal loved David. Here was another chance to trick David to risk his life in battle for a wife. This time Saul told his servants to speak to David as if in secret and tell him: "The king really likes you, and all his servants love you. Consent to be his son-in-law."
Again David protested, saying, "Does it seem a simple thing for me to be the king's son-in-law when I am a poor man and of little standing?"
Saul's servants promptly carried word back of David's reply. Saul said, "Tell David that the king does not desire any dowry but a hundred foreskins of the Philistines" — proof that 100 Philistines had been killed.
David could give that price, and he was pleased at the thought of marrying Michal, so he and his men went out to battle, and came back bringing the foreskins of not 100, but 200, Philistines. Saul had to give Michal to him in marriage — and David was still safe. Saul grew more afraid.

Look through chapter 18 and write down a contrast of the way the people were growing in their admiration of David and the way Saul was growing in his fear and hatred of David. For example: Jonathan loved him; the women sang in praise of him — while Saul became very angry. Also notice the verses that say the Lord was with David, and the ones that indicate He was not with Saul. List the verses where the contrasts are shown, giving a brief description of each contrast.

Jonathan pleads for David's life (1 Sam. 19:1-7):

Until this time, only Saul knew how much he hated David. Now Saul told his servants and his son Jonathan to try to kill David. But Jonathan loved David as dearly as he loved himself. Jonathan went straight to David and said, "My father is trying to kill you. Now please be on guard in the morning and hide in a secret place. I will go out with my father into the field where you are hiding and I will talk with him about you. If I find out anything, I will tell you."
Jonathan talked to Saul and reminded him of all that David had done. He reminded Saul of how David had risked his life to fight Goliath and how David had won victory after victory for Israel. He urged his father, "Do not sin by killing an innocent man like David for no reason."

Saul listened to Jonathan and he vowed, "As surely as the Lord lives, David will not be put to death."

Jonathan hurried to tell David the good news. David came back into court and everything seemed to be back to normal.

Michal helps David escape (1 Sam. 19:8-17):

Soon there was war again with the Philistines, and David went out and defeated them with a great slaughter. The Philistines fled before him.

It was not long before Saul had another bad day and David came in before him to play his music. Again, Saul threw his spear at him. David dodged, and the spear stuck into the wall. David fled from Saul and went to his own home. By now Saul was so determined to kill him he ordered men to guard David's house, intending to kill him the next morning.

Michal was sure David was in grave danger from her father. She said, "If you don't save your life tonight, tomorrow you will be slain." She helped him escape through a window and then hid an image in the bed and a shawl of goats' hair at the head of it, making it look as if a person were sleeping there *(a person with black hair, by the way, since they usually raised black goats)*.

The next morning when Saul sent for David, Michal told the servants, "He is sick."

They carried word back to Saul, but he said, "Bring him to me in his bed so that I may kill him."

The servants went back to Michal and discovered the image in the bed. Saul was furious. He sent for Michal and demanded, "Why have you deceived me like this and have let my enemy go, so that he has escaped me?"

She was afraid for her own life, so she said, "He told me, 'Let me go; why should I have to kill you?'"

Remember that Michal loved David at the time of their marriage. Now she has helped David escape from her father. There will be more about Michal in the book of 2 Samuel. The end of her story is sad. Remember to watch for it.

Psalm 59

Note the title at the beginning of Psalm 59. It commemorates this moment in David's life when Saul sent men to guard his house in order to kill him. This was the first time David was forced to leave home to save his life.

With all these historical Psalms, the question is: When did David actually compose them? Was it some time after the event, when he had more time to reflect on the matter? Or was it more or less on the spot? In most cases he probably wrote them at the time of the event, or at least while the emotion and dread was upon him. This would explain the fervor of emotion in the psalms, and in some of them, as in this one, the psalm reads as a prayer during a current trial. It is amazing that David could write such memorable poetry under such stress, but such ability was part of David's genius. David was a man of deep feelings and of marvelous musical and poetic ability. Such people find it natural to express themselves in their poetry and/or their music. The Spirit of God also worked in David to guide him in expressing his feelings and his thoughts at such times as these (1 Sam. 16:13; 2 Sam. 23:2).

> Deliver me from my enemies, O my God. Set me on high from them that rise up against me. Deliver me from the workers of iniquity, and save me from bloodthirsty men.

For, lo, they lie in ambush for my soul; the mighty gather themselves together against me, not for my transgression, nor for my sin, O Jehovah. They run and prepare themselves against me, though I have done nothing to deserve it.

Awake thou to help me, and look, even you, O Jehovah, God of hosts, the God of Israel. Arise to visit all the nations. Be not merciful to any wicked transgressors.

They return at evening, they howl like a dog and go around the city. Behold they belch out with their mouth, swords are in their lips, because they say, "Who hears us?"

But you, O Jehovah, will laugh at them. You will have the nations in derision. Because of my enemy's strength, I will listen to you. God is my high tower. My God will meet me with His mercy. He will let me see what I desire upon my enemies.

Slay them not, lest my people forget. Instead, scatter them by your power, and bring them down, O Lord our shield. For the sin of their mouth, and the words of their lips, let them even be taken in their pride, and for cursing and lying which they speak. Consume them in wrath, consume them, so that they shall be no more. Let them know that God rules in Jacob as far as the ends of the earth.

At evening let them return, let them howl like a dog and go around the city. They shall wander up and down for food, and stay all night if they be not satisfied.

But I will sing of thy strength. Yes, I will sing out loud of thy mercy in the morning, because you have been my high tower and a refuge in the day of my distress. Unto you, O my strength, will I sing praises, for God is my high tower, the God of my mercy.

David was the greatest song writer among the Israelites. About 75 of his psalms are recorded in the book of Psalms, which was the Jewish "song book." He wrote on many subjects, and under many different circumstances. Some, such as the one included here, were based upon some particular circumstance in his own life. These included psalms of distress when he cried to God for help; others were psalms of thanksgiving for deliverance. Then there were psalms that were used for specific parts of their worship to Jehovah; there were psalms of pure praise to Jehovah. The psalms give us a beautiful insight into David's heart as he turned to God in every emotion of life. As we look at his relationship with God, it will help us grow in our own dependence upon Him.

There were two periods of great trial from enemies in David's life: when he was a fugitive from Saul, and when he fled from Absalom during that rebellion. In both of these situations, David was forced to flee from one who should have been his friend. Many of the psalms obviously fit into one of these two periods, but determining which psalm fits which period is often impossible. In many cases, references to Jerusalem, Zion, or to David as king, show that the time was during Absalom's rebellion, since he did not become king until after the days when he was a fugitive from Saul. Several psalms, including 59, have inscriptions that connect them with specific events during the times of conflict in David's life. We have inserted those psalms at their respective places.

We list the other psalms here that seem fit this period when David was fleeing from Saul, but which cannot be definitely placed: 7, 13, 17, 22, 31, 35, 40. Sometimes the evidence is linguistic, and in some cases the evidence for the date is slight, but in each of these psalms there is at least some reason to place it in this period. As you continue to follow the history of Saul's hatred for David and David's flight from him, take time to look at these psalms. It will help you see into the heart of David and to see how he took comfort from his dependence upon the Lord in times of trial. Let us learn the lesson and depend upon Him also.

David flees to Samuel for safety (1 Sam. 19:18-24):

Meanwhile, David had fled from the city. He went to Ramah to Samuel and told him all that Saul had done to him. Samuel took him to Naioth in Ramah to keep him safe. *(It seems that Naioth was a school for young prophets in the city of Ramah.)*

Before long Saul learned where David was, and he sent some servants to bring him back. When the servants of Saul got to Naioth, the Spirit of God came upon them and they joined the young prophets in prophesying. Saul sent a second group, then a third group, and the same thing happened to all of them.

Finally, Saul himself went to Ramah. When he arrived at a well in Secu on his way, he inquired where he might find Samuel and David. He was told they were at Naioth in Ramah, but then the Spirit of God came upon Saul and he prophesied also. Saul stripped off his outer garment and lay all night prophesying. God was intervening to protect His servant David.

The proverb that had started when Saul was a young man and had just been anointed king (1 Sam. 10:12) received a new burst of meaning on this occasion: "Is Saul also among the prophets?" *(This proverb would fit anytime someone was doing something that seemed entirely out of character for that individual.)*

Label your map: Ramah

Jonathan warns David (1 Sam. 20:1-42):

David was able to escape from Naioth and he went back to Jonathan. He asked, "What have I done? Why is your father trying to kill me?"

Jonathan protested, "No, no, my father is not trying to kill you. He always tells me whatever he is planning to do. Why would he hide this from me?"

David said, "Your father knows you are my friend. He does not want to grieve you by telling you what he is planning. But as surely as you live, and as surely as God lives, there is only one step between me and death."

Jonathan told him he would do anything in his power to help. David suggested a plan whereby they might learn Saul's intentions. He said: "Tomorrow is the New Moon festival (Num. 28:11-15) and I am supposed to eat at the king's table. Instead I am going to hide in the field until day after tomorrow. You go to the feast just as usual. If your father inquires where I am, tell him that I have gone home to Bethlehem to the annual sacrifice. If he says, 'Very well,' then I am safe. But, if he is angry, you may be sure he is trying to harm me."

David continued, "Jonathan, please deal kindly with me because we entered into a covenant of friendship before the Lord. If I have committed some crime that is worthy of death, then please kill me yourself. Why hand me over to your father?"

Jonathan was grieved at the thought. "Don't you think I would tell you if I thought my father were trying to kill you? I promise I will sound out my father by this time day after tomorrow. Which ever way it is, I vow I will let you know. If you are in danger I will send you away safely."

David asked, "Who will tell me if your father answers your harshly?"

Jonathan swore to David, with God as his witness, "When I have sounded out my father by this time tomorrow, or the next day, I will send to you and let you know what my father answers. And may God be with you as He has been with my father."

Jonathan then asked David to make a promise to him. He said, "If I am alive, please show kindness to me, and do not cut off your loving-kindness from my family after God has destroyed all your enemies." They renewed their covenant of friendship, and swore their love and loyalty to each other.

David and Jonathan had to decide on a way Jonathan could let him know what he had learned if it were not safe for Jonathan to come directly to him. They agreed that Jonathan would go to the feast as planned while David hid. Then toward evening on the second day, David would go to the place where he had hidden when the trouble first began. Jonathan would go there as if he were going target practicing. He would take a lad with him to collect the arrows. When he sent the lad to find the arrows, if he told him, "Look, the arrows are on this side of you," then that would be the signal to David that all was safe. If Jonathan told the lad, "The arrows are beyond you," then David must flee for his life.

The next day came, and Saul made no comment about David's empty place; he said to himself: "Something has happened to him; for some reason he is unclean." The second day came, and Saul asked Jonathan at the table: "Why did the son of Jesse not come to eat yesterday or today?"

Jonathan replied, "David asked permission to go to Bethlehem for his family's annual sacrifice. He said his brother had commanded him to come, so he wanted to go and visit his family."

Saul became angry and began berating Jonathan. "You son of a rebellious woman! Don't you know that you will never be king as long as that man David lives? Now send for him, for he must die!"

Jonathan tried to plead with his father. "Why must he die? What has he done?" Saul was so angry he threw his spear at Jonathan, trying to kill his own son in his frustration and hatred for David! Now Jonathan knew that David was in grave danger. Jonathan was so upset he left the table without eating.

At the agreed time, Jonathan went to the field taking a lad with him. He told the boy to run find the arrows — and he shot the arrow beyond him. He called out, "Is not the arrow beyond you?" Then, lest there be a mistake and David not understand him, he called out, "Hurry! Go quickly! Don't stop!" The lad knew nothing beyond the fact that he had helped Jonathan in his target practice. Jonathan sent him back to the city while he himself went to find David.

After the boy was gone, David came from his hiding place and bowed three times before Jonathan. They kissed each other and wept together. Jonathan said, "Go in peace. We have sworn friendship between us. God is our witness between us and between our descendants."

David left, fleeing for his life, and Jonathan returned to the city, knowing that his father was obsessed with hatred for David.

Jonathan and David have made a vow of lasting friendship. Jonathan knows David will be king after Saul, and he has asked David to be kind to him and to his family. There will be more to this story in 2 Samuel. Keep watching for it.

David and Ahimelech (1 Sam. 21:1-9):

David is now parted from his best friend Jonathan. He has left his beloved wife Michal behind in the city. It is evident that there is no hope that Saul will relent and let David live in the king's court again. Yet, where is he to go? He has tried going to Samuel, and he was not safe. He is afraid to go home to Bethlehem because that would be the first place Saul would think to look for him. David is well known to the people of the land, so where is he even going to find food or spend the night without someone telling Saul where he is? He does not know whom he can trust.

Most of the people of the land still love David. Most have no idea that Saul hates him. Michal has learned it and has helped David get away. Jonathan did not believe it at first when David told him Saul was seeking his life, but now he knows it beyond a shadow of a doubt, and he has warned David to flee. Samuel knows it because David fled to him when he first left the city. The servants may have guessed something must be wrong because they have been sent after David a few times by now, but even they probably have very little idea what is in Saul's mind. David had been one of Saul's army officials so they would expect to call David in for special messages from the king. In this section, we will see how others begin learning of the conflict, and how they begin taking sides.

Saul is obsessed with hatred. He can think of nothing except killing David. Needless to say, his kingdom is being neglected.

When David left Jonathan, he was desperate. He needed food and weapons and he did not know where he could get them safely. He went to Nob which was a city of the priests. Ahimelech the priest came out to meet him. The priest was afraid, so he may have heard rumors of trouble between Saul and David, or he may have feared there was some other kind of trouble in the land. He said, "Why are you alone?"

David told him, "The king has commanded me to take care of a matter, and he warned me not to let anyone know about it. Therefore I have sent my assistants to wait for me at a certain place. Now what supplies do you have with you? Please give me five loaves of bread, or whatever you have available."

The priest said he had no food except the holy bread. He told David, "If your young men are not defiled, I can give you some of the holy bread to eat." David assured him that he and his men were not ceremonially unclean. So Ahimelech gave him the shewbread for food, since it was an emergency.

David said, "By the way, I was in such a rush to get away on my journey I did not bring a sword with me. Do you happen to have a sword?"

Ahimelech said, "I have the sword of Goliath whom you slew. I do not have another."

David was delighted and said, "There is no sword like that one. Let me take it."

David and Ahimelech carried on their conversation and business without noticing that a man named Doeg was observing what they did. Doeg was an Edomite servant of Saul's. He was Saul's chief shepherd.

Names to add: **Label your map:**
    Ahimelech   **Nob**
    Doeg

In the Holy Place in the tabernacle, there were three pieces of furniture. The little altar of incense stood on the west side, just in front of the curtain dividing the Holy Place from the Most Holy Place. A golden lampstand with seven lamps stood on the south side. A table made of wood and covered with gold stood on the north side. Every sabbath day twelve loaves of unleavened bread were prepared and placed on this table. It was called shewbread. The priests took the old bread from the table and ate it there in the tabernacle. No one else was to eat it. (See Leviticus 24:5-9.)

Jesus refers to this story when the Pharisees criticized His disciples for plucking grain on the sabbath day. The Jews did not criticize David for doing something that was expressly against God's law, yet they criticized Jesus when His disciples had broken the rules the Jews themselves had made about the sabbath. The Jews recognized it was an emergency when David was given the shewbread. It would have been carrying God's law beyond the point God intended if Ahimelech had refused to help David in his time of need. It was carrying the sabbath law further than God intended when the Pharisees said that the disciples could not meet their physical need by plucking grain to eat. (See Matthew 12:1-14; Mark 2:23-3:6; Luke 6:1-11.)

David before King Achish (1 Sam. 21:10-15):

When he left Ahimelech, David decided that he would not be safe anywhere in Israel, so he fled to the Philistine city of Gath. This was a mistake, as he soon found out, because his defeats of the Philistines had made him well known to them. The servants of Achish the king of Gath began asking, "Is this not David the king of the land? Isn't this the one they sang about saying, 'Saul has slain his thousands, and David his ten thousands'?"

Therefore they seized him and brought him before Achish. David was very afraid because he knew he was in great danger. To escape, he pretended to be crazy. He drooled spittle down his beard and scribbled on the walls. Achish took one look and said, "Do I not have enough crazy men around that you need to bring me another one? Get him out."

So David's life was spared one more time.

Label your map:	**Name for your chart:**
Gath	King Achish

Psalm 56

This psalm was written in memory of David's capture by the Philistines when they brought him before Achish king of Gath.

> Be merciful to me, O God, because man would swallow me up. All day long he fights, oppressing me. My enemies would swallow me up all day long. Many are they that would fight proudly against me.

> Those times when I am afraid, I will put my trust in you. In God (I will praise His word), in God I have put my trust. I will not be afraid. What can flesh do to me?

> All day long they twist my words. All their thoughts are against me for evil. They gather themselves together; they hide themselves, they dog my footsteps, even as they have waited in ambush for my soul.

> Shall they escape through their iniquity? In anger cast down the peoples, O God. You keep up with my wanderings. Put my tears into your bottle. Are they not in your book? Then shall my enemies turn back in the day that I call.

This I know, that God is for me. In God (I will praise His word), in Jehovah (I will praise His word), in God have I put my trust, I will not be afraid. What can man do to me?

Your vows are upon me, O God. I will render thank offerings to you, because you have delivered my soul from death. Have you not delivered my feet from falling, that I may walk before God in the light of the living?

Psalm 34
As the story shows, David was brought before Achish, and by pretending to be insane, he escaped, but he knew he owed his deliverance to God.

I will speak well of the Lord all the time. His praise shall continually be upon my lips. My soul shall make her boast in Jehovah. The meek shall hear thereof, and be glad. O magnify Jehovah with me, and let us exalt His name together.

I sought for Jehovah, and He answered me, and delivered me from all my fears. They looked unto Him, and were radiant; and their faces shall never be confounded. This poor man cried, and Jehovah heard him, and saved him out of all his troubles.

The angel of Jehovah encamps around them that fear Him and delivers them. Oh taste and see that Jehovah is good. Blessed is the man that takes refuge in him. Oh fear Jehovah, you saints of His, for there is no want among them that fear Him. The young lions do without, and suffer hunger, but they that seek Jehovah shall not do without any good thing.

Come, children, listen to me: I will teach you the fear of Jehovah. Which man among you wants to live, and loves many days so that he may see good? Keep your tongue from evil, and your lips from speaking guile. Depart from evil and do good. Seek peace, and follow after it.

The eyes of Jehovah are toward the righteous, and His ears are open unto their cry, but the face of the Lord is against them that do evil, to cut off the remembrance of them from the earth.

The righteous cried, and Jehovah heard, and delivered them out of all their troubles. Jehovah is nigh unto them that are of a broken heart, and saves such as are of a contrite spirit. Many are the afflictions of the righteous, but Jehovah delivers him out of them all. He keeps all his bones; not one of them is broken. Evil shall slay the wicked, and they that hate the righteous shall be condemned. Jehovah redeems the soul of His servants, and none of them that take refuge in Him shall be condemned.

David at the cave of Adullam (1 Sam. 22:1-5):
David was glad to get away from Gath with his life. When he got back to Israel, he hid in the cave of Adullam. Gradually word begin spreading about the conflict between David and Saul, and people began taking sides. His brothers learned he was at the cave and they and all his family joined him. Soon men from all over Israel began joining David. Anyone who was in trouble of some sort,

or in debt, or was discontented with conditions in the land joined him. Soon he had four hundred men.

Remember that David's parents lived in Bethlehem. They have joined David in Adullam, but he feared they would not be safe. Jesse is described as "old and advanced in years" at the time of the battle when David killed Goliath (1 Sam. 17:12), and this is some time later, so Jesse would not be able to take the rigors of hiding in caves and fleeing from one place to another, but neither was he safe from Saul in his own home. So in order to protect them from Saul, David took his parents to Moab. This was a reasonable move for David since his great grandmother Ruth was a Moabitess (Ruth 4:13-22).

David remained for a time in Moab in some kind of stronghold, but a prophet named Gad told him, "Leave, and go back to the land of Judah." So David returned and went into the forest of Hereth.

Label your map:
Cave of Adullam
Forest of Hereth
Remind yourself of the location of Moab

Psalm 142
When David returned to Judah from Gath, he went to the cave of Adullam where men began joining him from all Israel. This Psalm is written in honor of that time.

I cry with my voice to Jehovah. With my voice I make supplication to Jehovah. I pour out my complaint before Him. I show before Him my trouble.

When my spirit was overwhelmed within me, you knew my path. In the way wherein I walk they have hidden a snare for me. Look on my right hand, and see, for there is no man that knows me. Refuge has failed me. No man cares for my soul. I cried to you, O Jehovah. I said, "You are my refuge, my portion in the land of the living. Listen to my cry, because I am brought very low. Deliver me from my persecutors, for they are stronger than I. Bring my soul out of prison that I may give thanks unto your name. The righteous shall be all about me because you will deal bountifully with me."

Saul kills the priests of Nob (1 Sam. 22:6-19):

Meanwhile Saul was desperately seeking David. He bitterly reproached his servants for hiding David from him: "You men of Benjamin, do you think David will give you the kind of jobs I have given you when he becomes king? Have all of you decided to conspire against me and make a covenant with him? No one told me when Jonathan made a covenant with David. Does no one care about me anymore?" *(Saul was of the tribe of Benjamin, while David was of the tribe of Judah. If Saul were no longer king, then the tribe of Benjamin would no longer be the most favored tribe of Israel.)*

Finally Doeg the Edomite volunteered and said, "I saw the son of Jesse coming to Nob, to Ahimelech the son of Ahitub. Ahimelech inquired of Jehovah for him and gave him food, and gave him the sword of Goliath the Philistine."

Saul called Ahimelech and the priests to him to give an account for what they had done. "Why have you conspired against me, you and that son of Jesse, by giving him food and a weapon, and by inquiring of God for him so that he could rebel against me as he has this day?"

Ahimelech said, "Yes, I helped David. Is he not the servant of Saul? He is your most loyal servant, your son-in-law, the captain of your body guard, and highly respected in your household. Was that the first time I had inquired of God for him? Of course not! Please do not accuse me or my family of disloyalty, because I knew nothing about this whole affair."

But Saul was enraged against the priests and he commanded his soldiers to slay them. But they refused to obey this dreadful command. Saul then turned to Doeg and said, "You turn around and attack these priests."

Doeg, as an Edomite, did not have the respect for the priests that the Israelite soldiers had, so he turned and killed them. Not only did Doeg kill the eighty five priests that had come to Saul, he attacked the city of Nob and destroyed everything in it: men, women, children, and even the animals.

Abiathar joins David (1 Sam. 22:20-23; 23:6):

One of the priests managed to escape. Abiathar, a son of Ahimelech, got away and fled to where David was hiding. David was deeply grieved when he heard what had happened. He said, "When I saw Doeg the Edomite there that day, I knew he would surely tell Saul. I have brought about the death of every person in your father's house. Now, stay here with me, and do not be afraid, because the one who seeks your life is the same one who is seeking my life. You will be safe here with me."

When Abiathar fled that day, he took with him an ephod with the Urim and the Thummim by which he could communicate with God. The Urim and Thummim proved very helpful to David and his men.

New name: Abiathar

No one knows exactly what the Urim and Thummim looked like, or exactly how it was used. The High Priest wore a specially designed vest called an ephod. On it, there was a piece of cloth that had twelve precious stones on it, one for each tribe. This piece of material was folded double to form a pocket. The Urim and Thummim were kept in this pocket or breastplate as it was called (Exod. 28:30). By using the Urim and Thummim, the High Priest could ask God questions. Some have thought it might have been two stones, one white and black. If so, then the Priest asked the question, put his hand into the breastplate and drew out a stone. One color meant the answer was yes and the other color meant no. When God was answering them, then He controlled which color was drawn out just as He sometimes controlled how the results would turn out when lots were cast. (See Exod. 28:30; Lev. 8:8; Num. 27:21.) The priest could know whether God was controlling the answer by whether the same stone came out each time the same question was asked.

As we follow the fortunes of Abiathar we will also be observing the fulfillment of God's prophecy against Eli's house, because Abiathar was a descendant of Phinehas, one of the sons of Eli (1 Sam. 14:3; 22:20). Stay alert to the story of Abiathar, because we will meet him over and over in the story of David.

Psalm 52
This psalm was written by David when he learned of Doeg's heinous deed. David did not blame God for the terrible tragedy that had occurred. He placed the blame where it belonged: upon wicked men! His question was: how do you think you can get away with such wickedness?

Why do you boast about your wickedness, O mighty man?

The loving-kindness of God endures forever.

Your tongue devises wickedness, like a sharp razor, working deceitfully. You love evil more than good. You would rather lie than speak righteousness. You love all devouring words, O you deceitful tongue.

God will likewise destroy you for ever. He will take you up, and pluck you out of your tent, and root you out of the land of the living.

The righteous will see it, and fear, and shall laugh at such a man, saying, "This is the man that made not God his strength, but trusted in the abundance of his riches, and strengthened himself in his wickedness."

But as for me, I am like a green olive-tree in the house of God. I trust in the loving-kindness of God for ever and ever. I will give you thanks for ever in the presence of your saints, because you have done it, and I will hope in your name, for it is good.

David helps the city of Keilah, but has to flee again (1 Sam. 23:1-14):

Very soon David had an occasion when he needed to ask God's advice. He and his men heard that the Philistines had attacked the city of Keilah: "The Philistines are fighting against Keilah and are plundering their threshing floors."

David asked God, "Should I go and attack these Philistines?"

God replied, "Go and deliver Keilah."

David's men protested, saying, "We are afraid hiding here in Judah. How much more danger shall we be in if we go and openly attack the Philistines?"

David inquired of God again to be sure he was correct in his understanding. God said, "Go to Keilah, because I will deliver the Philistines into your hands."

So David and his men went to Keilah and fought the Philistines. Their victory was complete. They struck the enemy with a great slaughter, and led away their livestock. Thus David rescued the men of Keilah.

But when David defended the men of Keilah against the Philistines, Saul found out where he was. He rejoiced, saying, "God has delivered David into my hands, for he has shut himself up inside a walled city." Saul summoned all the people to assemble for war, and headed down to Keilah to besiege the city. *(Here Saul is ready to besiege one of his own cities in order to carry out his personal effort to rid himself of David. This illustrates just how complete this obsession had become.)*

David learned that Saul was on his way, so he called for Abiathar to bring the ephod in order to inquire of God. He said, "O Lord God of Israel, I, your servant, have heard that Saul is coming to destroy the city of Keilah for my sake. Will the men of Keilah turn me over to Saul? Will Saul really come as I have heard?"

God replied, "Yes, Saul will come; and yes, the men of Keilah will surrender you to him in order to spare themselves."

So David and his men were forced to flee again, searching for places of safety. They stayed in the sparsely populated areas of southern Judah, in first one stronghold and then another in the wilderness of Ziph. By now there were about 600 men with David. These six hundred men prove to be very loyal supporters of David throughout his lifetime.

When Saul learned that David had left Keilah, he gave up attacking the city, but he did not give up his pursuit of David. He knew David was still somewhere in the area, so he and his soldiers sought for him every day, but God protected David and did not deliver him into the hands of Saul.

Label your map:
  Keilah
  Wilderness of Ziph

Jonathan comforts David (1 Sam. 23:15-18):

While David was in Ziph, Jonathan came to see him and encouraged him in the Lord: "Do not be afraid, because my father Saul will not find you. You will be king over Israel and I will be next to you, and my father Saul knows that."

They renewed their covenant of friendship. David promised again that he would treat Jonathan's family kindly when he became king. Jonathan returned home and David remained in hiding from Saul. This was the last meeting between David and his good friend Jonathan.

The men of Ziph betray David (1 Sam. 23:16-29)

Soon the men of Ziph betrayed David to Saul. They went to Gibeah to tell Saul, "Is not David hiding with us in the strongholds?" — and proceeded to tell him exactly where David was hiding in their midst. They said, "Now come down and do whatever your soul desires, and we will surrender him to you."

Saul was very happy. He said, "May you be blessed of God, for you have had compassion for me. Now go home and make sure exactly where his haunt is, and that he is there, for he is very cunning. Learn all the places where he hides, and let me know the certainty of his location. I will go with you and we will search him out if he is hiding among all the thousands of Judah." So the men of Ziph returned home to watch David's movements, and Saul gathered an army to pursue him.

David's men kept him informed of Saul's every movement. He moved a few miles away to the wilderness of Maon, with Saul right on his heels. Day after day Saul searched for David, but God helped David, and Saul was not able to find him.

One time, Saul was on one side of a mountain, and David was on the other side. David knew Saul was there and was hurrying to get away. Just when the situation looked hopeless for David, a messenger came to Saul, saying, "Hurry and come, for the Philistines have made a raid on the land." So Saul was forced to withdraw his forces, and David was saved. Therefore, he called the spot the Rock of Escape.

David moved a little more to the east and hid in the strongholds of En-gedi, on the shores of the Dead Sea.

Label your map:
  Maon
  En-gedi
  Dead Sea

Though men might have built shelters in southern Judah to protect themselves from enemies, and David may have used one or more of these, most of these strongholds mentioned were caves or other such natural formations. Saul could more easily trap David in a man-made shelter than in a natural formation that would made a good hiding place. For example, a walled city was a very strong place for protection, but God advised David to get away from the city of Keilah because Saul could have come and besieged the city until the men of the city surrendered David to him. The Bible uses the term "wilderness" for any area that was mostly uninhabited. All of these places where David is hiding are in the southern part of Judah's territory, but they are mostly in rugged areas of woods or rough terrain where the population was scarce.

The prefix "En" on a Hebrew word means a spring. En-gedi was a large spring in the very rugged region immediately west of the Dead Sea. It is still there today and it forms a pool large enough for a group to swim in.

Psalm 54
After David's brief stay at Keilah he moved to Ziph and experienced the same ingratitude and deceit there. This Psalm reflects his feelings at the time.

Save me, O God, by your name, and judge me in your might. Hear my prayer, O God. Give ear to the words of my mouth. Because strangers are risen up against me, and violent men have sought after my soul. They have not set God before them.

Behold, God is my helper. The Lord is with them that uphold my soul. He will requite the evil unto my enemies. Destroy them in your truth.

With a freewill offering will I sacrifice unto you. I will give thanks unto your name, O Jehovah, for it is good. For He has delivered me out of all trouble, and my eye has seen my desire upon my enemies.

David spares Saul's life (1 Sam. 24:1-22):

It was not long before Saul learned that David was at En-gedi, so he came against him with his army. By this time, Saul had 3,000 specially chosen soldiers with him, against David's 600 who had joined him from all walks of life.

David and his men were hiding in the inner recesses of a cave. Saul went into the same cave to "cover his feet" *(a euphemism for using the bathroom)*. David's men urged him to kill Saul: "This is your chance. This is the day God has given your enemy into your hands."

David crept up to Saul in the darkness and cut a piece from his robe. But then David's conscience smote him for doing even that much. He told his men, "Far be it from me to lay my hand upon God's anointed. He is the one God chose to be king." So David prevented his men from harming Saul.

When Saul had gone out of the cave, and had moved a safe distance away, David went out and called to him. When Saul looked around, David bowed himself to the ground and said, "Men have told you, O king, that David seeks your life. But why do you listen? Behold this day the Lord gave you into my hands in the cave, and some wanted me to kill you, but I had pity on you. I said, 'I will not touch the Lord's anointed.' Now, my father, look. Do you see this piece of your robe? If I had been wanting to kill the king, I could have done so just now. Don't listen to the lies men tell you. Know and understand that there is no evil or rebellion in my hands. I have not sinned against you although you are lying in wait to take my life. The Lord will judge between you and me, and will avenge me of you, but I will never lift my hand against you. Against whom has the king come out? Whom are you pursuing? A dead dog, or a single flea? May the Lord see what you are doing and deliver me from your hand."

Saul looked at the piece of cloth in David's hand, and he knew that David spoke the truth. The king wept and cried out to David. "You have shown today what kind of man you are, because the Lord delivered me into your hands and you did not kill me. You are more righteous than I. The Lord will reward you, for I know that you will surely be king and that the kingdom will be established in your hand. Swear that you will not cut off my seed after me, or cut off my name from my father's house."

Since Saul was chasing David to try to kill him, he really was not in a good position to ask a favor from David, but David was a good man who held no hatred for Saul. So he swore he would show kindness to Saul's family, and they went their separate ways. Saul returned to his city, but David and his men remained in the stronghold. Saul's remorse did not last very long, so David remained a fugitive.

Psalm 57
The title of this psalm says of David: "When he fled from Saul, in the cave." Some refer this psalm to 1 Samuel 22 and the cave of Adullam, but it seems that the circumstances of David in the cave in 1 Samuel 24 fit the psalm better.

> Be merciful to me, O God, be merciful to me, because my soul takes refuge in you. Yes, in the shadow of your wings I will take refuge, until ordeals have ceased.

> I will cry unto God Most High, unto God who performs all things for me. He will send from heaven, and save me, when he that would swallow me up reproaches me. God will send forth His mercy and His truth.

> My soul is among lions; I lie among them that are set on fire, even the sons of men, whose teeth are spears and arrows, and their tongue a sharp sword.

> May you be exalted, O God, above the heavens; let your glory be above all the earth.

> They have prepared a net for my steps; my soul is bowed down. They have dug a pit before me. They are fallen into the midst thereof themselves.

> My heart is fixed, O God, my heart is fixed. I will sing, yes, I will sing praises. Wake up, my glory; wake up, psaltery and harp. I myself will wake up very early. I will give thanks unto you, O Lord, among the nations. For your mercy is great unto the heavens, and your truth unto the skies.

> May you be exalted, O God, above the heavens; let your glory be above all the earth.

David and Nabal (1 Sam. 25:1-44):
Samuel the prophet died and was buried in Ramah which had been his home for many years. All Israel wept for him.

David and his men moved into the Wilderness of Paran. A very wealthy man named Nabal had large flocks and herds of sheep and goats in Maon and Carmel, places in this area of southern Judah. From time to time, David and his men defended the animals and their shepherds from enemies who would have attacked them if David's men had not been there.

Time came for Nabal to shear one thousand goats and three thousand sheep. Sheep shearing time was a time for hard work, but it was usually a time for feasting also.

Finding food for his men was always a problem for David in the wilderness. So David decided that since he and his men had guarded Nabal's possessions, Nabal should be willing to give them some food. David could have taken what he wanted at any time, but he was an honorable man and would not do that.

David sent ten of his men to ask Nabal very courteously for some food. He instructed his men, "Greet Nabal in my name and tell him we have heard that he is shearing sheep. Tell him that we have been with his shepherds and have taken nothing from them nor hurt them in any way. Have him ask his young men, and they will tell him that I am telling the truth. Therefore, say to him, 'Let my young men find favor in your eyes, for we have come on a festive day. Please give us whatever you find at hand — to us and to your servant David.'"

When David's men spoke to Nabal, he was very rude to them. He sneered and said, "Who is David? You cannot be sure these days whom you are dealing with. There are runaway slaves all around. Surely you do not think I will take my bread, my water, and my meat that I have slaughtered for my servants and give it away to anyone who comes along."

David's men returned and told David the very insulting reply of Nabal. David was filled with rage and he said, "Every man put on his sword." Four hundred angry men headed for Nabal's house, while 200 remained behind with their possessions.

Now Nabal was harsh and evil in all his dealings, but he had an intelligent, beautiful wife named Abigail. When this exchange between Nabal and David's men took place, one of Nabal's servants hurried to tell Abigail what had happened: "David sent messengers to our master, and he was very rude to them. They have been good to us and have been a wall between us and our enemies while we were keeping the sheep. I wanted you to know about this because David will not take such treatment. I could not speak to our master because he is such a worthless fellow one cannot tell him anything."

Abigail was horrified to hear what her husband had done, so she had the servants prepare a large supply of food. They loaded the supplies on donkeys, and she set out to meet David and his men.

Make no mistake: David was furious! He said, "May God curse me if I leave even one child alive at Nabal's house by daybreak."

When Abigail met David, she fell on her face before him and pleaded for mercy. She said, "Let me take the blame for this. Please let me explain. My husband is named Nabal which means 'fool,' and that is what he is. Please do not pay attention to what he says and does. I did not know anything about this until your young men were gone. Do not let this make you guilty of bloodshed, my lord. Behold the present which I have brought you. Take it for yourself and for your men. I know that the Lord is going to preserve you and make you a sure house. Do not do anything now that will be a grief to you later. And when Jehovah has dealt well with you, remember me."

David's anger disappeared as he listened to Abigail's words. He said, "May you be blessed of God, because you have surely kept me from bloodshed today. As God lives, I had planned to wipe out every living soul of Nabal's house. Go in peace. I will do as you have said."

When Abigail returned home, Nabal was in the midst of a feast. He was very drunk, so she told him nothing. The next morning, however, she told him what she had done, and Nabal's heart died within him. Ten days later, Jehovah struck him so that he died.

When David heard of Nabal's death, he said, "Jehovah has returned Nabal's evil upon his own head and has kept me from wrong."

David remembered the beautiful woman of wisdom who had met him in the wilderness. He sent for Abigail to become his wife. When her servants brought her the word, she said, "Oh, I am not fit to wash the feet of his servants," — but all the while she was hurrying as fast as she could to get ready to go to him.

David had already taken a wife named Ahinoam since he had been running from Saul. Now he takes Abigail as well. These were in addition to Michal whom he was forced to leave behind when he fled from Saul. By this time, Saul had given Michal to a man named Paltiel.

Notice that Michal has been given to another man as his wife. David did not leave her by choice, and Saul has insulted David, pretending he was dead, to give her to another man. Continue to watch her story.

New names:　　　　　　**Label your map:**
　Nabal　　　　　　　　**Wilderness of Paran**
　Abigail　　　　　　　**Carmel (in southern Judah)**
　Ahinoam
　Paltiel

There is a Mount Carmel in northern Israel. It is the mountain that juts out into the Mediterranean Sea almost directly west of the Sea of Galilee. It is the Carmel that is best known in the Bible story. The Carmel mentioned here is in the Wilderness of Paran, near Maon, because Nabal's sheep are in that area. This is the only period of Bible history that mentions this Carmel. Seemingly it was a small village, or just an area with the name here in southern Judah. Probably this is the Carmel where Saul and his soldiers set up a monument to celebrate their victory over the Amalekites when Samuel was trying to find Saul to give him the message from Jehovah (see 1 Sam. 15:12). Saul had been in the very southern part of Israel when he fought the Amalekites, so this is the Carmel that would have been near his path back home.

David spares Saul's life again (1 Sam. 26:1-25):

David returned to the Wilderness of Ziph. The Ziphites told Saul that David was there, so Saul came after him with his 3,000 chosen men. David's scouts kept him informed where Saul was. David and his men kept out of sight, but when Saul made camp, David was waiting nearby. He carefully noted where Saul was preparing to sleep and where Abner his chief captain was beside him. Saul was sleeping in the very center of the camp of soldiers. His spear was stuck in the ground near his head, and there was a bottle of water nearby.

When the camp of Saul had settled down to sleep, David proposed a daring and dangerous plan. He said, "Who will go with me into Saul's camp?"

Abishai, Joab's brother and one of David's bravest men, said, "I will go with you."

David and Abishai picked their way silently through the slumbering forms to stand beside the sleeping king. Abishai begged David to let him kill Saul: "This is our chance. Let me smite him to the earth with the spear. One stroke, that is all it will take."

But David would not allow it. "As Jehovah lives, God will smite him, or he will die, or he will be killed in battle, but who can kill God's anointed without guilt? Now, take his spear and the water jug, and let us go." Then David and Abishai left as quietly as they had come. No one awoke to stop their progress because God was with them.

David went to the top of a hill a long way off and shouted, "Abner! Aren't you going to answer me, Abner?"

Abner answered, "Who are you?"

David said, "I thought you were a real soldier, Abner. This is not a good thing you have done. You have let men come into the camp to slay the king. You should die because you have not guarded your lord, God's anointed. See where the king's spear is, and the bottle of water which was at his head."

Saul's men were dumbfounded to see that the spear and water had been taken away. Saul cried out, "Is that you, David?"

David said, "It is, O King." David pleaded with Saul: "Why are you pursuing me? What have I done? What evil is in my hand? Please listen to my words. If the Lord has stirred you up against me, then let Him accept an offering at my hand. But if it men who have persuaded you, then let them be cursed before God, because they have caused me to be driven from my home and away from my inheritance. Now do not let my blood fall to the ground away from home. The king has come out to search for one flea, or as one hunts for a partridge in a mountain."

Saul said, "I have sinned! Return, my son David, for I will do you no more harm. I see that my life is precious in your eyes. I have been foolish, and have committed a serious error."

David said, "Here is your spear. Send one of your young men to get it. May the Lord give to every man according to his conduct. As your life was precious in my eyes today, so let my life be precious in God's eyes and let Him deliver me from all tribulation."

Saul blessed David, and they went their separate ways.

New name: Abishai

Notice that Abishai is a brother of Joab. We have not yet added Joab's name to our list because we have not yet met him in a specific story, though he was probably one of the men who joined David as early as the cave of Adullam. Abishai, Joab, and another brother named Asahel all play important roles in the life of David. Stay alert to their parts in the action because we will meet them again and again. Abishai is one of David's very loyal soldier.

Psalm 63

Though this psalm deals with the time when David was hiding out in the wilderness of Judah, verse 11 seems to indicate that it was written later, when David was king. It could fit any moment of the time when David was fleeing from Saul in the wilderness of Judah. We place it here just before he fled to Gath in Philistia.

O God, you are my God. Earnestly I will seek you. My soul thirsts for you, my flesh longs for you, in a dry and weary land, where there is no water.

Thus I have looked upon you in the sanctuary, to see your power and your glory. Since your mercy is better than life, my lips will praise you. So I will bless you as long as I live: I will lift up my hands in your name. My soul shall be satisfied as with marrow and fatness, and my mouth shall praise you with joyful lips, when I remember you upon my bed and meditate on you in the night-watches. Because you have been my help, and in the shadow of your wings I will rejoice. My soul follows close behind you. Your right hand holds me up. But those who seek my soul, to destroy it, shall go into the lower parts of the earth. They shall be given over to the power of the sword; they shall be a portion for jackals.

But the king shall rejoice in God. Every one that swears by Him shall glory, for the mouth of them that speak lies shall be stopped.

David among the Philistines (1 Sam. 27:1-12):

David still did not trust Saul. He was afraid that the longer he stayed in Israel the greater were his chances of being captured. Once again, therefore, he went to King Achish of Gath, but this time he had a company of 600 men and their families with him. By now the Philistines had learned of the enmity between Saul and David, so they welcomed him. They thought David hated Saul as much as Saul hated David. Saul learned that David had fled to Philistine territory, and did not continue to search for him.

At first David and his company remained in Gath with Achish, each man with his own household. But after a time, David went to Achish and said, "If I have found favor in your eyes, let me have a place of my own in one of the cities in the country. Why should your servant live in the royal city with you?" So King Achish gave David his own city, a place called Ziklag. David lived in Philistine territory for a year and four months.

During his time at Ziklag, David took his men and made raids on various enemies of the Israelites who lived in the South. He would leave no one alive to tell what had happened. Therefore, word never came to Achish that David was using his time at Ziklag to prepare for the day when he would be king over Israel. David planned to have no enemies on his southern border.

David would tell Achish that he had raided the south of Judah or one of the allies of Israel. Achish was very pleased because he thought this would make David an enemy of Israel forever and that he would remain a servant of Achish.

The expression translated "the South" refers to the area south of Beersheba and reaching about 50 miles to Kadesh-barnea. The geographic term for the area is "the Negev." It was a very dry region. During the winter rains, grass would grow, but then during the hot, parching heat of summer it was semi-desert. It was the buffer zone between the fertile lands of southern Judah and the true desert of the peninsula of Sinai. Various nomadic people moved through the region and would edge closer and closer to the rich lands during times of less strength in Israel. David was clearing out these potential threats to his kingdom.

Label your map:
Ziklag
The Negev

Others join David (1 Chron. 12:1-18):

The book of 1 Chronicles covers the same period of time as 2 Samuel, with a little overlapping with 1 Samuel also. The first nine chapters of 1 Chronicles give various genealogies and lists. There is no story given in those chapters. Chapter 10 tells of the death of Saul, overlapping with the last chapter of 1 Samuel. Most of the book tells about David's time as king, so most of the parallel starts with 1 Chronicles 11 and 2 Samuel 5. But there is some information given about David's mighty men that fits with this period while he was still fleeing from Saul. The picture would not be complete without including that information here.

From this time on in the study, if the event under consideration is told in both books, you will be given more than one passage to read. Be sure you read both accounts. Sometimes the accounts are nearly identical, but some details may be given in one passage that are not found in the other. Or, one book will include a particular story the other does not include. You must have both books to make the history complete. Since the two books do not always tell the events in the same order, we will use 1 and 2 Samuel (and then 1 and 2 Kings) as our pattern for which event to study next.

You will be studying two books of the Old Testament at once. Be sure your students know it if they are old enough to understand the point. Too often the books of 1 and 2 Chronicles remain a blank in our minds, even after we have a pretty good knowledge of the Bible story. The stories they include are as interesting as those in 2 Samuel and 1 and 2 Kings. This parallel continues all the way through the fall of Judah. We will try to combine the history given in both sources in its chronological place.

Men of Israel continued to take sides in the conflict between Saul and David. We have already observed as David's relatives joined him at the Cave of Adullam, then as others who were discontented with conditions in the land joined him. First he had 400 men, then 600. Those are the only ones specified in the book of 1 Samuel, but 1 Chronicles 12 tells of more who joined him.

While he was at Ziklag, some mighty men came to him. Some were even relatives of Saul. They were very skilled soldiers, able to use either hand slinging stones, and they were very capable with the bow. Some from the tribe of Gad joined David while he was still in the strongholds *(probably those in southern Judah before he went to Ziklag)*. They, too, were mighty men of valor. They had on one occasion crossed the Jordan River at flood stage and had put to flight enemies camped all along the valleys. All of these men were great assets to David, and they proved to be very loyal to him.

A group of men from the tribes of Benjamin and Judah came to David. Since Saul was of the tribe of Benjamin, David was not sure why these men were approaching him. Were they spies or soldiers from Saul who had come to capture him? He went out to meet them, saying, "If you have come peacefully to help me, then my heart will be united to you; but if you have come to betray me to my adversary, and there is no wrong that I have done, then may God decide between us."

The Spirit came upon Amasai, one of the group, and he said, "We are yours, O David. Peace be to you, and peace be to Him who helps you. Indeed, your God helps you." Amasai became one of David's choice men.

Then David received them with joy and made them captains of bands.

Saul and the Witch of Endor (1 Sam. 28:1-25):

The Philistines began gathering their forces for another battle. This time they moved up the coastal plain to Aphek north of Mount Carmel. Saul gathered his forces on Mount Gilboa to prepare to meet them in battle.

Find these places on your map. This was unusually far north for the Philistines to venture. That they feel strong enough to attack this far north lets us know just how badly Saul had been neglecting his own kingdom of Israel.

As time for the battle approached, Saul was terrified. He inquired of God, but God would not answer by dream, by the Urim and Thummim, or by a prophet. Saul was desperate to find out what would happen. Samuel was now dead; the Spirit of God had left Saul; and God would not communicate with him in any way. What could he do?

Saul had hunted out and destroyed all the wizards and those with familiar spirits that he could find in the land. This had been a good thing, because the Law of Moses specifically commanded that all such people be destroyed (see Exod. 22:18). But Saul was so desperate for information he told his servants to find someone who could communicate with the dead. They brought him word that there was a woman with a familiar spirit in Endor.

That night Saul disguised himself, took two of his men, and went to see the woman. When they arrived, Saul said, "Please use your familiar spirit to bring someone from the dead that I wish to speak with."

The woman said, "You know how Saul has cut off all those having familiar spirits. Why are you trying to trap me and get me into trouble?"

Saul swore, "As surely as the Lord lives, you will not be punished for this."

The woman agreed to help and she asked, "Whom do you want?"

"Samuel," was Saul's answer.

So, the woman went into her act.

The word translated "familiar spirit" is sometimes translated "leather bag" or "stomach." It describes the woman as one who "speaks from the stomach." She was a ventriloquist. She pretended to have a spirit in the realm of the dead with whom she was familiar, that is, on good terms with. Though she could not talk freely with the dead herself, her familiar spirit could. Through it, therefore, she could talk to any dead person she wished. All of this was pretense. She pretended the familiar spirit was talking, but she was really the one speaking. She was "throwing her voice."

This time, when she began her act, she suddenly screamed. She was terrified! You see, her act had never worked before. Something really was happening this time. She was more frightened than anyone else. The witch turned to Saul and said, "Why have you tricked me? You are Saul."

Saul said, "Do not be afraid. What do you see?"

She answered, "I see a god coming up out of the earth." *(She was using "god" here in the sense of some superhuman, unearthly being.)* When Saul asked what he looked like, she replied, "An old man is coming up, and he is covered with a robe." Saul knew it was Samuel and he fell on his face.

Samuel said, "Why did you disturb me?"

Saul said, "I cannot find out anything about the battle tomorrow. God's spirit has departed from me so that I cannot find out what will happen by prophet, or dream, or vision."

Samuel said, "Then why do you ask me, since the Lord has departed from you and become your adversary?" He reminded Saul of what God had said He would do and why He was doing it: "The Lord has torn the kingdom out of your hands and has given it to David. God has done this because you did not obey Him in destroying the Amalekites. Now, the Lord will hand all of Israel over to the Philistines tomorrow, along with you and your sons. You and your sons will be with me by this time tomorrow." *(Samuel did not mean Saul and his sons would be in heaven. He meant they would be in the realm of the dead.)*

Saul fainted when he heard these words, and Samuel disappeared. Saul had no strength left in him.

The woman insisted on preparing food for the king and his men. Saul protested, but then agreed to eat after the woman and his men insisted. He must have strength to lead his army in battle the next day — even though it would be a day of defeat. After eating, they arose and returned to camp to await the battle.

Label your map:
- **Aphek**
- **Mt. Carmel**
- **Mt. Gilboa**
- **Endor**

New name:
- **Witch of Endor**

This woman with the familiar spirit is commonly called the "witch of Endor," and we have used the term even though that specific word is not applied to her in the Bible text. There are several words used in the Bible to refer to a class of people who claimed to have miraculous power through evil spirits, and to the art they practiced. The terms include: witch, wizard, magician, sorcerer, one with a familiar spirit, witchcraft, divination, sorcery, and perhaps others. By whatever term they are identified, all such practices were strongly condemned by God (see Exod. 22:18; Deut. 18:9-14; 1 Sam. 28:3, 9; 2 Kings 23:24; Isa. 8:19; Acts 19:18, 19, and other passages).

There has been a good deal of disagreement about the facts in this story. Did the woman actually succeed in bringing Samuel back from the dead to deliver this message, or was it pretense on her part? Did she succeed by her "demonic" powers? Was the one speaking as Samuel really an evil spirit pretending to be Samuel? Most of these questions arise because of misconceptions about "demonic" powers, and because little attention is paid to the text itself. Consider these facts:

1. *One of the main arguments made by God to prove that He is real and other gods are false is that they are unable to do the things that God can do (Isa. 41:22-24). In the New Testament, the miracles were done by the power of God to confirm that the message of Jesus (see John 10:25, 33-38) and that of the apostles after Him was true and genuine (Mark 16:17-20; Heb. 2:3-4). Now if the demons can work miracles also, how does one know when a miracle is a "demonic" miracle or a God-caused miracle? Some one might say, if the miracle is good then it is God-caused, and if the miracle is bad then it is "demonic." But we would like an example of a bad miracle. Paul speaks of lying wonders in 2 Thessalonians 2:9. If "demonic" miracles are real, then why would they be <u>lying</u> wonders?*

2. *The text of 1 Samuel says, "When the woman saw Samuel," not when she <u>thought</u> she saw Samuel. It is the inspired historian who said she saw Samuel. The text says, "And <u>Samuel</u> said to Saul." Again, it is the inspired historian who observes this fact. Throughout the conversation, the inspired historian continues to say, "And <u>Samuel</u> said..." Finally, in verses 19 and 20, the historian says that "Saul fell straightway his full length upon the earth, and was sore afraid, <u>because of the words of Samuel</u>." It would be denying the word of inspiration to say this was pretense on the part of the woman, or that some evil spirit was impersonating Samuel. The only explanation that agrees with the testimony of the inspired historian is that Samuel himself delivered this message from God.*

3. *There is no proof at all that the woman knew who Saul was when he arrived with his request, but what she saw somehow let her know who her visitor was.*

4. *After Saul replied to Samuel's question of why he had disturbed him, Samuel proceeded to tell Saul why Jehovah had abandoned him (28:15-19). He included in his explanation things that Samuel would have known well, but it is unlikely that a demon could have given such a clear answer to Saul.*

5. *Samuel was able to foretell what was going to happen to Saul and to his sons the next day. Demons cannot know the future. If they could then Satan could have known what Jesus was going to do, and how God was going to save the world, but he did not know it, and could not know it (1 Cor. 2:8).*

Scripture, as well as reason, strongly affirm that this story occurred just as it is recorded. Samuel was sent back by God to give His final answer to Saul, an answer of condemnation and judgment.

David among the Philistine army (1 Sam. 28:1-2; 29:1-11):

Meanwhile, the Philistines had been organizing their forces. King Achish was part of the group. He had brought David and his men with him to fight on the Philistine side, because he had said, "Know assuredly that you and your men will go with me to help us fight." David had been so successful in deceiving him, Achish was sure that David was now completely on the Philistine side. David had agreed, saying, "You shall know what your servant can do."

The other Philistine lords were not so deceived, however. When the soldiers marched before the lords, they demanded, "What are these Hebrews doing here?"

Achish replied, "Oh this is David and his men who have been with me these years now, and he is very loyal to me."

But the Philistine lords would not hear of letting David's men be included in their army. "Is this not David, of whom they sang to one another, saying, 'Saul has slain his thousands, and David his ten thousands'? Will he not join with the Israelites again in the battle? Send him home!"

King Achish protested, but he finally sent David back to Ziklag. The Philistines and Israelites moved their forces nearer to each other while David went on his way.

The Philistine lords were wiser than King Achish, because David had never become an enemy of Israel in his mind or in his actions. Achish was the one deceived.

David finds Ziklag destroyed (1 Sam. 30:1-31):

It was the third day before David and his men reached Ziklag. The battle between the Israelites and Philistines took place during this same time. The inspired historian takes us home with David first, before returning to tell what happened in the battle on Mt. Gilboa.

When David and his men got back in sight of Ziklag, they were horrified to find their village in ashes. Amalekites from the desert had raided the city and had stolen their possessions and had taken their families captive. The men were so upset they lifted up their voices and wept aloud until there was no strength left for weeping. They were so upset they talked of stoning David. *(This implies they had not wanted to go with the Philistine army when David had suggested it.)* Of course, David's own wives had been taken also.

David called for Abiathar to bring the ephod. When he inquired of God, God replied, "Pursue the Amalekites, for you will surely recover everything." So David's men set out in pursuit of the raiding band, across the barren wilderness. By the time they came to the brook Besor, 200 of the men were so tired David decided to leave them there with the supplies. The other 400 continued their chase.

After a time they found a man who had been left to die by the Amalekites. He was an Egyptian who had been a slave of an Amalekite. His master had left him behind when he became sick, and he had not had food or water for three days. David gave him food and water and asked him if he could show them the Amalekite camping places. The slave agreed to help if David's men would promise not to kill him themselves, or to return him to his master. David agreed.

With the young man's help, they found the Amalekites feasting, drinking, and dancing. They were celebrating their successful raids upon the Philistine and Israelite cities, and rejoicing over all the spoils they had managed to take. David and his men fell upon them unawares and wiped them out except for 400 young men who escaped on camels. They recovered everything: their wives, their children, and their possessions. In addition, they found an enormous booty the Amalekites had gotten from other raids. What joy there was among David's men!

Soon they came back to the 200 men who had stayed at the brook Besor. Some of the 400 did not want to share the booty with them, but David set forth a rule to stand from that day forward: "Everyone shares in that which we take in battle, whether he goes to war or stays with the baggage."

As a good will gesture, David sent gifts from the spoils of war to various southern cities of Judah. He sent each gift to the elders of the city, with these words: "Behold, a gift to you from the spoil of the enemies of the Lord." These cities were in the territory where David and his men had hidden from Saul, and David knew these gifts would help pave the way for his shortly becoming king.

Still more join David (1 Chron. 12:19-22):

Soldiers from the tribe of Manasseh defected from Saul and joined David's forces as the armies gathered for this last battle of Saul's. They were in David's group when the Philistine lords had seen them pass as they were organizing their forces, and they were sent away when the lords refused to let David's forces join theirs. Though 1 Samuel does not tell of their being in the group who returned to Ziklag to find it burned, 1 Chronicles tells that they were with David's men and helped in the raid against the Amalekites. The story of 1 Samuel concentrates on those 600 who lost their families and possessions and were, therefore, so upset and grieved over the attack that had been made upon their village. These men who were accompanying them had not lost their possessions, but they helped the others to regain theirs.

It is evident that David has not been forgotten by the people of Israel. They did not share the hatred that Saul felt. It will not be long before he has their full loyalty.

Saul's last battle (1 Sam. 31:1-13; 1 Chron. 10:1-14):

Meanwhile, the battle between the Philistines and Israelites was taking place. Just as Samuel had said would happen, Israel was smitten. The soldiers were soon fleeing before the Philistines. The Philistines chased Saul and his sons. Jonathan, Abinadab, and Malchishua, the sons of Saul, were caught and slain.

Saul was critically wounded by the Philistine archers. He was afraid the Philistines would find him before he died and torture him, so he asked his armor-bearer to kill him. The young man protested because he was afraid, so Saul fell on his own sword. When the armor-bearer saw that his king was dead, he, too, fell on his own sword and died. Thus the king's three sons died, Saul himself died, and his armor-bearer with him.

The people in the nearby cities learned that the army was fleeing and that Saul and his sons were dead. They began fleeing across the Jordan to save their lives, and the Philistines moved into the cities behind them. The Israelites were defeated and in disgrace.

The next day when the Philistines went out to search the dead bodies for spoil, they found Saul and his sons. They cut off Saul's head, stripped him of his weapons, and sent them throughout the land of Philistia to spread the good news of their victory. They put Saul's weapons in the temple of their god, and fastened his head in the house of Dagon. They fastened his body, and those of his sons', to the wall of the city of Beth-shan.

When the men from Jabesh-Gilead learned what the Philistines had done to their bodies, they risked their lives to put an end to Saul's shame. During the night, a group of valiant men of the city slipped across the Jordan, through the Philistine lines, and took the bodies down from the wall. They returned to Jabesh, burned the bones, and buried them there under a tree. They mourned and fasted seven days for their king and his sons.

This was a sad end to a king who could have been great if only he had been faithful to God. Saul died because he did not keep the word which Jehovah commanded him, and because he sought advice from one who had a familiar spirit instead of Jehovah.

Do you remember why the men of Jabesh-Gilead would have a special feeling of kindness for Saul? Remember this story, because we will come to more about it some years after David becomes king.

Label your map:
    Beth-shan — See how far the Philistines are from their usual borders.
    Compare the location of Jabesh-Gilead to Beth-shan.

The Reign of David
2 Samuel 1-24; 1 Chronicles 11-29

Outline of Bible history:
Look at the outline of Bible history once more. We are still in the period of the United Kingdom, but Saul is now dead, and David is ready to become king.

Creation Stories
Flood
Scattering of the People
The Patriarchs
The Exodus
Wilderness Wandering
Conquest of the Land
Judges

*United Kingdom

    Saul
    *David
    Solomon

Divided Kingdom
Captivity
Return from Captivity
Years of Silence
Life of Christ
Early Church
Letters to Christians

Set the stage:
Remember that 1 Samuel ends with Saul's last battle with the Philistines. The Israelites were severely beaten; Saul and his three sons were killed; the Israelites in the cities of the Jezreel Valley fled across the Jordan, and the Philistines moved into the cities behind them. The Philistines nailed the bodies of Saul and his sons to the walls of the city of Bethshan. The men of Jabesh-Gilead came by night, took the bodies down, took them back to Jabesh, burned the bones, and buried them.

Remember that, prior to the battle between Saul's army and the Philistine forces, David was included with the Philistine army at first, not because he was no longer loyal to Israel, but because King Achish of Gath thought David was loyal to him. The other Philistines refused to let David go to battle with them. David and his men went back to Ziklag, found it burned, and pursued the Amalekites who had raided it. The book of 2 Samuel begins with David's return to Ziklag after his battle with the Amalekites.

David mourns for Saul and Jonathan (2 Sam. 1:1-27):

While David was chasing the Amalekites who had raided Ziklag, Saul was fighting his last battle with the Philistines. On the third day after David returned to Ziklag, a man arrived from Saul's camp. He had dust on his head, his clothes were torn, and he bowed low before David.

David said, "Where have you come from?"

The man answered, "I escaped from the Israelite camp."

"What happened?" was David's eager question.

The man told him all the dreadful news: "Our soldiers have fled; many of our people are dead, and Saul and his son Jonathan are dead."

David asked, "How do you know Saul and Jonathan are dead?"

He said, "As I was going along on Mount Gilboa, I came upon Saul leaning on his spear. The Philistines were almost upon him. Saul asked me to kill him because he was wounded and yet his life was still in him. I knew he could not live, so I killed him. This is his crown and bracelet which I took from him to bring to you."

This man's story of Saul's death is not the same one given by the inspired historian in 1 Samuel 31 and 1 Chronicles 10. It seems this man wanted David's favor and thought he could win it by saying that he had slain Saul. He probably found Saul dead, as the record says he was in 1 Samuel 31:4-6 and in 1 Chronicles 10:4-6, and took the crown and bracelet to use as evidence that he killed Saul.

David was very upset to hear of the death of Saul and Jonathan. He rent his garments, and he and his men mourned. He asked the young man, "Who are you?"

The young man said, "I am a sojourner, an Amalekite."

David said, "Why were you not afraid to put your hand upon God's anointed?" Then, since David had no other information about Saul's death, he ordered the young man killed. He said: "Your blood be upon your own head. Your own mouth testified against you when you said you killed the Lord's anointed."

Then David wrote a song of lament over Saul and Jonathan, and taught it to the men of Judah. The song said:

How are the mighty fallen in the mountains!
Tell it not in Gath and Ashkelon lest the Philistines rejoice.
Let there be no rain or dew upon Mount Gilboa because it was there that Saul and Jonathan were slain.
They were mighty in battle. Saul and Jonathan were united in battle and in death.
Weep, O daughters of Israel, over Saul who clothed you in scarlet with ornaments of gold.
How are the mighty fallen! I am distressed for my brother Jonathan, for his love to me was great, even greater than the love one has for a wife.
How are the mighty fallen and the weapons of war perished!

Name to add: The young Amalekite

David becomes king in Hebron (2 Sam. 2:1-7, 11):
David asked God what his next move should be, and God told him to go to Hebron. It had been a few years since God had told David through Samuel that he would be king after Saul's death; the time had come for that plan to be accomplished.

David took his two wives, Ahinoam and Abigail, and his men and their families, and moved to Hebron. This was in the midst of the territory of Judah, David's own tribe, and the men of Judah anointed him king in Hebron. But there was still trouble ahead.

Word came to David that the men of Jabesh-Gilead had buried Saul. David appreciated their showing kindness to Saul, so he sent messengers to thank them and to tell them the men of Judah had made him king. The message said: "May you be blessed of the Lord because you have shown kindness to Saul and have buried him. May God show you kindness, and I will show kindness to you also. Now let your hands be strong, and be valiant, because your master Saul is dead, and the house of Judah has anointed me king over them."

David remained in Hebron as king over Judah for seven years and six months.

Label your map: Hebron

Ish-bosheth becomes king in Mahanaim (2 Sam. 2:8-3:1):

Meanwhile, Abner, the captain of Saul's army, took Ish-bosheth, a surviving son of Saul's, and made him king in Mahanaim. He claimed that Ish-bosheth was king over all Gilead, over the tribe of Ashur, over all the valley of Jezreel, over Ephraim, over Benjamin, and over all Israel. He remained king for two years, but the tribe of Judah remained loyal to David.

Look on your map. Mahanaim was on the east side of the Jordan River. Saul's capital had been at Gibeah on the west side of the River. Abner claimed that Ish-bosheth was king over "all Israel," but the fact he was not in the old capital indicates it was an empty claim. It was not long before the expected battle between the two kings erupted.

Abner led Ish-bosheth's men out from Mahanaim and went to Gibeon to fight David's men. Joab, the son of Zeruiah, was in charge of David's men. David's men were from the tribe of Judah, and Abner's men were mostly from the tribe of Benjamin. They met at the pool of Gibeon. The two armies sat down on opposite sides of the pool, and tried to negotiate at first in order to avoid civil war.

Abner suggested that they let some of the young men from each side fight in hand-to-hand combat in front of them to settle the dispute: "Let the young men arise and hold a contest before us." Joab agreed, and the contest began with twelve men from each side prepared to fight.

It seems this was to be a sort of tournament, a contest of strength between the sides instead of a full battle. But tempers were hot that day, and the tournament soon turned into a battle. The twelve young men from each side killed each other, and the battle was in full swing. They named the place "the field of sword-edges" because of the slaughter of the men assigned to the contest.

Very soon Abner's forces were fleeing for their lives. A young man named Asahel set out after Abner himself. Asahel was a brother to Joab and Abishai. These three men were sons of Zeruiah who was an older sister of David's (see 1 Chron. 2:13-17); therefore they were David's nephews.

Abner had been a trained soldier for many years, so the young man Asahel was no match for him in fighting skills. Abner said, "Turn aside, Asahel; take on one of the younger men and strip him of his weapons." But Asahel refused to turn aside.

Abner protested again, "Stop chasing me! Why should I strike you down? How could I look your brother Joab in the face?" But Asahel continued to follow him. Finally, Abner stabbed backward with the butt end of his spear and killed Asahel in his tracks. David's men felt deep grief as they came along and found Asahel dead, but it only made Joab and Abishai pursue Abner more fiercely.

When evening came, the remaining men of Benjamin rallied around Abner on top of a hill. Abner called to Joab: "Must the sword devour forever? Don't you realize that this will end in bitterness? How long before you order your men to stop pursuing their brothers?"

Joab answered, "As surely as God lives, if you had not spoken, my men would have continued the pursuit until morning." Then he blew his trumpet and stopped the battle. *(In other words, Joab accepted Abner's call as a surrender on Ish-bosheth's side.)*

Abner's men marched all night to get back to Mahanaim. Joab's men waited and went to check the dead. They found that David had lost twenty men, including Asahel, and that Abner had lost 360 men. They buried Asahel in the tombs of his father in Bethlehem. Then Joab's men marched all night to return to Hebron.

Time passed, and there was continual conflict between David's forces and Ish-bosheth's. David's forces grew stronger while Ish-bosheth's grew weaker. *(There was not widespread open warfare, but the conflict continued so long as both kings were upon their thrones.)*

Names to add:	**Label your map:**
Joab	Mahanaim (Compare its location to Gibeah.)
Asahel	Gibeon

Look at your map of the land in Saul's day. By the time Saul died, the Philistines had invaded far north beyond their normal boundaries. Now one king, Ish-bosheth of the family of Saul, is ruling in Mahanaim on the east side of the Jordan, while David of the tribe of Judah is ruling in Hebron on the west side of the river. Enemies have crowded in on all sides of the Israelites.

Compare this map with a map showing the land as it was divided among the tribes in Joshua's day. If the people had remained faithful to God, they could have held the entire land nearly enemy free. Instead, there are enemies all around and right in their midst. The land of Israel included about 12,000 square miles as it was given to the tribes in Joshua's day. By Saul's death, he possessed about 6,000 square miles, and his right to that portion was being contested by the Philistines.

Abner negotiates with David (2 Sam. 3:6-21):

During the time of conflict between the house of Ish-bosheth and the house of David, Abner continued to strengthen his own position in Ish-bosheth's kingdom.

After a time, Ish-bosheth accused Abner of adultery with Rizpah, one of Saul's concubines. Abner became very angry at the charge, and said: "Am I a dog's head? Am I loyal to Judah? I have been loyal to you and to your father's house this whole time and have not delivered you over to David. Yet you accuse me of sin with this woman! I am going to help David get the throne that the Lord promised him on oath! I am going to transfer the kingdom from the house of Saul and establish David's throne over all Israel from Dan to Beersheba."

Ish-bosheth was afraid of Abner, and could not answer a word.

It is unclear whether Abner was indeed guilty of sin with Rizpah or not. To take a wife or a concubine from a king was declaring great power to one's self. Abner may have been flaunting his power and was angry because Ish-bosheth had questioned his right to have her. Notice that when Abner responded angrily to Ish-bosheth, the response from Ish-bosheth was not an apology because he learned that his charge was not true — instead the Bible text says Ish-bosheth was <u>afraid</u> of Abner. He did not press the charge. Add Rizpah's name here even though she is only mentioned. There will be a story about her later.

Name to add: Rizpah, the concubine of Saul's

Abner sent messengers to David saying, "Whose land is this? Make an agreement with me, and I will help bring all Israel over to your side."

David sent word back, "Good. I will be glad to negotiate with you. But I demand one thing: Do not come into my presence unless you bring Michal my wife, the daughter of Saul, to me."

To strengthen his demand, David also sent a message to Ish-bosheth, saying, "Send me Michal my wife." He reminded Ish-bosheth that he had won the right to Michal's hand by providing proof he had killed 100 Philistines for Saul.

Ish-bosheth was afraid to do otherwise, so he gave order that Michal be taken from her husband Paltiel and returned to David. Paltiel followed along weeping behind the men who were taking Michal, until Abner ordered him to leave. He had no choice, so he returned to his own home.

At the time of their marriage, Michal loved David and helped him when she thought her father was about to kill him. But years have passed since the night Michal helped David escape from Saul. She had been given to Paltiel as his wife. Almost certainly, Saul had done all he could during those years to poison Michal's mind against David. By now Paltiel loves her and wants to keep her, but the matter of her marriage to David has become a political issue. Neither Michal or Paltiel had any control over where she would be taken. And by all rights, she still belonged to David.

Abner conferred with the elders of Israel and then the men of Benjamin *(Saul's tribe)*. He said, "For some time you have wanted to make David your king. Now do it! The Lord promised that He would deliver His people from the hand of the Philistines and from all other enemies by His servant David."

Then Abner took twenty men with him to meet David in Hebron, in order to tell David all that seemed good to Israel and to the whole house of Benjamin. David gave a feast in his honor, and they talked together. The meeting went smoothly, and Abner left planning to gather all Israel for David to make a contract with them so that he might rule the whole land.

Abner is killed (2 Sam. 3:22-39):

Meanwhile, Joab and a band of men had been out on a raid. They returned to Hebron from a successful raid immediately after Abner had come and gone. Joab learned what had happened and he rushed in before David, saying: "What have you done? Abner came to you, and you let him go in peace! Don't you know he only came to deceive you and to observe your every move?"

Joab rushed back out of the king's presence and sent messengers after Abner to bring him back. When Abner returned, Joab took him aside as if to talk privately. But instead of talking, Joab stabbed him and killed him. The Bible states specifically that Joab killed Abner to avenge the blood of his brother Asahel — not because he feared Abner would not be good for David's kingdom. It also adds blame to Abishai for the plot against Abner.

David was horrified when he learned what Joab had done. He declared himself and his kingdom free from the blood of Abner. He vowed that Joab's family would bear the blame forever. Then David forced Joab and the people with him to put on sackcloth and to walk in front of the funeral procession while David himself walked behind the body.

All the people wept at the grave of Abner, and David wept also. He lifted up his voice in a lament for Abner:

> Should Abner die as a fool dies?
> Your hands were not bound, nor your feet put in fetters.
> As one falls before the wicked, you have fallen.

Thus Abner was buried as a great man, in the city of Hebron. All the people of the land saw how David acted, and they were pleased. In fact, everything the king did pleased them. They all understood that it had not been the will of the king to put Abner to death.

David said, "A prince and a great man has fallen today in Israel. I am weak today, though anointed king. These sons of Zeruiah are too difficult for me. May the Lord repay the evildoer for his evil."

Refresh your memory, and the memory of your students, on the part Abner has played in the story of Saul and David.

At first glance, it would seem that Abner set Ish-bosheth up as king out of a deep sense of loyalty to Saul's house. But it is obvious from such verses as 2 Samuel 3:10 and 3:18 that he knew God had planned for David to be king. Therefore, his action was in direct conflict with God. He was trying his best to thwart God's plan.

There is no way to know whether Abner would have been loyal to David. His past life certainly did not indicate he would be. He had been Saul's chief captain while Saul and his army chased David. Now he was the power behind Ish-bosheth's throne. There seems to have been some political wisdom behind Joab's action, but that was not the reason Joab killed him. Abner had killed Asahel in the midst of a battle; in revenge, Joab murdered Abner by using treachery. That is why David was so upset over his actions. As the story progresses, you will find other times when Joab decided to take personal revenge and to act directly against David's stated plan or command.

Ish-bosheth is killed (2 Sam. 4:1-12):

When Ish-bosheth heard that Abner was dead, he lost all courage. The Israelites with him became alarmed also because they realized their cause was nearly lost.

Ish-bosheth had two men who led raiding bands for him. They were Baanah and Rechab, sons of Rimmon of the tribe of Benjamin. One day, these two men came into the house as if they were getting a supply of grain. It was in the heat of the day, at the time when the king took his noonday rest. Baanah and Rechab went into his bedroom and killed Ish-bosheth in his bed. They cut off his head and hurried to take it to David.

When they got to Hebron after traveling all night, they told David, "Here is the head of Ish-bosheth, the son of the man who tried to kill you. The Lord has avenged you against all your enemies this day."

David answered, "As surely as the Lord lives, who has delivered me out of all my troubles, when a man told me Saul was dead, thinking he had brought me good news, I seized him and put him to death. That was the reward I gave him for his news! And now you come telling me you have killed an innocent man in his own house and on his own bed. Should I not demand his blood from your hands and rid the earth of you?"

David gave order for Baanah and Rechab to be killed. Their hands and feet were cut off, and their bodies were hanged by the pool of Hebron. Then they took Ish-bosheth's head and buried it in Abner's tomb.

It had been two years since Saul had died (see 2:10).

Names:
   Baanah
   Rechab

David becomes king over all Israel (2 Sam. 5:1-5; 1 Chron. 11:1-3; 12:23-40):

David became king over the tribe of Judah very quickly after Saul died, but at that time his right to rule over the whole land was contested by Ish-bosheth whom Abner had set up as king. Now, with Ish-bosheth's death, there is no one left to contest his right to the throne.

The book of 1 Chronicles does not tell about the conflict between David and Ish-bosheth. It picks up the history with the men of Israel coming to make David king over the whole land. Be very conscious of the parallel accounts, and read all passages given.

The tribes of Israel came to David in Hebron and said, "We are your own flesh and blood. In the past, even while Saul was king over us, you were the one who led us on our military campaigns. We know the Lord said that you would shepherd His people and that you would become our ruler.

Now, please be our king."

First Chronicles 12 tells of the mighty men of valor and wisdom who were part of this group who came to ask David to become king over all Israel. A very large group came, one that could draw up in battle formation. These men came with "a perfect heart" to make their request to David. They were representative of all the people of the land who wholeheartedly wanted him to be their king.

For three days the company of men were in Hebron with David, negotiating, rejoicing, and eating together, for their kinsmen had sent food they had prepared for them. Other Israelites who lived near brought vast quantities of food for the company to share. It was a time of great joy in Israel.

David made an agreement with them and became ruler over all Israel. David was thirty years old when he became king, and he ruled a total of forty years. He reigned over Judah in Hebron seven years and six months and over all Israel in Jerusalem thirty-three years.

David was described as "a lad" when we first met him back in 1 Samuel 16. At that time he stayed home with the sheep instead of going to the sacrifice/feast with his father and older brothers. Obviously, some years have passed since Samuel anointed him king, and this point when he actually becomes ruler over the whole land. By now he is thirty years old. This is the only indication of how much time passed while David was first a hero in Israel and then a fugitive as King Saul sought his life.

There is one little point that it is hard to be sure about. How long did David reign over Judah alone? The struggle with Ish-bosheth lasted two years (2 Sam. 2:10). Abner had already started negotiating with the men of Israel to make David king before he died (3:17-18). Now, after Ish-bosheth's death, the men of the other tribes come to David at Hebron (5:1) and make arrangements for him to rule over the whole land. The implication is that they came soon after Ish-bosheth died.

But notice 2 Samuel 5:5. It says that David reigned "over Judah" in Hebron for seven years and six months. Therefore, there may have been a period of time after the conflict with Ish-bosheth ended before the men of Israel came to him and he actually became king over the whole land. Or, the passage may be merely stating that the capital remained at Hebron for about five more years after he became king over all Israel. Such questions are not necessary to settle, so do not spend time arguing the point either way.

David makes Jerusalem his capital (2 Sam. 5:6-12; 1 Chron. 11:4-9; 14:1-2):

The walled city of Jerusalem had never been in the hands of the Israelites. Joshua's army killed the king of Jerusalem in one of their battles (see Josh. 10), and, according to Judges 1:8, Jerusalem was burned by the men of Judah, but the Israelites had never occupied the city itself. It had remained in the hands of the Jebusites until this point in history. At this time, it was a small city (sometimes called Jebus) on the border between the tribes of Benjamin and Judah (Josh. 15:8; 18:16). David decided to capture the city and make it his capital. This was a wise move politically, because the city had never belonged to any tribe; therefore no tribe could be jealous of the other because Jerusalem was chosen to be the capital. It was also easily defended because it was located on top of a mountain.

David and his army approached the city, and the Jebusites taunted them: "You can't take our city! Even the blind and the lame can defend these walls against you."

David told his men to go up through the watercourse and smite those "blind and lame" *(not literal blind and lame people, but the Jebusite guards who had flung down their insults)*. David promised that the one who got inside the city first would be the captain of his host from that time forward. Joab was the one who succeeded in getting in first. David kept his promise, and Joab became his chief captain.

David moved into his new city and named it the City of David. He enlarged it and strengthened it on all sides. The city of Jerusalem became the most important city in the land. God was with David and he grew more and more powerful.

King Hiram, the Phoenician king of Tyre, heard of David's growing strength and he sent messengers to greet him. He also sent cedar trees, carpenters, and stone masons to help David build a palace. So David prospered. It was evident that God had established his throne and that God had exalted his kingdom for the sake of all Israel.

Label your map:　　**Names to add:**
 Jerusalem   **King Hiram of Tyre**
 Phoenicia   **Jebusites**
 Tyre   **Phoenicians**

Psalm 30

Psalm 30 is entitled: "A Song at the Dedication of the House. A psalm of David." The "House" could not be the temple, since it was built by Solomon, not David. Almost certainly the psalm was written to commemorate the dedication of David's own house (2 Sam. 5:8-12). According to verse 12, "David perceived that Jehovah had established him king over Israel, and that He had exalted his kingdom for His people Israel's sake." In other words, the completion of David's palace was a symbol to him that the Lord had fulfilled His promise to establish David upon his throne. The psalm is a song of joy, thanksgiving, and praise to Jehovah.

I will praise thee, O Lord, for you have lifted me up. You have not let my enemies rejoice over me. O Lord, I cried to you for help, and you healed me. You brought up my soul from the realm of the dead.

Sing praises to the Lord, and give thanks to His holy name. For His anger is but for a moment; His favor is for a lifetime. Weeping may last for the night, but a shout of joy comes in the morning.

The Bible does not tell the details of the conquest of Jerusalem, but archaeology has some very interesting facts to add. The city was built on a mountain ridge. In the days of David, the spring Gihon flowed out of a cave in the side of the mountain outside the city wall. The Jebusites had dug a tunnel from inside their city to a point where they could drop a vertical shaft into the cave where the spring was. They would walk down their tunnel to the shaft, lower their vessels to the water, and pull them back up full. This seems to have been the watercourse David was talking about when he told his men to go up it to conquer the city. David's men (with Joab leading them) made their way up this shaft (likely at night) to the inside of the city. From there, they could easily unlock the city gates to let in the rest of the soldiers. Many years later, a king named Hezekiah sealed the outside opening to the cave to keep an enemy army from using the water. He dug another tunnel to divert the water into a pool inside the city (called the Pool of Siloam in New Testament days, John 9:7). (See 2 Chronicles 32:1-4, 30.) The tunnel still exists today. Travelers can visit the tunnel and see the old Jebusite shaft and the later tunnel of Hezekiah.

The original city of Jerusalem that David conquered was small in comparison to its later size. David enlarged it and fortified it, and called it the City of David. His son Solomon greatly enlarged the city when he built the temple and his palace next to it. The temple was on another mountain peak, outside the walls of the original City of David. The city reached the peak of its glory under Solomon, at least so far as its wealth is concerned.

The Jebusites and the Phoenicians were both Canaanite tribes. The Jebusites were a small tribe living in the central portion of the land with Jerusalem as their main city. Most of the Jebusites were likely killed when David took the city. The remaining Jebusites joined other Canaanites in the land and became absorbed into those living intermingled among the Israelites. They were never again a problem as a distinct people.

The Phoenicians were Canaanites who lived on the narrow coastal plain north of Mount Carmel, at the foot of the very high Mount Lebanon. They had excellent harbors at Tyre and Sidon, and they turned to sea trade very early in their history. They were very skilled ship-builders and sailors, and they took their merchandise far and wide. Therefore, their influence was felt all around the Mediterranean world. In fact, the name "Phoenician" came to them from a particular purple dye that they sold. They kept their distinct identity even after the other Canaanite tribes were absorbed into one group.

As Canaanites, both the Jebusites and the Phoenicians should have been destroyed when the Israelites entered the land under Joshua. Instead, the Israelites did not have the faith and the determination to do as God asked. The day came when God said He would no longer help them drive out the remaining enemies. The remaining Canaanites were left to try Israel to see if they would be faithful to God in spite of the idols all around them (see Judg. 2). Israel failed the test in nearly every generation.

David's family (2 Sam. 3:2-5; 5:13-16; 1 Chron. 14:3-7):

Before we go further in the history of David's rule over Israel, let us take time to look at his family. You remember that he married Michal the daughter of Saul first, but then he had to leave her behind when he fled from Saul. He was not reunited with her until after Saul's death (see 1 Sam. 19:12; 2 Sam. 3:13-16). During the time he was a fugitive, he married Ahinoam and Abigail the widow of Nabal (see 1 Sam. 25). There were other wives and concubines as the years passed, as was the custom of that day.

David had six sons born during the seven years his capital was at Hebron. Listed in the order of their birth, they were: Amnon, Chileab, Absalom, Adonijah, Shephatiah, and Ithream. Chileab must have died young because he is never mentioned again. Remember the others named, particularly Amnon, Absalom and Adonijah. Even the order of their birth plays a part in the later story.

After he moved his capital to Jerusalem, David had more sons. They were: Shammua, Shobab, Nathan, Solomon, Ibhar, Elishua, Nepheg, Japhia, Elishama, Eliada, and Eliphelet. The only one of these who plays a part in the later story is Solomon, though Nathan is mentioned in the New Testament.

The genealogy of Jesus that is found in Matthew 1 gives Jesus' lineage through Solomon (Matt. 1:6-7). This lineage was His legal lineage through Joseph, thus making Him legal heir to David's throne. In Luke 3:31, the lineage is given through Nathan the son of David. Usually a person's lineage was given only through his father's line, but Jesus was in a unique position. It was necessary for Him to be the legal heir to David's throne, but Joseph was not His true father. It was necessary to show that Mary also was of the lineage of David to prove that Jesus' bloodline fulfilled the prophecy that He would be of the family of David (Rom. 1:3). Therefore, Joseph's lineage is given in Matthew, and Mary's lineage is given in Luke.

Names to add:
    Amnon   **Solomon**
    Absalom **Nathan (the son of David)**
    Adonijah

David defeats the Philistines (2 Sam. 5:17-25; 1 Chron. 14:8-17):

The Philistines have been Israel's most persistent enemy since the days of Samson the judge. When David began ruling as king in Hebron, the Philistines had just defeated Israel in a major battle, and they had laid claim to cities in the Jezreel valley (1 Sam. 31). Nothing is said about what the Philistines did while David ruled in Hebron, but now, with his move to Jerusalem and his becoming king over the whole land, the Philistines decide to attack.

The Philistines gathered in full force in the Valley of Rephaim west of Jerusalem. David took his army out to the stronghold to meet them. He asked God, "Shall I go up against the Philistines? Will you deliver them into my hand?"

God answered, "Go, for I will surely give the Philistines into your hand."

So, David attacked them and thoroughly defeated them. The Philistines were beaten so badly they left the images of their gods behind them. David gave orders for the images to be gathered and burned.

Again, the Philistines attacked in the Valley of Rephaim. This time, when David asked God what he should do, God told him to go around behind the Philistines and wait near the mulberry trees. God said: "When you hear the sound of marching in the tops of the mulberry trees, then rise up to battle because that will be the sign that the Lord has gone out before you to smite the host of the Philistines."

David did exactly as God instructed and drove the Philistines back to their own borders. The fame of David went out into all the lands around, and they all feared him.

David brings the Ark of the Covenant to Jerusalem (2 Sam. 6:1-23; 1 Chron. 13:1-14; 15:1-29; 16:1-6, 43):

In the early days of Samuel the judge, in a battle with the Philistines, the Israelites were defeated, Hophni and Phinehas the sons of Eli were killed, and the ark of the covenant was captured by the Philistines. When Eli heard the dreadful news, he fell over backward and broke his neck.

The ark stayed in Philistine territory about seven months. During that time, God afflicted the Philistines with a plague so that many of them died. They sent the ark back to Israel on a new cart. It arrived in Beth-shemesh, and then it was taken to Kiriath-jearim where it remained until David decided to move it to Jerusalem. (See 1 Samuel 4:1-7:1.)

David called for all his army officers and he said, "If it seems good to you, let us call for all our brethren throughout the land and have them join us to bring the ark of our God back to us. We did not inquire of it during the whole reign of Saul." After building his own house, David had prepared a place for the ark in Jerusalem by pitching a special tent for it.

The whole assembly liked the plan, and arrangements began to be made. Word went out and the people gathered from one end of the land to the other, and they set out from Jerusalem to Kiriath-jearim (also called Baalah) to get the ark. It was at the house of Abinadab. This was to be a day of great joy.

The law taught that the Levites were to carry the ark on their shoulders (Exod. 25:14; Num. 3:31; 4:4-6, 15-16), but David and the people ignored those instructions. Instead they built a new cart for it. That is the way the Philistines had sent it home many years earlier, so the Israelites seemed to think it would be all right if they carried it the same way.

The Israelites put the ark on their new cart, and the sons of Abinadab, Uzzah and Ahio, drove the oxen pulling the cart. David and the whole house of Israel went along celebrating with all their might, singing and giving praise to God, and playing all sorts of musical instruments. When they got to the threshing floor of Nacon, the oxen stumbled enough to make the cart lurch. Uzzah put out his hand to steady the ark, and God smote him dead for showing irreverence by touching His ark. All joy ended!

David was angry because of God's wrath, and he named the place Perez-Uzzah *(meaning "breach, or outburst against Uzzah")*. He was deeply afraid, and said, "How can I ever bring the ark of God to me?"

Since he was afraid to take the ark farther, he turned aside and put it in the house of Obed-Edom. David and the rest of Israel went home much subdued.

Three months passed, and someone brought word to David: "The Lord has blessed the house of Obed-edom and all that belongs to him, because the ark of God is there." That meant that the mere presence of the ark did not mean disaster.

So David did what he should have done first. He looked into the law to see how the ark was supposed to be handled. Then he called for the priests, Zadok and Abiathar, and six of the leading Levites and said: "You are the heads of the families of the Levites. Now consecrate yourselves so that we can bring up the ark of the Lord to the place I have prepared for it. No one but the Levites may carry the ark. God smote us earlier because we did not carry the ark as He said."

The Levites agreed, and preparations began again. This time there were a few hundred Levites who took the lead in the activities of the day. Some were specifically designated to carry the ark upon their shoulders; others were appointed as singers and musicians; the priests were appointed to blow trumpets before the ark; and still others were designated as gate-keepers for the ark.

Again the people gathered from all over the land for a day of joy and celebration, but this time the ark would be carried correctly on the shoulders of the priests, and the celebration would be led by the Levites. When the bearers of the ark had gone only six paces, the whole company stopped and offered a sacrifice to Jehovah. As the ark was carried along, the Levites sang and played music. More sacrifices were offered all along the way. All Israel rejoiced as they brought it into Jerusalem. David himself dressed in a linen robe like the priests, and he leaped and danced with joy along with the people as the ark was borne along.

When the ark was set in its place, final sacrifices for the day were offered. David blessed all the people in the name of the Lord and he gave gifts of food to everyone present. The people departed for their own homes, and David went to his home to bless his own household. It had been a day of great celebration for all the people.

Meanwhile, David's wife Michal had been watching from her window. She saw David dancing and rejoicing in the midst of his people and she "despised him in her heart." When David got home, she met him with sarcasm, "How glorious was the king of Israel today who got out and uncovered himself before the eyes of his handmaids as some tramp." *(In other words, she did not think he had kept the dignity of a king before his people.)*

David's joy was suddenly gone. He told Michal, "I was rejoicing before Jehovah, who chose me above your father. I may play before Him again. I may be even lower than I have been today, and I may amount to nothing in my eyes, but I will be held in honor in the eyes of my handmaids whom you mention."

Michal remained in David's household, but he never regarded her as his wife again. Therefore she never had a child, even to the day of her death.

This is the end of the story about Michal. What could have been a happy marriage between two people who loved each other has ended with strife and discord. She despises him, and he has only distaste for her.

Names to add: **Label your map:**
Uzzah **Kiriath-jearim**
Obed-edom

1 Chronicles 16:7-36;   Psalm 105

On that day of celebration, David gave a new psalm to be sung. Part of it is quoted in 1 Chronicles 16:8-36. It is given in its full length in Psalm 105.

Oh give thanks to the Lord; call upon His name; make known His doings among the peoples. Sing praises to His name and think about all His marvelous works. Glory in His holy name. Let the heart of them that rejoice seek the Lord. Seek the Lord and His strength. Seek His face always.

Remember His marvelous works that He has done, His wonders, and the judgments of His mouth, O you seed of Israel His servant, you children of Jacob, His chosen ones. He is Jehovah our God; His judgments are in all the earth.

Remember His covenant for ever, the covenant which He made with Abraham, and with Isaac, and confirmed to Jacob for a statute, to Israel for an everlasting covenant, saying, "Unto you will I give the land of Canaan, the lot of your inheritance." He did it when you were but a few men in number and sojourners in it. And they went about from nation to nation, and from one kingdom to another. He allowed no man to do them wrong. He reproved kings for their sakes, saying, "Do not touch my anointed ones, and do my prophets no harm."

Sing to the Lord, all the earth. Show forth His salvation from day to day. Tell of His glory among the nations, His marvelous works among all the peoples. For great is the Lord, and greatly to be praised. He is to be feared above all gods. For all the gods of the peoples are idols, but the Lord made the heavens. Honor and majesty are before Him. Strength and gladness are in His place. Ascribe unto the Lord glory and strength, you kindred of the peoples. Ascribe unto the Lord the glory due to His name. Bring an offering, and come before Him. Worship the Lord in holy array. Tremble before Him, all the earth. The world is established that it cannot be moved. Let the heavens be glad, and let the earth rejoice, and let them say among the nations, "The Lord reigns." Let the sea roar, and the fullness thereof. Let the field exult, and all that is therein. Then shall the trees of the woods sing for joy before the Lord, for He comes to judge the earth.

O give thanks unto the Lord, for He is good, for His mercy endures for ever. And say, "Save us, O God of our salvation, and gather us together and deliver us from the nations, to give thanks unto your holy name, and to triumph in your praise." Blessed be the Lord, the God of Israel, from everlasting even to everlasting.

And all the people said, "Amen," and praised the Lord.

Psalm 24

This psalm refers either to the bringing of the ark into Jerusalem on this occasion (2 Sam. 6), or to its being brought back to Zion after accompanying the army to battle. Either way, the psalm may have been used regularly on occasions when the ark was taken out with the army and then returned to the city in victory. It is a glorious song and describes the King of Glory entering Zion. We place it here. Psalm 101 may also fit at this time, but the evidence is scant and indecisive.

The earth is the Lord's, and the fullness thereof; the world, and they that dwell therein. He has founded it upon the seas, and established it upon the floods.

Who shall go up into the hill of the Lord? And who shall stand in His holy place? He who has clean hands, and a pure heart; he who has not lifted up his soul unto falsehood, and has not sworn deceitfully. He shall receive a blessing from the Lord, and righteousness from the God of his salvation. This is the generation of them that seek after Him, that seek your face, even Jacob.

Lift up your heads, O you gates, and be you lifted up, you everlasting doors, and the King of Glory will come in. Who is the King of Glory? The Lord strong and mighty, the Lord strong in battle. Lift up your heads, O you gates. Yes, lift them up, you everlasting doors, and the King of Glory will come in. Who is this King of Glory? The Lord of hosts, He is the King of Glory.

David organizes the Levites (1 Chron. 16:37-42):

At this time, David organized the Levites into groups and assigned them certain tasks. Some were singers, some were door-keepers (guards), etc. The arrangements of David at this time reflect the presence of the ark in Jerusalem, while the tabernacle of the Lord was in Gibeon. There will be further organization of the Levites late in David's reign, as he prepares the way for Solomon to build the temple.

Though the ark of the covenant was now in the special tent in Jerusalem that David had prepared for it, the tabernacle with the altar of burnt offering was at Gibeon. That is where all sacrifices were offered, so that is where the priests presided. In this passage, Zadok and his relatives are specified as the priests who offered the regular sacrifices there. In 1 Chronicles 15:11, as the Levites were being prepared to move the ark into the city, Zadok and Abiathar are both listed as priests. We will discuss their roles more later, but it seems these two men shared in the duties of high priest during the reign of David.

Remember that Abiathar has been with David since Doeg killed the priests of Nob at Saul's command (1 Sam. 22:20-23). Zadok must have begun as priest under Saul at that same time. Watch for the work of these two priests under David.

It is on this occasion that we meet the chiefs of the singers. There were three. Asaph was appointed as the leader of the Levite singers in Jerusalem, where the ark was. Two others, Heman and Jeduthun (also called Ethan), served with Zadok and his relatives at Gibeon, where the tabernacle was located. Asaph is the best known of these singers because twelve of the psalms are attributed to him: Psalm 50 and Psalms 73-83. Psalm 88 is attributed to Heman, and Psalm 89 to

Ethan. Though in the titles of the Psalms they are called Heman the Ezrahite and Ethan the Ezrahite, they are probably the same as the well-known singers. *(See further information in the Appendix on the Psalms.)* In addition, Psalms 39 and 62 are written by David but are said to be "for Jeduthun (Ethan)." There is never a story about the specific actions of either of these men, though their names are mentioned on different occasions in connection with the work of the Levites.

First Chronicles 6 gives more information about these three Levite singers. Asaph was of the family of Gershon (or Gershom, 1 Chron. 6:39-43), Heman was of the family of Kohath (1 Chron. 6:33), and Ethan was of the family of Merari (1 Chron. 6:44) — the three branches of the tribe of Levi. This chapter in 1 Chronicles, though found earlier in the book, tells of the arrangement of the singers in the days of Solomon, when the temple was finished. By that time the priests and Levites and singers were all together in Jerusalem at the temple. The singers played important roles in all public worship, celebrations, and feast days as they sang specific psalms associated with the occasion, and led the whole congregation in singing praise to God. Heman seems to have been the chief of the three because he stood with the center group of singers. Asaph and his group were on Heman's right (1 Chron. 6:39), and Ethan and his group were on Heman's left (1 Chron. 6:44).

Names to add:
Zadok
Asaph
Heman
Jeduthun (Ethan)

When the Israelites took the land of Canaan in the days of Joshua, they set up the tabernacle at a place called Shiloh (Josh. 18:1). It was still there in the days of Eli (1 Sam. 1:3). No one knows exactly what happened to Shiloh, or when the tabernacle was moved from there to Gibeon. Jeremiah tells the people of his day to go to Shiloh and look at what the Lord did there because of the wickedness of the people. Jeremiah warned the people of his day that the same thing was about to happen to Jerusalem where the temple was then located (Jer. 7:12-15; 26:6, 9). So, obviously, God had a direct hand in the destruction of Shiloh, though we are given no details about the event. The tabernacle stayed at Gibeon until the temple was completed and the furniture and treasures were moved to Jerusalem (see 2 Chron. 1:3; 5:1-5; 1 Kings 3:4; 8:3-5).

David offers to build God a house (2 Sam. 7:1-29; 1 Chron. 17:1-27):

After David was secure in his kingdom, he began thinking about how he lived in a fine house of cedar, whereas the ark of the covenant of God remained in a tent. This situation bothered David because he had a deep reverence for God. He did not think it fitting for him to live in a better house than God's ark was in, so he spoke to Nathan the prophet about it: "Here I am, living in a palace of cedar, while the ark of God remains in a tent."

Nathan said, "Whatever you have in mind, go ahead and do it, for the Lord is with you."

But that night, God spoke to Nathan, saying:

> Go tell my servant David that I have not required him to build me a house. Since the day that I brought Israel up out of Egypt, I have not dwelt in a house, but in a tent. Did I ever ask any of the leaders of my people, "Why have you not built me a house of cedar?"

Then God continued His message to David:

> I took you from following the sheep to be the leader of my people. I have been with you wherever you have gone and I have cut off all your enemies from before you. Now I will make your name great, like the names of the greatest men of the earth. I will establish a place for my people Israel where they can be safe from all their enemies. I will give you rest all about.
>
> Furthermore, David, I will establish a house for you. When you are dead, I will raise up your son to reign after you and I will establish his kingdom. He is the one who will build a house for My name and I will establish the throne of his kingdom forever. I will be his father, and he will be my son. If he sins, I will punish him, but my mercy will not be taken from him as I took it from Saul whom I removed from before you. Your house and your kingdom will endure forever before me, and your throne will be established forever.

David was overwhelmed and awed by this great promise. He went in and sat before the Lord and prayed:

> Oh Lord, who am I, and what is my family that you have brought me this far? You have made far-reaching promises, and what can I say? This is your own decision and you are the great God. There is no other like you. Neither is there any nation like Israel whom you took for yourself out of Egypt and established as your own people, and you became their God.
>
> And, now, please do this thing that you have promised and let my name be magnified. Because you have made this promise, your servant has found courage to pray this prayer. You are God, and your words are trustworthy, and you have promised to do this great thing for me! Please continue your blessings upon me and upon my house forever.

Name to add:
Nathan, the prophet

Let 2 Samuel 7 (and its parallel passage in 1 Chronicles 17) become an important link in your understanding of the development of the scheme of redemption. Think about the significance of the passage and learn its location so well you can call it to mind readily.

As we analyze this promise that God has made to David, let us break it down into its various components. There are at least three distinct elements in the promise. We will analyze each one briefly.

David's son will build a house (a temple) for Jehovah:

This is the simplest element of the promise. David has decided he wants to build a house for the ark of God. God's answer to David is, "No, I do not want you to build a house for me. I have never asked any leader of my people to do so, and I have not asked you to do it either. But your son will reign after you, and I will allow him to build me a house." God does not at this time specify which son of David will reign after him, but He later specifies that it will be Solomon (1 Chron. 22:9).

As David tells Solomon about the promise that God made and as he lays the charge to build the temple upon his son, he adds a detail that is not found in 2 Samuel 7. He says:

> *As for me, it was in my heart to build a house unto the name of Jehovah my God. But the word of Jehovah came to me, saying, "Thou hast shed blood abundantly, and hast made great wars: thou shalt not build a house unto my name, because thou hast shed much blood upon the earth in my sight. Behold, a son shall be born to thee, who shall be a man of rest; and I will give*

him rest from all his enemies round about; for his name shall be Solomon [peaceful], and I will give peace and quietness unto Israel in his days. He shall build a house for my name, and he shall be my son, and I will be his father; and I will establish the throne of his kingdom over Israel for ever." Now, my son, Jehovah be with thee; and prosper thou, and build the house of Jehovah thy God, as He hath spoken concerning thee (1 Chron. 22:6-11; see also 1 Chron. 28:2-10).

David understood God's promise in this regard, and from that day forward, David gathered supplies for the temple that would be built in the days of his son, though he did not know immediately which son it would be who would reign. As the history progresses, we will see Solomon build that temple just as God promised.

God promised to establish David's family as the ruling dynasty:
This promise to David began to be fulfilled in the reign of his son Solomon. It is obvious from such passages as 1 Chronicles 22:6-11 and 28:2-10 that David himself applied the promise to Solomon. Later Solomon quoted the promise, applying it to himself (see 1 Kings 8:17-21; 2 Chron. 6:7-11). After Solomon, the royal line of David's descendants continued in the kingdom of Judah for about 300 years. That means that, including the reigns of David and Solomon, David's family remained on the throne in Jerusalem in an unbroken chain for about 400 years.

When Jacob, the grandson of Abraham, was nearing his death, he called his twelve sons before him and gave each of them a blessing. To Judah he said, "The scepter shall not depart from Judah, nor a lawgiver from between his feet, until Shiloh come; and unto him shall the gathering of the people be" (Gen. 49:10). That is, the sign of rulership was to be in the house of Judah until Christ should come.
Many years passed from the time of that prophecy before a king was anointed in Israel. The first king, Saul, was from the tribe of Benjamin instead of Judah. His family could have been established as the family that would rule forever in Israel if Saul had been faithful (1 Sam. 13:13-14), but he failed to please God and his kingdom was rejected. God chose David, a "man after His own heart," from the tribe of Judah. Now God has promised to establish David's throne forever, thus fulfilling the promise to Judah.

This prophecy and its fulfillment illustrates God's foreknowledge. There are some prophecies in the Bible of things God intended to <u>cause</u> to happen. There are other prophecies of things God foresaw happening, things which He did not directly cause. God did not make a mistake when He selected Saul as the first king, but He had foreseen the events that would lead to the rejection of Saul and the choosing of David.

As we continue to watch the history of Israel, we will see Solomon build the temple. But then we will also see Solomon forsake the Lord. The kingdom divided following Solomon's death into the north and the south. For 200 years this situation continued until Israel in the north was taken away into Assyrian captivity (721 B.C.). David's descendants ruled in Judah after the fall of Israel for a little more than 100 years. But his descendants became more and more wicked until, in 586 B.C., Jerusalem and the temple were destroyed, and the people of Judah were taken into Babylonian captivity. Since the fall of Judah, never again has a descendant of David sat upon a throne ruling over the land and kingdom of Israel. In fact, the prophet Jeremiah said that no descendant of Coniah, or Jehoiachin as he is also called (the last of the direct royal line of David to reign in Jerusalem), would ever prosper again, sitting on the throne of David or ruling again in Judah (Jer. 22:30).
What about the promise to David that his kingdom would be established forever? Did God forget it? No! Look again into the promise made in 2 Samuel 7. Right in the midst of the promise about David's

dynasty, God said, "I will be his father, and he shall be my son: if he commit iniquity, I will chasten him with the rod of men, and with the stripes of the children of men; but my loving kindness shall not depart from him, as I took it from Saul, whom I put away before thee" (2 Sam. 7:14-15). The prediction of punishment was built into the whole promise. It would be totally foreign to God's justice if He made a promise that allowed men to become wicked with no consequences to pay. God was establishing David's family as the reigning dynasty. When his descendants sinned, God would punish them, but He would not do it the way He had punished Saul. When Saul sinned, God removed the position of king from his family. God did not intend to remove the position from David's family, even when it became necessary to punish them for their wickedness.

God delayed sending the kingdom of Judah into captivity even when the kings began to be wicked. For example, look at the description of the reign of Jehoram the son of Jehoshaphat in 2 Chronicles 21. Jehoram was terribly wicked, and God punished him severely: "Howbeit, Jehovah would not destroy the house of David, because of the covenant that He had made with David, and as He promised to give a lamp to him and to his children alway" (2 Chron. 21:7). God waited until "there was no remedy" before allowing the king of Babylon to destroy Jerusalem and take the people away into captivity (see 2 Chron. 36:14ff).

God will establish David's house, his kingdom, and his throne <u>forever</u>:
But David and the later writers knew that the ultimate fulfillment of this promise was more than just Solomon's rule, or even the rule of the kings after him. As one who loved God's word and all His promises, David knew of the promises to Eve, to Abraham, to Isaac, and to Jacob concerning One who was to come who would bless all families of the earth (Gen. 3:15; 12:3; 26:4; 28:14). He knew this promise God had made to him was a step in the fulfillment of the promise to Judah (Gen. 49:10). Let us look at some of the things David wrote, plus some of the things others wrote concerning this promise.

Psalm 89

Note, for example, the words of Ethan the Ezrahite in Psalm 89. Ethan flourished in the days of David and Solomon (1 Chron. 6:44; 16:39-42). He began the 89th Psalm saying, "I will speak of the mercy of the Lord for ever." He then chooses, however, to speak of the specific mercy the Lord showed to David in His promises.

In verses 3 and 4, Ethan quotes God who says:
I have made a covenant with my chosen, I have sworn to David my servant: "Thy seed will I establish for ever, and build up thy throne to all generations."

In the verses that follow, through verse 18, Ethan praises Jehovah, the incomparable One, who alone can make such far-reaching promises.

He takes up his emphasis upon God's promise to David again (89:19-21):
You spoke in vision to your saints, and said, "I have laid help upon one that is mighty; I have exalted one chosen out of the people. I have found David my servant; with my holy oil have I anointed him: with whom my hand shall be established; my arm also shall strengthen him."

Concerning David, God says (89:28-29):
My loving-kindness will I keep for him for evermore; and my covenant shall stand fast with him. His seed also will I make to endure for ever, and his throne as the days of heaven.

The promise clearly involves David, his seed, and his throne. David's children are involved because God says (89:30-33):
If his children forsake my law, and walk not in my ordinances, if they break my statutes, and keep not my commandments, then will I visit their transgression with the rod, and their iniquity with stripes. But my loving-kindness will I not utterly take from him, nor suffer my faithfulness to fail.

The unfaithfulness of David's children would not invalidate God's promise to him, nor would it prevent God from carrying out His promise.

Listen to the scope of God's promise again (89:34-37):
My covenant will I not break, nor alter the thing that is gone out of my lips. Once have I sworn by my holiness: I will not lie to David. His seed shall endure for ever, and his throne as the sun before me. It shall be established for ever as the moon, and as the faithful witness in the sky.

The last of the Psalm, verses 38-52 takes quite a turn. The circumstances fit the time of Rehoboam, when the larger part of the kingdom was torn away. Ethan, who could easily have survived into the first of Rehoboam's reign, asks the Lord:
"Lord, where are your former loving-kindnesses, which you shared unto David in thy faithfulness?" (89:49).

This Psalm shows clearly that what constituted the hope of David was God's promise regarding his <u>house</u> and his <u>throne.</u> No matter what happened to a given descendant of David, God's promise was sure.

Psalm 132

Let us look at another of the important psalms concerning this point: Psalm 132. There is no title at the first of this psalm to tell us who wrote it. Peter refers to a verse from it in Acts 2:30 and indicates it was written by David himself. If it were written by someone else, he was by inspiration expressing the thoughts of David.

The writer tells us of David's vow to build a house for the Lord (132:1-5):
Jehovah, remember David who vowed he would not rest until he had found out a place for Jehovah, a tabernacle for the Mighty One of Jacob.

A few verses later, he writes (132:10-12):
For thy servant David's sake turn not away the face of thine anointed. Jehovah has sworn unto David in truth; He will not turn from it: of the fruit of thy body will I set upon thy throne. If thy children will keep my covenant and my testimony that I shall teach them, their children also shall sit upon thy throne for evermore.

The rest of the Psalm praises Jehovah who chose Zion for His abiding place, and who blesses His people who serve Him there (132:13-18).

It is from this Psalm that Peter quotes on the day of Pentecost, saying of David, "Being therefore a prophet, and knowing that God had sworn with an oath to him, that of the fruit of his loins he would set one upon his throne ..." (Acts 2:30).

Psalm 16

Now consider this: Though we do not know how much David understood about the ramifications of the promise, the Spirit revealed to him that the resurrection of one from the dead would be required for the promise of God to be fulfilled that the throne of David and his kingdom would be prolonged as the days of the moon and sun.

Preserve me, O God, for I take refuge in thee. I said to the Lord, "Thou art my Lord; I have no good besides Thee." Sorrows are multiplied for those who give their sacrifices to another god. I will not give them my sacrifices, nor will I have their name upon my lips.

The Lord is my inheritance; indeed, my heritage is beautiful to me.

I have set the Lord continually before me; because He is at my right hand, I will not be shaken. Therefore my heart is glad; my flesh will dwell securely. For you will not leave my soul to Sheol; neither will you suffer your holy one to see corruption.

After quoting Psalm 16:8-10 on the day of Pentecost, Peter explained it this way: "Brethren, I may say unto you freely of the patriarch David, that he both died and was buried, and his tomb is with us unto this day. Being therefore a prophet, and knowing that God had sworn with an oath to him, that of the fruit of his loins He would set one upon his throne; he foreseeing this spake of the resurrection of the Christ, that neither was He left unto Hades, nor did His flesh see corruption" (Acts 2:29-31).

Note two things in particular: (1) David <u>knew</u> that God had sworn with an oath that of the fruit of his loins, He would set one upon his throne. (2) David <u>foresaw</u> this, and, being a prophet, spake of the resurrection of the Christ. David realized that for one to reign forever, then that one must live forever. These words indicate that David was given some understanding of the special nature of God's promise to him, and of the special measures it would take to fulfill it.

Psalm 110

David predicted God would make One both Ruler and Priest, joining the roles of king and high priest.

The Lord said to my Lord: "Sit at my right hand, until I make your enemies a footstool for thy feet." The Lord will stretch forth your scepter from Zion, saying, "Rule in the midst of thine enemies."

The Lord has sworn and will not change His mind. "Thou art a priest forever after the order of Melchizedek."

The Lord is at thy right hand. He will shatter kings in the day of His wrath.

Peter quoted from this psalm as he declared that God had raised Jesus whom the Jews had crucified and had exalted Him to sit at His own right hand as Ruler and Christ (Acts 2:33-36).

Let us put together the information we have so far. The scriptures show that David and his contemporaries, as well as later writers, understood that God's promise concerned the future of his house (family), the future of his throne, and the future of his seed. In unmistakable language the Bible stresses the exceedingly long time the kingdom and throne of David would last. It is clear, however, to any Bible student that the earthly kingdom and throne of David did not last any unusual length of time, and that the descendants of David have not occupied any earthly throne since the fall of Judah. But look at the prophecies about the future of David's house even as it was falling into decay in the Old Testament.

Toward the close of the Old Testament, the prophet Amos predicted that a day would come when the tabernacle of David that was falling into decay in his day would be raised up (Amos 9:11-12). James applied this prophecy to the church, and, therefore, to Jesus' sitting upon David's throne (Acts 15:13-18).

After saying that no descendant of Coniah would reign in Judah (Jer. 22:30), only a few verses later Jeremiah said, "Behold, the days come, saith Jehovah, that I will raise unto <u>David</u> a righteous Branch, and <u>He shall reign as king</u> and deal wisely, and shall execute justice and righteousness in the land..." (Jer. 23:5). In other words, Jeremiah had just said that no descendant of David would sit upon a throne in physical Jerusalem, but then he says there <u>would</u> be a king to come to fulfill the ultimate promise to David, One who would reign in righteousness.

When the angel appeared to Mary, he told her that the child she would bear would be given the throne of His father David, and that He would reign forever (Luke 1:32-33). In Acts 2, on the day of Pentecost, Peter declared that God had raised up Jesus and had exalted Him to His own right hand, making Him both Lord (Ruler) and Christ. Thus the promise to David in 2 Samuel 7:11-14 was ultimately fulfilled in Jesus. Today, Jesus is reigning in heaven on David's throne. Indeed, David's throne is established "forever."

David subdues all his enemies (2 Sam. 8:1-18; 1 Chron. 18:1-17):

Just as there was a summary of Saul's victories over his enemies in 1 Samuel 14:47-48, there is now a summary of David's victories. There will be more details given about some of the battles later. This summary is to show that God was with David everywhere he turned, and gave him victory on every hand.

David defeated the Philistines early in his reign when they attacked in the Valley of Rephaim (2 Sam. 5:17-25). Later David attacked the city of Gath and took it and its surrounding villages *(even though it was in Gath where David found refuge with King Achish when he was fleeing from Saul)*. Gath is called the "mother city" in 2 Samuel 8:1, so this must have been a key victory in conquering the Philistines. There were later battles with the Philistines during David's reign when three more giants of the same family as Goliath were killed (see 1 Chron. 20:4-8).

The Philistines never became subject to David as other surrounding peoples did, but they were driven back into a narrow strip on the coastal plain. There will be border conflicts between the Israelites and the Philistines throughout all the history of the kings, but they were never again a major enemy to the Israelites. God gave Israel victory over this persistent enemy in David's day.

It is interesting that even though David took his parents to Moab for safe-keeping while he was fleeing from Saul (1 Sam. 22:3-4), he did not spare the Moabites when it came time to fight. He killed two thirds of them, and the Moabites became subject to him.

David had major battles with the Syrians (or Arameans) of Zobah. Hadadezer (or Hadarezer) tried to wrest control of the territory northeast of Israel. David defeated him. By defeating Hadadezer, David established his rule all the way to the Euphrates River — far north beyond Israel's usual boundaries. By the time the battle was over, David had succeeded in taking 1,000 chariots with their horses, 7,000 horsemen, and 20,000 foot soldiers. David kept enough horses for 100 chariots, but he hamstrung the rest of the horses.

When the Syrians from Damascus came to help Hadadezer, David defeated them also and stationed Israelite soldiers in the city of Damascus. So, the Syrians became subject to David. God gave victory to David wherever he went.

There will be more information about the conflicts between David and the Syrians, or Arameans as they were also called, in 2 Samuel 10 and in 1 Chronicles 19.

Why would David hamstring these horses? There was a very distinct reason — he was obeying a law God had made for kings many years earlier. In Deuteronomy 17:16, as God looked toward a day when the Israelites would ask for a king and was giving rules for that king to follow, He said: "Moreover, he shall not multiply horses for himself..." God did not give a reason for His instruction there, but it seems to fit with the trust a king was to place in God. Chariots and horses were the strongest instruments of warfare for the people of that day, since battles were fought with hand to hand combat. God did not want His people to rely upon multiplying horses and chariots for their strength in battle. He was their strength. David did not kill these horses — he cut the hamstring (the tendon) in the back leg of each horse. Thus he made them so that they could be good work animals, but they could no longer be swift in battle. Remember this incident about David and the horses he conquered. Compare it to the way Solomon handled horses.

The king of Hamath was glad when he learned that Hadadezer had been defeated because they had been at war with one another. Therefore, King Toi (or Tou) of Hamath sent his son Joram with vessels of silver and gold and brass to David. The people of Hamath were not conquered by David, but they were at peace with him.

Abishai, one of David's captains, conquered Edom and brought it under David's control. Many were killed, and David put garrisons throughout the Edomite territory.

David took the spoils which he took in war, plus the gifts such as those sent by Toi of Hamath, and dedicated them to Jehovah. Notice the expressions that indicate how much treasure David was taking in these battles: he took "the shields of gold" and "exceeding much brass *(bronze)*" from the servants and cities of Hadadezer. The gift from Toi of Hamath included silver, gold, and brass — and gifts from one king to another under these conditions were vast. These precious metals were used later in the building of the temple and in its furnishings. The account in 1 Chronicles 18:7-8 specifies that this bronze was used by Solomon in making the bronze sea, the pillars at the front of the temple, and for the bronze utensils used in the temple service.

It seemed David was invincible. He ruled righteously and executed justice in all the land. The general of his army was Joab; the one who recorded his history was Jehoshaphat; Zadok and Ahimelech *(the one called Abiathar in other passages)* were high priests; Seraiah was the official secretary; Benaiah was captain of the Cherethites and Pelethites; and his sons were chief aides.

Names to add:
  Benaiah
  Cherethites and Pelethites

We have already added Joab's name to our list, and we have already mentioned Zadok and Abiathar as priests, but we have not yet added the other names given in this list of chief officials under David. Jehoshaphat and Seraiah never play a significant role in the story of David, so we do not need their names on our list. There is no story here about Benaiah and the Cherethites and Pelethites, but we will come to them again in David's life, so add their names here.

The Cherethites and Pelethites are mentioned over and over in David's story, but very few details are given about exactly who they were. It is obvious from the references to them that they were a group of soldiers, and Benaiah was their captain. It seems that they were a special group who served as David's body guard, or perhaps a group of soldiers who stayed near enough to the palace to be ready for call at a moment's notice. They were definitely the inner core of David's loyal men.

Psalm 60

This psalm was written during the campaign against Edom, and apparently at a time when the war was not going well. Verses 5-12 are combined with Psalm 57:7-11 to compose Psalm 108. This latter psalm bears the inscription, "A Psalm of David," though it is a combination of two of his earlier psalms. Either David himself combined the two into one to serve a particular purpose, or a later writer combined them to serve a particular need.

O God, you have thrown us away. You have broken us down. You have been angry. Oh restore us again. You have made the land to tremble. You have torn it. Heal the breaches of it, for it is shaking. You have shown your people hard things. You have made us drink the wine of staggering. You have given a banner to them that fear you that it may be displayed because of the truth in order that your beloved may be delivered. Save with your right hand, and answer us.

God has spoken in His holiness: "I will exult. I will divide Shechem, and measure out the valley of Succoth. Gilead is mine, and Manasseh is mine. Ephraim also is the defence of my head. Judah is my scepter. Moab is my wash-pot. Upon Edom will I cast my shoe. Philistia, shout because of me."

Who will bring me into the strong city? Who has led me unto Edom? Have you not thrown us away, O God? And you do not go forth, O God, with our hosts. Give us help against the adversary, for vain is the help of man. Through God we shall do valiantly, for it is He that will tread down our adversaries.

Psalms of the Wars

There is some uncertainty about which psalms fit in this period. Possibly the following Psalms belong here: 2, 9, 18, 20, 21, 110. These psalms are songs of victory and expressions of thanksgiving to God for His deliverance from enemies. They express David's confidence in God's dominion. His rule is sure.

Prepare a new map:

Look at the study map on the next page. Note that the map showing David's empire covers much more territory than is normally shown in a map of Canaan. Find and label all the places David conquered on your blank map. Compare it to the map you labeled showing the land in Saul's day. Compare the map of David's territory to the map of the land as it was divided to the tribes in Joshua's day. Do you see that David controlled much more than was conquered in Joshua's day?

Compare the information given here about David's victories to the information given in 1 Samuel 14 about Saul's victories. Saul was victorious also. He, too, defeated the Moabites, the Ammonites, the Edomites, the kings of Zobah, the Philistines, and the Amalekites. There was one difference in

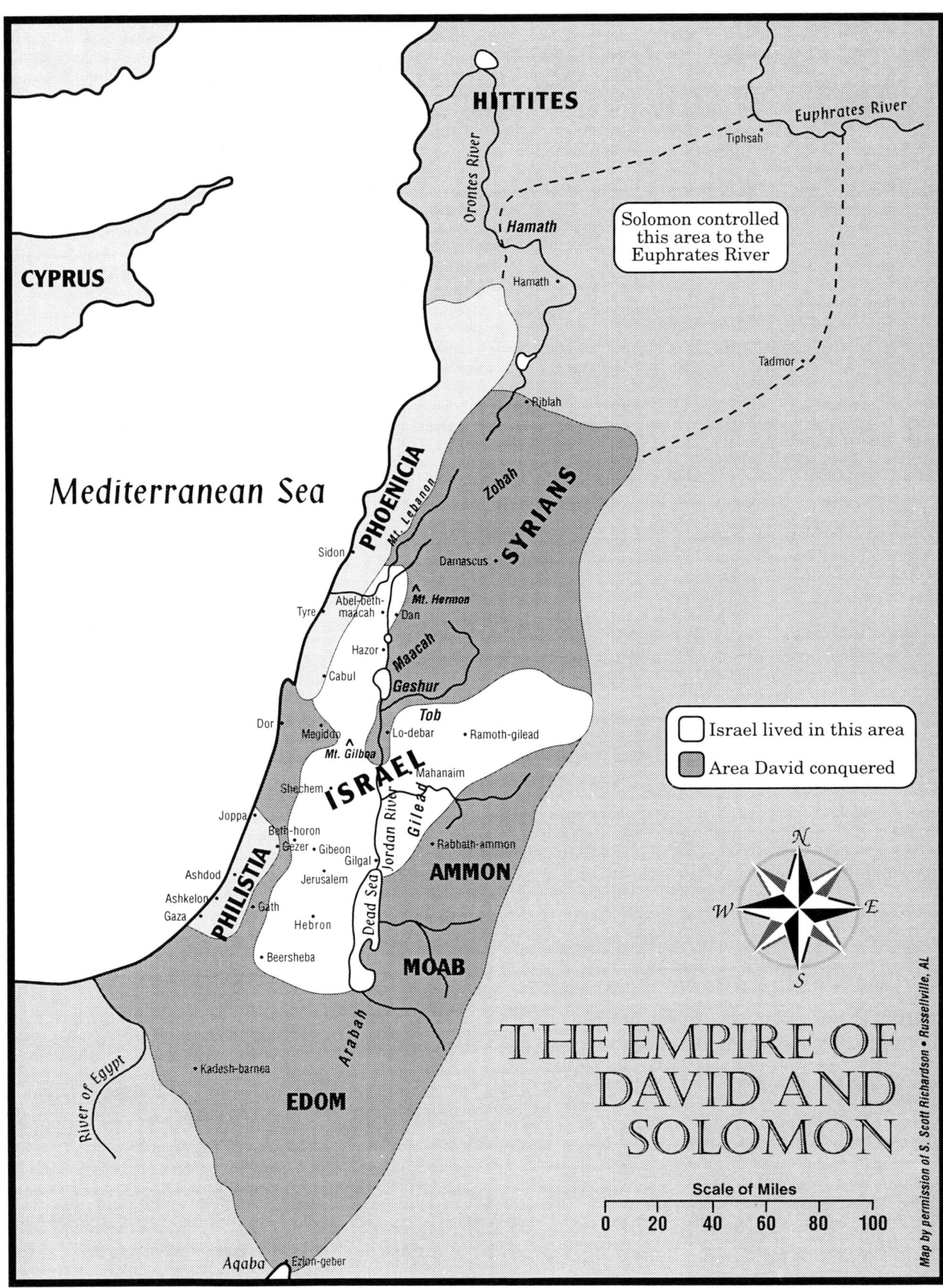

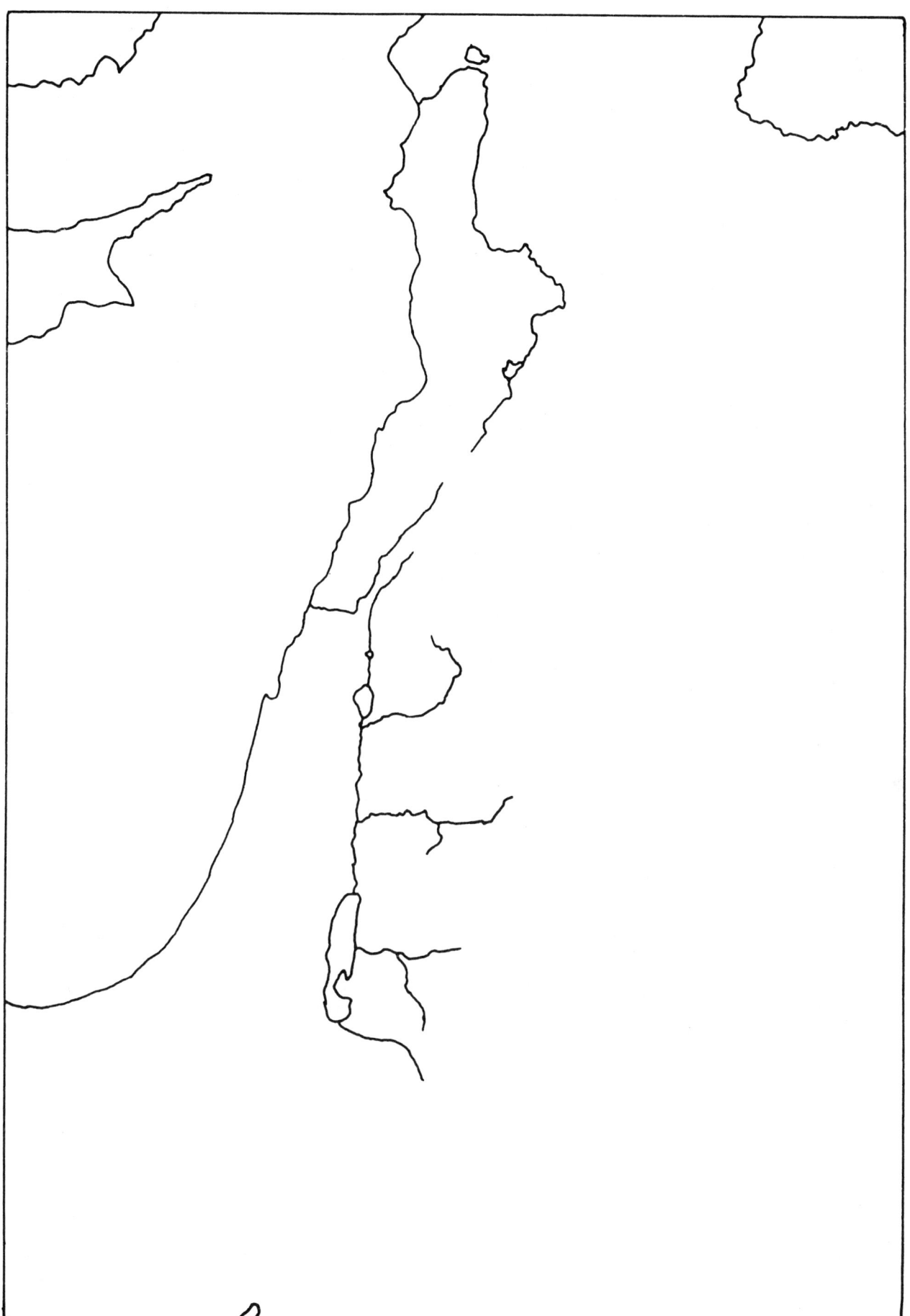

their victories, however. Saul fought his neighbors only enough to convince them to leave the Israelites alone. In contrast, David defeated them and made them subject to him. Soon David controlled all the territory from the tip of the Gulf of Aqaba to Hamath. Saul only controlled 6,000 square miles by the time of his death, and even that portion was being claimed by the Philistines. David controlled about 60,000 square miles by the time of his death.

>**Label your new map:**
>   **Jerusalem (David's capital)**
>   **Philistine territory**
>   **Gath (a main Philistine city)**
>   **Moab**
>   **Zobah**
>   **Hamath**
>   **Euphrates River**
>   **Damascus**
>   **Edom**

David shows kindness to Mephibosheth (2 Sam. 4:4; 9:1-13):

Do you remember that David made a covenant of friendship and loyalty with Jonathan? Jonathan knew that David would be king after Saul died, and he asked that David show kindness to him and to his family (see 1 Sam. 20:14-16). David was glad to make the promise, but Jonathan died at the same time his father died, so David did not have the opportunity to show kindness to Jonathan himself. Now some years have passed, and David wanted to do something to fulfill his promise to Jonathan.

David asked if there were anyone left of the house of Saul to whom he could show kindness for Jonathan's sake. His servants told him of a man named Ziba who had been Saul's servant. So, David sent for him.

When Ziba came in, David said, "Is there anyone of the house of Saul to whom I may yet show kindness?"

David was thrilled when the servant said, "There is a son of Jonathan. He is lame in both his feet."

David asked, "Where is he?"

Ziba replied, "In the house of Machir the son of Ammiel in Lo-debar."

Mephibosheth was five years old when his father Jonathan and his grandfather Saul were slain in battle on Mount Gilboa (1 Sam. 31). When the news came that day, Mephibosheth's nurse picked him up to flee and, as they were hurrying to get away, he fell and became lame in both his feet. By now Mephibosheth was the father of a young son named Mica, so probably fifteen or more years had passed since that day. It seems that Machir in Lo-debar had provided for Mephibosheth's needs during these years.

Mephibosheth was sent for, and he came and bowed low before David. The king said, "Mephibosheth, I want to show kindness to you for the sake of your father Jonathan. I am giving you the land that belonged to your grandfather Saul and you will eat bread at my own table."

This was a great honor which David gave to Mephibosheth, and he was impressed. He said, "What am I that you should even notice such a dead dog as I am?"

David called Ziba back to him and said, "All that Saul had I have given to Mephibosheth. You and your sons are to farm the land for him and bring in the harvest for Mephibosheth so that he may be provided for. But Mephibosheth himself, the grandson of your master, will eat at my table as if he were my own son."

Ziba replied, "I will do all that you have commanded." So Ziba and his fifteen sons and twenty servants cultivated Saul's land for Mephibosheth, while Mephibosheth lived in Jerusalem as part of David's family.

Names to add:
  Ziba
  Mephibosheth
  Machir

Label your new map:
  Lo-debar

War with the Ammonites and the Syrians (2 Sam. 10:1-19; 11:1; 12:26-31; 1 Chron. 19:1-20:3):

The Ammonites had been enemies of Israel since the Israelites first came into the land of Canaan. They lived east of the Jordan River on the fringe of the Arabian Desert. God did not allow the Israelites to fight them at the time of the Exodus, because they were descendants of Lot, and God said He gave them their land (see Deut. 2:16-23). As is true of all nations, their power fluctuated. When they were powerful and Israel wicked, they afflicted Israel, as in the days of Jephthah the judge (Judg. 11), and in the early days of Saul (1 Sam. 11). The King Nahash whose death is mentioned here may have been the same king whom Saul fought when he attacked Jabesh-gilead. The name "Nahash" was a title for Ammonite kings, so we cannot be sure. It would be possible, but this was fifty or more years since that battle between Saul and Nahash.

Nahash, king of the Ammonites, died and David decided to extend courtesy to the king's son Hanun by sending messengers carrying his condolences. David said, "I will show kindness to Hanun the son of Nahash, just as his father showed kindness to me."

But the princes of the Ammonites said to Hanun, "Do you really think that David is honoring your father? His men are here to spy out our city, trying to see how they can cause it to fall."

Hanun listened to his princes and followed their advice. He took David's messengers and shaved off half their beards, cut off their clothes up to their buttocks, and sent them home.

When David was told about this, he sent more messengers to meet his men, because they were greatly humiliated. David told them to stay at Jericho until their beards had grown out.

No king could ignore such an insult, so David began making preparations for battle. When the Ammonites realized they had become a "stench in David's nostrils," they began hiring men to help them. They hired 20,000 Syrian foot soldiers from Beth-Rehob and Zobah, plus 1,000 men and 32,000 chariots from the king of Maacah, and 12,000 from the king of Tob. *(All these places were city states among the Syrians, or Arameans.)* David sent Joab and his entire army to meet them.

The battle began. The Ammonites came out of their city *(probably their capital city Rabbah)* and drew up in battle formation, while the Syrian forces took up their position in the field. David's men found themselves between the two forces.

Joab divided his men and took the very best of the fighting men with him to face the Syrians. He put the rest of the soldiers in the hands of Abishai his brother to fight against the Ammonites. Joab said: "If the Syrians prove too strong for me, then you come to my rescue; but if the Ammonites are too strong for you, I will come to your rescue. Everyone be of good courage and fight like men for our people and the cities of our God."

Joab and his men defeated the Syrians and drove them away. When the Ammonites saw this, they withdrew and fled into their city.

The Syrians took their defeat personally. Their pride was injured, so their king Hadadezer (or Hadarezer) sent and had Syrian troops brought from beyond the Euphrates River. Under the leadership of Shobach the captain of the host, they met Israel in battle at Helam. David defeated the Syrians, killing 40,000 horsemen and the crews of 700 chariots. Shobach was slain also. All the kings that were subject to Hadadezer hastened to make peace with David. After this, the Syrians were afraid to help the Ammonites anymore.

To finish the conflict with the Ammonites, in the spring, at the time when kings go to war, Joab led out the armed forces. He laid waste the land of the Ammonites and went to Rabbah and besieged it. Meanwhile, David stayed in the city of Jerusalem.

After a time, Joab sent a message to David: "I have fought against Rabbah and I have taken its water supply. Now muster the rest of the troops and come take this city, or I will take it in my own name."

So, David called out his army, went to Rabbah, and captured it. He took the crown from the king and placed it upon his own head, thus declaring himself king of the Ammonites. He took a great amount of plunder from the city. The crown itself was made from a talent of gold and inlaid with precious stones. David brought out the people from the city and assigned them to task work with saws, iron picks, axes, and brick-making. Not only was Rabbah so treated, the other towns of the Ammonites were treated the same way. Then David and his army returned to Jerusalem.

Label your map:
Ammonite territory
Rabbah (or Rabbath-Ammon)

David commits adultery with Bathsheba (2 Sam. 11:1-27):

This story begins a chain of events that can be traced through the rest of David's life. Up until this point, David's reign had prospered, and God had been with him everywhere he turned. David let down his guard, he sinned, and spent the rest of his life reaping the consequences. The book of 1 Chronicles does not record this story, nor the struggles that followed it.

Did you notice in the last section that David remained in Jerusalem while Joab and the army were besieging Rabbah of the Ammonites (see 2 Sam. 11:1; 1 Chron. 20:1)? This story with Bathsheba took place while David was in Jerusalem on that occasion.

One evening, David got up from his bed and took a walk on the roof of his house *(their roofs served as porches or patios)*. From the roof, he saw a very beautiful woman taking a bath. David continued to watch until he desired the woman very much. Lust had been conceived in David's heart.

He sent to find out who the woman was. He was told, "She is Bathsheba, the wife of Uriah the Hittite."

Uriah was one of David's mighty men (see 2 Sam. 23:39; 1 Chron. 11:41). He was included in the list of men who helped David when he fled from Saul and who helped make him king. At that moment, Uriah was with the army at Rabbah trying to take a city for David.

Even after finding out that Bathsheba was the wife of one of his closest supporters, David's desire was so strong he sent messengers to the woman to have her come to him. Bathsheba came, he committed adultery with her, and she returned home.

Before long, there was a complication. Bathsheba sent word to David: "I am with child."

This was a major problem. Caught in a net, David sought for a way to cover what he had done. Finally, he sent for Uriah.

When Uriah came, David asked him, "How are my soldiers getting along? How goes the siege?" But David was not really interested in those things at that moment. He told Uriah, "Go to your home and rest a while." David assumed that Uriah would go home, go to bed with his wife, and then everyone would think the baby was Uriah's. But Uriah did not go to his home. Instead he slept with David's servants.

Next day, David found out that Uriah had not been to his house. This was very frustrating to him. "Uriah, haven't you been away from home for a long time? Why don't you go home for a while and see your wife?"

Uriah replied, "The ark of the Lord is in a hut, and my lord Joab and all my comrades are in the field unable to be at home. I will not go to my house to eat and to drink and to go to bed with my wife while my fellow soldiers are in the field."

David had Uriah stay in Jerusalem two more nights. David even had Uriah eat with him and made him drunk. Uriah still would not go home. By now David was desperate. So David wrote a letter to Joab and sent it back by the hand of Uriah. The letter said: "Set Uriah in the place where the battle is the hottest, then pull the soldiers back and leave him to be killed."

What questions this strange letter must have raised in the mind of Joab! But Joab did as he had been commanded, and Uriah was killed in battle.

When Joab sent a messenger to report the news of the battle to David, he said, "If you see the king is getting angry, and he says, 'Why did you go so close to the city? Did you not know they would shoot from the walls? Don't you remember that Abimelech, the son of Gideon, was killed when a woman dropped a stone upon his head from the wall?' (see Judg. 9:50-55). If the king starts to get angry, then tell him, 'Uriah the Hittite is dead also.'"

The messenger came to David, but he did not wait to see if the king would get angry. He said, "The men overpowered us and came out against us in the open, but we drove them back to the entrance of the city gate. Then the archers shot arrows at your servants from the wall, and some of the king's men died. Moreover, your servant Uriah the Hittite is dead."

David was so relieved to have covered his evil deeds he was not concerned about the unsuccessful skirmish, or the death of some of his men. He said, "Go back and tell Joab not to worry. The sword devours one as well as another. You are just going to have some reversals in war. So just press the battle and overthrow the city and everything will be fine."

When Bathsheba learned that Uriah had been killed, she wept and lamented. After her time of mourning was over, David sent for her to come to his house to become his wife. Months passed, and she bore him a son.

David thought he had taken care of everything. All his tracks were covered — except for one thing: "The thing David had done displeased the Lord."

Names to add:
   Bathsheba
   Uriah the Hittite

David confesses his sin and the child dies (2 Sam. 12:1-25):

God sent Nathan the prophet to David. Nathan began by telling David a story:

> There were two men who lived in a certain city; one was very rich and the other was poor. The rich man had many flocks and herds, but the poor man had nothing but one ewe lamb which he had bought. He raised it, and it grew up with him and his children. It shared his food, drank from his cup, and even slept in his arms. It was like a daughter to him.
>
> One day, the rich man had a visitor for whom he prepared a meal. But instead of taking one of his many sheep and preparing it, he took the poor man's lamb and dressed it for his guest.

David had been a shepherd. He knew of the affection one could develop for a lamb. He was so angry he said, "As Jehovah lives, the man is worthy of death! He shall restore the lamb fourfold."

As the hot words of David died away, there was a moment of silence as Nathan looked at him. Then the prophet said, "Thou art the man." Nathan continued:

> This is what the Lord says, "It is I who chose you to be king, and it is I who saved you from Saul's hand. I gave your master's house into your hand and your master's wives into your bosom. I gave you the house of Israel and the house of Judah, and if that were not enough, I would have added more. Why then have you despised the word of Jehovah to do such an evil thing? You have slain Uriah with the sword. You have taken his wife and have killed him with the sword of the Ammonites. Therefore, the sword will never depart from your house. I will raise up evil against you from your own household. I will take your wives and give them to one who is close to you, and he will lie with them in broad daylight. You did what you did secretly, but I will do this thing before all Israel."

Instantly the dam David had built to hold back his guilt burst. David said, "I have sinned against the Lord." This confession was merely the vanguard of the grief and shame that came pouring forth. David knew how the sin had robbed him of his precious relationship with God.

Nathan answered, "God has put away your sin so that you will not die. But you have given a great opportunity to the enemies of Jehovah to blaspheme. Therefore, the child that is born will die." With these dreadful words, Nathan left and went to his own home, no doubt with his own heart broken.

The law of Moses stated: "If a man be found lying with a woman married to a husband, then they shall both of them die, the man that lay with the woman, and the woman: so shalt thou put away the evil from Israel" (Deut. 22:2). God's message through Nathan was that He was forgiving David so that he would not be put to death, but that there would be consequences that must be paid.

Sure enough, the baby became very ill. David fasted and prayed, spending the nights on the ground. The elders came and tried to cheer him, but he would not rise up nor eat bread. After seven days the child died.

David noticed that the servants were whispering among themselves. They were afraid to tell him the news: "While the child was still living, we spoke to David but he would not listen to us. How can we tell him the child is dead? He may do something desperate."

David saw their fear and he asked, "Is the child dead?"

They replied, "Yes, he is dead."

To their astonishment, David got up, washed, anointed himself, changed clothes, and went to the house of God to worship. Then he called for bread to be brought and he ate. The servants were mystified. Finally they asked, "How is it that while the child was alive you fasted and wept, but now that the child is dead you get up and eat?"

David replied, "While the child was still alive, I prayed because there was a chance that God might be gracious and let him live. But now that the child is dead, why should I fast? I cannot bring him back. I shall go to him, but he will never return to me."

After this, Bathsheba conceived again. She brought forth a son, and David named him Solomon which means "peace." God sent word by Nathan to name him Jedidiah also because he was "beloved of God."

In saying that this baby was "beloved of God," God was saying He accepted this baby, in contrast to the baby that died. The first baby was illegitimate; his birth was the result of sin. By now Bathsheba is David's wife, and this baby is legitimate. Even though it will be Solomon who will reign after David, there is nothing said here about the position of king. God is not specifying here that this is His choice as the next king.

Name to add: Solomon

Psalms about the event

There are several psalms thought to be associated with this event in David's life, though only Psalm 51 has an inscription specifically designating it as belonging to this period. These psalms are very descriptive of the way a righteous man feels after he has sinned, whether David wrote them about this particular sin, or another. After looking at Nathan's message to David, and David's own confession, read the following psalms in sequence and watch as David pours out his heart to Jehovah. (The psalms are summarized here.)

Since we can be confident that Psalm 51 fits the event, read it together in class. It gives a beautiful, but poignant, insight into the heart of David as he reels from his sin. He knew he had sinned against Bathsheba, against Uriah, and against all who respected him — but he knew those involved were as nothing in comparison to his sin against Jehovah. David would have been glad to offer many sacrifices to God if that would blot out his sin, but he knew that would not be sufficient. The only thing David could offer to God was a broken and contrite heart. That is all any of us can offer God, no matter what our sin may be. In the psalm, we see David falling back upon the same refuge he always depended upon in time of need, the Lord who was his shepherd.

Psalms 6 and 38 express deep penitence. Read them, looking at David's grief. Psalm 32 is a psalm of praise to the Lord for His forgiveness. Likely it was written after the death of the child that was born from the adultery of David and Bathsheba. The book of Romans quotes from Psalm 32:1-2 to show a lesson David learned. He learned that the man who is blessed by God is the forgiven man, not the perfectly sinless man (see Rom.4:6-8). We will all have to rely upon God's mercy and His forgiveness to get to heaven, just as David did.

Psalm 6: *The prayer of one who lies awake in grief because of sin.*

O Lord, do not rebuke me in your anger. Be gracious to me, O Lord, for I am pining away. My soul is greatly distressed.

Return, O Lord, rescue my soul; save me because of your loving-kindness.

I am weary with my sighing. Every night I make my bed swim; I dissolve my couch with my tears. My eye has wasted away with grief.

Depart from me, all you who do iniquity, for the Lord has heard my weeping. He has heard my supplication and has received my prayer.

Psalm 38: *Another psalm of deep grief, and a cry for God's mercy.*
O Lord, do not rebuke me in your anger. For your arrows have sunk deep into me; your hand has pressed me down. There is no health in my bones because of my sins. My iniquities have gone over my head. They are like a burden too great for me to bear. My wounds grow foul and fester because of my folly. I mourn all day long. I am numb and badly crushed. I groan because of the agitation of my heart.

Lord, all my desires are before you and my sighing is not hid from you. My heart throbs, my strength fails, and my eyesight is gone. My loved ones, my friends, and my relatives all stand aloof in the time of my plague. Those who seek my life set snares for me. They threaten destruction, and devise treachery all day long.

But I am like a deaf man, and do not hear them. I am like a dumb man who does not open his mouth to answer them. For I hope in you, O Lord. You will answer me, O God. For I said, "May they not rejoice over me, those who would magnify themselves over me when my foot slips." For I confess my iniquity. My enemies are strong, and they oppose me because I follow good.

Do not forsake me, O Lord. O my God, do not be far from me. Hurry to help me, O Lord, my salvation!

Psalm 51: *David's earnest prayer for forgiveness.*
Have mercy upon me, O God, according to your loving-kindness, according to the greatness of your compassion, blot out my transgressions. Wash me thoroughly from my iniquity, and cleanse me from my sin.

For I am conscious of my transgressions, and my sin is ever before me. Against you alone have I sinned, and done that which is evil in your eyes. So you are just when you speak, and pure when you judge.

Behold, I was brought forth in the midst of iniquity and, surrounded by sin, my mother conceived me. Behold, you desire truth in the depths of the heart, and in the hidden part you will make me to know wisdom.

Oh, purge me with hyssop, and I shall be clean; wash me, and I shall be whiter than snow. Make me to hear joy and gladness, that the bones that you have broken may rejoice. Hide your face from my sins, and blot out all of my iniquities.

Create in me a clean heart, O God, and renew a steadfast spirit within me. Cast me not away from your presence, and do not take your Holy Spirit away from me.

Restore to me the joy of your salvation, and uphold me with a willing spirit. Then I will teach transgressors your ways, and sinners shall be converted to you.

Deliver me from the guilt of blood, O God of my salvation, and my tongue shall sing aloud of your righteousness. O Lord, open my lips, and my mouth shall declare your praise. For you do not delight in sacrifice, or I would have given it. You have no pleasure in burnt offering. The sacrifices God wants are a broken spirit and a contrite spirit. A broken and a contrite heart, O God, you will not despise.

Do good as you please unto Zion; build up the walls of Jerusalem. Then you will take delight in the sacrifices of righteousness, in burnt offering and whole burnt offering. Then will they offer bullocks upon your altar.

Psalm 32: *A psalm of praise to Jehovah for His forgiveness.*
How blessed *(happy)* is the one whose transgressions are forgiven, whose sin is covered! How blessed is the man to whom the Lord does not put iniquity on his account, in whose spirit there is no deceit!

When I kept silent about my sin, my body wasted away. For day and night your hand was heavy upon me. My strength drained away as with the heat of summer.

I confessed my sin to you, and I did not hide my iniquity. I said, "I will confess my transgressions to the Lord," and you forgave me.

Therefore, let everyone who is godly pray to you in a time when you may be found. Surely then the flood of great waters will not reach him. You are my hiding place; you preserve me from trouble.

I will instruct you and teach you in the way you should go *(David's advice to others)*. Do not be as the horse or as the mule which have no understanding, who must have a bit and bridle to hold them in check. Many are the sorrows of the wicked, but he who trusts in the Lord will be surrounded by loving-kindness. Be glad in the Lord and rejoice, you righteous ones. Shout for joy, all you who are upright in heart.

This is one of the saddest stories of the Bible. David was one of the greatest men of God who ever lived. Including the chapters specifically about his life and the psalms which he wrote, there are more chapters about his life than any other character in the Bible. (Of course, the whole Bible is about Jesus, but there are more chapters about David than there are chapters in the gospel accounts about Jesus.) He was a man who feared God, who loved God, who was the man after God's own heart. Note that he was called a man after God's own heart before he was anointed king (1 Sam. 13:14), but he was also called by the same title in Acts 13:22, long after this sin was committed. He was not a mean, wicked man because he committed this sin. He was a righteous man who made a grievous mistake and had to pay the consequences for his sin.

Note the difference between Saul's sins and David's sins. Saul denied his guilt until he was forced to admit it by indisputable evidence (see 1 Sam. 15). After he had sinned and his kingdom had been rejected, instead of repenting and asking for forgiveness, he allowed his jealousy and hatred for the one who would take his place to consume him completely. On the other hand, David sinned just as grievously, but his sin and guilt devastated him. He poured out his heart to the Lord, asking His forgiveness.

Even though David was forgiven, he was told that there would be consequences. Note them very carefully. As we follow the rest of David's life, we will see each one of these predictions come true. You might make a chart of these predictions and put them up before your class so that you may watch carefully for their fulfillment. The wages of sin are severe, even in this life (Prov. 13:15).

1. *The sword will never depart from David's house.*
2. *Trouble will arise from David's own family.*
3. *His wives will be lain with openly.*
4. *The child will die. Already in our story, the child has died.*

Amnon's sin with Tamar (2 Sam. 13:1-22):

We have already been introduced to David's family. Do you remember that Amnon was his oldest son? He was the son of Ahinoam. His brother Absalom was the son of Maacah. They were, therefore, half-brothers. (See 2 Sam. 3:2-3.) Absalom had a very beautiful sister named Tamar. As time passed, Amnon allowed himself to conceive a lust for his half-sister Tamar. He was so consumed with his desire he became frustrated to the point of illness.

Amnon had a first cousin named Jonadab who was his close friend. Jonadab could tell something was bothering Amnon, so he asked, "Why do you, the king's son, look so haggard morning after morning? Why not tell me about it?"

Amnon said simply, "I love Tamar." He did not have to say more. Jonadab could see the problems.

Jonadab suggested a plan whereby Amnon could get Tamar alone and commit fornication with her. He said, "Lie down on your bed and pretend to be sick. When your father comes to see you, ask him to send Tamar to prepare food for you."

Amnon immediately put this plan into operation. When David came to see him, Amnon said, "Let Tamar come and fix me a couple of cakes of bread that I may eat from her hand."

David sent word to Tamar to go to Amnon's house and prepare him food. In all good faith, Tamar went to Amnon, kneaded dough, and made cakes of bread as he watched. When the cakes were ready, she brought them to him, but he refused to eat.

"Send everyone out of here," said Amnon. Then he told Tamar to bring the food into his bedroom so that he might eat from her hand.

Tamar took the bread in as he requested. But instead of eating, he seized her, and said, "Come, go to bed with me, my sister."

Tamar was horrified: "No, my brother, don't force me. You should not do this terrible thing. What will I do? Where will I carry my shame? And you will be considered as one of the wicked, foolish ones in Israel." In desperation, she told him to ask David their father for permission to marry her, but Amnon would not listen. So, he raped his sister!

Amnon's "love" for Tamar was no more than lust and, as soon as he had satisfied his lust, he could not stand the sight of her. She was contemptible to him. He told her, "Get up and get out of here."

She was devastated and did not know where to go. She said, "Do not thrust me from you, because that will be an even greater wrong than what you have already done."

But Amnon cared nothing for her pleas. He called to his servant and said, "Put this woman out of my house and bolt the door after her."

As Tamar went along the way, she put ashes on her head and tore the beautiful garment that she wore identifying her as the king's daughter. She wept aloud as she went home.

When Absalom saw her, the first thing he asked was, "Has Amnon been with you?" Obviously, Absalom had heard some talk, or had evidence of some kind that Amnon was up to no good. He comforted Tamar and took her into his own house where she remained desolate. Remember that Tamar and Absalom were full brother and sister. For this reason Absalom had a special concern for Tamar.

David heard what had happened and was very angry, but he did nothing about it.

Absalom hated Amnon for what he had done. He refused to speak to him because he had disgraced his sister.

Names to add:
   Tamar
   Jonadab

For the first time in his life David is indecisive. According to the law of Moses, Amnon deserved to die (see Deut. 22:25-27), but David did nothing. According to that same law David himself had deserved to die just a short time earlier (Deut. 22:22). His own feeling of guilt tied his hands in dealing with Amnon. Therefore, David did nothing. There was, however, one important difference between David's sin and Amnon's sin: David was deeply grieved over his sin and prayed for forgiveness. The Bible does not tell of any sign of remorse on the part of Amnon.

It is a little hard for us to understand how Amnon could have a desire like this for his sister, but their family life was very different to ours. In a king's household, each wife and her children had her separate quarters. Amnon would have grown up seeing his half-sister Tamar the way we might see a good friend at school. Their relationship would have been no closer than we might have with a cousin whom we saw often.

Absalom's revenge (2 Sam. 13:23-39):

Two years passed.

Absalom had sheep-shearers in Baal-Hazor near the border of Ephraim. It was customary to have a feast when the shearing was finished, so Absalom invited all his brothers, his father, and the king's officials to the feast.

David protested, "No, my son. All of us should not go; we would only be a burden to you." Even though Absalom pressed him to go, David would not agree, but he gave Absalom his blessings.

Then Absalom said, "If you are not going, please let my brother Amnon come with us."

David was suspicious: "Why do you want him to go?" But Absalom urged him, and he agreed for Amnon to go with his other brothers.

So, all the brothers of Absalom were at the feast. It seemed to be an ordinary feast until Absalom gave his servants a strange order. He said, "Watch Amnon carefully and when you see his heart is merry with wine, strike him down, then kill him. Don't be afraid for I have given you the orders to do so."

The servants of Absalom waited and watched and then carried out their dreadful orders. The rest of the king's sons fled in panic.

While the sons were still on their way, terrible news came to David: "Absalom has struck down all the king's sons; not one of them is left." David's grief was without bounds. He tore his clothes and lay upon the ground. His servants stood around with their garments rent also.

But Jonadab, David's nephew, was there and heard the news. Do you remember that Jonadab was the one who advised Amnon how to get Tamar alone? He told David, "Let not the king think that they have killed all the king's sons. Amnon is the only one dead because Absalom has been waiting to do this since the day Amnon raped his sister Tamar. So do not let the king grieve that all his sons are dead, for they are not. Only Amnon is dead."

It was not long before the watchman on the wall saw a group of men coming. Jonadab said, "Look, the king's sons have come. They are safe just as I said."

As the sons greeted their father, they wept and David wept with them. It was a time of deep grief.

Absalom, however, fled from the country. His mother was the daughter of the king of Geshur (see 3:2), so he fled to his grandfather. He remained there three years.

As time passed, David's heart went out to Absalom because he was comforted over Amnon's death.

Label your map: Geshur

David knew Amnon had done wrong and that he needed to be punished, but he waited until one brother killed the other instead of dealing with the matter himself. Now David is still paralyzed. Secretly, he is glad for what Absalom did, and yet he allows him to languish in Geshur for three years. Indeed, we see a different David now, an indecisive one — particularly in dealing with his own sons. We also see the seeds of later trouble already sown.

Absalom returns to Jerusalem (2 Sam 14:1-24, 28):

Joab could tell that David's heart longed for Absalom, so he tried to think of a way to persuade the king to bring his son home. He went to the city of Tekoa and persuaded a woman known for her wisdom to help him. He told her: "Pretend you are in mourning. Dress in mourning clothes, and do not use any cosmetic lotions. Act as if you have spent many days grieving for the dead. Then go before the king, and I will tell you exactly what to say."

The woman agreed and went before the king. She bowed low before him and said, "Help me, O King!"

David asked, "What is your problem?"

She began her story, following Joab's exact instructions: "My husband is dead. I had two sons who got angry with each other. They got into a fight out in the field, and no one was there to separate them. One of them struck the other and killed him. Now the whole family has risen up against the one who is left to put him to death. If they kill him, they will destroy the heir to my estate, they will put out the only burning coal I have left, and they will leave my husband neither name nor descendant upon the earth."

David told her not to worry: "Go home, and I will issue an order in your behalf."

David had not yet committed himself as firmly as the woman wanted, so she pursued the matter further. She said, "Let any guilt for your action be upon me and upon my father's family; let the king and his throne be guiltless."

"If anyone gives you any problem about this, bring him to me and he will not bother you again," David answered.

She still wanted a more specific statement, so she said, "Then let the king give an order from

God to prevent the avenger of blood from killing my son." (See Numbers 35:15-28.)

David answered, "As surely as the Lord lives, not one hair of your son's head will fall to the ground." Now David's commitment was complete.

The woman said, "Let me speak a word to my lord the king." David agreed, and she continued:

> Why have you acted as you have toward your banished son? In what you have said about my son, you have made yourself guilty. We all die, and when we die, we are like water spilled upon the ground which cannot be gathered up again. Neither does God take away life; instead He devises ways so that the one who is banished will not remain an outcast. That is why I came to the king. The people made me afraid and I thought, "Perhaps the king will hear my request and deliver my son." And now the word of my lord the king brings me rest, for the king is like a messenger of God in discerning good and evil. May God be with you.

David was shrewd and he guessed what had happened. He said to the woman, "Now answer my question: Did Joab have a hand in this? Did he send you here?"

The woman answered, "No one can outsmart the king. Yes, Joab put these words in my mouth. My lord is wise as an angel of God to know everything."

David called Joab in and said, "I have done as you have said. Go, bring back the young man Absalom."

Joab was overjoyed and bowed before the king. He went to Geshur and brought Absalom home.

The total problem was not solved however. David allowed Absalom to come home, but he still would not receive him in good standing. He sent word for Absalom to go to his own house, but the king refused to see him. This state of affairs continued for two more full years.

Name to add: Woman of Tekoa

Count the time that is passing. Amnon raped Tamar; Absalom was very angry, but did nothing just then. Two full years passed, and then Absalom ordered his servants to kill Amnon. Absalom fled from the country and was gone three more years. Through Joab's intercession, David gives his consent for Absalom to come home, but refuses to see him for two more years. That makes a total of seven years since Amnon's crime. Do you see how resentment would be building in Absalom's mind?

Absalom is reconciled with David (2 Sam. 14:25-33; 18:18):

The Bible describes Absalom as a very handsome young man. There was not a man in all Israel as highly praised for his looks. From the top of his head to the sole of his foot there was no blemish in him. He cut his luxuriant hair once a year because it became too heavy. The part cut off would weigh about 200 shekels. *(A silver shekel equalled one-half ounce according to Brown, Driver and Briggs' Hebrew Lexicon; therefore, the part of Absalom's hair that was cut off weighed about six pounds.)*

At this point in the history, Absalom had three sons and one daughter. He named the daughter Tamar, and she grew to be a beautiful woman. It is interesting to note that Absalom later erected a monument to his memory in the King's Valley because he said he had no son to carry on the memory of his name. Therefore, the sons mentioned here must have died young.

By the time Absalom had been back in Jerusalem for two years, he grew tired of the strained relationship with his father. He sent for Joab to get his help in persuading David to see him, but

Joab ignored the summons. Absalom sent for him a second time with the same results. By now Absalom was annoyed. He called for his servants and said: "Look, Joab's field is next to mine, and he has barley planted there. Go, set it on fire." As usual, his servants did as they were commanded.

Now Joab came. He demanded, "Why have your servants burned my field?"

Absalom calmly answered, "I sent word for you to come to me and you ignored me. Now go to the king and ask him why he let me return from Geshur. It would be better for me if I had remained there. I want to see the king's face. If I am guilty of anything, then let him put me to death. If not, let this matter be resolved!"

So Joab went to David and told him what Absalom had said. David listened to the plea, and he sent for Absalom. When he came, Absalom bowed before his father. David kissed him, and all seemed to be well again.

Absalom rebels against his father (2 Sam. 15:1-12):

Four more years passed. During this time Absalom set out to win the hearts of the people of Israel.

The circumstances of the last few years had caused Absalom to lose all love for his father. By the end of these four years, it had been 11 years since Amnon's sin, and the beginning of the conflict between Absalom and David. With Amnon the oldest son dead, Absalom was next in line for the throne. He decided he did not want to wait until his father died. (Look back to 2 Samuel 3:2-5: Amnon was the firstborn son, Chileab was second, and Absalom was third. As we noted in the section about David's family, Chileab is never mentioned again, and Absalom considered he had a right to the throne, so it seems that Chileab died young, as so many children did in that day.)

Absalom prepared a special chariot and horses for himself, and he hired fifty men to run before him. This measure was designed to make him appear as a great man before the people — the crown prince. He would get up early and go stand by the side of the road leading to the city gate. As someone approached with a complaint to be placed before the king, he would call out, "What town are you from, and what is your complaint?"

The person would explain his problem, and no matter what it was, Absalom would say, "Look, your claims are valid and proper, but, unfortunately, my father has not provided a man to hear such cases." Then he would add, "Oh, if only I were appointed judge in the land! Then anyone who had a complaint or a problem could come to me and I would see that he gets justice." Or if someone approached Absalom and bowed in honor of the king's son, Absalom lifted him up and kissed him as a friend.

Naturally the person who heard Absalom's words would go home discouraged, not trying to discuss his matter with David because he thought it hopeless. He felt Absalom was his friend, and would wish Absalom were in control. "So Absalom stole the hearts of the men of Israel."

By the end of four years, Absalom was ready to make his move. He went to the king and said, "Please let me go to Hebron to fulfill a vow I made to God. While I was in Geshur, I promised that if God would bring me back to Jerusalem I would worship Him in Hebron."

David said, "Go in peace."

So Absalom made his arrangements. He took two hundred carefully selected guests with him. They went innocently, having no idea what Absalom had in mind. He also sent secret spies throughout the land. At the proper moment, they were to say, "As soon as you hear the sound of the trumpets, you are to shout 'Absalom is king in Hebron.'"

While Absalom was offering his sacrifices in Hebron, he sent for one more man to join his forces: Ahithophel, one of David's wisest and most trusted counselors. Thus, Absalom's conspiracy gained strength rapidly.

Name to add:	**Label your map:**
Ahithophel	Hebron

How could such a thing happen? How could Absalom rebel against his own father? How could the Israelites forget their love for their hero David?

Many years have passed since the young man David went out and faced the giant Goliath. David is no longer the young, exciting figure he was then. In contrast, Absalom is young, handsome, shrewd, and totally unscrupulous. As we watch the events unfold, it seems clear that even David expected Absalom to be the one who would take his place upon the throne. But Absalom does not want to wait. David is still a very wise king in controlling everything about his kingdom (except for dealing with his own sons), but Absalom has undermined the people's confidence in David by his own crafty measures. It is a very sad story.

And do you remember Nathan's predictions? Trouble has certainly arisen from within David's own household, and the sword has not departed from his house. When God makes a promise — whether for good or bad, it comes true!

David flees from Jerusalem (2 Sam. 15:13-37):

A messenger came to David in Jerusalem and said, "The hearts of the men of Israel are with Absalom."

David told his officials, "Come! We must flee, or none of us will escape Absalom. Hurry lest he catch us and smite the city with the edge of the sword." *(David did not want to be caught inside the walled city of Jerusalem, because then he would have access to those in the city with him — and no more. Absalom's forces could besiege the city and force them to surrender.)*

The officials said, "We are ready to do whatever the king requires."

David left ten concubines to keep the house, but the rest of his household went with him. David started out of the city and then halted just outside to see who was coming with him. As he observed, all his men passed before him. There were the Cherethites and the Pelethites, his personal body guard. One group who followed him surprised David. It was a group of six hundred men from the city of Gath (Gittites) with their leader Ittai. They had been in David's service for some time. David protested to Ittai: "Why do you want to go with us? Go back and remain with King Absalom. You are a foreigner, an exile from your homeland. This is not your battle. You only came recently, so why should I make you wander with me when I do not know where I am going? Go back, and take your men with you."

But Ittai admired David and was loyal to him. He answered, "As surely as the Lord lives, and as my lord the king lives, wherever the king is, whether it means life or death, there will I be also." David was pleased to have the help of these loyal men, so he told them to move ahead.

Of course, news of what was happening was spreading fast. The people along the route David's men were taking wept aloud as they saw the people pass. By now, the king and all his company had crossed the Kidron Valley just outside the walls of the city, and were starting up the side of the Mount of Olives. They were heading east toward the deep cleft of the Jordan Valley.

Zadok, Abiathar, and the Levites who were on duty, came bringing the ark of the covenant with them. They set the ark down, and Abiathar began offering sacrifices and continued to do so until all the people accompanying David passed by.

It must have been deeply comforting to David for these priests to show their loyalty to him by their willingness to come, but David sent them back into the city. He said: "Take the ark of God back into the city. If I find favor in the Lord's eyes, He will bring me back and let me see it and His dwelling place again. But if He is not pleased with me, then I am ready for whatever comes. Let God do with me whatever seems good to Him."

The priests could be of more help to David by staying inside the city than they could by going with him. David told them, "You are seers (prophets). Go back into the city in peace. Zadok, you have your son Ahimaaz and Abiathar's son Jonathan with you. I will wait at the fords of the Jordan until I hear word from you."

Zadok and Abiathar returned to the city with the ark. The beginning of a spy system had been established. The priests would learn all they could and then send word to David by their sons.

As David was going up and over the Mount of Olives, he and all the people with him wept. Here he was fleeing for his life again — and this time from his own son! Someone came bringing him more bad news, "Ahithophel is among the conspirators with Absalom."

This was indeed very bad news because Ahithophel was exceedingly wise. David prayed, "O Jehovah, I pray thee, turn the counsel of Ahithophel to foolishness."

At the crest of the hill, still another of David's counsellors met him. This was a man named Hushai. He had dust on his head and his garment was rent. *(From David's comments to him, it seems Hushai was an old man.)* David told him, "Hushai, if you go with me you will be a burden to me. You can serve me much better by remaining behind to defeat the counsel of Ahithophel. Tell Absalom, 'I will be your servant just as I have been your father's servant.' The sons of Zadok and Abiathar are in the city with you. Whatever you learn, tell it to Zadok and Abiathar, and they will send their sons to tell me." Thus, another very important link in David's spy system was established.

Hushai returned to Jerusalem, approaching from the east, just as Absalom and his company was arriving from Hebron in the south. Absalom had come in triumph. His rebellion was going strong. David and his men had gotten away from the city just in time. They were just a little out of sight over the crest of the Mount of Olives.

Names to add:
   Ittai and the 600 Gittites
   Ahimaaz
   Jonathan (the son of Abiathar)
   Hushai

Troubles along the way (2 Sam. 16:1-14):
As David and his supporters continued their flight, others came out to meet them. One of them was Ziba, the steward of Mephibosheth's property. Ziba was leading a string of donkeys, saddled and loaded with food supplies.

David asked, "Why have you brought these?"

Ziba replied, "The animals are for the king's household to ride, the supplies are for the people to eat, and the wine is for anyone who becomes exhausted on the trip."

Then David inquired, "Where is Mephibosheth?"

Ziba answered, "He is staying in Jerusalem, because he thinks, 'Today the house of Israel will give my grandfather's kingdom back to me.'"

How disappointing to David! He had shown kindness to Mephibosheth for Jonathan's sake, and now Mephibosheth was returning the kindness this way! David told Ziba, "All that belonged to Mephibosheth is now yours."

"I humbly bow," said Ziba. "May I find favor in your eyes, my lord the king."

David had no evidence to refute Ziba's word at this point. Remember this event, however, because we will learn more about Mephibosheth and Ziba later.

As David was approaching Bahurim, a relative of Saul's named Shimei came out against him. Shimei cursed David as he went along. He threw rocks at David and at his company even though David's special troops and guard were all around him. As he cursed, Shimei said: "Get out, get out, you man of blood, you scoundrel! The Lord has repaid you for all the blood you shed in the household of Saul, in whose place you have reigned. The Lord has handed the kingdom over to your son Absalom. You have come to ruin because you are a man of blood!"

Abishai was filled with anger and said, "Why should this dead dog curse the king? Let me go over and cut off his head."

David said, "What am I going to do with you sons of Zeruiah? If my own son seeks my life, why shouldn't this Benjamite curse me? It may be that Jehovah has sent him to curse me. Or, it may be that the Lord will see my distress and repay me with good for the cursing I am receiving today." So Shimei followed along, going parallel to them, cursing them and throwing rocks and dirt at them.

Finally, the whole company reached the edge of the Jordan River and stopped to rest. They were exhausted by then.

Name to add: Shimei

Hushai and Ahithophel advise Absalom (2 Sam. 16:15-17:14):

Let us leave David and his company at the fords of the Jordan River and go back to the city to see what is happening with Absalom and his company. By now Absalom and all the men with him have arrived in Jerusalem. Remember that Ahithophel, David's very wise advisor, is with Absalom. And remember that David has sent Hushai, another very wise advisor, to pretend loyalty to Absalom in order to try to defeat the counsel of Ahithophel.

Hushai, David's friend, came to meet Absalom, saying, "Long live the king! Long live the king!"

Absalom was surprised: "Is this the way you treat your friend? Why did you not go with your friend?" It was a crucial moment for Hushai and for the cause of David.

Hushai replied, "Oh no, the one chosen by the Lord, by these people, and by all the men of Israel — his will I be, and I will remain with him. Besides, you are your father's son. Why should I not serve you?" Absalom liked the answer and accepted Hushai with no more questions.

Then Absalom turned to Ahithophel: "What should I do first?"

Ahithophel knew that if Absalom crossed the point of no return in his father's eyes, there would be no turning back in the rebellion. The people with him would know they were obligated to see it carried to completion. One way to demonstrate that Absalom was now king was to take over the wives of his predecessor, so Ahithophel said: "Go in and lie with the concubines your father left to take care of the palace. Then all Israel will hear that you have made yourself a stench in your father's nostrils, and the hands of everyone with you will be strengthened."

So they spread a tent on the roof of the palace and Absalom committed adultery with his father's concubines in the presence of all Israel. *(Remember the prediction Nathan made to David about his wives? See 12:11-12.)*

Ahithophel had the reputation of giving such wise counsel that it appeared as if it had come straight from God. That is how both David, and now Absalom, regarded his advice.

Next it was time to plan their battle strategy. Ahithophel said: "Let me choose 12,000 men and set out tonight in pursuit of David. Let me attack him while he is tired and weary. I will make a surprise attack and cause terror in his camp. I will kill only your father so there will be a minimum of bloodshed. If we kill the one man you seek, then the rest of the people can be brought back to you, and everything will be under control."

This was indeed wise counsel. If Absalom accepted it, then David would surely be caught. David was only a few miles away; the troops with him were weary and discouraged, and he had not had time to gather additional support. Absalom was very pleased with Ahithophel's advice, and so were the elders of Israel with him.

Nevertheless, Absalom wanted to hear Hushai's advice also before he took any action. More than anyone else present, Hushai knew just how deadly Ahithophel's advice would be for David. Ahithophel had gauged the situation correctly and had given the very best advice to further Absalom's cause. How could Hushai make that advice sound bad? Realizing that men often allow their emotions to overcome wisdom, he decided to prey upon a very powerful emotion of Absalom's — that is, fear. He said:

Ahithophel has not given good advice this time. You know your father and his men; they are fighters and as fierce as a wild bear that has been robbed of her cubs. Besides, your father is an experienced fighter. He will not spend the night with his troops. He is probably already hidden in some cave. If you send a small force, and there is even one skirmish in which your father is not captured, and some of your men are killed, then the rumor will spread that "Absalom's men have really taken a beating," and all with you will lose courage and forsake you because all Israel knows how brave a fighter your father is.

This is what I advise: Let all Israel, from Dan to Beersheba, be gathered. Gather an army as numerous as the sand on the seashore. Then go out to meet David, with you personally in command. You will come upon your father as the dew upon the ground and you can kill all his men. Even if he is in a city by then, we will take ropes and pull the walls down into the river till not one stone is left, and you will defeat your father.

Absalom was afraid of his father's prowess, and his pride liked the idea of the enormous army very much. So he and his men said, "The counsel of Hushai is better than that of Ahithophel this time."

God was still protecting His servant David. God had determined that Ahithophel's advice would be defeated on this occasion.

David's spy system is put to use (2 Sam. 17:15-29):

Even though Absalom decided that Hushai's advice was better than Ahithophel's about the battle strategy, Hushai was very afraid he would yet change his mind. Hushai knew that David must get as far away as possible before Absalom decided to attack. Therefore, he began trying to send a warning to David. The time had come to use the spy system David had set up.

Hushai told Zadok and Abiathar, the priests, all that had transpired. He told what advice

Ahithophel had given to Absalom and how he himself had tried to counteract it. Then he said, "Send quickly and tell David that he must not spend the night at the fords of the Jordan. Tell him to go across the river as quickly as possible lest he be captured."

Jonathan and Ahimaaz, the sons of Zadok and Abiathar, were waiting at a spring called En-Rogel which was located just outside the city wall. They were afraid to be seen going in or out of the city. A servant girl was used to carry the message to them. Unfortunately, a young man saw the girl talking to them and guessed she was giving them a message for David. He went back into the city and told Absalom what he had seen. Absalom immediately sent men after them.

Jonathan and Ahimaaz knew they were in danger, so they hurried away toward Bahurim. They came to the house of a man who had a well in his courtyard. They climbed down into the well, and the woman of the house put a cover over the well and spread grain on it as if she were working with it.

Very soon, Absalom's men came by. They saw the woman working and asked, "Where are Ahimaaz and Jonathan?"

She answered, "They crossed over the brook." The men hurried on their way, but they could not find anyone. Soon they gave up and returned to Jerusalem.

As soon as they could, the two young men climbed out of the well and hurried to warn David. "Pass quickly over the river because Ahithophel has advised Absalom to come after you now before you get completely away."

So David and all the people with him set out and crossed the Jordan that night. By daybreak, all the company was on the eastern side of the river heading north.

When Ahithophel saw that Absalom was not following his advice, he knew Absalom would lose the struggle with David. Knowing this as surely as if it had already happened, and knowing what would happen to him for his part in the rebellion, he went to his house, made some last arrangements of his affairs, and hanged himself!

David finally arrived in the city of Mahanaim. There he was met by several supporters including Shobi (the son of Nahash the king of the Ammonites), Machir of Lo-debar (the man Mephibosheth lived with before joining David), and a man of Gilead named Barzillai. They brought bedding, eating vessels, and food of all kinds.

Meanwhile, Absalom was preparing his own forces for battle. He gathered his army and he, too, crossed the Jordan into Gilead. He chose a man named Amasa as his chief captain. Amasa was the grandson of a woman named Nahash who was a sister to Zeruiah the mother of Joab and also a sister to David. Thus, Absalom, Amasa, and Joab were all cousins, and all relatives of David. (See 1 Chronicles 2:16-17.)

Names to add:
- Shobi
- Machir
- Barzillai
- Amasa

Label your map:
- Mount of Olives
- Jordan River
- Mahanaim
- Gilead

Psalm 3

By inscription we know that Psalm 3 fits in the period of Absalom's rebellion. Also thought to belong to this period are Psalms 4, 5, 11, 12, 23 (even though we chose to quote this one earlier in the story of David), 25, 26, 27, 28, 41, 55, 58, 61, 62, 63, 86, 122, 140, 141, 143. The factors that play a part in determining that these psalms belong to the time of Absalom's rebellion are:

1. *David is in deep trouble.*
2. *He feels betrayed by those closest to him, especially by his former "friend," thought by many Bible students to be Ahithophel. The rebellion itself originated with David's own son, so that too may have been in his mind.*
3. *When there is some indication of David's being king, or Jerusalem being the capital, or the ark's being in Jerusalem, then the time of David's affliction referred to would have to be Absalom's rebellion rather than Saul's persecution of David, because in Saul's day, David was not king, Jerusalem was not his capital, and the ark was not in Jerusalem.*

Jehovah, how many are my enemies. Many rise up against me. Many say of my soul: "There is no help for him in God."

But you, Jehovah, are a shield around me, my glory, and the one who lifts up my head. I cried unto Jehovah with my voice, and He answered me out of His holy hill.

I laid down and slept. I woke up, because Jehovah sustains me. I will not be afraid of ten thousands of the people that have set themselves against me all about me.

Rise up, O Jehovah, help me, O my God. For you smite all my enemies upon the jaw. You have broken the teeth of the wicked. Salvation belongs to Jehovah. Let your blessing be upon the people.

Absalom is defeated (2 Sam. 18:1-18):

By the time of the battle between the forces of David and Absalom, David had put together a sizable army. He organized his men into three groups and placed them under three commanders: Joab, Abishai, and Ittai the Gittite.

As the army prepared to go into battle, David said, "I will go forth to fight with you."

But his followers objected: "No, because if we have to flee, Absalom's army will not care about us; or if half of us die, that will not matter because there are thousands of us, but there is only one of you. Stay here and be ready to help us from the city." David agreed to do as they said.

David stood by the city gate and watched as all his troops passed before him. Then, there before the whole army, he told his commanders, "Deal gently with the young man Absalom for my sake." All the troops heard the instructions.

The Bible says the battle took place in the Forest of Ephraim, yet in 2 Samuel 17:24-26, it specifically says that Absalom and his army had crossed the Jordan and were in Gilead. Ephraim's territory was on the west side of the river, and Gilead was on the east side. Either the armies crossed the river as the battle grew hotter, or else there was a forest in Gilead named for Ephraim. Most students today believe the latter is the correct explanation.

Absalom's men were no match for David's forces, so they were soon fleeing in all directions. The slaughter was immense. Absalom was soon fleeing also. As he was riding his mule through the forest, he passed under an oak tree, and his head caught in a limb. His mule ran on ahead and left Absalom hanging in the tree.

One of David's soldiers saw Absalom and went to tell Joab, "Behold, I saw Absalom hanging in a tree."

Joab answered, "What? You saw him helpless and did not kill him? I would have given you ten pieces of silver and a warrior's belt if you had killed him."

The soldier replied, "Not even for a thousand pieces of silver would I have killed him, because we all heard the king tell you and Abishai and Ittai not to harm Absalom. If I had killed him, and the king had learned of it, as I am sure he would have, you would not have defended me."

Joab said, "I do not have time to waste talking to you." And he rode away to find Absalom. He took three darts and thrust them into Absalom. Ten young men with Joab surrounded the helpless Absalom, beat him, and killed him.

Joab then blew the trumpet to end the battle. The people took Absalom's body and cast it into a large pit there in the forest. Then they piled up a big heap of rocks to mark the spot. We have already noted that Absalom had built a monument to himself in the King's Valley to keep the memory of his name alive.

Meanwhile, Absalom's men fled to their homes in defeat.

David mourns for his son (2 Sam. 18:19-33):

Ahimaaz, the son of Zadok, wanted to run to carry the news of the victory to David, but Joab knew that whoever took the news of victory would also have to tell of Absalom's death. Ahimaaz was the son of David's friend, so Joab did not want him to be the bearer of such bad tidings. Therefore Joab sent a Cushite runner to tell David. *(In the KJV the runner is called Cushi, as if that were his name.)*

When the Cushite left, Ahimaaz begged to be sent. Joab said, "Why will you run, my son, since you have no news to report that will bring you a reward?" But Ahimaaz insisted, and Joab agreed. The young man set out, went a different way, and reached Mahanaim ahead of the Cushite.

David was anxiously awaiting news. Finally the watchman sounded the cry, "Behold, I see one man running alone."

David said, "If he is alone, he carries news."

Then the watchman said, "Behold, another man comes."

"He also brings news," David said.

The watchman said, "The first one runs like Ahimaaz the son of Zadok."

David replied, "He is a good man and brings good news." That was why Joab had not wanted to send Ahimaaz. He knew that David was fond of Ahimaaz and would assume that since he had been chosen as the runner the news must be good.

Ahimaaz called out to the king as he approached, "All is well." He bowed before David and said, "Blessed be Jehovah who has delivered up the men that lifted up their hand against the king."

David was interested in only one question: "Is the young man Absalom safe?"

Ahimaaz answered, "I saw a tumult just as Joab was about to send me, but I do not know what it was about."

David said, "Stand aside and wait here." Together they waited for the Cushite and his message.

The Cushite arrived and said, "My lord the king, hear the good news! The Lord has delivered you today from all who rose up against you."

David asked, "Is the young man Absalom safe?"

Sadly, tactfully, the Cushite replied, "May all the enemies of my lord the king be as that young man is."

David's heart was broken. His victory meant nothing. His son was dead. He slowly went up to the chamber over the gate and wept. As he went, he cried, "O my son Absalom, my son, my son Absalom! If only I had died instead of you. O Absalom, my son, my son!"

Joab reproves David (2 Sam. 19:1-8a):

Joab heard, "The king is weeping and mourning for Absalom."

The whole army heard the same message. Instead of coming into the city in triumph as they should have after winning such a victory, they began stealing back as if they were in shame over defeat. And David continued to lament: "O my son Absalom, O Absalom, my son, my son!"

Joab went straight to David and delivered a stinging rebuke: "Today you have put to shame the very ones who saved your life, the lives of your sons and daughters, and the lives of your wives and your concubines. You love those who hate you and hate those who love you. You have made it clear that the commanders and their men mean nothing to you. I see that you would be pleased if Absalom were alive today and all of us were dead. I am telling you: you had better get up and go speak encouragingly to your servants or I swear by the Lord that you will not have a man left to you by nightfall. Then you will be in worse trouble than you have been from your youth until now."

David meekly accepted the rebuke. He knew Joab was right. So he got up and sat in the gate where he could be seen and where he could greet his soldiers. Word spread rapidly that "the king is sitting in the gateway," and the soldiers hurried to greet him. Even though David was personally grieved over the loss of his son, it was indeed a day of great victory for the kingdom.

In every kingdom, in every situation where one is in high authority, there are those who advise the chief, but who would hesitate to rebuke him when he makes a mistake. Then, there are a very few select ones who are close enough to the king or chief to be able to walk in and say the thing that everyone knows needs to be said, but has been hesitating to say. Such was the relationship between Joab and David. Though there is much to criticize in Joab's life, this is one time his rebuke was needed. David was allowing his personal grief to interfere with his wisdom in guiding his nation.

David returns to his kingdom (2 Sam. 19:8b-40):

This is one time when your list of names will prove to be of great value to you. Look on your list and remind yourself of the role various ones have played during the rebellion of Absalom. Then watch to see what happens with each one as David returns to Jerusalem. Particularly observe these:

Amasa and Joab, Shimei, Ziba and Mephibosheth, Barzillai, and the ten concubines.

The battle with Absalom is over, but the whole nation was still in turmoil. There was strife and quarreling, and no one knew exactly what to do. They argued among themselves, saying, "The king delivered us from the Philistines and from all our enemies. He fled from Absalom, but now Absalom, the one we appointed to rule over us, is dead." The people were in limbo. They could not follow Absalom because he was dead; and they still had affection for David; but they needed something to move them to action to bring the king back.

Meanwhile, David was hearing the rumors that were going through the land. He sent a message to Zadok and Abiathar: "Ask the men of Judah, my own tribe, why they are the last to talk of bringing the king back to the palace? All Israel is talking of bringing me back. You are my bone and my flesh. Why are you not in the lead to bring me home?"

He continued with a special message for Amasa who had served as the captain of Absalom's host. Amasa must have been fearing punishment since he had served as captain of the rebellion. But Amasa was David's nephew. The king sent word: "Tell Amasa that he is my bone and flesh also. May God deal with me, be it ever so severely, if from now on you are not captain of my host instead of Joab."

So, David won the hearts of the men of Judah. They sent word to him saying, "Return to us, you and your servants."

Though David does not put it into words as he makes this promise to Amasa, part of his reason for making Amasa captain instead of Joab seems to have been because Joab had disobeyed his order about showing kindness to Absalom. It would have been difficult for there ever again to be a good relationship between David and his rebellious son, so from a political viewpoint, Joab may have made the right decision to kill Absalom. But David was Joab's king, and he had given a direct order to his army and his captains. Joab deliberately disobeyed the order.

David and the company with him set out for the Jordan River. This time, instead of making the trip in flight from an enemy, they were returning in pomp. The men of Judah assembled on the west side of the Jordan at Gilgal, waiting to welcome their king home.

Visualize the scene. David's headquarters had been in Mahanaim during this time he had been in exile (2 Sam. 17:24), so we assume he and his company came from there to the Jordan. The men of Judah have assembled to await the king at Gilgal. There was a Gilgal in the central hill country near Bethel, Ramah, and such places. It is the Gilgal that is mentioned most often in the scriptures. But that Gilgal would have been too many miles from the Jordan River to fit this story. The men of Judah who are welcoming David are on one side of the river while David and his company are on the other side. Therefore, this must be the Gilgal that was the Israelites' first camping place when they crossed the Jordan River on dry land in the days of Joshua (Josh. 4:19-20). It was located in the valley of the Jordan, just a little east of Jericho. It would be close enough to the river's edge to fit the description here.

Label your map: Gilgal (in the Jordan Valley)

In addition to the men of Judah, Shimei (the one who had cursed David as he fled) was there with a thousand men from the tribe of Benjamin. Ziba was there with his fifteen sons and twenty servants. A ferry boat was used to carry David and his household over the river, and it seems that these men with Shimei and Ziba were the ones primarily operating the boat to transport David's company and all their possessions across the river.

Shimei was the first to run to meet David as he reached the shore *(seemingly on the east side of the river, before David even crossed over)*. He fell on his face before David and said, "I hope the king will pay no attention to the silly words I said. Let not the king hold me guilty. Do not remember how ugly I acted. I know I did wrong and that is why I am the first of the house of Joseph to come down to meet my lord the king."

Abishai asked, "Shouldn't this man be killed because he cursed God's anointed?"

Abishai could remember that David would not kill Saul because he was God's anointed. David had also killed the Amalekite who claimed to have killed Saul. It was a good question, but David did not want the day of his home-coming to be marred by bloodshed. So he said: "What am I going to do with you, you sons of Zeruiah? Are you going to be my adversaries? No man will be put to death this day in Israel." Then David swore to Shimei that he would not kill him, but David did not forget the incident. We will learn more about Shimei later.

Shimei was of the tribe of Benjamin. He was not from Ephraim or Manasseh, the two tribes of Joseph. Why then did he say he was of the house of Joseph? It was because Benjamin was Joseph's full brother, so the tribe of Benjamin was closely associated with the two tribes which came directly from Joseph.

Next came Mephibosheth. He had not changed the wrappings on his feet, nor trimmed his beard, nor washed his clothes from the day the king left until he returned. When they met, David said, "Why did you not go with me, Mephibosheth?"

Mephibosheth answered, "My servant deceived me, O King. Since I am lame, I asked my servant to saddle a donkey for me so that I could go with you. But he left me and slandered me to you. My lord the king is like an angel of God; so do whatever pleases you. All my grandfather's descendants deserved nothing but death from the king, but you gave me a place among those who sit at your table. Why should I complain? What right do I have to make any more appeals to the king?"

David did not know which one told the truth, Ziba or Mephibosheth, so he said, "You and Ziba will divide the land."

Mephibosheth said, "He may have it all. I am just relieved that the king has come home."

Barzillai of Gilead had provided supplies for David in Mahanaim, because he was a very rich man and loyal to David. Now he escorted David across the Jordan, and David urged him to go to Jerusalem and remain with him.

But Barzillai answered, "How much time do I have left to enjoy such things? I am eighty years old. I no longer enjoy eating, nor can I hear well enough to enjoy the singers. It would be a waste for me to go with my lord the king. Why should you have the extra burden of caring for me? Let me go back and die in my own city and be buried by the grave of my father and my mother. But I have here my son Chimham. Let him go with the king, and do with him what seems good to you." David agreed to this and he kissed Barzillai and they parted in peace.

Thus David and his company crossed the Jordan. The men of Judah and part of the men from the other tribes had greeted him.

Name to add: Chimham

Rebellion of Sheba (2 Sam. 19:41-20:26):

David had been brought back to be king, but the trouble was still not over. Even the simple operation of bringing him across the river caused strife between Judah and the other tribes.

The men of Israel came to meet the company and demanded of the men of Judah, "Why have you gathered to steal the king away to bring his household across the Jordan?"

The men of Judah replied, "Because the king is closely related to us. Why are you angry? Have we eaten any of the king's provisions? Have we taken anything for ourselves? We have received no special treatment from him."

The others answered, "Well, we have ten shares in the king, so we have more right to him than you. Why did you ignore us? We were the first to talk of bringing back our king."

The quarrel grew heated and the words of the men of Judah were fiercer than those of the men of Israel. A trouble maker by the name of Sheba happened to be in the group. He was of the tribe of Benjamin. After a time, he blew a trumpet and shouted, "We have no portion in David. Every man to his tents, O Israel." The other tribes followed Sheba, but Judah remained loyal to David and continued to accompany him from the Jordan to Jerusalem.

When David arrived in Jerusalem, the first thing he did was to take care of the ten concubines he had left behind to care for the palace (the ones Absalom had molested). He put them in seclusion from the rest of the wives and concubines. He provided for their needs the rest of their lives, but he no longer regarded them as his concubines. They were treated as widows.

Then David turned his attention to the rebellion of Sheba and the ten northern tribes. He called Amasa to him and said, "Gather the men of Judah to me within three days, and you be here also."

Amasa set out to obey David's order, but he was not back within the three days. David was worried that the rebellion would get completely out of control. He called Abishai to him and said, "If we do not do something quickly, Sheba will do us more harm than Absalom did. Take my own servants and go after him before he gets into a fortified city and escapes us."

Therefore, Joab's men, the Cherethites, the Pelethites, and all the mighty men who normally stayed near David, set out after Sheba. Note that they were under the command of Abishai rather than Joab this time.

As they came to the great stone in Gibeon, Amasa showed up. Joab knew that David had sworn to make Amasa captain of the host in Joab's place. Joab was prepared for battle with his armor on, and strapped to it at his waist was a belt with a dagger in its sheath. As Joab stepped forward to greet Amasa, he allowed the dagger to drop out of its sheath, as if by accident. Joab picked it up as he said: "Is it well with you, my brother?"

Then Joab pretended to be about to give Amasa a kiss of greeting. Amasa paid no attention to the naked dagger in Joab's hand. Suddenly, with no warning, Joab thrust his weapon into Amasa's abdomen. Amasa fell to the ground and died.

Joab turned to pursue Sheba as if nothing had happened, and his brother Abishai accompanied him. One of Joab's young men stood beside Amasa. He saw that as the troops approached the place where Amasa lay in his blood, they all stopped in horror. So the young man dragged the body from the road into a field and covered it with a garment. Then he called out, "Whoever is on Joab's side and on David's side, let us follow Joab." So the people turned from the horrible sight and followed Joab to capture Sheba.

Sheba had fled to the north to a city called Abel of Beth-maacah. As Joab passed through the tribes of Israel, others joined his band so that by the time they reached the city where Sheba was, they had an army able to surround and besiege the city. Immediately efforts began to be made to destroy the walls. A full scale siege was underway — of an Israelite city.

Then a wise woman from Abel called out: "Listen! Listen to me. Please tell Joab to come here so that I can speak to him."

Joab was fetched and he came to the woman. She said, "Are you Joab?"

He said, "I am."

She said, "Hear the words of your handmaid. In old times it was said, 'Seek counsel at Abel and that will settle the matter.' We have been known for our wisdom. We are the peaceful and faithful in Israel. Why have you come to destroy a city and a mother in Israel? Why will you swallow up Jehovah's inheritance?"

Joab, clearly impressed by the woman, said, "That is the last thing we wish to do. That is not what we are after. You see, a man named Sheba, the son of Bichri, has raised his hand against the king, even against David. He is the only one we want. Deliver him up and we will leave."

This cultured, genteel woman said, "If you will give us just a minute, his head will be thrown to you over the wall."

The woman went and told the people what was needed. They cut off Sheba's head and threw it out to Joab. Then, true to his word, Joab blew the trumpet, and the militia was dispersed. And

Joab went back to the king in Jerusalem.

So the kingdom of David was fully restored, and things continued as they had been: Joab was chief captain over the army; Benaiah was over the Cherethites and the Pelethites; Adoram was over the forced labor; Jehoshaphat was the recorder; Sheva was scribe; and Zadok and Abiathar were priests; and a man named Ira the Jairite was also listed as a priest for David.

Names to add:
  Sheba
  Wise woman of Abel Beth-maacah

Label your map:
  Abel Beth-maacah

The rebellion of Sheba was so short-lived it was not of major significance in itself. But the unrest in Israel that led to the rebellion was. We have just had two rebellions, Absalom's and now Sheba's. We will soon have another, Adonijah's. Each of these rebellions was put down, and the kingdom held together. But there were distinct jealousies and unrest between the tribes. About forty more years passed from this point until the kingdom divided. Note that the words said here at the beginning of Sheba's rebellion (20:1) are almost the same words said when the ten northern tribes rebelled in Rehoboam's day (1 Kings 12:16). The rebellion in Rehoboam's day was a permanent one. The kingdoms were never reunited after that.

By now, Joab has killed three men against David's wishes. First he killed Abner just after Abner had negotiated with David to unite the kingdom (2 Sam. 3:22-39). At that time, the Bible specifically states that Joab killed Abner because Abner had earlier killed Joab's brother Asahel in battle. Then Joab killed Absalom, even though David had specifically forbidden it (2 Sam. 18:1-15). Now, Joab has killed Amasa who had been Absalom's chief captain.
Did he kill these men out of loyalty to David, or out of personal revenge and dislike? In the case of Absalom and Amasa his motives are not stated. There were times when Joab gave David badly needed advice, such as the time he was grieving over the death of Absalom instead of greeting his victorious soldiers. Likely David listened to Joab in a way he would not have listened to anyone else because Joab was kin to David and also one of his most trusted soldiers. Their working relationship was very close.
Would these men have been loyal to David? Abner had been Saul's chief captain and had opposed David in every way possible. Absalom had rebelled against his father and likely would have continued to be a source of trouble. Amasa had joined the rebellion, so it is surprising that David would put him in such a trusted position as the chief captain.
But look at Joab's methods. He pretended to call Abner back for a special message — and then treacherously stabbed an unsuspecting man. Absalom was hanging helplessly in a tree while Joab and his men stabbed him repeatedly. This time, Joab pretended to be greeting his cousin Amasa with a kiss. Instead, he stabbed him to death. None of the actions fit that of an honorable soldier. Besides, even after David specified that Solomon was the son who would succeed him, Joab joined Adonijah's rebellion as soon as he thought David was dying, which shows just how loyal he was to David. It is almost as if Joab thought he was in such a close relationship with David that his commands and wishes did not apply to Joab himself. He walked by his own self-made rules.

David avenges the Gibeonites (2 Sam. 21:1-14):

A severe famine struck Israel. When it had gone on for three years, David inquired of God about the cause of the famine. God said, "It is because of Saul and his bloody house; it is because he put to death the Gibeonites."

The Gibeonites were not Israelites; they were of the remnant of the Amorites who lived in the land when the Israelites took it in the days of Joshua. At that time, the Gibeonites tricked the Israelites into making a covenant with them even though they were from a city in Canaan. The Israelites honored the agreement to let them live, but they made the Gibeonites slaves to hew wood and carry water for the sacrifices and for the worship of Jehovah (Josh. 9:1-21). Saul, in his on again, off again zeal for God, had decided to carry out the command in the law of Moses that the inhabitants of Canaan be destroyed (Deut. 20:16-18). Therefore, he had tried to kill the Gibeonites even though a solemn covenant had been made with them.

Obviously, all the Gibeonites had not been slain, because David asked them, "What shall I do to make correction for what has been done so that you may bless the inheritance of Jehovah?"

The Gibeonites replied, "It is not a matter of silver or gold. Nor do we wish for any Israelite in general to be slain. Give us seven sons of the man who tried to destroy us, and we will hang them up before the Lord in Gibeah of Saul."

David said, "I will give them to you."

David inquired about the remaining descendants of Saul. He spared Mephibosheth because of his covenant of friendship with Jonathan. He found two sons of Rizpah, a concubine of Saul. *(This was the same concubine Ish-bosheth accused Abner of committing adultery with in 2 Samuel 3:6-8.)* He also took five sons of Merab the daughter of Saul (see 1 Sam. 18:19) and gave them with Rizpah's two sons to the Gibeonites. They executed them and hanged them on trees. It was at the beginning of barley harvest.

Poor Rizpah was deeply grieved. She spread sackcloth on a rock and camped there day and night to keep scavengers away from the bodies of her sons. Someone told David what Rizpah was doing. David sent and had the bones of Saul and Jonathan brought from Jabesh-gilead, and he took the bones of the seven who had been hanged and buried them all in the sepulchre of Kish the father of Saul. Then God's justice was satisfied for the land.

From the beginning of the world, God made the shedding of man's blood a crime which could only be satisfied by the shedding of the murderer's blood (Gen. 9:6). In the law of Moses, God repeated this rule. Saul broke this law and also forsook the covenant which Israel had made with the Gibeonites. All Israel had known of Saul's deed, but nothing had been done to atone for it. According to God's law, the deaths of the slain Gibeonites could only be atoned for by the shedding of the blood of the guilty party. Saul was dead, so the requirement of the shedding of blood was satisfied with his sons and grandsons.

All these measures are required by God to maintain respect for human life. If human life were to be viewed as cheap, then the death of Christ itself would be cheapened in the eyes of men.

David counts the fighting men (2 Sam. 24:1-25; 1 Chron. 21:1-22:1):

There is one more actual story about David's reign as king that is told in the book of 2 Samuel, then there are some summary accounts about his mighty men, his organization of his people, and two more psalms that he wrote. The last part of the book of 1 Chronicles summarizes the preparation of supplies for the temple and David's charge to Solomon and then to the people about the plans for the temple.

But before we look at those summary materials, let us skip to 2 Samuel 24 and to 1 Chronicles 21 to get this story about David counting the soldiers of his day.

An "adversary" stood up against Israel and caused David to decide to count the fighting men of Israel. David said to Joab, "Go throughout the tribes of Israel from Dan to Beersheba and enroll the fighting men, so that I may know how many there are."

Joab protested, "May God multiply the troops a hundred times over, and may the eyes of the king see it happen, but why count them? Why do you need to know? Why bring guilt upon Israel?"

Nevertheless, David insisted, and Joab and his men set out to obey the order. The numbering took nine months and twenty days. Joab was so unhappy with the command he did not count the Levites or the Benjamites. There were over a million men in the age bracket to be soldiers.

After the task had been finished, David's conscience smote him. He knew he had done wrong in ordering the count. He prayed to God, saying, "I have sinned greatly in what I have done. Forgive me, I pray, for I have done foolishly."

God sent the prophet Gad to David, saying, "Tell David that I am giving him three choices. Tell him to choose one of them to be carried out against him."

Gad went to David and asked him, "Shall three (or seven) years of famine come upon the land? or would you flee from your enemies for three months while they pursue you? or would you have three days of pestilence in the land? Think it over and decide which you choose."

David said, "It is difficult to decide, but I had rather fall into the hands of Jehovah, for His mercies are great. Please do not let me fall into the hands of men."

God, therefore, sent a great plague upon the land and seventy thousand men died. When the angel of the Lord had passed through the land and had stretched out his hand toward Jerusalem to destroy the men there, God said, "It is enough! Now relax your hand." The angel stopped at the threshing floor of Araunah (or Ornan) the Jebusite. There he stood between heaven and earth with his drawn sword extended toward Jerusalem. It was a terrifying sight! Araunah and his sons hid themselves, while David and the elders of Jerusalem fell on their faces before God.

David cried to God, "Am I not the one responsible for this sin? Did not I command it? It is I who have done wrong. These people are but sheep who have done nothing. Let the Lord's wrath be upon me and upon my father's house, but do not let this plague remain on the people."

God sent Gad to tell David to build an altar and offer sacrifices there at the threshing floor of Araunah. So David went to carry out the instructions.

Araunah and his sons had been threshing wheat when they saw the angel of destruction and had hidden themselves in terror. Now they saw the king coming to them. Araunah went out and bowed low before David, asking, "Why has my king come to his servant?"

David said, "Let me buy the site of your threshing floor so I can build an altar to the Lord, so that the plague against the people may be stopped. Sell it to me for its full price."

Araunah said, "Take it! Do whatever pleases you. Look, I will give the oxen for the burnt offerings, the threshing tools for the wood, and the wheat for the grain offering. You may have it all."

But David answered, "No, I insist on paying the full price. I will not take what is yours to offer to God as my sacrifice, nor will I offer to God something that costs me nothing."

So David bought the threshing floor of Araunah for 600 shekels of gold. There he built an altar and offered burnt offerings and peace offerings. He called upon God, and God answered by sending fire upon the altar. The Lord commanded the angel of destruction and he put his sword back in its sheath. Thus the plague was stopped.

At this time, the tabernacle with its altar of burnt offering was located at Gibeon. David did not go there to offer this particular sacrifice, because this one was offered to stop the plague where the angel had stopped. When David finished his sacrifices, he declared: "The house of God is to be built here, and also the altar of burnt offering for Israel."

Names to add:
Gad, the prophet
Araunah (or Ornan)

An "adversary" stood up against Israel and moved David to take a census (1 Chron. 21:1). "Adversary" in Hebrew comes from the word which is often transliterated as "Satan." That is why most translations render the word Satan. It probably <u>was</u> Satan on this occasion and not some ordinary adversary. In other words, Satan tempted David to do wrong. In 2 Samuel 24:1, the text says that God moved David to count the people (see ASV). God must have been angry with David about something that is not specified in the text, and He "moved David" by allowing Satan to entice him to count the people.

What was wrong with counting the soldiers? Many years earlier in Israel's history, there had been two counts made. One was at Mount Sinai about one year after the people came out of Egypt (Num. 1:2-49). The other was at the end of the forty years of wandering in the wilderness, just before they crossed the Jordan River into the land of Canaan (Num. 26:2-51). Both of those times, the numbering was specifically commanded by God. Otherwise, God considered the numbering a source of pride. He had promised to be with His people no matter whether the number was few or many. (See Leviticus 26:3-8 and 1 Samuel 14:6.) He did not want the Israelites to rely on numbers for their strength. He wanted them to rely on Him. Therefore, why did David need to know how many men he had? It was either a lack of faith in God's power, or more likely in this case, a matter of pride on David's part. Therefore, God disapproved.

David was forgiven each time he sinned, and repented, and prayed to God for forgiveness, but he still had to pay consequences. All sin carries a price that must be paid in consequences (see Prov. 13:15). Some sins just have more far-reaching consequences than other sins.

The total number of warriors given in 2 Samuel differs from the total given in 1 Chronicles. This is only one example of the times when there is a discrepancy in numbers. In all languages numbers are notoriously difficult to copy from one document to the other. Most discrepancies in the Bible text are in different numbers given, or in the spelling of names. These discrepancies were not in the original text but have come about as the manuscripts have been copied through the years. Even so, the purity of the Bible text is remarkable. Do not let anyone tell you otherwise.

David's song of praise (2 Sam. 22:1-51):

There are two songs, or psalms, recorded in this section. These are just as surely psalms as the others we have looked at, even though they are recorded here in the last of the history about David, and not in the book of Psalms.

David's song of praise was written after God delivered him from the hands of his enemies and from the hand of Saul. It is a majestic song of thanksgiving and praise because God listened to his pleas for help and responded. The imagery is vivid and beautiful. There is no way to be sure exactly when this psalm was written, because it would fit at so many moments in David's life.

Jehovah is my rock, my fortress, and my deliverer, in whom I take refuge. He is my shield, the horn of my salvation, my high tower, my refuge, and my savior. I call upon the Lord, who is worthy to be praised, and I am saved from my enemies.

For the waves of death encompassed me; the floods of ungodliness made me afraid; the snares of death came upon me.

In my distress I called upon Jehovah. He heard my voice out of His temple. My cry came into His ears.

Then the earth shook; the foundations of heaven quaked, because He was wroth. There went up a smoke out of His nostrils, and fire from His mouth devoured. He bowed the heavens and came down. Thick darkness was under His feet. He rode upon a cherub, and did fly. He was seen upon the wings of the morning. He made the darkness pavilions round about Him. At the brightness before Him coals were kindled. Jehovah thundered from heaven; He sent out arrows and scattered them. He sent lightning and discomfited them. The channels of the sea were revealed and the foundations of the earth were laid bare by the rebuke of Jehovah, by the blast of His breath.

He sent from on high and drew me from many waters. He delivered me from my strong enemy. They were too mighty for me, but Jehovah was my stay. He brought me into a large place because He delighted in me. He rewarded me according to my righteousness, according to the cleanness of my hands. For I have kept the ways of Jehovah, and I have not wickedly departed from my God. All His laws were before me, and I have kept them. Therefore, God has recompensed me according to my cleanness in His sight.

With the merciful, you will show yourself merciful; with the perfect man you will show yourself perfect; with the pure you will show yourself pure. But with the perverse man you will show yourself froward. You will save the afflicted, but your eye is upon the haughty to bring him down.

You are my lamp, O Jehovah. You lighten my darkness. By thee I shall run upon a troop; I will leap over a wall.

God's way is perfect; His word is tried. He is a shield to all who take refuge in Him. For who is God, save Jehovah? And who is a rock, save our God?

And so he continues with his beautiful description of God's help in time of need. It is a beautiful description of God's power and love, and a beautiful expression of faith on the part of David. We would do well to imitate David's trust in Jehovah.

David's last words (2 Sam. 23:1-7):
Since these are described as David's "last words," this must have been the last psalm he wrote. Look at the ways he identifies himself. Then notice he states that the Spirit of Jehovah spoke by him — that is, he is declaring that he has spoken by the inspiration of the Holy Spirit. David is rejoicing over the great blessing God had given to his household — that of the everlasting covenant we studied back in 2 Samuel 7.

David the son of Jesse, the man who was raised on high, the anointed of the God of Jacob, the sweet psalmist of Israel, declares:

The Spirit of Jehovah spoke by me, and His word was upon my tongue. The God of Israel said: "One that rules over men righteously, that rules in the fear of God, shall be as the light of the morning, when the sun rises on a cloudless day. He will be like the tender grass springing out of the ground after a rain."

Though my house is not like that, yet He has made an everlasting covenant with me, one ordered in all things and sure.

But the ungodly shall be like thorns to be thrust away, because they cannot be handled with the hand. One must be armed with iron and the staff of a spear to touch them. They will be utterly burned with fire in their place.

David's mighty men (2 Sam. 21:15-22; 23:8-39; 1 Chron. 11:10-47; 20:4-8):

We have already learned many of the exploits of David and his mighty men. In the references for this section, we find a summary of David's most valiant warriors and a few of their most noteworthy foes. The list includes men who were with him in his earliest days as well as those who joined him later. There are no stories related in these passages about most of the characters named. We will mention only those about whom stories are told.

In their battles with the Philistines, David and his men met a number of giants. David fought one named Ishbi-Benob. The giant was armed with a great spear and a new sword and boasted that he would kill David. During the fight, David became exhausted and Abishai came to his rescue. Abishai smote the giant and killed him. After this the men of David said, "Never again will you go out with us to battle, lest the lamp of Israel be extinguished."

Three other Philistine giants were defeated by David's men: A giant named Saph was killed by Sibbecai the Hushathite at Gob. Elhanan the Bethlehemite slew another giant named Goliath, who was from Gath. In still another battle at Gath, a nephew of David named Jonathan killed a giant with six fingers on each hand and six toes on each foot. The giant had been taunting Israel. All four of these giants were descendants of the giant in Gath.

At the top of the list of David's mighty men were two ranks of three men each. The first rank included the three mightiest men of all: Jashobeam, Eleazar, and Shammah. The next rank included both Abishai and Benaiah.

Jashobeam slew three hundred enemies in one battle. Eleazar stood when there were no others to fight and fought against the Philistines until there were no more. He fought until he could not open his hand from his sword hilt. Jehovah gave a great victory through him. Shammah and Eleazar were with David at the battle of Ephes-dammim (1 Sam. 17:1) where the Philistines were gathered for war. The people fled from the barley field where the battle took place, and these mighty men stood in the midst of the plot and defended it against all comers.

One time David and his band were in a stronghold at the cave of Adullam while a Philistine garrison held the city of Bethlehem *(David's home town)*. David got to thinking about how good water from the well at the gate of Bethlehem would taste. He said, in an idle manner, "Oh, if somebody would just give me a drink of water from the well down there at the gate of Bethlehem."

Jashobeam, Eleazar, and Shammah slipped away from the stronghold, fought their way through the Philistines, got David some water from the well, and brought it back to him. They said, "Here is the water you wanted."

David was horrified to think that they would take a casual comment he had made and risk their lives to get him some water. He was awed at their devotion to him. At the same time he felt that water gained at such a price was too valuable to drink. Therefore he used the water for the most valuable purpose he could think of, as a drink offering to Jehovah.

Abishai was one of the mightiest of David's men. He was fiercely loyal to David all his life. We have already been observing the loyalty of Abishai as we have followed the story. Among his exploits was the slaying of 300 enemies. But Abishai's feats did not match those of the mighty man of the first rank of three, but he was one of the second rank.

We have already met Benaiah as the captain of David's personal bodyguard: the Cherethites and Pelethites. His deeds included the slaying of the two sons of Ariel of Moab. The word "sons" is not in the Hebrew text. Ariel means "lion of God" and was a title given to a particularly valiant man. The meaning of the expression here probably is that Benaiah slew two heroes of Moab who bore the title Ariel, Lion of God. Then, during a time of snow, Benaiah found a lion in a pit. He went down into the pit and killed the lion. He also fought against an Egyptian who was seven and a half feet tall. Benaiah had a staff; the Egyptian had a spear with a shaft the size of a small log. Benaiah wrested the spear away and killed the Egyptian with his own spear.

There were a total of thirty mighty men of special place in the life of David. Their names are given, though we have no story about most of them. As you read down through the list, notice certain names: There is Asahel, the brother of Joab and Abishai, who was killed by Abner in battle. And there is Uriah the Hittite whose death was ordered by David himself as he tried to cover his sin with Bathsheba.

Names to add:
   Ishbi-Benob
   Saph
   Goliath the Gittite
   Jashobeam
   Eleazar
   Shammah

David prepares for the building of the temple (1 Chron. 22:2-23:1):

Early in David's reign, God promised that one of David's sons would reign after him (2 Sam. 7:11-16). At that time, no son was specified as the one to follow David. Amnon was the oldest of David's sons and was the heir until he molested Tamar and was killed by Absalom. Then Absalom thought he had the right to the throne, and he sought to take it even before his father died. Since David wept so at his death, it seems he, too, had expected Absalom to be his heir. But now Absalom is dead also. Who will be the king? At some point, God specified which son He wanted as the next ruler. It was to be Solomon (1 Chron. 22:9). Every specific reference to Solomon as the successor comes after the rebellion of Absalom, so it is probable that God told David which one it was after Absalom's death. If David had known it would be Solomon, he would have objected when Absalom hired the fifty men to run before him to indicate he was the son to be honored. Solomon was the second son of David and Bathsheba, even though he was the eleventh of seventeen sons of David (see 2 Sam. 3:2-5; 5:13-16). From this time on, there was no question in David's mind about his successor. God had spoken. It was up to David to work toward that end by preparing his son Solomon for the task before him and by preparing the people to accept him.

From the time God made His promise that David's heir would build a temple for Jehovah, David had gathered treasures for it. Look back to the summary of David's victories in 2 Samuel 8. When he conquered kings and took treasures from them, or when he received precious metals in tribute, he dedicated those things for the future temple (2 Sam. 8:11). But now that David knows his life is coming to an end, and he knows that Solomon will be the one in charge of the task, he makes very detailed preparations.

David knew that building the temple would be a great undertaking for his son Solomon because he was young and inexperienced. He planned for it to be a magnificent structure, so he helped by preparing for the building of it. He found artisans to hew the stone; he gathered iron and brass (bronze) without measure; he collected cedar trees without number from the people of Tyre and Sidon; and he laid up a vast amount of gold and silver.

Then David called Solomon to him privately and charged him to build the temple of Jehovah. He said:

> I wanted very much to build God's house, but because I was a man who had shed much blood, Jehovah would not let me. Instead He said He would give me a son who would be a man of peace, and he would build God's house. You are that son. You therefore must build the house of God. Now, my son, may the Lord be with you so that you may be successful in the task before you. And may God give you discretion and understanding, so that you will be careful to obey God. If you will walk in all His ways, He will bless you in all you do. Do not be afraid or be dismayed by the task before you.
>
> In my declining years I have prepared for God's house 3,750 tons of gold (100,000 talents), 37,500 tons of silver (1,000,000 talents), and brass (bronze) and iron too much to be weighed, and wood and stone in abundance. Now begin the work, and may God be with you.

David commanded the leaders of Israel to help Solomon. He said, "Is not the Lord your God with you? Has He not granted you rest on every side? Now devote your heart and soul to seek God. Go ahead and get started building God's house so that you may bring the ark of the covenant and the sacred vessels of God into the temple that will be built in the name of Jehovah."

Thus David officially proclaimed that Solomon would be his successor.

David organizes the people (1 Chron. 23:2-27:34):

Not only did David gather materials for the temple, he also organized the people to be ready for the work. First he called the Levites together and counted all the men thirty years old and older. There were a total of 38,000. David specified that 24,000 of these were to be directly involved in doing the work around the temple. In addition, 6,000 were to be officials and judges throughout the land, 4,000 were to be gatekeepers or guards, and the other 4,000 were to lead the people in singing praise to God.

As you look at this section on the organization of the Levites, remind yourself and your students that all priests were Levites, but not all Levites were priests. In order to be a priest, one must be of the tribe of Levi, of the branch of Kohath, and of the particular family of Aaron (see Exod. 28:1; Num. 3:10; 18:1-7). Even more specific was the position of High Priest. In order to be High Priest, one must be of the family of Aaron, and the direct descendant of the High Priest, usually passed from the Priest to his oldest son. Other Levites served in various capacities connected with the worship, but they did not offer the animal sacrifices or the incense (see Num. 18:3; cf. Num. 4:15, 19-20).

David went one step further in his organization and divided the Levites into their separate families (the descendants of Gershon, Kohath, and Merari, the sons of Levi). Each family was told its exact assignment. The Levites would not be needed to move the tabernacle nor its furnishings after the permanent temple was built, so their duties had changed a little since the law was given in the wilderness in the days of Moses. David outlined the duties they would have from that day forward: they were to help the priests who were Levites of the family of Aaron; they were to be in charge of the courtrooms and the side rooms of the temple; they were to see that all sacred things were kept clean and purified so that they would be ready for use; they were to prepare the bread regularly that was used on the table of shewbread. In addition, they were to measure out the exact portions of flour, grain, bread, or whatever was to be offered in the sacrifices. They were to lead in prayer and thanksgiving to God each day when the regular sacrifices were offered and at times when the whole assembly had gathered for special festivals. Their duties did not include offering the sacrifices themselves nor offering the incense, but they were to do all the steps to have things ready for the priests to do their work. (See 1 Chronicles 23:24-32; 26:20-27.)

By this time, there were many descendants of Aaron who were qualified to be priests so David organized them also. He divided them by families and cast lots to see which family would have their turn first. There were a total of twenty-four families.

In David's day, there were two men serving as high priests — Zadok and Abiathar. Aaron had four sons: Nadab, Abihu, Eleazar, and Ithamar. Nadab and Abihu died before they had children (see Lev. 10:1-2; Num. 3:1-3). Therefore, all priests came through the families of Eleazar and Ithamar. Zadok was of the family of Eleazar, and Abiathar was of the family of Ithamar. Through most of Israelite history, there was only one high priest, who served until he died. Under him, the twenty-four courses of priests took turns serving in the temple. They came for their turn, and then returned home. The other Levites were divided into courses also and took their turns for their assigned jobs, either as helpers in the temple work, as singers, gatekeepers, or officials.

David also organized the rest of the people in the kingdom. He divided the army into divisions with 24,000 men in each division. He made twelve such groups so that one group could serve before the king each month, and then go home until its turn rolled around the next year. In addition, he appointed officers over each tribe and overseers over various aspects of the work to be done.

God was not displeased over the counting of the Levites in order to organize them into efficient groups to do their work. Neither did He object to organizing the rest of the people for their work. In fact, from 1 Chronicles 28:13, it seems that God instructed David in exactly how to organize the Levites and priests. God had objected to the counting of the people in order to learn the total number of soldiers that existed in the land. David did not need to base his strength on that number.

Look back to 1 Samuel 8 to the occasion when the people asked for a king. Remind yourself and your students about the warnings God gave them at that time. He said that the day would come when they would work for their king, instead of working for themselves. "The king will take your sons and make them his horsemen, his soldiers, and his servants to work his fields, to make his weapons of war, and to make his equipment for his chariots. He will take your daughters to be his perfumers, his cooks, and his bakers." God continued His warning to say that when they were tired of working for their king, and wanted relief, God would not listen to their pleas. The people still wanted a king, in spite of the warnings, and God chose Saul to be their leader. Saul had a very small standing army, and the problem of working for their king did not seem very bad. David has had a much larger standing army, but they have been victorious in most of their activities, so that still has not seemed bad. Now David has organized his people into a very precise arrangement — because there is a very large task before them, that of building the temple. All the people are looking forward to having their magnificent temple, so they still do not mind working hard to carry out the king's plan. But do not forget this warning God gave about their king. Be alert to this situation that seems so innocent at the moment, and watch as the people grow tired of the arrangement.

David assembles Israel to tell them his plans (1 Chron. 28:1-29:22a):

The king assembled all the princes, captains, officers, and all the influential men of the kingdom. He stood before them and said:

> Listen to me, my brethren, and my people. I had it in my heart to build a house for Jehovah our God, but He would not let me because I have been a man of war. Nevertheless Jehovah chose me out of my father's house to be king over Israel forever. He chose Judah to be the leader; and from within Judah, He chose my father's house; and from my father's son, He took pleasure in me to make me king. And of my sons God has chosen Solomon to rule after me.
>
> Furthermore Jehovah has said, "Solomon will build my house, for I have chosen him to be my son and I will be his father. And I will establish his kingdom forever, if he will obey my commandments." Let me therefore publicly encourage all of you to do the commandments of the Lord so that you may possess this good land and leave it as an inheritance for your children.

David then turned to Solomon and said, "Solomon, my son, come to know the Lord, and serve Him with a ready mind. If you serve Him faithfully He will always be near to help you, but if you forsake Him, He will cast you off forever. Be careful now. Jehovah has chosen you to build His house. Be strong and do it."

Before the whole assembly, David gave Solomon the pattern for the temple and for all that was in it. This pattern was given by the Spirit of God. The pattern included a blueprint for the building itself, information regarding the courses into which the Levites were divided, and it listed the various articles to be made and told how much gold was to be used for each one. David said, "All of this I have written by the guidance of Jehovah according to the understanding He gave me."

Upon giving Solomon this information, David said again, "Be strong and of good courage to do this work. Jehovah is with you. He will not fail or forsake you until all this work is done. All the people are before you and will be entirely at your command."

Then David addressed the assembly: "Solomon my son is young and inexperienced, and the work before him is great. After all, the temple is not for man but for Jehovah God. Now I have laid up great amounts of gold and silver for God's house. In addition to all I have gathered for the temple, I give of my own gold and silver for the house of my God. Who among you would like to give a gift for God's house?"

The princes and nobles had come prepared, and they gave liberally for the service of the house of Jehovah. They gave 190 tons of gold, 185 pounds of gold in coin, 375 tons of silver, 675 tons of bronze, and 3,750 tons of iron. The people rejoiced greatly as they gave for they gave willingly. David also rejoiced greatly.

David led the assembly in prayer: "O Lord, we praise you from everlasting to everlasting. Yours is all the power and glory and majesty, for everything is yours. You are ruler over all things and we praise your glorious name. But how can we, nomads and strangers, give such gifts as these? You have blessed us with such great treasure, and we have given it to build your house. You know our hearts, that we have offered willingly. O Lord, please keep your people's heart close to you and also bless my son with a perfect heart that he may keep your commandments always and that he may build the temple for which I have prepared."

David commanded the assembly to praise God and they fell on their faces and worshiped Jehovah and honored the king. That day great sacrifices were made of a thousand bullocks, a thousand rams, and a thousand lambs with appropriate drink offerings, and the people ate and drank before Jehovah with great gladness.

The Reign of Solomon
1 Kings 1-11; 2 Chronicles 1-9

Outline of Bible History:
Look at your outline once more. We are still in the period of the United Kingdom. It is time for Solomon to become king.

Creation Stories
Flood
Scattering of the People
The Patriarchs
The Exodus
Wilderness Wandering
Conquest of the Land
Judges

*United Kingdom

    Saul
    David
    *Solomon

Divided Kingdom
Judah Alone
Captivity
Return from Captivity
Years of Silence
Life of Christ
Early Church
Letters to Christians

Set the stage:

The book of 1 Chronicles ends with David's death, and we have not yet covered it in our account of the history, but there is one more story that fits before we tell of his death. There is one more rebellion, but it is actually against Solomon rather than against David himself, so we are including it under this heading rather than the preceding one.

Look carefully at the conditions in Israel as 2 Samuel and 1 Chronicles close, and as 1 Kings and 2 Chronicles open. David has been promised by Jehovah that one of his descendants will reign upon the throne. At first God did not specify which son that would be, but He has now specified that He has chosen Solomon as the one to rule (1 Chron. 22:9), though he is David's eleventh son (2 Sam. 5:13-16). That made the choice official in David's eyes. David called his leading men together and told them who was to be king and urged them to help Solomon in the huge task before them of building the temple (1 Chron. 22:17; 23:1-2; 28:1-8). After David delivered the blueprint for the temple and all its furniture and utensils to Solomon in front of the officials, they rejoiced before the Lord and did homage to their new king (1 Chron. 29:1-25).

So Solomon is officially slated to be the new king as soon as his father dies, but he has not begun his work when the book of 1 Kings opens. David is still living, though he is very frail and very near death. The books of Chronicles do not tell of this one more problem that arises in David's life.

A brief survey of the life of Solomon:

Before we proceed with the narrative of Solomon's reign, let us survey the two portions of scriptures that describe his reign. The history of Solomon is recorded in 1 Kings 1-11 and in 2 Chronicles 1-9.

In 1 Kings 1 Solomon is enthroned as king and the rebellion of Adonijah is crushed. In chapter two, Solomon deals with the enemies of David and of his kingdom.

Chapter three tells about the Lord appearing to Solomon at Gibeon, where Solomon asked God for wisdom. Chapter four is a general description of Solomon's officers and of his kingdom. Chapters five through seven describe the building of the temple. Chapter eight is Solomon's prayer at the dedication of the temple. Chapter nine tells of the second appearance of God to Solomon. It also tells of Solomon's payment to Hiram for his help in building the temple. Chapter ten tells of the visit of the Queen of Sheba and of the amazing wealth of Solomon. Chapter eleven tells of Solomon's marriages with many foreign wives, of his falling away from God, and of his death.

Note the contrast in 2 Chronicles. Chapter one tells of Solomon's prayer for wisdom at Gibeon. The next six chapters (2-7) tell of the building of the temple and of its dedication. Chapter eight tells of the works of Solomon and gives even more information about the temple. Chapter nine tells of the visit of the Queen of Sheba, of the incredible wealth of Solomon, and of his death. In 1 Kings, out of eleven chapters about Solomon, four are devoted to the building of the temple. In 2 Chronicles, out of nine chapters, six are devoted to the building of the temple and its dedication.

The rebellion of Adonijah (1 Kings 1:1-53; 1 Chron. 29:22b-25):

By the time the book of 1 Kings opens, David was very frail. He was only 70 years old, because he began his reign when he was 30 years old, and he reigned a total of 40 years (2 Sam. 5:4; 1 Kings 2:11). But the years had been trying years, and David was worn out. He was bedfast, and dying.

One of his servants thought it might help the king recover heat in his body if he could lie with a young virgin. The idea was that David could absorb vitality and energy from contact with the young woman. So a search was made for a beautiful, young virgin. Abishag the Shunammite was found and brought to the king. She became one of his wives, though there was never a true marriage relationship between them. But there was no improvement in David's health. Abishag continued to serve as David's nurse.

Name to add: Abishag

Meanwhile, Adonijah saw that his father was dying. According to custom, Adonijah was next in line to be king. David's sons had been born in the order of Amnon, Chileab, Absalom, and Adonijah. The first three were dead. Adonijah was next in line, except that he knew, along with all Israel, that Solomon was designated to be the next king and that it was God who had chosen him. The knowledge that Solomon had been chosen did not stop Adonijah from making his own plans. He declared, "I will be king."

David had never exercised discipline over his sons, so Adonijah had always been able to do as he chose. He was very handsome, and he was sure he could win his way. Therefore, he prepared a chariot and fifty men to run before him. He conferred with Joab and Abiathar, and they gave him their support. But Zadok, Benaiah, Nathan, and David's mighty men did not join him.

Adonijah held a special sacrifice and feast at En-rogel just outside the city wall of Jerusalem. He invited Joab, Abiathar, his brothers, some of the leading men of Judah, and the officials of the king whom he thought would be loyal to his cause. But he did not invite Nathan, Benaiah, the special guard, or Solomon.

Be sure you can identify each of these people mentioned. What part has each one played in the life of David?

When Nathan the prophet learned what Adonijah was doing, he went to Bathsheba and said, "Have you heard that Adonijah is reigning, and David does not know it? Let me advise you how to save your own life and the life of your son Solomon. Go in to David and ask him if he didn't swear to make Solomon king. Then ask him why Adonijah is reigning." Nathan promised that he would come into David's room at that point and confirm what she said.

Bathsheba saw the wisdom of Nathan's advice and lost no time before going to David. She went into the sickroom where Abishag was waiting on the ailing king. Bathsheba bowed before the king and said just what Nathan had advised: "My lord, you swore to your handmaiden, saying, 'Surely your son Solomon will be king after me and will sit upon my throne.' But now, behold, Adonijah is king and you do not even know it." She continued by telling the full story of what was happening: "Adonijah has slain oxen and sheep in abundance and has called all your sons together, along with Abiathar and Joab, but he has not invited Solomon. Now all Israel is watching to see what you will do about it. They want to know who is to follow you on the throne. Otherwise, when you die, my son Solomon and I will be counted as criminals."

According to plan, Nathan arrived at that moment and was granted an audience with the king. He too bowed with his face to the ground and he confirmed the words of Bathsheba: "Did you say that Adonijah should be king? Everyone is saying 'Long live King Adonijah,' for he has gone down today to sacrifice oxen, and fatlings, and sheep in abundance. He has invited all the king's sons, the commanders of the army, and Abiathar the priest, and they are all eating and drinking and rejoicing before him as they proclaim him king. But he has not called me, Zadok, Benaiah, or Solomon. Is this what you wanted?"

Bathsheba had left when Nathan had been admitted to the room. David said, "Call Bathsheba to me." When she came, David said, "As Jehovah lives, I have already sworn that Solomon will reign after me, so I will make it official this very day." Bathsheba bowed low before David in gratitude.

David called for Zadok, Nathan, and Benaiah. He said, "Take with you my servants and let Solomon ride upon my mule, and bring him to the spring Gihon. Let Zadok the priest and Nathan the prophet anoint him king over Israel, and blow the trumpet and say, 'Long live King Solomon.' Then you will come up after him, and he shall come and sit upon my throne, because he shall be king in my place. I have appointed him to be leader over Israel and Judah."

Benaiah said, "So be it. It will be done exactly as you have ordered. May the Lord be with Solomon as he has been with you, and may his kingdom be even greater than that of King David."

So Zadok, Nathan, and Benaiah took the Cherethites and Pelethites and escorted Solomon to Gihon (*the spring just outside the city wall*) and anointed him king. This is what the people had been waiting to see. When they blew the trumpet and shouted, "Long live King Solomon," the people joined the celebration with such enthusiasm that Adonijah and his company heard the noise.

Joab said, "I wonder what is causing the uproar in the city."

Just then, Jonathan the son of Abiathar came running into their midst. Adonijah was still in an excellent mood, thinking himself to be king. He said, "Come in. You are a worthy man so you must be bringing good news."

But Jonathan's news was not good at all for Adonijah and his co-conspirators. "The king has sent Zadok, Nathan, Benaiah, the Cherethites, and the Pelethites to anoint Solomon king. All the king's servants have come to bless David and Solomon, so Solomon is now sitting on the throne of the kingdom."

The rebellion ended very abruptly. Everyone fled in terror. Adonijah, of course, feared most of all, so he fled to the altar of the Lord and took hold of the horns of the altar. This action was a plea for mercy. Someone told Solomon, "Adonijah is afraid of the king; he has seized the horns of the altar and says that he will not let go until the king swears that he will not slay him with the sword."

Solomon sent word to him, saying: "If he will show himself a worthy man, not a hair of his head will fall to the ground, but if any wickedness is found in him, he will die."

When Adonijah heard these words, he came before Solomon and bowed in submission. Solomon said to him, "Go to your house."

Thus the last rebellion in David's reign was ended, and Solomon began his duties as king. He was seated upon the throne of the Lord, in his father's place. He prospered in all he did and all Israel obeyed him. All the officials, the mighty men, and all the sons of David pledged their allegiance to him. The Lord highly exalted him and bestowed on him royal majesty that neither of the kings before him had seen.

It is not surprising that Joab joined Adonijah, because he had been an opportunist all along. He often disagreed with David's decisions. But Abiathar had been such a long-time supporter of David, it seems strange that he would forsake him. This rebellion, however, was not against David personally, but against Solomon as the one chosen to be king after him. They were missing one important point, though: Solomon was God's choice. David was not the one who had chosen him. Therefore, this rebellion was in direct disobedience to God, even if the participants were not stopping to think of that.

David's last charge to Solomon (1 Kings 2:1-12; 1 Chron. 29:26-30):

David gave Solomon some parting advice. As he had done several times before, David told Solomon to be strong and of good courage. He said:

Be sure to obey God's commandments as they are written in the law of Moses so that you will prosper and succeed in all that you do. Live so that God can keep the promise He made to me: "If your descendants will watch how they live, and walk faithfully before me with all their heart and soul, you will never fail to have a man upon the throne of Israel."

Then David gave Solomon advice about specific people in his kingdom. He said:

You know what Joab did to me, and what he did to Abner and to Amasa, two commanders in Israel. You know how he slew them with treachery, shedding the blood of war in peace. Deal with him according to your wisdom, but do not let his gray head go down to the grave in peace.

Show kindness to the sons of Barzillai the Gilleadite. Let them be among those who eat at your table, for they assisted me when I fled from your brother Absalom.

You also have with you Shimei, the Benjamite from Bahurim, who called down bitter curses upon me when I went to Mahanaim. When he came to meet me at the Jordan upon my return, I swore not to kill him. But do not consider him innocent. You are a man of wisdom. You will know what to do. Bring down his gray head to the grave in blood.

After this David died and was buried in the City of David. He died at a good old age, having enjoyed a long life, wealth, and honor. He had reigned a total of forty years. The events of his life were recorded by Samuel the prophet, by Nathan the prophet, and by Gad the prophet.

Psalms of David too indefinite to date
There are several psalms of David's that simply cannot be dated with any certainty for a variety of reasons. Of course, scholars differ somewhat about this, so do not be surprised to read

that one of them knows exactly where a given psalm fits. Following are psalms we do not feel comfortable trying to fit with specific times in his life: 8, 14, 15, 16, 19, 29, 36, 37, 39, 53, 64, 65, 68, 69, 70, 109, 124, 131, 133, 138, 139, 144, and 145.

A very few of the psalms labeled "of David" may not be his work. Remember that these titles of the Psalms, while old, are not inspired. Psalm 108 is a combination of Psalm 57:7-11 and Psalm 60:5-12. That means it was probably put together by someone after the time of David. Original composers do not usually create a new piece in this manner. It is beyond the scope of this study to go into the study of criticism to determine the fine points about when these psalms may have been written. The student may consult the commentaries if he wants more information about these things.

These psalms that we cannot date include some of his most beautiful works, and we certainly do not want to minimize their beauty by not looking at them in more detail. They just do not fit directly into the historical narrative of David's life. Take time to look at them in your own study. Through the psalms, we see David's deep love for Jehovah and we see more clearly than any other way why he is called a man after God's own heart. Let us look at just a few phrases from a few of these psalms to remind ourselves of their beauty:

Psalm 8: O Lord our Lord, how excellent is thy name in all the earth!... When I consider thy heavens, the work of thy fingers... What is man, that thou art mindful of him? and the son of man, that thou visitest him?

Psalms 14 and 53: The fool hast said in his heart, There is no God...

Psalm 19: The heavens declare the glory of God; and the firmament showeth His handiwork... There is no speech nor language, where their voice is not heard.

Psalm 37: Fret not thyself because of evildoers... but those that wait upon the Lord, they shall inherit the earth... I have been young, and now am old; yet have I not seen the righteous forsaken, nor his seed begging bread.

Psalm 133: Behold, how good and how pleasant it is for brethren to dwell together in unity!...

Psalm 139: O Lord, thou hast searched me, and known me... Whither shall I go from thy spirit?... If I ascend up into heaven, thou art there; if I make my bed in hell, behold, thou art there. If I take the wings of the morning, and dwell in the uttermost parts of the sea; even there shall thy hand lead me, and thy right hand shall hold me...

Psalm 145: I will extol thee, my God, O King; and I will bless thy name for ever and ever... One generation shall praise thy works to another, and shall declare thy mighty acts...

Solomon secures his kingdom (1 Kings 2:13-46):

Adonijah did not remain cautious for very long. He decided that he wanted Abishag, the young woman who had ministered unto David in his last days, for his wife. He went to ask Bathsheba to intercede with Solomon in his behalf.

Bathsheba said, "Do you come peacefully?"

Adonijah said, "Yes." He continued: "As you know, the kingdom was really mine. All Israel looked to me as king. But things did not work out, and the kingdom went to my brother because it was given to him of the Lord. Now I have one little request. Do not refuse me."

"Go ahead and make it," she said.

"Please ask Solomon — he will not refuse you — to give me Abishag the Shunammite for my wife."

"Very well," replied Bathsheba. "I will speak to the king for you."

When Bathsheba came to Solomon, he was glad to see her, and he had a throne placed for her as a sign of respect. She sat down on his right hand and said, "I have one small request to make of you. Do not refuse me."

Solomon replied, "Make it, my mother. I will not refuse you." But Solomon had not heard the request!

Bathsheba said, "Let Abishag the Shunammite be given to your brother Adonijah for his wife."

At that request Solomon was enraged, not at his mother particularly, but at Adonijah. He said, "Why do you only ask that he might have Abishag? Why not go ahead and request the kingdom as well, for he is my older brother; yes, for him, and for Abiathar the priest, and for Joab the son of Zeruiah!"

Then Solomon vowed, "May God do so to me and more if Adonijah does not pay for this outrage with his life. As surely as Jehovah lives, Adonijah will die today!" Solomon ordered Benaiah to go and execute Adonijah. So Benaiah went and slew him.

Why was it so bad for Adonijah to ask for Abishag as his wife? When a man became king, he inherited his predecessor's harem of wives. Therefore, to ask for one of David's wives was to ask for one of the privileges only David's successor had the right to possess. Even though Abishag was David's widow, she was now one of Solomon's wives. Adonijah had no right to her. Solomon interpreted Adonijah's request for David's wife as a subtle request for Solomon's position.

Notice the wording of Adonijah's request. He indicated he still thought the kingdom should have been his, and he still thought all Israel would have been glad to have him as king. Notice, however, that he too realized that God was the One who had chosen Solomon as king. If he had proper respect for Jehovah, that should have settled the matter, and Adonijah should never have questioned it again.

Solomon decided to make a clean sweep of his enemies. To Abiathar the priest, he said, "Go back to your fields in Anathoth. You deserve to die, but because you carried the ark of the Lord before my father David and shared in all his afflictions, I will spare your life." So Solomon removed Abiathar from the priesthood of the Lord, fulfilling the prophecy God had spoken at Shiloh concerning the house of Eli.

God said He would remove the house of Eli from the priesthood, that is, from the position of high priest (1 Sam. 2:27-36; 3:12-14). Aaron (Exod. 28:1), Eleazar the son of Aaron (Num. 20:22-29), and Phinehas the son of Eleazar (Judg. 20:27-28) were the first three high priests of Israel. The Bible does not tell who the high priests were between Phinehas and Eli (1 Sam. 1:9). At some point, however, during the time of the judges, the line of the high priesthood jumped from the line of Eleazar, the son of Aaron, to the line of Ithamar, another son of Aaron.

This is evident because 1 Chronicles 24:3-6 tell that Ahimelech and his son Abiathar were descendants of Ithamar, and Ahimelech was high priest at the time David fled from Saul (1 Sam. 21:1). We are not given enough information to trace the lineage from Eli to Abiathar, but we know they shared a common lineage. The connection between Eli and the family of Ithamar is established because the casting out of Abiathar is specifically said to fulfill the word spoken about Eli's house (1 Kings 2:27). The prophecy to Eli included not only his own family, but all those in his "father's" house, that is, in the lineage of Ithamar.

All through the reign of David, we have observed that two priests served simultaneously: Zadok and Abiathar. Zadok was of the lineage of Eleazar and Abiathar was of the lineage of Ithamar (1 Chron. 24:1-3). It was very unusual for there to be two men serving at once, and it would not have happened in David's day if it had not been for unique circumstances. Abiathar's father Ahimelech helped David as he was first fleeing from Saul, and was murdered by Doeg at the command of Saul. Abiathar fled for his life and joined David, taking with him the ephod that was part of the equipment for the high priest (1 Sam. 21:1-9; 22:6-23). It seems Zadok became the new high priest under Saul. But out of loyalty to his friend Abiathar, David made him high priest with Zadok when he became king. Therefore, with this banishment of Abiathar, the line of high priest reverted to the original line of the family of Eleazar.

The problem of Joab was next on Solomon's list. When news reached Joab of Solomon's actions against Adonijah and Abiathar, he fled to the tent of the Lord and took hold of the horns of the altar to beg for mercy just as Adonijah had earlier. King Solomon was told where Joab was, and he instructed Benaiah: "Go put Joab to death."

When Benaiah arrived at the tent, he said, "The king says for you to come out."

Joab said, "No, I will die here."

Benaiah went back and told Solomon what Joab had said. Solomon replied: "Do as he says. Put him to death and bury him. That will clear me and my father's house of the blood he shed of two men who were better than he: Abner, commander of Israel's army, and Amasa, commander of Judah's army. May the guilt of their blood rest on the head of Joab and his descendants forever." Benaiah did as he was commanded. He went and killed Joab and buried him on his own land in the wilderness.

Solomon put Benaiah in Joab's place as commander of the army, and he put Zadok in Abiathar's place as priest.

Solomon had not forgotten Shimei. The story of Shimei is all told here even though the end of the affair did not come for three more years.

Solomon called Shimei in before him and said, "Build yourself a house here in Jerusalem and live there, but do not go anywhere else. The day you leave and cross the Kidron Valley, you will surely die, and your blood will be upon your own head."

Shimei was glad to be spared under any condition, so he said, "What you have said is good. I will do as you have commanded."

Shimei stayed in Jerusalem without leaving for a long time. Three years passed. Then two of Shimei's slaves ran off to King Achish of Gath. Shimei learned where he could find his slaves, so he saddled his donkey and rode to Gath to recover them. When he had found them, he brought them back to Jerusalem.

When Solomon heard what had happened, he summoned Shimei before him. "Did I not make you swear by the Lord that you would not leave Jerusalem to go anywhere else? Did I not say that on the day you left you would surely die? And you agreed and said that was good and you would obey. Why then have you not kept your oath to the Lord and obeyed the command I gave you?"

Solomon continued, "You know in your heart all the evil you did to my father David. Now the Lord will repay you for your wrong-doing. But I will be blessed, and David's throne will remain sure before the Lord forever."

Solomon commanded Benaiah to put Shimei to death, and Benaiah slew him. The kingdom was now firmly established in Solomon's hands. The trouble-makers left from David's reign were gone.

Solomon was not acting merely as an individual as he dealt with his enemies. He was the civil authority responsible for enforcing God's law, and that included the punishment for murder (Joab's murder of Abner and Amasa), and the punishment for cursing God's anointed (Shemei's cursing of David). He executed Adonijah because when Adonijah asked for Abishag, he showed that he still had his dream of taking over as king.

Solomon makes a treaty with Egypt (1 Kings 3:1; 9:16, 24; 2 Chron. 8:11):

Solomon made numerous treaties of peace with neighboring peoples during his time as king. The first such treaty that is mentioned was made with Egypt. To seal the alliance between Solomon and the Pharaoh of Egypt, Solomon married the daughter of the king.

Pharaoh captured the city of Gezer from the Canaanites and gave it to his daughter and to Solomon as a wedding gift. Pharaoh had killed the inhabitants and burned the city, so Solomon rebuilt it as an Israelite city.

Solomon kept Pharaoh's daughter in the City of David until he had built the temple, his own palace, and the wall of Jerusalem. Then he brought her up from the City of David to a special palace which he had built for her. He said, "My wife cannot live in the palace of David king of Israel, because the places where the ark of the Lord has been are holy."

Many admire the wisdom and diplomacy of Solomon in making his numerous treaties with the nations around Israel. Usually these treaties were sealed by a marriage, as it was in this case with Egypt. In God's sight, however, it was not wise or pleasing for Solomon to marry foreign wives who would turn his heart away from God (see Deut. 7:1-5; 17:17). Neither was it right for Solomon to depend upon such alliances instead of God to strengthen his kingdom (compare 2 Chron. 15:7-10).

Solomon asks for wisdom (1 Kings 3:2-15; 2 Chron. 1:1-13):

At the beginning of Solomon's reign the people sacrificed in various places of worship rather than at one central location as the law commanded (see Deut. 12:1-14). Solomon was following God's law carefully at this point in his life, but he too participated in the sacrifices at the various high places. The temple had not yet been built and, as a matter of fact, all the things associated with the old tabernacle were not in one place. The tabernacle itself and the bronze altar of burnt offering were at Gibeon, whereas the ark of the covenant was at Jerusalem.

There are strong indications that there was also an altar that had been built in Jerusalem by this time at the tent of meeting that David set up for the ark of the covenant. There are times when sacrifices are mentioned as being offered there, or the priests were on duty in Jerusalem (see 2 Sam. 15:24-29). Adonijah and Joab seem to have been nearby when they were holding to the horns of the altar, begging for mercy. The altar in Jerusalem was not, however, the original altar of burnt offering that Bezalel built for the tabernacle in the days of Moses. That altar was still at Gibeon.

Solomon assembled all Israel at Gibeon, the primary place of worship, in order to offer sacrifices unto Jehovah. It was appropriate that at the beginning of Solomon's reign, he and all the people should seek the favor of God. Solomon offered a thousand burnt offerings on the altar.

That night the Lord appeared to Solomon in a dream. He said, "Ask whatever you want and I will give it to you."

Solomon said, "Oh God, you have been merciful and very kind to my father David because he was faithful and righteous unto you. You have continued this great kindness by giving him a son to sit upon his throne this very day. Now you have made me king in the place of my father and I am like a little child. I do not know what I should do. Here I am among your people, the ones you chose as your own, a great people, too numerous to count. Therefore I pray that you will give me wisdom that I may judge all this great people and that I may be able to distinguish between right and wrong."

God was very pleased at this excellent request. He said, "Since you have asked for wisdom and not for wealth or long life, I will give you what you have asked for. I will give you a wise, intelligent mind such as no other man has ever had, or ever will have after you. I will also give you what you have not asked for, both riches and honor, so that while you live, you will have no equal among the kings of the earth. And if you follow my word, I will also give you a long life."

When Solomon awoke, he realized God had spoken to him in a dream. He returned to Jerusalem, stood before the ark of the covenant and sacrificed burnt offerings and peace offerings to the Lord and made a feast for all his servants. *(Here again is a verse that shows that an altar had been erected for sacrifices in Jerusalem where the ark of the covenant was located.)*

Solomon asked for his wisdom in order to accomplish very important goals: He wanted to know how to judge his people wisely and to know how to distinguish right from wrong in his judgment. As we continue looking at the history of Solomon, watch and see if he uses his wisdom for the purposes for which he asked. This would be another good chart to make and keep before your class.

God has promised Solomon wisdom greater than any before or after him. God increased Solomon's intelligence far beyond normal, to that of great genius, but God left it in Solomon's hands to determine how that intelligence would be used. God has promised great riches and honor, and Solomon receives those in abundance as his life continues. But notice there is an if before the next promise: "<u>If you will follow my word</u>, I will give you long life." Solomon reigned forty years, but he began his reign as a young man, so he did not have an unusually long life. His age is never given, but even if he were as old as twenty (which may be guessing the age a little high) when he began to reign, that would make him only sixty when he died. Watch his story and see why he does not receive this blessing.

Two women and a baby (1 Kings 3:16-28):

An opportunity soon came for Solomon to demonstrate his wisdom. Two prostitutes came before the king to ask him to settle a dispute between them.

One of the women said, "This woman and I live in the same house. I gave birth to a baby boy. Three days later she also gave birth to a baby boy. There was no one else in the house with us. In the night her baby died because she rolled over on him and smothered him. She discovered what had happened, and, in the middle of the night, she got up and took my son from my side while I was asleep and put him by her breast. She put her dead son by my breast. When I got up to nurse my son the next morning, he was dead. But when I looked more closely in the morning light, I saw it was not my son."

The other woman said, "No! The living baby is my son. The dead one is yours."

But the first one insisted, "No! The dead one is yours; the living one is mine." Since there were no witnesses, it was one woman's word against the other's.

Solomon said, "Each one claims the living baby. Bring me a sword."

They brought a sword to the king, and he said, "Cut the living child in two and give half to one and half to the other."

The mother of the living son cried out, "Please, my lord, give him to her. Do not kill him!"

But the other woman said, "Neither one of us can have him. Cut him in two."

Solomon, seeing this, said, "Give the living baby to the first woman. She is his mother."

When Israel heard of Solomon's verdict, they held the king in awe because they knew then that God had indeed given him wisdom to deal justly.

Solomon organizes his kingdom (1 Kings 4:1-28):

The names of Solomon's chief officials are given in the first part of 1 Kings 4. Let us look at just a few of the positions. Zadok and Abiathar were still high priests at the beginning of Solomon's reign, but Abiathar was soon banished from his office. It seems that Zadok soon "retired," but he remained an honorary priest while his son Azariah served as high priest. Benaiah became the chief captain of the host. Two sons of Nathan the prophet were given important positions in the kingdom. Adoniram was placed in charge of the forced labor. This is the first time we meet Adoniram, but we will hear more about him later, or at least about one wearing the same title. The word means "exalted lord" and could have been a title for the supervisor of all forced labor.

Solomon divided his kingdom into twelve districts which were responsible for providing food for the king's household for one month each. Each district was under a prince. These provisions required an enormous amount of food. Each day the king, his household, and his court consumed about 185 bushels of fine flour, 375 bushels of meal, ten fattened oxen, twenty pasture fed oxen, one hundred sheep, and many deer, gazelles, roebucks, and choice fowl. The supply officers of Solomon also provided the barley and the straw for the many horses that belonged to Solomon.

Solomon had peace on every side. He ruled over all the kingdoms from the Euphrates River to the border of Egypt. All the surrounding kings paid him tribute and served him all the days of his life. God's promise of peace for him had come true.

All Israel was prosperous, happy, and secure. Every man lived under his own vine and fig tree, from Dan all the way to Beersheba. The future looked glorious. No reign of any king ever began with so much promise.

Label your map:
    Euphrates River
    Border of Egypt
    Dan
    Beersheba

Name to add:
    Adoniram

Though there were twelve tribes of Israel with distinct tribal territories, and there were twelve districts placed under these twelve princes, the lines were not the same. Each family knew which tribe it was from and could trace its own ancestry, but the old tribal territory lines were no longer of primary importance in organizing the kingdom.

Be alert to what is happening. Each prince with his district was responsible for providing food for the king and his court for a full month. Each district must also supply feed for all of Solomon's horses. Even one day's supply was enormous; thirty days would be even more so. That means that each family within each district had to supply their own needs, plus a huge portion that went to the king. Do you remember the prediction Samuel told the people when they asked for their first king? As Solomon's reign is beginning, and as he sets up these districts, the people are prosperous and happy. It is still no big problem to work for their king. Keep watching.

The cities of Dan and Beersheba are mentioned over and over in the Old Testament to describe the land from one end to the other. These cities were approximately 150 miles apart. Though Solomon controlled much more land than Israel proper, the people continued to live in their own territory. The surrounding peoples were subject to Solomon in the sense that they paid tribute to him regularly; they were his peaceful allies.

Solomon's wisdom (1 Kings 4:29-34):

Solomon's request for wisdom was granted lavishly by God. Solomon became a mental giant. The breadth of his mind was like the sand on the seashore. His wisdom far excelled that of the most famous wise men of his day. He spoke three thousand proverbs and wrote one thousand five songs. His observations and comments covered all nature — that of trees, plants, animals, birds, creeping things, and fish. He also explored the heights and depths of human experience. He wrote or collected most of the book of Proverbs. In addition, Solomon wrote the Song of Solomon, Ecclesiastes, and a couple of the psalms (72, 127). The fame of Solomon's wisdom spread in all directions. Men from all nations came to hear his words.

At least, all the writings listed are attributed to him. Some scholars think someone else wrote the book of Ecclesiastes and used Solomon and his wealth as his role model, or viewpoint from which to write. All of this type literature is referred to as "wisdom literature." The information they include advises us on every aspect of "life under the sun." It stresses the fact that there is no meaning to life without God. Consult the appendix on Wisdom Literature for further information.

Solomon arranges to build the temple (1 Kings 5:1-18; 7:13-14; 2 Chron. 2:1-18):

King Hiram (Huram) of Tyre had been a friend and ally of David's. When he learned that Solomon had followed his father upon the throne, Hiram sent congratulations to him.

Solomon responded by sending word back to Hiram, saying, "You know that because of the wars my father waged, he was not able to build a house for our God. But now Jehovah has given me complete peace. I intend to build the temple for the name of Jehovah my God." Then Solomon requested help from King Hiram, saying:

> This temple must be great because our God is greater than all other gods. But who can build a temple in which Jehovah could truly dwell? The heavens and the highest heavens cannot contain Him. Therefore I will build this place where I can burn sacrifices before my God. Send me, therefore, cedar logs as you sent to my father David. In addition, I will need cypress *(possibly fir or pine)* and algum timber from Lebanon. My men will work with your men to cut the logs because no one cuts logs like the Sidonians. I will need plenty of lumber, so I will supply all the food needed by the workmen.
>
> I will also need a man who is a skilled craftsman able to work in gold, silver, bronze, and iron, and in purple, crimson, and blue yarn. He must also be skilled in the art of engraving. He will work with the skilled craftsmen my father David provided.

Hiram rejoiced when he received the word from Solomon. He sent his response to Solomon's request for help, by a letter, saying:

> Because the Lord loves His people, He has made you king over them. Blessed be the Lord today, who has given David such a wise son over this great people, who will build a house for Jehovah and a royal palace for himself.

I am sending you a skilled man named Hiram who is endowed with understanding. His mother is from the tribe of Dan and his father is a Phoenician from Tyre. He is skilled in all manner of work with metals and fine cloth and he can make any kind of engravings and can execute any design given him.

I have heard your request, and I will do all you desire concerning the lumber. My servants will bring the logs down from Lebanon to the sea, and will make them into rafts to float down to Joppa. We will break the rafts apart, and your men can take them to Jerusalem from there. In return, you send us the wheat, barley, olive oil, and wine you have promised us as wages.

Things went well between Solomon and King Hiram. Solomon sent the food he had promised year by year (about 125,000 bushels of wheat and 115,000 gallons of olive oil), and Hiram supplied Solomon with all the lumber he wanted. Solomon took King Hiram's suggestion and sent for the skilled craftsman, who was also named Hiram. He came and performed all the work Solomon needed him to do.

To provide workers in the mountain, Solomon drafted 30,000 Israelite men. These were divided into three shifts of 10,000 men. Each shift would spend one month in Lebanon and two months at home. Adoniram was in charge of these workers.

In addition, Solomon figured the number of all the aliens (non-Israelites) in Israel according to the census of David. There were 153,600. He assigned 70,000 of these to be porters (carriers), and 80,000 to be stonecutters in the hills, with 3,600 foremen to oversee their work.

Large quantities of finished stone were taken from the quarry. Craftsmen of Hiram and Solomon, aided by men from Gebal (Byblos), cut and prepared the timber and stone for the temple.

Label your map:
  Mt. Lebanon
  Joppa

Name to add:
  Hiram, the skilled craftsman

The plan for transporting the lumber from Lebanon to Jerusalem was an efficient one. Mount Lebanon is a high peak in a mountain range that begins miles to the north of Israel and runs south all the way through the land and on into the peninsula of Sinai. It would have been very difficult to move the logs overland. But the peaks of Lebanon are only a few miles from the Mediterranean coast. The workers hauled the logs down the mountain to the shore, made them into rafts, floated them south to Joppa, took them apart, and then transported them across land only from Joppa to Jerusalem.

Hiram, the skilled craftsman who is described here, is the man upon whom the whole foundation of the Masonic Lodge rests. According to their accounts, he was the greatest of all masons, and they have fabricated a whole system of history and religion around him. There is only one problem — the whole thing is a fabrication! The Bible gives only the barest information about him, and secular history gives even less. He was merely the man hired by Solomon to work with his own skilled men to perform the task of building the temple and the articles for its use. Do not be deceived.

The construction of the temple (1 Kings 6:1-7:50; 2 Chron. 3:1-4:22):

All preparations were complete and the time had come for the people to begin their work. The building of the temple began on the second day of the second month of the fourth year of Solomon's reign (about 960-958 B.C.). It had been four hundred and eighty years since the Israelites came out of Egypt. Solomon built the temple on the site of the threshing floor of Araunah the Jebusite on Mount Moriah where the Lord appeared to David on the occasion of the plague caused by David's sin in counting the soldiers (2 Samuel 24:16-17; 1 Chron. 21:15-16).

It took seven years to finish building the temple. It was a grand and beautiful structure, with a cost beyond calculation. It was the symbol of God's presence among His people. God told Solomon, as he began the construction of the temple: "If you will keep my commandments and statutes, I will fulfill the promise I made to your father David. I will live among the Israelites and I will not abandon my people" (1 Kings 6:11-13). This was a repetition of the covenant that God had made with His people from the days when He brought them out of the land of Egypt and made them His own (see Exod. 6:6-7; 19:4-6). The people wanted God to dwell in their midst and count them as His chosen people, but they tended to forget that the covenant began with an *if clause* — "If you will walk in my statutes and execute my ordinances and keep all my commandments by walking in them..."

It is difficult to visualize the temple. The data given in the text does not describe all details of the temple's construction or appearance. What we have enables us to have only a general picture of the way it looked. There are many more details given back in Exodus about the tabernacle, because it tells first about the instructions Moses was given about how to build each piece, then it describes the way the people actually did the work, and then it gives still more details as it describes how they set up the tabernacle and put each piece of furniture in its place. By combining all the accounts, we can come to a fairly good picture of how the tabernacle looked. But the temple is not described in such detail. Though there is an account in 1 Kings and another in 2 Chronicles, the details are still vague. Therefore, as you start to describe the temple to your class, you may find yourself frustrated in picturing it in your own mind, or in finding visual aids that might help you. Those who draw the pictures that are found in the visual aid packages have the same problem you and I have in finding enough details to know exactly how it looked. This temple was totally destroyed in the days of Nebuchadnezzar from Babylon (2 Kings 25), so even the archaeologists can be no help in describing it.

The structure was magnificent. There is no way we could place a value on it in terms of our modern money. Some of the most elaborate buildings of our day may cost millions, or even billions, of dollars — but we cannot conceive of a building completely <u>lined</u> with pure gold! Therefore, in our description, let us stand back as if it were from a distance, and describe its grandeur and only include the details that are given. Let us not grow frustrated beyond that.

To clarify the descriptions as much as possible, we are breaking it down into different categories, though the details we include are scattered in the passages given. Read the accounts carefully in both Kings and Chronicles as you make your study.

The exterior of the temple:

The main part of the building was ninety feet long, thirty feet wide, and forty-five feet high. These were the dimensions of the temple proper, not including the porch on the front, or the storerooms on the side. On the front, a porch (or portico) extended fifteen feet from the front door. It was as wide as the building itself (30 feet). The exterior walls of the temple were made of great blocks of stone. These blocks were dressed so carefully at the quarry that no hammer, chisel, or any iron tool was heard at the building site.

Along either side of the temple there were rooms. These rooms were three stories high, each story seven and a half feet high — making the store rooms on the sides a total of twenty two and a half feet high, one half the height of the temple proper. The outside wall of these rooms was straight up and down, but the *inside* wall of the rooms was the *outside* of the temple wall. In order that the beams of the ceiling and floor of each story of rooms not be actually attached to the temple, the outside wall of the temple was offset at each level so that the ceiling and floor beams rested on

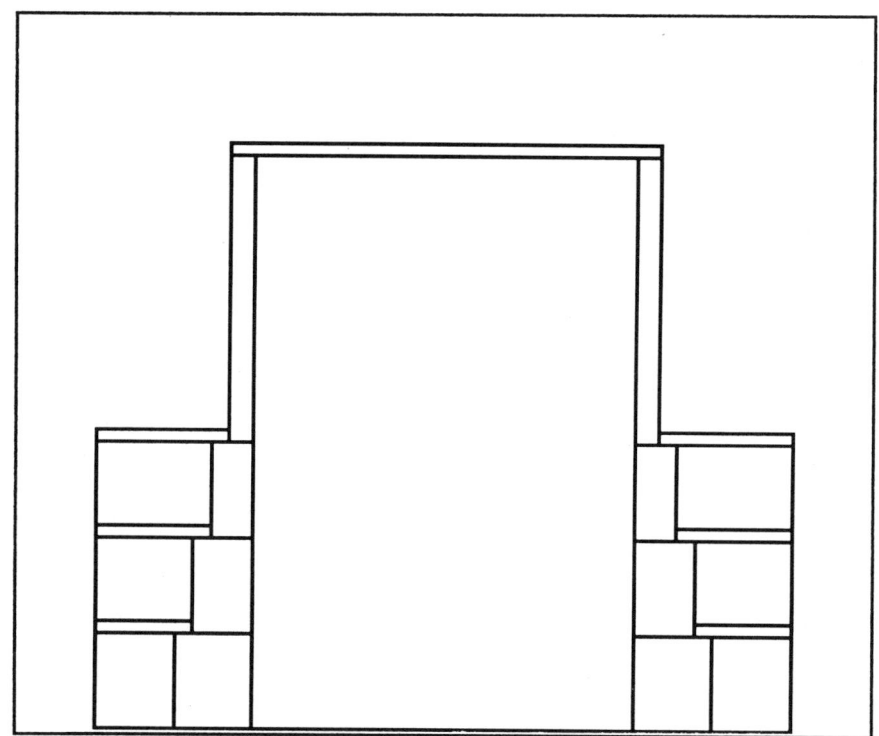

Cut-away view of temple wall and side rooms

the wall which jutted out eighteen inches for each floor. Thus the first story of rooms was seven and a half feet wide; the second story was nine feet wide; and the top floor was ten and a half feet wide. These rooms served as store rooms for the temple and held grains and other supplies for the regular sacrifices, as well as treasures dedicated to the Lord. The door to the store rooms was on the right side of the temple, and the upper rooms were reached by way of a winding stairway.

A great bronze pillar stood on either side of the front doors. Each pillar stood twenty-seven feet high and was eighteen feet in circumference. Each pillar had a capital on top of it seven and half feet high, making the total height of the pillars approximately thirty-five feet. The pillar on the right was called Jachin (He shall establish) and the one on the left was called Boaz (In it is strength). These were cast by Hiram of Tyre, the workman sent by King Hiram. All the items of bronze were cast in the clay ground on the plain of the Jordan between Succoth and Zarethan. Forms were shaped in the clay into which the molten bronze was poured to make each item, even these enormous pillars (1 Kings 7:46).

These huge molten pillars were not only big, they were very elaborate in design. The capitals are described as "lily-shaped," or "lily-designed." That must mean they were shaped as huge open flowers. In addition there were "nets of network (checker-work) and twisted threads of chain-work," seven for each pillar. Two hundred pomegranates were shaped in rows around each one. It is difficult to visualize the exact designs, but it is evident they were beautiful. Imagine the work it took to shape the clay into the forms to make each of these designs.

There were windows in the temple. They were over twenty-two and a half feet above the floor, above the roof of the store rooms on the sides. They were narrow on the outside and wide on the inside. These allowed for light and ventilation, but no one could see in or out of them.

The front doors to the temple were of pine with frames of olive wood. These were decorated with carvings of cherubim, palm trees, and blossoms, and covered with gold hammered evenly over the carvings.

The inside of the temple proper:

The inside of the temple proper was divided into two great portions. First was a great hall thirty feet wide, forty-five feet high, and sixty feet long. Beyond this was a room thirty feet long, thirty feet wide, and thirty feet high. The first room corresponded to the Holy Place that is described in the tabernacle. This is where the daily sacrifices of incense were offered. The innermost room was the

Most Holy Place. The ark of the covenant was placed here. From the day when the ark of the covenant was first set into its place in the Most Holy Place in the tabernacle, God's presence was said to rest above it (see Exod. 25:10-22, particularly verse 22). That is why this room was "most holy."

Inside the building, the stones which formed the walls were covered with cedar paneling on the walls and ceiling. Pine wood covered the floor so that no stone could be seen inside. Moreover, all the wood — ceiling, walls, and floor — was covered with gold plate. Even the ceiling beams and door frames were covered with gold. Figures of gourds and flower blossoms, cherubim and palm trees, were carved on the walls, and then the gold plate was gently beaten and shaped to conform to these figures. That means that if you could have stepped inside the temple, you would have seen only gold on all sides — and that gold was shaped and molded over intricate carvings all over the walls. Beauty beyond anything we have experienced!

The outer sanctuary:

The windows were located in the first sixty foot long room (the windows were higher than the inner room ceiling). The two doors to the sanctuary are described as being of cypress (pine) wood, intricately carved just as all the rest, and covered with gold. There were four-sided doorposts on either side of the doors, and the doors turned on gold pivots (hinges). These doors are almost certainly the same doors described as the front doors of the temple, but the details are unclear about whether the porch was enclosed or open.

In the tabernacle, there was one table of shewbread and one lampstand located in the Holy Place. In the temple, there were ten tables and ten lampstands. Five of each were placed on either side of the room. The tables were of wood covered with gold, and the lampstands were of pure gold. In addition to the furniture for the Holy Place, there were one hundred golden bowls, plus golden lamps, tongs, and other utensils prepared for the lampstands and tables.

The inner sanctuary:

Six hundred talents of gold were used in covering the walls, ceiling, and floor of the inner room. Even gold nails, or spikes, weighing a total of one and one-fourth pounds were used. Notice that the room was a perfect cube in shape: twenty cubits wide, high, and long (30x30x30 feet). That means its ceiling was fifteen feet lower than the outer room.

Within the inner sanctuary were two cherubim made of olive wood overlaid with gold. These cherubim were fifteen feet high. They stood with wings extended left and right. Their wing tips touched each other in the middle of the room, and the other wing of each cherub touched the outer wall on either side. They faced the main hall. The ark of the covenant was placed beneath their wings. No new ark of the covenant was built. The old one was kept and carefully placed in its position when the time came for the dedication of the temple.

Between the two rooms there were doors, a veil, and a gold chain. Again, the details are unclear. Could the veil be seen from the first room, or the doors? The gold chain(s) is described as being across the front of the room, from the top of the pillars (the doorposts?), with one hundred gold pomegranates worked into it. But exactly where was it? The answers are unclear. The veil was of fine linen with cherubim of blue, purple, and crimson yarn worked into it. The two doors were made of olive wood, beautifully carved and overlaid with gold. There were five-sided doorposts on either side of the doors, and they too were covered with gold, as was the lintel above the doors.

An altar of incense was made of cedar and plated with gold. It is described in connection with the description of the inner room, but if the rules concerning its use were the same as in the days of the tabernacle, it must have stood just outside the doors to the inner room. This is where the priests came twice each day to offer incense before the Lord. Since the sacrifice of incense was offered directly before the presence of the Lord, its function was very closely tied to the inner room. (See Hebrews 9:1-5.)

The courtyard of the temple:

An outer courtyard was surrounded by a wall made of three rows of cut stone, with a row of cedar beams at the top. Its doors were overlaid with bronze.

The furniture and vessels used outside of the temple were made of bronze (brass). Besides the two great pillars, there was a great bronze altar for offering all the sacrifices, except the incense which was offered inside on the little altar. The bronze altar was thirty feet long, thirty feet wide, and fifteen feet high. Many bronze basins, and shovels, and bowls were prepared for service at the altar. The original bronze altar of burnt offering that was built for the tabernacle was seven feet wide and seven feet long, and four and a half feet high (Exod. 27:1-8).

Hiram the artisan made a great sea of cast bronze. It was circular in shape and had a lip which curved out like the blossom of a flower. It was forty-five feet across the brim, seven and a half feet deep, and it held about 17,500 gallons of water. Below the rim, figures of knops or gourds encircled the sea in two rows, ten knops every eighteen inches. The sea rested on the backs of twelve bronze bulls, three facing north, three south, three east, and three west. This great sea was placed in the courtyard in front of the temple, on the right side toward the southeast. It was to be used by the priests for washing themselves (2 Chron. 4:6b).

Ten stands with wheels were made of bronze. Each supported a basin holding about 230 gallons of water. These stood five on the north side of the temple and five on the south side. They were used to rinse the items used in the burnt offerings (2 Chron. 4:6a). The huge brazen sea and these ten basins for water took the place of the laver that had been made for service in the tabernacle and stood in its courtyard (Exod. 30:17-21).

When Hiram had finished making all the items of bronze there were: the two huge pillars that stood in front of the building, with their two great bowl shaped capitals, the two sets of network with the total of four hundred pomegranates worked into the net decorating the tops of the capitals, the great brazen sea with its twelve bulls under it, the ten stands for water, and all the innumerable objects and vessels for the temple service. All of these items were cast in clay molds in the plains of the Jordan. There was so much bronze used they made no attempt to weigh it.

There are several differences between 1 Kings and 2 Chronicles in the details about the temple and its furnishings. For example, for the capacity of the Sea, 1 Kings 7:26 has 2,000 baths, while 2 Chronicles 4:5 says 3,000 baths. According to Keil and Delitzsch, this discrepancy is simply a confusion by some copyist between the Hebrew letter gimel which is also the number "3" in Hebrew, and the letter beth which is the number "2" (<u>Keil and Delitzsch</u>, Vol. 2, p. 597). From the dimensions given, it is thought that the figure of 2,000 baths is the correct one. Those given to math may do some figuring and find that it would be difficult to get even 17,500 gallons (2,000 baths) into a vessel of the circumference given. For this reason, some speculate that the sea was not perfectly spherical but bulged out somewhat in the shape of a caldron all the way around. As we said about the temple, details are not sufficient for us to know the exact explanations for our questions.

Another difference is the knops (figures of gourds), which 1 Kings says surrounded the bronze sea beneath the brim (1 Kings 7:24), and oxen or bulls, which 2 Chronicles says surrounded it (2 Chron. 4:3). Again, according to Keil and Delitzsch, this difference is explained by the fact that a scribe substituted a word similar to gourd in the 2 Chronicles account (<u>Keil and Delitzsch</u>, Vol. 2, p. 597).

The temple is finished and dedicated (1 Kings 6:37-38; 7:51-8:66; 2 Chron. 5:1-7:10):

When all the work was finished on the temple, Solomon brought the treasures his father David had dedicated and placed them in the treasuries of the Lord. David had prepared so much gold and silver, there was much more than was needed for the construction. (Compare 1 Chronicles 22:14 with 2 Chronicles 3:8-9.) By now it was the eighth month of the eleventh year of Solomon's reign. It had taken seven years to complete the work.

The time for celebration had come. Solomon called for all the elders of Israel, the heads of the tribes, and the chiefs of the Israelite families to come to him. They all came together in the seventh month at the time of the yearly festival (of atonement). When the people had assembled, the priests brought the ark of the covenant from its resting place in the City of David to the new temple. The old Tent of Meeting was brought from Gibeon with all its old furnishings and vessels. As the priests and Levites carried them into place, all Israel assembled around the king before the ark. They sacrificed so many sheep and cattle in celebration they could not be counted. All the priests present that day had dedicated themselves to be ready to help with the sacrifices, no matter what course they were from *(in other words, no matter whose turn it was)*. The Levites singers, Asaph, Heman, and Jeduthan, were there leading the people in songs of praise to God, with one hundred twenty priests blowing trumpets. The whole assembly lifted up their voices in song, to the accompaniment of trumpets, cymbals, and instruments of music as they sang, "Praise the Lord, for He indeed is good, for His loving-kindness is everlasting."

The priests carried the ark of the covenant inside and placed it in the Most Holy Place under the wings of the cherubim. The moment they had all been waiting for had arrived: the ark of God had a final resting place. The poles for carrying it were left in place. Nothing was in the ark at this time except the two stone tablets that Moses had received at Mount Sinai. When the ark was in its place, a cloud filled the temple of the Lord. The priests could not perform their work for a time, because God's presence had filled the temple. (See Exodus 40:34-35. God's glory filled the tabernacle also just as they finished setting everything is its place, and Moses could not continue for a time.)

Solomon saw the cloud of God's presence and he said, "God said He would dwell in a dark cloud; indeed I have built a magnificent temple for God to dwell in." Then he turned to the people and declared that God had fulfilled His promises:

> Praise be to the Lord, for He has fulfilled what He promised to my father David. God said He had never chosen a city for a temple to be built, but He chose David to rule as king. David wanted to build a house for God, but God would not let him do so. Instead, God said He would allow David's son to build it. And God has kept that promise. Here I am today, having succeeded my father on the throne, and, according to the promise, I have built a temple for our God. I have provided a place for the ark, in which is the covenant which the Lord made with our fathers when He brought them out of Egypt.

Solomon was standing on a bronze platform he had built and placed in the courtyard of the temple so that all the people could see him. After his statement of joy that God had kept His promise, Solomon knelt before the whole group, spread out his hands toward heaven, and prayed:

> O Lord God, there is no God like you in all heaven and earth who can keep His covenant with His servants as you do. You have kept your promise to David that the temple would be built; now may you also keep the promise that he would always have one of his

descendants to sit upon his throne, if only they will be careful to serve you with a whole heart.

But will God really dwell on earth with men? The heavens, even the highest heavens, cannot contain you. Much less this temple I have built! Yet please hear our prayers and our pleas for mercy. May your eyes be open toward this temple day and night, toward this place where you said you would place your Name. May you hear the prayers and supplications that your servants pray toward this place. Please hear from heaven, your dwelling place; and when you hear, please forgive.

No matter what our problem is, or what our need may be at that moment, if we pray toward this place, please hear us. If one man wrongs another and brings a sacrifice, or if we have been defeated in battle, or if there is a drought and we pray for rain, or if there is famine or plague in the land, please hear our petitions toward this place and forgive our iniquities so that we may be blessed again.

If even a foreigner comes to this place and prays toward this temple, please hear his prayer and grant his request so that all the people of the earth may fear your great Name. If we go out to war, and we pray toward this city from wherever we are, please help us and uphold our cause. If we sin and are taken captive by an enemy to a land even far away, and if we repent there in that land and pray toward this place, please hear us from your dwelling place in heaven and forgive us.

May your eyes and your ears be ever attentive to prayers offered in this place.

When Solomon finished his prayer, he rose from before the altar and turned to bless the people. He called out in a loud voice:

Praise be to the Lord who has given rest to his people Israel. Not one of the good promises God made through Moses has failed. May God continue to be with us; may He never forsake us nor leave us. May He turn our hearts to seek Him always and to keep all the commands and laws we have been given. And may God hear the prayer I have offered so that He will hear all prayers offered to this place. But you must be fully committed unto God to live by His decrees and obey His commands, as you are at this time.

As Solomon finished his prayer, fire came down from heaven and consumed the burnt offerings and sacrifices being offered, and the glory of the Lord filled the temple. The priests could not enter the house of the Lord, because the glory of the Lord filled the temple. This was God's way of saying He had accepted the prayer and that He had indeed placed His Name in the temple. God had also sent fire down upon the altar many years earlier at the end of the dedication of the tabernacle at Mount Sinai (Lev. 9:23-24). When all the Israelites saw the fire and glory of God, they fell on their faces and worshiped God, saying, "Truly He is good, truly His loving-kindness is everlasting."

The king had dedicated a large area of the ground of the courtyard because there were too many sacrifices to be offered on the altar even though it was thirty feet long and thirty feet wide. In addition to the numberless sacrifices already offered as they brought the ark to its resting place, and all those brought by the people, Solomon offered 22,000 cattle and 120,000 sheep. It was, indeed, a great celebration.

The festival continued for seven days. People were there from Lobo-Hamath up near the Euphrates River to the Wadi of Egypt on the southern edge of the arable land in Canaan. It was a time of great joy for all the people as well as for the king. They had worked hard for seven years, but they had accomplished a magnificent task. The feeling of accomplishment overshadowed everything else. On the twenty-third day of the month, they returned to their homes rejoicing over all the good things that God had done for David and Solomon and for all Israel.

Mark 1 Kings 8 and 2 Chronicles 6 as the high point of all Israelite history. They are at their peak. God has blessed them greatly. Their magnificent temple is finished. They are at peace on every side. The territory the Israelites controlled is at its very largest. The king and the people are serving God, happy to worship Him in their new temple. The king is rich beyond our comprehension. The people of the land share in that wealth. They are prosperous and happy from one end of the land to the other. Oh, if only their history could have continued that way! Even the glory and grandeur which Israel had at this point was only a glimpse of the blessings God had in store for His people if they remained faithful.

Label your map:
- **Lobo-Hamath**
- **Euphrates River**
- **Wadi of Egypt**

Sacrifices are offered regularly (1 Kings 9:25; 2 Chron. 8:11-16):

Solomon and the people were careful to offer all the regular sacrifices to the Lord on the altar that had been built at the temple. They did so according to the daily sacrifices commanded in the law, plus all those commanded for the sabbaths, the new moons, and for the three annual feasts — the Feast of Unleavened Bread, the Feast of Weeks, and the Feast of Booths. (See Numbers 28 and 29.)

According to the ordinance of David, Solomon appointed all the divisions of the priests and Levites to their proper roles. The priests were divided into their courses for service, and the Levites were set for their duties as singers, as ministers before the priests, and as gate-keepers for the temple. They did not depart from all the commandment of the king in regard to their service, or in regard to the storerooms.

Thus all the work of Solomon related to the temple was complete. The building itself was built and dedicated, and all the service of the Levites and priests was established.

Solomon builds his own palace (1 Kings 7:2-12; 10:18-20; 2 Chron. 9:17-19):

After the temple was finished, Solomon built his palace complex. Its description is fitted right into the midst of the description of the temple. It took thirteen years to complete, in contrast to the seven years it took to build the temple. The palace complex was next door to the temple grounds.

The palace was a vast structure 150 feet long, 75 feet wide, and 45 feet high. Four rows of cedar columns supported cedar beams, and the building was roofed with cedar. The palace was called "The House of the Forest of Lebanon," because it had so many cedar posts in it. A colonnade 75 feet long connected the various parts of the palace with one another. The exterior walls were made of high grade stones which were cut to size with saws. The foundation included some stones fifteen feet and some twelve feet long.

Solomon built a great throne hall to serve as the place where he judged the people. It was covered from floor to ceiling in cedar. His living quarters were built the same way, and so were the quarters of Pharaoh's daughter.

In the throne room the king placed a great throne made of ivory and overlaid with pure gold. Six steps led up to the throne itself, and there was a gold footstool attached to the throne. On each side of the seat there were armrests with a lion standing beside it. *(The lion was the symbol of the tribe of Judah.)* Lions also stood on each side of the six steps, making twelve lions on the steps. Nothing like it could be found in any other kingdom.

God appears to Solomon a second time (1 Kings 9:1-9; 2 Chron. 7:11-22):

When Solomon had completed the temple and his own house, God appeared to him by night and said:

> I have heard your prayer and have chosen this place for myself for a house of sacrifice. Whatever condition my people are in, if they humble themselves and seek my face and turn from their evil ways, I will hear from heaven and will forgive their sin and heal the land.
>
> As for you, if you will walk before me as David did, and will keep my commandments, then I will establish the throne of your kingdom just as I promised to your father when I said, "You will not fail to have a man to be ruler in Israel."
>
> But if you or your children turn away from me and do not obey my commandments, I will cut off Israel from this land, and this house which I have made holy, I will cast it out of my sight. And though it is so great now, people will pass by and be amazed. They will say, "Why has Jehovah done such things to this land and to this house?" The answer will be: "Because they forsook Jehovah who brought them up out of Egypt and worshiped other gods. That is why Jehovah brought upon them all this calamity."

God has heard Solomon's prayer, and He promises to hear every prayer His people offer toward the temple — so long as His people remain faithful. But notice how clear God's warning is about what will happen if they turn away from Him. Even though the building of the temple and its dedication mark the high point of all Israelite history, God knows that Solomon and the people need the warning about the future if they turn away from Him.

Do not let anyone deceive you by saying that God did not keep His promises to the Israelites, because they lost their land. God <u>did</u> keep His promises! His promises <u>included</u> the promise of punishment and the promise that they would lose their temple and their land if they became wicked. Do not need to ask why the temple was destroyed and the land devastated. God answered that question in prophecy long before it happened.

King Hiram is displeased with his pay (1 Kings 9:10-14; 2 Chron. 8:1-2):

The construction of the temple and of the royal palace took twenty years. Solomon paid Hiram king of Tyre by giving him twenty cities in Galilee. Hiram came to see them and did not like what he saw.

He said, "What kind of towns have you given me, my brother? They are Cabul (worthless)."

Hiram had given Solomon a present of four and a half tons of gold. He felt he was very much the loser in the deal. Hiram may have just given the cities back to Solomon saying, "They are not worth my time and trouble" (see 2 Chron. 8:1-2).

Other works of Solomon (1 Kings 9:10-27; 2 Chron. 8:3-10, 17-18):

By the time Solomon had completed only two of his building projects, the temple and his palace, about half of his forty years' rule was gone. His building projects continued at a frantic pace. He captured the city of Hamath in the far north of his dominion and fortified Tadmor on the main trade route from Mesopotamia to Israel. He fortified and enlarged Hazor, Megiddo, Gezer, upper and lower Beth-horon, and Baalath. He extended the walls of Jerusalem to include Mount Moriah and the temple. Some of these cities were built specifically to house Solomon's chariots and horses.

All the remnant of the Amorites and Canaanites were drafted for slave labor before he began his very first building project, the temple. Solomon did not enslave the Israelites, but he used them extensively for his soldiers, his servants, his officials, his officers, his chariot commanders, his horsemen, and his captains.

Solomon even had navies in two seas. These navies worked in co-operation with King Hiram and the Phoenicians. One navy operated in the Mediterranean, sailing to Tarshish *(on the southern coast of what is now Spain)* and back once every three years. The other operated in the Red Sea and the Indian Ocean with Ezion-geber at the head of the Gulf of Aqaba as its home port.

Label your map:
  Hamath
  Tadmor
  Hazor
  Megiddo
  Beth-horon
  Baalath
  Mediterranean Sea
  Gulf of Aqaba
  Ezion-geber

Tarshish is too far across the Mediterranean Sea to be included on this map. It was on the southern edge of what is now Spain, where the Mediterranean meets the Atlantic Ocean. The Gulf of Aqaba was the eastern gulf at the northern end of the Red Sea. The ships sailed south in the gulf, into the Red Sea, and on into the Indian Ocean. Look on a larger map and find where Solomon's ships sailed.

The splendor and wealth of Solomon (1 Kings 10:11-12, 14-29; 2 Chron. 9:13-28):

Nowhere is the splendor of Solomon's reign more emphatically shown than in his ceremonial trappings. He had 200 large shields made of gold. Each shield was made from seven and a half pounds of gold. There were 300 smaller shields of about three and three-fourths pounds of gold each. These were used on ceremonial occasions by an honor guard.

Gold is measured in ounces today, and each ounce is costly. Let this thought be vivid in your mind as you read of the <u>pounds</u> and <u>tons</u> of gold that describe Solomon's wealth.

The navies of Solomon brought him much wealth. Every three years his ships would carry cargo to Tarshish, trade, and return with gold, silver, ivory, apes, and peacocks. From Ophir in southern Arabia, his navy brought him sixteen tons of gold. The weight of gold Solomon received from his trading ventures was twenty-five tons each year. He also received enormous taxes, tributes from the nations subject to him, and fees from the numerous caravans which passed through his kingdom.

Solomon did a thriving business in horse trade. He was the middle man for all the horses which left Egypt going to Mesopotamia and Asia Minor. Solomon would buy a herd of horses from Egypt and then sell them to the kings of Syria and to the kings of the Hittites. He also handled the chariot trade. Each chariot sold for about fifteen pounds of silver. The horses sold for about three and three-fourths pounds of silver. Solomon had 4,000 stalls for horses and chariots and 12,000 horsemen. He stationed part of them in the chariot cities he had built and part of them in Jerusalem.

(Remember that each of the twelve districts that provided the food for the king and his court for one month out of the year also had to provide the feed for all the king's horses.)

People came from all the earth to see Solomon's kingdom and to hear his wisdom. No one came without a gift: vessels of silver or gold, clothes, armor, spices, horses, and mules. Solomon ate and drank only from gold vessels. Silver was not esteemed as valuable in Solomon's day, because it was as common as stones in the streets of Jerusalem. He made cedars as plentiful as sycamore trees that grew in the lowlands.

Look one more time at the warning Samuel gave when the people first asked for a king (1 Sam. 8:11-18). Until that time each man lived on his own farm and worked for his own needs. Samuel warned that if they had a king, he would take their sons and their daughters and make them serve him. He would take the best of their fields and their vineyards and give them to his servants. He would take the best of their animals for his own use. He would take a tenth of all their possessions for himself. Do you remember, also, that God warned that when they grew tired of their king, He would not listen to their pleas to remove him?

Look at what has happened. King Saul had some servants, and he had a standing army for the first time in Israelite history, but the number of people involved was small. King David had more servants and a more highly organized government, but still most lived in their own places and did as they wished. But Solomon organized his whole kingdom into a work force. He did not make slaves of the Israelites — but they worked for him year in and year out. They might be serving in Lebanon in the forests bringing out wood, or they might be serving in the navy away from home for three years, or they might be one of his supervisors over the other workers. If they were at home for a time, they had to work hard to help supply the portion of food their district was assigned to provide for the king and his animals one month out of the year.

The Israelites were glad to work hard to build the temple, because it was a national shrine to their God. There was unmixed joy on the day it was dedicated. But the work did not stop. Next it was the palace that must be built, then some city to be fortified, or some city to be built for the king's horses. The people grew weary as the years passed. The warnings God gave through Samuel had come true.

Do you remember the reasons why Solomon asked for wisdom? He wanted wisdom to know how to rule his people wisely. He was given wisdom in abundance, but do you think he used it to rule wisely? Do you think his people thought so?

The Queen of Sheba (1 Kings 10:1-13; 2 Chron. 9:1-12):

One of the most illustrious visitors Solomon ever had was the Queen of Sheba. Her kingdom was in the very southern part of Arabia, directly across the Red Sea from Ethiopia. The journey was a dangerous, arduous undertaking. A very large escort would have been necessary to guard the riches the queen carried to Solomon. Her large caravan reached Jerusalem with a vast cargo of spices, gold, and precious stones.

The queen conversed with Solomon, plying him with all the questions she had. Solomon answered them with ease. She beheld his court, his servants, the food on his table, his officials, and the sacrifices at the temple and she was completely overwhelmed.

In stunned amazement, she said, "I had heard in my own country of your greatness, but I did not really believe all the things I heard. But now that I see them with my own eyes, I must say that not even half the truth was told me. You are far greater in wisdom and in wealth than I had heard. How happy your men must be to have you for their king. God is to be praised who has delighted in you and placed you upon the throne of Israel. Because of His eternal love for Israel, He has made you king to uphold justice and righteousness."

The queen of Sheba gave Solomon four and a half tons of gold, precious stones, and more spices than were ever brought to him by anyone else. In turn, Solomon gave her all she desired and asked for, besides what he gave her as a voluntary gift. Then she left and returned to her own country.

Though the queen of Sheba said, "How happy your men must be," she would have gotten a very different impression if she had gone out into the villages and cities and asked the people their opinion of Solomon. The common people shared in the wealth of the kingdom. Indeed, we are told that silver was as common in Jerusalem as stones (1 Kings 10:27), but the constant forced labor and the endless taxes were grinding the people down. Unrest was building in the kingdom. The bubble of splendor was about to burst.

Solomon falls away from God (1 Kings 11:1-40):

Solomon's wives became, by far, the greatest cause of his downfall. Not only did he marry wives to seal treaties, as we have mentioned, he "loved many foreign women besides Pharaoh's daughter." He married Moabites, Ammonites, Edomites, Sidonians, and Hittites. All these were from nations about which God had warned Israel: "Do not intermarry with them because they will surely turn your hearts away unto other gods" (see Deut. 7:3-4). Solomon had a total of seven hundred wives and three hundred concubines.

As Solomon grew older, his wives turned his heart away unto other gods. On the east side of Jerusalem, he built high places for the worship of Chemosh, the detestable god of Moab; for Molech, the abomination of the Ammonites; and for all his wives who worshiped their various gods. This is the same man who had built a temple for Jehovah God just a few short years earlier! Solomon followed after Ashtoreth, the goddess of the Sidonians, and Molech, the god of Ammon. It is absolutely incredible that Solomon could do such a thing.

Jehovah was angry with Solomon. He had appeared to Solomon twice, had given him wisdom, and had showered all sorts of blessings upon him, yet Solomon did not heed the warning against following other gods. Therefore God said:

> Because you have turned away from me and have refused to keep my covenant and my statutes, I am taking the kingdom away from you and I will give it to one of your servants. Nevertheless, for the sake of David your father, I will not take it away during your lifetime. I will tear it out of the hand of your son. I will not take the whole kingdom away, but will leave him one tribe for the sake of David my servant and because of Jerusalem which I have chosen.

How sad! No king ever had a greater opportunity to accomplish wonderful things for his people than Solomon had. No one ever had a father who had taught him and warned him as many times to obey God's commandments as Solomon had. No king ever had the relationship with God which Solomon was offered in which he was told to ask for whatever he wanted. No king ever had the incredible wisdom and ability Solomon was given to rule wisely and to distinguish between good and evil.

There is an even more serious problem than the unrest of the people. Look back to Deuteronomy 17:14-20 to the laws God gave for a king. Read the passage with your students in your class. God said:

> *When the day comes that you say, "I will set a king over me like all the nations around us," then be sure it is a king whom God has chosen from among your own people. Do not put a*

foreigner over yourselves.

Your king must not multiply horses for himself, nor shall he cause his people to go to Egypt in order to get horses. Neither shall he multiply wives for himself, lest his heart turn away from God. He must not greatly multiply gold and silver for himself.

The king shall write for himself a copy of the law of God and keep it ever before him. He must read it regularly all the days of his life so that he may learn to fear the Lord, by carefully observing all its laws and statutes. His heart must not be lifted above his countrymen and he must not turn to the right or to the left from serving the Lord, so that he and his sons may continue long in his kingdom in the midst of Israel.

Solomon broke every warning given by God. He traded extensively in horses with Egypt; he greatly multiplied silver and gold; and he multiplied wives. Worst of all, he gradually forgot God's law. Solomon's life can be summed up by four W's: wisdom, works, wealth, and wives.

Adversaries began to arise (1 Kings 11:14-40):

God began to allow adversaries to rise up against Solomon. When David had destroyed the men of Edom, a boy named Hadad, of the royal lineage, had fled to Egypt with some Edomite officials who had served his father. The Pharaoh of Egypt gave Hadad a house and supported him. When Hadad was grown, Pharaoh was so pleased with him he gave him a sister of Pharaoh's own wife, Queen Tahpenes, in marriage. She bore him a son Genubath who was reared in the royal palace with Pharaoh's own children.

In Egypt, Hadad heard of the death of David and Joab, and he asked Pharaoh, "Let me return to my own country."

Pharaoh protested, "What have you lacked here that you want to return to your own country?"

Hadad replied, "Nothing, but let me go anyway." So Pharaoh allowed him to return to Edom. That meant Hadad was in place waiting for the opportunity to rebel.

In the area north of Israel proper, a man named Rezon gathered forces together and established headquarters in Damascus. He joined Hadad in causing problems for Israel. It seems there were no open battles in Solomon's day, but the neighboring forces were waiting for their chance to declare their independence.

In addition to these enemies, a man named Jeroboam, the son of Nebat, had come to the notice of Solomon as a good worker. Solomon had placed him in charge of the labor force of Ephraim and Manasseh.

One day as Jeroboam was leaving Jerusalem, a prophet named Ahijah from Shiloh met him. Ahijah was wearing a new cloak. The prophet stopped Jeroboam. He took his new cloak, tore it into twelve pieces, and said to Jeroboam:

Take ten of these pieces because this is what the Lord says: "I am going to tear the kingdom away from Solomon and give you ten tribes because he has forsaken me and worshiped Ashtoreth, Chemosh, and Molech, and has not followed my commandments.

"I will not, however, take the kingdom from Solomon himself for the sake of David my servant whom I chose and who obeyed my commands and statutes. But I will take it from his son and will give you ten tribes. I will give one tribe to his son so that David my servant will always have a lamp before me in Jerusalem where I have chosen to put my Name.

"Now, if you will walk before me as David did, I will establish your throne, and I will make your family to rule upon your throne just as I have done for David. I will humble David's descendants but not forever."

When Solomon heard of these things, he tried to kill Jeroboam, but he fled into Egypt where he enjoyed the protection of a new Pharaoh whose name was Shishak. Jeroboam remained in Egypt until Solomon's death.

Names to add:
   Hadad, the Edomite
   Rezon, the Syrian
   Jeroboam
   Ahijah
   Shishak, the Egyptian

Notice this promise to Jeroboam carefully. Just as all the other promises from God have come true, this one will also come true as the kingdom divides: Jeroboam become king over ten of the tribes very soon after Solomon dies. But look at the part of the promise to him that includes an if clause: "If you will walk before me as David did..." then your family will be established as the reigning dynasty over the ten tribes. As you study the divided kingdom, watch to see if that part of the promise comes true. If not, look at the reason why.

Solomon's death (1 Kings 11:41-43; 2 Chron. 9:29-31):
Solomon reigned for forty years. He died and was buried with his fathers in the city of David. Among those who wrote records of Solomon's life were Nathan the prophet, Ahijah the Shilonite, and Iddo the seer. Solomon's son Rehoboam succeeded him as king.

Distinct cracks in the kingdom:
Distinct cracks were all over Solomon's kingdom when he died. To casual observers, the kingdom might have looked as strong as ever. Externally it was still whole, but it would require very little shaking to reveal just how fragile the kingdom was. That shaking would come within days of Solomon's death.

One's overwhelming feeling as he contemplates the end of Solomon's life is, "How sad!" "What a shame!" "If only..." But Solomon showed that no ordinary son of man could be the ideal chosen one of God. For one truly to occupy the throne of David, to rule in justice and righteousness, not for just a year, or a decade, but forever, would require the Son of Man who was also the Son of God, the Messiah, the Son of David who would rule forever upon His father's throne. The lesson is that only God can adequately rule His people. For God to have allowed other kings to rule was just His way of proving that.

Appendix

The Wisdom Literature

The Book of Job
Psalms
Proverbs
Ecclesiastes
Song of Solomon

The Wisdom Literature

The Wisdom Literature:

Job: Why do men serve God? Is it for gain, or is it because of devotion and commitment?

Psalms: the Jewish hymnal.

Proverbs: a collection of principles and axioms containing the distilled wisdom of the ages.

Ecclesiastes: What is the meaning of life under the sun? What really matters?

Song of Solomon: a love song.

The books of Job, Psalms, Proverbs, Ecclesiastes, and Song of Solomon, are collectively called by different terms. When children are taught the simple classification of the various portions of the Bible, these books are usually called *poetry*. Though the books are poetic, it is misleading to call them the books of poetry because there is much poetry elsewhere in the Bible also. A more compelling reason to use a different term, however, is the content of these books. They deal with man's approach to life on earth in all its aspects. Therefore, they are among the most practical of books one can study on the subject of life. A better name for them is *Wisdom Literature*.

The Hebrew word for *wise* is *chakam* or *hakam*. The word for *wisdom* is *chokmah* or *hokhma*. I deliberately mention these different spellings because they can be confusing when one is reading material about this literature. The initial letter of both *hakam* and *hokhma* is a guttural *h*. Some transliterate it with merely the *h*, while others transliterate it with the *ch* to bring out the guttural pronunciation of the letter. We will refer to the books as wisdom literature, with no further mention of the Hebrew words.

Since these books are written as poetry, there are phrases and expressions in them that are harder to understand than the books of history. Most of us feel more comfortable interpreting prose than we do poetry, because we deal with the prose style of writing so much more, but the messages of the books can be understood. Overlook the obscure expressions, and look for the message of the passage.

English poetry has rhyming words, and it usually has a rhythm or meter in the syllables of each line. But Hebrew poetry is not like that. If it were the rhyming sounds and rhythm of their language that made it poetry, then its beauty would have been lost when it was translated into other languages. Instead, Hebrew poetry has rhyming thoughts. A thought is expressed, then it is repeated in different words with perhaps a little more intensity in the meaning. Or a thought is expressed, with the second line expressing an opposite as a contrast.

Time of the writing of the books:

Wisdom literature flourished in the days of David and Solomon, particularly in the days of Solomon. The Bible says, "Solomon's wisdom excelled the wisdom of all the children of the east, and all the wisdom of Egypt. For he was wiser than all men; than Ethan the Ezrahite, and Heman, and Calcol, and Darda, the sons of Mahol: and his fame was in all the nations round about. And he spoke three thousand proverbs; and his songs were a thousand and five. And he spoke of trees, from the cedar that is in Lebanon even unto the hyssop that springeth out of the wall: he spake also of beasts, and of birds, and of creeping things, and of fishes" (1 Kings 4:30-33).

Therefore, it seems that most of the material in the five books of wisdom literature was collected or written during the period of history that we call the United Kingdom. However, since two of the books, Psalms and Proverbs, are collections, they were not all written at the same time. For example, the book of Psalms includes a psalm written by Moses who lived close to 500 years earlier than King Solomon (Psalm 90). One section of the book of Proverbs is made up of proverbs that were collected by Solomon, but were copied in their present form by men in the days of King Hezekiah, who lived over 200 years after Solomon (Prov. 25-29).

Purpose for the books:

Although there is an overlapping in subject matter, each book serves its own purpose. The dialogues of Job explore why men serve God: is it for gain, or is it because of devotion and commitment?

The book of Psalms was the Jewish hymnal. It contains praise and prayers couched in the most beautiful language imaginable. Its figures and metaphors are among the most sublime and familiar in the English language. Generations of mankind have drawn comfort from these poems and songs for three thousand years. The psalms are the musings and overflowing of the most devout minds. They give us the words to express our most sacred and holy thoughts.

Proverbs is a collection of principles and axioms containing the distilled wisdom of the ages. Such principles and axioms are found among all civilizations, but the ones included here are the principles of wisdom that God's Spirit deemed of enough value to save for the guidance of all generations. The Proverbs emphasize that the beginning of wisdom is the fear of Jehovah. Not only is there information on how to conduct one's business affairs, there is a spiritual slant on all the advice given. Every young person would do well to read carefully the book of Proverbs and then determine to follow its principles throughout his whole life. Each of us will be a wiser, happier person by learning from the experiences of others and practicing the principles of life that work best.

Ecclesiastes is the most philosophic of the books of wisdom literature. The author looks for meaning in life *under the sun*, that is, life on earth. He explores all the activities one may busy oneself with and concludes that only one thing really matters in life: whether one serves God — all the rest is vanity, empty, without substance, a dead end street.

The Song of Solomon is a love song. The writer deals beautifully and chastely with the feelings of affection, romance, and sexual attraction which enter into the courting process and into marriage. Not once is sexual immorality even hinted at. It is hard for people in such a wanton, lustful age as ours to realize that such feelings as love and physical attraction can be described in a holy manner, yet what a powerful, helpful lesson to learn!

The scope of our study here:

This series of eight books covering the whole Bible is a survey of the narrative cycle of the Bible story, a survey of the scheme of redemption that God designed for mankind. Therefore it is beyond the scope of this study to delve into the wisdom literature in detail. Just as other books in the series place the writings of the prophets into their place in history and give an introduction to the prophet's message, so we place these books of wisdom literature into their place in the chronology of the Bible. We will survey each book and give the gist of its message, with its primary lessons. We will discuss briefly the time of writing and authors of each book. Our hope is that this introduction to the books will lay a foundation for later, more detailed studies.

The Book of Job
Will a Man Serve God for Nought?

A brief summary of the story of Job:

The book of Job begins and ends with a section of prose. The first two chapters set the stage for the rest of the book by describing Job as a righteous man who had been blessed by God, and then by telling of the slander Satan made against his character. The poetic section begins in chapter 3 and continues through all the speeches that were made, through the first half of the last chapter. The last half of the last chapter returns to the style of prose, as Job is vindicated.

Job was a righteous man who served God with all his heart, and God blessed him with many riches, a large family, and the respect of many friends. One day when Satan came before God, God asked if he had observed Job. Satan responded by accusing Job of serving God only because God had blessed him. Satan said that if Job were stripped of his blessings, he would curse God to His face.

God did not let the challenge go by. He allowed Satan to strip Job of everything he had: all of his possessions and all of his children — but Job did not sin. He kept his relationship with God intact.

Satan threw down his challenge again. He said Job would give up his possessions, but that he would quickly curse God if his health were taken away. God allowed Satan to smite Job with great affliction — but Job remained faithful.

To add to his misery, three of Job's acquaintances came to comfort him, and remained to accuse him of wickedness. They were: Eliphaz the Temanite, Bildad the Shuhite, and Zophar the Naamathite. There are three rounds of speeches, except that in the third round, Zophar does not speak. In each round, one man speaks, and Job answers him; then another man speaks, and Job answers him.

The three men took the position that since God is absolutely just, and no man is righteous before God, then Job's affliction proved that Job was wicked, or his trouble

---

Do men serve God only for the blessings He gives?

Is suffering always a sign of God's wrath?

Or, is prosperity always a sign of God's pleasure?

Do we have a right to question God about why He does the things He does, or why He allows the things He allows?

God is Sovereign!

Job had a covenant with God, and he remained faithful to his covenant, even when he did not understand what was happening to him.

Job never learned why he was suffering. He learned he was to pass the test even though he did not understand why the test had come.

would not have come upon him. They admonished him to repent and confess his wrong-doing, and God wouldforgive and restore him.

Job answered the charge by protesting his innocence, and by showing the utter fallacy of his friends' arguments. He pointed out that calamity comes upon the righteous, and that prosperity comes to the wicked. Job protested that, though he was not a perfect man, he had not sinned some great sin that had brought on his calamity. He declared that if only he could talk to God, and argue his case with Him, then God would vindicate him.

After three rounds of speeches by the friends, and Job's answer to each one, a man named Elihu speaks up. He had listened to all the others had said, and he objected to the fallacies that each of the men had made in his reasoning.

Finally God spoke out of a whirlwind and addressed Job. His point was: Job, you are in no position to question me, or what I do. God did not deal with who was right, Job or his friends, in His speech to Job. He dealt with Job's utter inability to contest anything with God. In utter humility, Job accepted God's rebuke. The story between Job and God is that of two partners in an agreement, who have some difficulties that test their relationship, but which do not destroy it, because of their mutual commitment to that relationship.

Then, in vindication of Job, God rebuked the three friends for falsely accusing Job and He demanded that they seek forgiveness by offering sacrifices through the hand of Job. God restored Job's wealth, giving him twice as much as before. He gave Job seven sons and three daughters again, and Job's brothers and sisters and friends sought him as they had before.

Introduction to the Book

With this brief summary in mind, let us look at some information about the book itself, and at some of the primary lessons taught. Then we will return to the text and give it a fuller survey.

There are many obscure passages in the book of Job. For example, there are Hebrew words found in the book that are found no where else in the Bible. That means it is very difficult for the translators to decide what the words mean. Then, since most of the book is written in poetic style rather than prose, it is more difficult to understand than the books of history. Try to overlook the things that are difficult to interpret, and look for the point each speaker is making. That overall message can be understood.

In order to simplify the thoughts, we have expressed the speeches in prose. But in doing so, we lose the beauty of the book. Look at our short explanations of the primary thoughts of the passage to help you understand what is being said, but then read the book carefully to see its beauty. Help your students see that same beauty. Let us be the first to say that we have the same trouble interpreting the obscure phrases that others have. Sometimes there is a line in a speech that we do not know how to express, because we do not know exactly what the speaker had in his mind at that moment. Our analysis is a simple interpretation of the book; ours is no more inspired than some other explanation you may see. Use this work, and any other works by men, as a spring board to help you do your own study of the book. But please do your own study. Do not let the difficult passages frighten you against learning its great lessons.

Date of the writing of the book:

Most conservative scholars date the writing of the book in the Solomonic age when Biblical wisdom literature flourished. The issues dealt with in the book match similar material in Psalms and Proverbs. Also, the vocabulary of the book fits well with the vocabulary of other wisdom literature of the day. The story itself, however, is much older, going back to the age of the patriarchs. Three reasons may be given for this conclusion:

1. The Chaldeans were still leading a nomadic lifestyle in the days of Job (1:17). They were a wandering tribe in the Arabian desert before they moved into the lower Euphrates River valley and established a settled existence in and around the city of Babylon.

2. There is no evidence of any connection between Job and Abraham, and certainly no evidence that Job was a part of the covenant between God and Abraham's descendants. Instead God spoke to Job directly, as He dealt with all faithful men before He chose Abraham for His chosen family (38:1; 42:7). Job definitely acted the part of a patriarch, offering sacrifices for his children and for his three friends (1:5; 42:7-9).

   When God separated Abraham from the rest of mankind in order to develop a special nation that could become His own, and after He gave His law to the Israelites on Mt. Sinai, He continued to communicate with others as He had during the whole patriarchal era. It is possible, therefore, that Job was a faithful servant of God even though he was not an Israelite. Most of the world outside of God's chosen people turned their backs on Jehovah very early in their history, but we do meet a few worshipers of Jehovah who were not part of His nation — such as Melchizedek (Gen. 14:18-20). But the lifestyle described in the book of Job certainly fits the style of the early patriarchs.

3. The third, and perhaps most telling reason, is that Job lived a much longer life than was common after the early patriarchs. Job had lived a full life up until the time of his ordeal. He had ten children, and they were grown (Job 1:4-5). Yet he lived 140 years after his ordeal (42:16). Abraham lived to be 175 years old, Isaac, 180 years, and Jacob, 147 years. Yet by the time of United Kingdom, David was described as an old man when he was only 70 years old. These facts argue that Job lived well back in the patriarchal age.

The story was, therefore, already old in Solomon's day. Nothing is told of the historian and poet who wrote it in the form which we have. Whoever it was, he had a very loyal devotion to Jehovah, because the real message of the book is that Job did not give up his faith in God during his troubles. His relationship to God was not based on his own condition from one day to the next, or upon his feelings. It was based upon the covenant (the agreement, the promise) that existed between himself and God.

Let us outline the book in this way:
I. Satan's challenge: "Will Job serve God for nought?" (1:1-2:10)
   A. His possessions and family are taken away.
   B. His health is taken away.
   C. But Job remains faithful to God.

II. Job's friends come to comfort and stay to accuse (2:11-31:40).
   A. Job's friends come to comfort him (2:11-13).
   B. The first round of speeches:
      1. Job's lament; he wishes he had never been born (3:1-26).
      2. Eliphaz speaks; and Job answers him (4:1-7:21).
      3. Bildad speaks; and Job answers him (8:1-10:22).

  4. Zophar speaks; and Job answers him (11:1-14:22).
 C. The second round of speeches:
  1. Eliphaz speaks; and Job answers him (15:1-17:16).
  2. Bildad speaks; and Job answers him (18:1-19:29).
  3. Zophar speaks; and Job answers him (20:1-21:34).
 D. The third round of speeches:
  1. Eliphaz speaks; and Job answers him (22:1-24:25).
  2. Bildad speaks; and Job answers him (25:1-26:14).
  3. Job continues with his cry before God (27:1-31:40).

III. Elihu speaks (32:1-37:24).
 A. He is angry with Job for justifying himself and blaming God for his calamity.
 B. He is angry with the three friends because, though they could not refute Job's arguments, they condemned him.

IV. God challenges Job (38:1-42:6).
 A. Job, you are in no position to question my actions (38:1-41:34).
 B. Job humbly accepts God's rebuke (42:1-6).

V. Job is vindicated (42:7-17).
 A. God rebukes the three friends.
 B. Job's blessings are returned.

Analysis of the main lessons of Job:

  The first subject that leaps to our minds when we think of Job is the matter of suffering. What causes suffering? How should I interpret it when I am doing my best to serve the Lord, and yet suffering enters my life? Is God angry with me? Is my suffering the result of some sin that I do not know I have committed? Or, is God not really just after all, and all my service vain? Why can I look around me and see good people who are suffering, and I can see wicked people who are prospering? Is there an answer? At some point in our lives, every person who has lived to adulthood has had to deal with the matter of suffering of some kind: whether it is sickness, death of a loved one, financial reversal, or something else. Therefore questions about the "whys" of suffering arise in every generation, and in every life. That means that the questions that Job and his friends raise are of utmost importance to us. We need to study the book to see their questions, and to see their misconceptions as well as their correct interpretations so that we can analyze our own thinking in times of trial.

  But the lessons about suffering are not the primary point of the book of Job. The question of suffering forms the basis for the conflict in Job's mind about his relationship with Jehovah, but his attitude toward that relationship is the basic lesson of the book. Look at Satan's accusations when God asked him if he had observed Job. Satan said, "Does Job serve God for nothing? Have you not made a hedge around him so that nothing bad can happen to him? You have blessed everything he has touched. If you put forth your hand and took away his possessions, he would curse you to your face!" Then when Job remained faithful after losing all his wealth and all his children, Satan appeared before God again and said, "Skin for skin! A man will give up everything he owns for his life. Put forth your hand now and touch his bone and flesh, and he will curse you to your face!" So God allowed Satan to smite Job with great physical suffering, but Job remained faithful to God.

Why did Job serve God anyway? Why do any of us serve God? Most people treat God as an occasional friend, or as a wandering pet that shows up from time to time, or as an insurance policy that is left in the desk drawer until it is needed. Some look upon God as some sort of fairy who will pour great riches upon us if we will only do certain things to win His favor. In contrast, the Bible emphasizes that God wants a constant relationship based on mutual commitment to a covenant made between Himself and each human being. Therefore every aspect of life and living, including suffering and even death, must come under that covenant relationship.

In the days of the United Kingdom there was much discussion about the proper pursuits in life and the meaning of life. In this context, the book of Job shows that the search for the meaning of life in all its aspects will be vain and unsuccessful unless it is guided by the religious perspective of man in his constant covenant relationship with God.

Therefore the great theme of Job is not suffering. It is, rather, that Job had made an agreement with God, and because of that agreement, he remained faithful to God even when he did not understand why his sufferings had come upon him, even when he thought God had sent his sufferings. Job, then, becomes an example to us of faithfulness and of constancy in a relationship. Job determined to serve God because of who He is, and because of all that He is. I am to make that same determination. He is my Creator; He gave me life; I therefore owe Him respect, honor, and obedience even if there were no blessings at all in return for my service. But in return for my commitment, God promises to be my God, to be my Father, and to give me a home in heaven itself. Each person who has ever served God faithfully will be greatly blessed — but not, necessarily, by outward physical blessings during life on earth. Even if I have only the barest necessities of life, even if I wrestle with sickness and physical handicaps all my life, even if I must lose every single one of my family to death, even if I face severe persecutions as a result of my service to God — my covenant relationship with Jehovah is worth it. This was Job's attitude. When the New Testament speaks of Job's patience, this is what it is talking about (James 5:11). It was not that Job did not express grief and pain over his sufferings — because he did. It was not that Job did not wonder why all the troubles had come upon him — because he did. He was *patient* because he remained steadfast in his relationship with God, even when things looked their darkest. This is the primary lesson of the book of Job. This is the primary lesson each one of us must learn.

Notice a few verses which show clearly that Job had a defined relationship with God, a covenant with Him. The Lord said to Satan, "Hast thou considered my servant Job?" (1:8; 2:3). That God called Job His slave or servant shows that He considered Job to be His in a special way. Job had called upon God, had relied upon Him, and God had answered him (12:4). Job said God was his witness, the One who vouched for him (16:19). Job was committed to the obedience of God's commandments as a way of life (23:11-12). In contrast to the godless, Job called upon God at all times (27:8-10).

Also notice some verses that show that Job remained faithful to that commitment. When he lost everything he had in one severe blow after another, he said, "Naked came I out of my mother's womb, and naked shall I return thither: the Lord gave, and the Lord hath taken away; blessed be the name of the Lord." In all this, Job did not sin nor charge God foolishly (1:21-22). When boils broke out all over his body, and even his wife thought he should curse God and die, Job said, "Shall we receive good at the hand of God, and shall we not receive evil?" In all this, Job did not sin with his lips (2:10). When Job was longing for death, he said he had one consolation: "I have not denied the words of the Holy One" (6:10). "Though He slay me, I will hope in Him" (13:15). "I have kept His way and not turned aside…" (23:10-12). "For as long as life is in me…my lips certainly will not speak unjustly… Till I die I will not put away my integrity, I hold fast my righteousness and will not let it go" (27:1-6).

Another lesson from the book of Job is that one of the realities of life is that God can be known only as He reveals Himself, and He has the final say in determining to what extent He chooses to do so. God has never promised to answer all our questions in this life. This understanding must be in the person who seeks to interpret life under the sun.

The book does not reveal to Job the *why* of his sufferings, but it presents a framework of hope that will help us face our sufferings. Through Job's example, we receive considerable enlightenment concerning the variety of causes of suffering. We learn that suffering or prosperity cannot be the basis for determining whether a man is wicked or righteous. We learn that there are many causes for suffering, and that often we cannot know the reasons. What we must do is maintain our commitment to God and trust in Him with our whole being. We, like Job, must learn that we are to pass the tests that come our way, even when we do not understand the causes behind the tests. Faith fills the gap between our understanding of why something is happening and our acceptance of it. Faith gives us the assurance that God is still in control, and that our service and loyalty to Him is worth whatever comes our way.

A Fuller Analysis of the Book

Satan's challenge (1:1-2:10):

Job was blameless and upright before God, one who feared God and turned away from evil. God was pleased with him and had blessed him greatly. Job had seven sons and three daughters, and he had great wealth: 7,000 sheep, 3,000 camels, 500 yoke of oxen, 500 female donkeys, and very many servants. He was the greatest of all the men of the east.

His sons and daughters feasted together often in the homes of the sons, and after each feast, Job would rise early in the morning and offer sacrifices for each of them. He said, "Perhaps my sons have sinned and cursed God in their hearts."

One day when the sons of God presented themselves before Jehovah, Satan came also. The Lord said, "Satan, have you noticed my servant Job? There is none like him on the earth: a blameless and upright man, fearing God and turning away from evil."

Satan replied, "Does Job fear God for nothing? You have built a hedge around him and around all he has. Everything he touches prospers. But if you took away the blessings you have given him, he would curse you to your face."

If God had let Satan's slander of Job's character stand, then Job could never have proven himself truly faithful. So God said, "Behold, everything he has in your power. You may take away his blessings, but do not touch Job himself." So Satan left the presence of God.

A day came when the sons and daughters were feasting, this time at the home of the oldest son. Job was at home when a messenger came to him saying, "The Sabeans have attacked and taken your oxen and your donkeys. They have killed all your servants, and I am the only one who has escaped to come and tell you."

While he was still telling his news, another messenger came saying that fire had fallen from heaven and had burned up Job's sheep, with the servants attending them. While he was still talking, a third servant came telling that the Chaldeans had raided and taken Job's camels and had killed that group of servants. And worst of all, still another messenger came with the horrible news that a wind had struck the house of Job's oldest son and had killed all his children and their servants.

Job arose and tore his clothes and shaved his head as signs of deep grief, but he fell to the ground and worshiped the Lord, saying, "I was naked when I came from my mother's womb, and I will be naked when my life ends. The Lord gives and the Lord takes away. Blessed be the name of the Lord." Job had passed the test. He did not sin as Satan had predicted he would.

Again Satan came before God, and God asked, "Satan, have you seen my servant Job? There is none like him in all the earth. He is blameless and upright, he fears God and turns away from evil. And he still holds fast to his integrity, even though you caused him to be ruined without a cause."

Satan was not convinced. He said, "Skin for skin! A man will give up everything he has if he can but spare his life. But put forth your hand and touch his body and he will curse you to your face!"

God accepted the challenge again in order to allow Job to clear the slander against his character. He said, "He is in your power, only you must spare his life."

So Satan struck Job with severe boils over all his body, from the sole of his foot to the top of his head. Job was in such misery he sat in the ashes and scraped himself with a broken piece of pottery.

This time even his wife said, "Are you still holding to your integrity? Curse God and die!"

But Job replied, "You speak as one of the foolish ones! Shall we accept only good from God, and not adversity?" In all of this, Job did not sin with his lips. He had passed the test again!

Job's friends come (2:11-13):

Job's friends and acquaintances heard of all the trouble that had come upon him. Three of his friends came to comfort him: Eliphaz the Temanite, Bildad the Shuhite, and Zophar the Naamathite. While they were still a distance away, they looked and saw Job sitting among the ashes. Job looked so bad they could hardly recognize him. The three friends lifted up their voices and wept. They tore their clothes and sprinkled dust upon their heads as signs of deep distress. They sat down near Job, but they were so overcome by his condition they did not talk to him for seven full days. They could tell his pain was too great.

The first round of speeches (3:1-14:22):
Job's lament (3:1-26):

Let the day of my birth be cursed. Let it be blotted out of the calendar, because it did not shut the door of the womb against me to hide trouble from my eyes. Why did I not perish at birth? Why were there knees to receive me and breasts to feed me? If I could have been buried as a stillborn child, then I could already be at peace with the kings and wise men who have lived and died before me. Even captives and slaves have peace there. Why is light and life given to those who suffer? Why can the one who seeks death like a hidden treasure not find it? My worst fears have come upon me.

Eliphaz speaks (4:1-5:27):

Will you be impatient with me if I speak? Yet I must speak! You have taught others, but now that trials have come your way, you are impatient. Think of it now: Who ever perished being innocent? When were the upright ever destroyed? It is those who plow iniquity who harvest it. God destroys the wicked by His own breath.

I had a dream that made me tremble. In the dark of the night a spirit passed before my face and made the hair of my flesh stand up. It stood still, but I could not see its form clearly. There was silence, and then I heard a voice, saying, "Can mankind be just before God? He does not even put His trust in His own servants, and He brings charges against His angels. Those who live on this earth are broken in pieces between morning and evening. They die, and still do not gain wisdom."

I have seen the foolish taking root, but it has not lasted. His sons are far from safety; they are oppressed in the gates. His harvest is eaten by others; the schemers take his wealth. For affliction does not just come from the dirt, nor trouble spring from the ground.

As for me, I will seek God. He does great and wondrous things. He sets on high those who are lowly, but He captures the cunning in their own devices. He saves the poor from the mighty and gives the helpless hope.

Do not despise this discipline that the Almighty has brought upon you. He inflicts pain, but then He heals. He will deliver you from all your trials when He has reproved you. We have investigated the matter carefully, so hear it and know it for yourself.

Job answers Eliphaz (6:1-7:21):
I have a right to complain! If my anguish and misery could be weighed on a scale, it would be heavier than the sand of the seas. The terrors of God are arrayed against me. Does a wild donkey bray when it has grass? Does an ox bellow when it has fodder? I have reason to cry out.

Oh that God would grant my request! Oh that He would loose me and let me die! I still have this consolation: I have not denied the words of the Holy One. But how can I endure longer?

A despairing man should be shown kindness from his friend, but my brothers have been as undependable as a water branch that dries up in the summer heat. There is plenty of water in it when everything is wet; but when things get dry, and its water is needed, it dries up. And, indeed, that is the way you have become. You see a terror, and you are afraid. Have I asked you to give me something? Have I asked for your wealth? Teach me, and I will be silent. Show me where I have erred. Look at me and see if I lie to you. Is there injustice on my tongue? Cannot I recognize calamities?

My life is like that of a slave who wishes his life could end. I lie down, and I say, "When shall I arise?" But the night continues, and I toss until dawn. My flesh is covered with worms and a crust of dirt; it is broken and loathsome. My days are swifter than a weaver's shuttle, and come to an end with no hope. Remember, O God, that my life is but a breath and my eyes will never see happiness again. The one who dies never returns; he does not come home again. Therefore, I will not keep silent. I will cry out in my anguish. If I say my bed will comfort me, then I have terrible dreams that frighten me. My soul would choose death rather than my pains. Leave me alone, for my days are but a breath.

Why single me out for attention, O God? Will you never turn your gaze away from me? Have I sinned? What have I done to Thee? Why have you made me your target? Why do you not pardon my transgressions?

Bildad speaks (8:1-22):
How long are you going to keep talking like this? Does God pervert justice? If your sons sinned against Him, then He delivered them to the reward for their transgressions. They got what they deserved! If you would seek God and beg for his mercy, surely He would arouse Himself and restore the estate you had while you were righteous.

Inquire of past generations and learn the lessons of our fathers. We've only lived since yesterday and do not yet know anything. Learn these lessons: Can the papyrus grow where there is no marsh? Can the rushes grow without water? So are the paths of all those who forget God. The hope of the godless will perish. His confidence is as fragile as a spider's web. God will not reject a man of integrity, nor will He support the wicked man. If you will seek for Him, He will fill your mouth with laughter.

Job answers (9:1-10:22):
I know God blesses the man of integrity and punishes the wicked, but how can a man be right with God? If I wished to dispute with Him, I could not answer Him one time out of a thousand. I see Him do marvelous things on every side: He removes mountains; He shakes the earth; He commands the sun not to shine; He stretches out the heavens, and tramples down the sea; He made the constellations. But even if He passed right by me, I would not see Him. If He snatched something away, who could stop Him? Who could say to Him, "What are you doing?"

God will not turn back His anger. How then can I answer Him, or choose my words to speak to Him? Even if my words were right, I would have to beg for the mercy of my judge. If I called Him, and He answered, I could not believe that He is listening to what I say, because He bruises me with a tempest. He will not even let me get a breath, because He saturates me with trouble. If it is a matter of strength, He is the strong one; if it is a matter of justice, who can challenge Him? Though I am righteous, my words would condemn me. I am guiltless, but He destroys the innocent with the wicked. If it is not God who does so, then who is it?

My days are passing faster than a runner, and I see no good. Though I say, "I will forget my complaint, and I will be cheerful," I am afraid of my own pain. I am treated as a wicked one, but what shall I do about it? If I should wash myself with snow and scrub myself with lye, yet you would plunge me into the pit.

God is not a man whom I can answer, or whom I can take to court. There is no umpire between us who can lay his hand upon us both. Please let Him remove His rod from me, and then I will not be afraid of Him.

I hate my life! I will say to God, "Do not condemn me. Let me know *why* you contend with me. Is it right for you to oppress me and reject all the labor of my hands? Are you looking with the eyes of men as you look at me? Are you seeking for my guilt and searching for my sin? You know I am not guilty, yet there is no deliverance from your hand. O God, your hands formed me. Now will you also destroy me? You granted me life and loving-kindness. If I sin, you take note of me and will not acquit me of guilt. If I am wicked, then woe to me! But even if I am righteous, I dare not lift up my head. You hunt me like a lion, and you show your power against me. Hardship after hardship is with me."

Why was I born? Oh that I had been carried from the womb to the tomb. Will God not let my few days alone? Please withdraw from me so that I may have a little joy before I die, before I depart for the land of darkness from which there is no return.

Job thinks that God is the One who is inflicting his pain and suffering, and he does not understand why. He knows there is no huge sin in his life to cause God to punish him — yet the suffering appears to be a punishment. Why? He wants to talk to God, to argue his point with Him, but he acknowledges that he would not know how even if he had a chance. There is no one to even mediate for him. But notice that God is still his God; he does not understand God's actions, but he does not sever the relationship.

Zophar speaks (11:1-20):
Listen to the multitude of words! Do you think you can talk yourself out of your troubles? You say you are innocent in your own eyes, but oh that God might speak! God has even *forgotten* some of the wickedness you have done!

Can you discover the depths of God, or His outer limits? They are as high as the heavens and as deep as the realm of the dead. What can you know? If He passes by, or if He closes something, or if He calls an assembly, who can stop Him? For He knows false men, and He sees wickedness without investigating. If you would direct your heart right, and put wickedness away from you, then you could lift up your face without defect. You would be able to forget your troubles as surely as you forget water that has already passed by you in a stream. Your life would be brighter than noonday. You could trust again because you would have hope. You could lie down and none would disturb you. But the eyes of the wicked will fail and there will be no escape for him. Their only hope for release is death.

Zophar is making up words for the Lord. He says that God would declare Job wicked if He spoke aloud, but look back to 1:8 and 2:3 to see how God really described Job.

Job speaks (12:1-14:22):

Truly you are the people, and wisdom will die with you! I have as much intelligence as you; I am not inferior. But I am a joke to my friends. The one who relied upon God has become a joke. The one who is at ease holds calamity in contempt.

But look around you: The destroyers prosper; those who provoke God are secure; the wicked are not always experiencing trouble. The things around us in nature all work out according to God's plan. The life of every living thing and the breath of all mankind is in His hand. God is the source of all wisdom and might. He tears down and it cannot be rebuilt. He causes things to happen which cannot be undone. Both the misled and the misleader belong to Him. He can make the counselors walk barefoot (in disgrace), and He can make fools of judges. He deprives the trusted ones of speech, and He takes away the discernment of the elders. He makes nations great, and then destroys them. He can put the chief of the people out to wander in the wilderness. My eyes have seen all these inequalities of life, just as your eyes have seen them. What you know, I also know. I am not inferior to you.

I want to speak with God, to argue my point. All you are doing is smearing me with lies. You are worthless physicians. I wish you would just be silent! Will you speak deceitfully for God? Aren't you afraid to speak for Him? Hasn't His dread fallen upon you? Your memorable sayings are proverbs of ashes. What you say does not apply to me. Be silent while I speak. Though God slay me, I will still hope in Him. But I want to argue my ways before Him. This is my hope. A godless man has no right to approach God, but I do have. I have prepared my case to present before Him and I know I will be vindicated.

O God, please do these two things for me: Remove your hand from me so that I will not be terrified of you, so that I may call upon you and you will answer. And, O God, tell me what I have done wrong so that I will know why you are hiding your face from me. You are making me suffer for every iniquity I have committed from my youth until now.

Life is short and full of trouble! There is hope for a tree that is cut down. Its stump may grow old and dry, but then when the moisture comes it will sprout again. But when a man dies, he never returns. It is like water that evaporates into the air. Oh that you would hide me in that place of the dead! Hide me until your wrath returns to you. But you watch my every step. My transgressions are sealed up in a bag. Mountains fall after a while; water wears down stones. You wash away what grows in the dirt, and you destroy what man builds. But my sins are sealed up; they are still here. My suffering continues.

The second round of speeches (15:1-21:34):

All four men continue making the same points, except they intensify their arguments each time. The three friends continue to say that Job must be wicked and they press him to repent. He denies he is guilty of some sin that would prompt punishment from God, but he thinks God is afflicting him, and he continues longing to present his case before God. Job also continues to argue that one cannot tell by looking at the circumstances of a person's life whether he is righteous or wicked.

Eliphaz speaks (15:1-35):

Your mouth is like the east wind — you are blowing hot air! It pours out iniquity. Were you the first man ever born? Does God tell you His secrets? What do you know that we do not know? There are men here much older than you. Why do you turn away from God and let such words pour out of your mouth? What is man that he can be pure before God? Even the stars are not clean in God's sight. How much more filthy is man who drinks up iniquity like water.

Listen to me and I will tell you what wise men have been told by their fathers: Wicked men have pain as long as they live. They wander around looking for food. Constantly in trouble, anguish, and fear, they live in shacks. Nothing they attempt will succeed. Fire consumes the tents of the corrupt.

Job responds (16:1-17:16):

Sorry comforters are you all! Is there no end to your words? What makes you keep on arguing? I could talk like you if I were in your position, but I would not. I would try to comfort you and lessen your pain.

God has wasted me. He has turned me over to the wicked. They glare at me, and gnash on me with their teeth, and smite me on the cheek. I was at ease, but God took me and shattered me. He took me by the nape of the neck and has shaken me to pieces. He has brought out all His archers and set me up for them to use as target practice. I have cried until my face is flushed and deep darkness is upon my eyelids. I do not understand why it has come upon me because there is no violence in my hands and my prayers are pure.

O Ground, do not hide my blood! I know that heaven *does* hear my pleas, because my Witness is there. My friends scoff at me, but my weeping is to the Lord, and not to them. O that I might plead with God the way one can plead with a neighbor. Soon I can leave this world and never come back. O God, please stand security for me. Do not exalt these friends, because you have hidden understanding from them.

God has made me a byword, one upon whom men spit. The upright are appalled when they learn about me. Nevertheless the righteous will hold to his way and only grow stronger.

But come now, all of you. I do not find a wise man among you. My days are passed; everything I had hoped for is gone; my only hope now is the grave.

Bildad speaks (18:1-21):

How long will you keep hunting for words? Show some understanding and then we can talk to you. You tear yourself with anger, but do you think the rocks will run from your anger?

Indeed, it is the *wicked* who suffer! He has no light; his vigor is shortened; his own schemes bring him down; he falls into a trap. Terrors frighten him; his strength is famished; his skin is devoured by disease; his tent is destroyed. Memories of him pass from the earth; no one even remembers his name; he has no children left behind him. All who hear of his fate are appalled. This is the place of the one who does not know God.

Job answers (19:1-29):

How long will you torment me? These ten times you have insulted me. Even if I have sinned, you are not helping. My sin is still here; it is my problem. Know then that God has wronged me; I do not deserve what has happened.

I shout for help, but there is no justice. He has made a wall against me so that I cannot pass; He has stripped my honor from me; He breaks me down on every side; He has uprooted my hope like a tree; He has kindled His anger against me and has treated me as His enemy. He has taken away my brothers, my acquaintances, my relatives, and all my intimate friends. My servants ignore me when I tell them to do something. My breath is offensive to my wife; even young children despise me. Everyone I love has turned against me. My bone clings to my flesh, and I have escaped by the skin of my teeth. Pity me, O my friends! For the hand of God has struck me.

Oh that my words were written in a book! May they be engraved on a rock forever! I know that my Redeemer lives and that at the last He will stand upon the earth. Even after my flesh is destroyed, I will see Him. *(Job is saying, I know that someday my Redeemer will stand upon the earth and vindicate me, even if it is after I am dead.)* If you continue to persecute me, then you had better be afraid of God's wrath also.

Job still thinks God is the source of his affliction. He says that God is treating him like the wicked, but Job is saying, "<u>I do not deserve it!</u>"

Zophar speaks (20:1-29):

The wicked man's triumph is short. He may reach to the heavens for a little while, but then he perishes like garbage. Those who knew him will forget him as if he had been a dream. His son has to learn to show kindness to the poor, and his hands will give back all his father stole. Though evil seems sweet as food to savor in his mouth, yet it turns to poison in his stomach. He swallows riches, but he will vomit them up. He gets no pleasure out of the things he has taken. God will rain His fierce anger upon him while he is eating at his table. He may try to flee from the weapon, but it will catch up with him. Complete darkness is held in reserve for his treasures, and the fire will devour him. This is the wicked man's inheritance from the Lord.

Job replies (21:1-34):

Put your hand over your mouth and let me speak; then you can mock me again. What you say about the wicked is not always true. When I think about the wicked, I am disturbed and horrified. Why is it that the wicked still live and become very powerful? Their children and grandchildren grow up around them and prosper; their houses are safe from fear. The wicked man's bull never fails; his cow never miscarries. His children play and sing in the streets. And suddenly he dies with no calamity having come upon him. Yet he said to God, "Leave me. I do not want to know of your ways. Who is the Almighty, that I should serve Him? What would I gain if I prayed?"

How often do you see the wicked reap the calamity they deserve? You say that God is storing away their punishment to bring it upon their sons; but that will not fit, because what do the wicked care if their children suffer? For it to serve any purpose, God must bring the calamity upon the wicked one himself.

One person dies in his full strength, having lived a life of ease and luxury. Another dies with a bitter spirit, never having tasted anything good. Both are buried in the same graveyard, and both are eaten by the worms.

You can ask anyone at all, even the wayfarer passing through, and he will tell you the wicked is reserved for the day of calamity. Yes, he will be punished, but not necessarily in this life. What good is all this comfort you offer? You are only telling lies!

Think about it. Can you tell whether a person is righteous or wicked by looking at his house? Can you tell by looking at his bank account? That is not the way God punishes the wicked.

The third round of speeches (22:1-31:40):
Eliphaz speaks (22:1-30):
Can a man be of use to God? Have you increased God's pleasure if you are righteous? What would He gain if you were blameless? Do you think He has reproved you because of your righteousness?

Your wickedness is great: you have taken pledges from the poor; you have stripped men naked; you have given no food or water to the hungry or thirsty; you have sent widows away empty handed and have crushed orphans. That is why there are snares all around you and your way is so dark you cannot see.

Isn't God in the highest part of heaven? Do you think He cannot see through the clouds to see your deeds? Are you going to keep walking in the paths of the wicked? They told God, "Depart from us. What can you do to us?" But the righteous will rejoice when they are cut off and their abundance has been consumed with fire.

Yield now to God, and good will come to you. Receive instruction at His mouth, and you will be restored. Place your ill-gotten gold in the dust, and the Almighty will become your gold and silver. Then you will be able to lift up your face to Him, and He will hear you. Humble yourself and He will save you.

Notice that the speeches are getting much harder. The three are stern in saying it is only the wicked who suffer. All three of them are saying that all the righteousness Job had shown earlier was only a sham. They think he prospered for only a short time, and that his horrible wickedness has caught up with him. They are no longer just implying there is a hidden sin, they are openly accusing him of fitting into the category of the grossly wicked and disobedient — deserving every pain and grief that has come upon him. They are looking at Job as we might look at a friend who had just been exposed as a serial killer. They had thought of Job as a righteous man before, but if all this calamity has come upon him, he must be terribly wicked. It is this kind of sin that Job is denying; he is not saying that he has never sinned, but he is denying that he has done some great crime that deserves this kind of punishment.

Job replies (23:1-24:25):
My complaint today is rebellion, because God's hand is still heavy upon me. Oh, that I knew where I could find God, so that I might come before His presence. I would present my case before Him, and I would see what He answers. Would He oppose me with His great power? No, surely He would pay attention to me, and I know I would be delivered from my Judge.

But I cannot find Him. If I go forward, He is not there; if I turn backward, I cannot see Him; when He is doing something on my right side, or on my left side, I cannot see Him. He can see me with no problem. But I know that when He has finished trying me, I will come forth as refined gold, because I have kept His ways and I have not departed from the command of His lips. I have counted His words as greater than the food I eat.

He is unique; He stands alone. Who can oppose Him? Whatever His soul desires, that He does. Therefore, I would be dismayed in His presence. When I think about it, I am terrified of Him. The Almighty has terrified me by His actions, but I am not silenced by the deep darkness and deep gloom that covers me.

Why are there not times of judgment set by the Almighty? I see wicked people who remove the landmarks to increase their land; I see them seize animals from the poor. They push the needy out of their path, and make the poor hide themselves for protection. The poor have to harvest the fields for the wicked rich, but then have to spend the night with no covering from the cold. They have to carry the sheaves for the rich and tread their wine presses, but they do not have enough food and wine for their own needs. The souls of the wounded cry out, but God does not pay attention to them. Others rebel against the light of God, and refuse to walk in His ways. The murderer rises at dawn to kill another, and the adulterer watches for the night so that he can continue his wickedness in secret. But nothing is done!

Job was right to think that God would listen to his pleas, but Job was out of place when he thought he could fill his mouth with arguments to tell God why He should not have acted as He had. Job is looking at all the injustices that exist in this life, and he is indicating God is unconcerned and unjust because He is not punishing the wicked immediately.

Bildad speaks (25:1-6):
Dominion and awe belong to God; He establishes order in the universe. How then can a man be just before God? Even the moon and the stars are dim in comparison to Him, so how can a man have any glory before Him? Man is no more than a maggot, a worm!

Job replies (26:1-14):
In sarcasm, Job says: "What a help you are to the weak! What helpful insight you have provided! Who told you all these words of wisdom?"

Even the dead tremble before God. He stretches out the north over empty space, and hangs the earth on nothing. He wraps up water in the clouds, and they do not burst under the weight. He hides the face of the full moon with a cloud. He has marked out a circle on the surface of the water *(the horizon)*, as the boundary between day and night. The pillars of heaven tremble before Him. But these are only the fringes of His ways. How small a whisper we hear and understand about Him! Who can understand the thunder of His might?

Job continues his cry before God (27:1-31:40):
As my God lives, who has taken away my right, and the Almighty, who has embittered my soul, for as long as my life is in me, my lips will not speak unjustly, nor will my tongue utter deceit. Far be it from me that I should declare you right in what you have done, but I will never put away my integrity. I will hold fast to my righteousness and will not let it go. My conscience will not reproach me for my days.

May my enemy be treated as the wicked. For what hope do the godless have when he dies? Will God hear his cry when distress comes upon him? Will he take delight in the Almighty, and call upon Him at all times? This is the portion of the wicked man before the Almighty: though he has many sons, they will die by the sword; his survivors will die from the plague. Though he piles up silver and gathers many clothes, the just will wear the clothes and the innocent will divide the silver. Terrors overtake him like a flood; the east wind carries him away and he is gone.

Surely there is a mine for silver, and a place where they refine gold; iron comes from dirt, and copper from rocks; food comes from the earth, and sapphires from stones. But where does wisdom come from? Where can understanding be found? The deep says, "It is not in me." The sea say, "It is not with me." Pure gold cannot be given in exchange for it; silver cannot buy it. Its value cannot be measured by even the gold of Ophir, or by precious stones. The getting of wisdom is of much greater value than pearls. Where then does wisdom come from? It is hidden from the eyes of all the living. Destruction and death say, "We have heard of it." Only God knows its way, and He knows its place. For He looks to the ends of the earth and He sees everything under the sky. He saw it and declared it; He established it and searched it out. And to man He says, "Behold, the fear of the Lord, that is wisdom; and to depart from evil is understanding."

Oh, how I long for the days that are passed, for the days when God watched over me, when His lamp shone over my head. I was in my prime when the friendship of God was over my tent, when the Almighty was with me, and my children were around me. When I went to the gates of the city, the young men saw me and stepped aside; the old men stood in my presence; the princes stopped their talking to hear my words. Because I delivered the poor who cried for help; I helped the orphan; I made the widow's heart rejoice. I was eyes to the blind and feet to the lame; I was a father to the needy. Then I thought I would die in my own home at the end of a long life. I thought my root was spread out to the waters and that the dew would be all night on my branches. My friends waited and listened to my words as if they were the spring rain. I smiled on them, and I chose a way for them, and I sat as their chief.

But now the young men mock me — the sons of the ones who used to be so far below me they had to roam the wastelands and search for food. And now I have become a taunt to them, a byword! They abhor me, and stand aloof from me; they even spit in my face. Because God has loosed His bowstring and has afflicted me. They profit from my destruction, and no one stops them. Terrors are turned against me. They pursue my honor as the wind, and my prosperity has passed away like a cloud. My soul is poured out; days of affliction have seized me; my gnawing pains take no rest. He has cast me into the mire, and I have become like dust and ashes. O God, I cry to you for help, and you do not listen! I stand up before you, and you turn your attention away. You have become cruel to me. I know that you will bring me to death.

Yet doesn't the one in a heap of ruins stretch out his hand for help? Have I not wept for the one whose life was hard, and was I not grieved for the needy? When I expected good, evil came; when I waited for light, darkness came. I am seething, the churning inside of me never stops. I go about mourning with no comfort; I stand up in the assembly and cry for help, but I am no more than a brother of jackals. My skin turns black, and my bones burn with fever. Therefore my harp is turned to mourning and my flute to the sound of weeping.

I made a covenant with my eyes that I would not gaze upon a virgin in lust. And what have I received from God above? Does He not see my ways, and number my steps? If I have walked in falsehood, then let Him weigh me in the scales. If my step has turned from the way, then let me sow my fields and another eat the crop. If my heart has been enticed by a woman, or if I have lurked by my neighbor's door for his wife, then let my wife become another man's. For that would be a lustful crime, and I should be punished. If I have been cruel or unkind to my servants, then what could I do when God called me to account? He made my servants as surely as he made me. If I have kept the poor from fulfilling his desire, or if I have eaten food the needy hungered for, if I have lifted up my hand against the orphan, then let my arm fall from my shoulder. I did not do these things, because the thought of calamity from the Lord was a terror to me. If I have put my confidence in gold, and boasted because of my wealth, if I have looked to the sun or moon to worship it, then that would be an iniquity calling for punishment because I would have denied God above.

But have I done that? Have I rejoiced when my enemy faced some evil? No, I have not allowed my mouth to sin by asking for his life in a curse. The men of my tent have always been satisfied with their share of food; the stranger could always find lodging at my house. Have I tried to hide my sins and transgressions because I was afraid of the scorn of the crowds?

Oh that I had someone to hear me! Behold, here is the signature on my defense! Let the Almighty answer me! Let Him bring His indictment against me! I would put it on like a crown. I would tell Him of my ways; I would approach Him like a prince! If my land cries out against me, if I have eaten of its fruits without money, or have caused its owners to lose their lives, then let briars grow instead of wheat, and stinkweed instead of barley!

The words of Job are ended.

Elihu speaks (32:1-37:24):

The speeches by Job and his three friends have ended. The friends stopped, because Job was righteous in his own eyes, and they could not convince him he was a sinner. Now another man speaks up: Elihu. He spoke out of a feeling of anger against each man. He was angry with Job because he justified himself and blamed God with his affliction. He was angry with the friends because, though they could not answer Job's arguments or prove him guilty of sin, they condemned him. Elihu had been there the whole time, listening to what the other men had said, but he had not spoken earlier because he was much younger than they. But now that they stop, he speaks up to express the thoughts pent up inside him.

Though Elihu is a much younger man, he rebukes the three friends for showing a lack of wisdom. He thinks Job has sinned, but not in the way the others have said. He rebukes Job for exactly the same thing for which God will soon rebuke Job. He tells Job that he has no right to call God into question for His actions, that God does not owe Job an answer. He says that Job is wrong to blame God for his afflictions as if God were unjust. Notice that after God speaks to Job, He rebukes the three friends for their words, but He does not rebuke Elihu. Elihu says that he had stayed quiet because he thought he would find wisdom in the aged, but that it was not there. Though Elihu does not have God's wisdom either, he shows more wisdom than the older men have shown.

The three friends have said that Job is being punished for some extremely wicked deed he has committed. Elihu does not deal with the original cause of Job's suffering. He does not accuse Job of sin worthy of punishment, nor does he say Job is innocent of sin. What he says is that, no matter the cause for the affliction, Job is wrong in blaming God and accusing Him of injustice. It is true that Job has said it is God's fault, that God has brought the affliction, and that He had no right to do so.

Elihu says:

I am young, and you are old, so I was shy to speak. I thought the aged should speak and teach wisdom, but it is the breath of the Almighty that gives wisdom. It is not always the old who are wise or who understand justice. So I say: Listen to me now, and I will tell you what I think. I listened patiently to your words, and I thought carefully about what you were saying, but not one of you refuted Job's arguments. Do not say, "We have already found wisdom, and God will refute Job." Job has not directed his arguments against me, and I will not answer him with the arguments you have used.

You three men have hushed; words have failed you. But should I be quiet just because you are? I will tell you my thoughts because I am full of words. My spirit constrains me; I am like a wineskin about to burst. Let me speak so that I can get relief. I will be partial to no one, nor will I flatter any one of you.

Job, listen to what I have to say. I speak from an upright heart. The Spirit of God made me and the Almighty gives me life. Now answer me if you can. Array yourself before me, take your stand. I belong to God just as you do; I too am made out of clay, so you do not need to be afraid of me.

Think about what Elihu is saying. Job has been saying that he has his arguments prepared and he wants to present his case before Jehovah. Job is sure he could win his case if only God would listen, but Job also expresses fear at the idea of standing before Jehovah. So Elihu is saying, "You say you have your case ready to present, so present it to me. I will pretend to be God, and I will try to give the answers God would give. But you do not need to be afraid of me because I am a man just like you. Now let us hear your arguments." But then, rather than waiting for Job to make his arguments again, Elihu takes up the arguments Job has already made and answers them.

Job, you have said in our hearing that you are pure before God, and that He is inventing pretexts against you in order to afflict you. But let me tell you, you are not right. God is greater than man. Why do you complain against Him because He does not give you an account for everything He does? God *does* speak, but men do not always listen. He speaks sometimes in dreams, so that He may turn men from their misconduct, or from their pride. He may chasten a man upon a bed of pain, making his flesh waste away to nothing, and bringing him very near death. But if there is an angel who serves as a mediator for the man, to remind him what is right, and he says to God, "Let this man live, for I have found a ransom for him," then his flesh is restored again. Then the man will pray to God, and He will accept him. The man will sing before his friends and will say, "I sinned and perverted what is right, but God redeemed my soul from death, and my life shall see light." Behold, God does these things to men to bring their souls back from the pit, in order to teach them the light of life.

Job, if you can answer my arguments, then speak up because I want you to be cleared. If not, then listen to me more and I will teach you wisdom. Listen to me, you wise men — those of you who know so much. Let your ears test my words the way the mouth tastes food.

Job says, "I am innocent, I am righteous — but God takes away my right; He denies me justice. My wound is incurable, though I am without transgression." What man is like Job? He puts himself in the company of the wicked when he says it does not profit a man when he is pleasing to God.

Listen to me, you men of understanding: God does not do wickedness; the Almighty does not do wrong. He pays a man according to his works. Surely the Almighty will not pervert justice. *(Elihu is saying, "Job, even though you do not understand why your afflictions have come upon you, you must not take the position that God is being unjust to you.")* Who gave God His authority over the earth? If He chose to do so, He has the right to destroy all flesh before Him and let man return to the dust. *(God is under no obligation to prolong life at all upon the earth.)* Will you condemn the just and mighty One? Is He not the One who says to kings, "You are worthless," and to princes, "You are wicked"? Isn't He the One who shows no partiality to the rich or the poor? In a moment, they all die and the mighty are taken away in the night.

His eyes are upon man; He sees his every step. There is no dark spot where the wicked can hide. He does not need a man to come before Him to present his case in judgment before Him, because He already knows all that a man does. He will break a mighty man in pieces without asking questions, and will set another in his place. He strikes a wicked one in a public place, because he has turned aside from the ways of God. But if He should choose to remain quiet, who can condemn Him? If He hides His face, who can see Him? He is over man and nation alike.

One says to God, "I have been punished; I will not sin again. Teach me what I do not see. If I have done wrong, I will do it no more." Should God then reward you on your own terms? You must decide the answer, not I.

Job speaks without knowledge. He ought to be tried to the limit, because he adds rebellion to his other sins. He speaks like a wicked man, and heaps up his words against God.

Do you think this is just? Do you say you are more righteous than God? For you say, what profit shall I have for serving Him, more than if I had sinned? I will answer you. Look to the sky above and behold how much higher the clouds are than you. If you have sinned, what harm have you done to God? Or, if you are righteous, what great blessing have you given to Him? Your wickedness affects only a man like yourself, and your righteousness only the sons of men.

People cry out when they are oppressed; but no one asks where God is when they have songs of happiness. Who gives Him thanks for giving us more wisdom than the animals and birds? Surely God will not listen to an empty cry. How can you expect Him to listen to you when you say you do not see Him. Your case is before Him, and you must wait for Him!

Job does not know what he is talking about.

Bear with me a little longer, for there is more to be said in God's behalf. I will give my Maker credit for my knowledge.

Behold, God is mighty, but He does not despise anyone. He does not keep the wicked alive, and He gives the afflicted their rights. If men are bound in fetters because of their sins, He tells them what they have done wrong. If they hear Him, and return from evil, they shall end their days in prosperity. But if they do not, they will die by the sword. But the godless in heart lay up anger, because they do not cry to Him for help in time of trouble. They die in their youth. God delivers the afflicted; He speaks to them in their affliction.

God is trying to call you back to Him, to call you to a spacious place where you may have comfort. But you are full of the judgment due to the wicked. Be careful that no one entices you to scoffing; do not let some great ransom turn you aside from God. Will riches keep you from distress? Be careful, lest you turn to evil. It seems you have preferred evil to affliction.

Behold, God is exalted in His power. Who is a teacher like Him? Who has the right to say to Him, "You have done wrong"? You should exalt His work. The number of His years is unsearchable. He draws up the water and pours down rain from the clouds. Can anyone understand how the clouds spread, or how He thunders from His booth? He spreads the lightning about Him, and covers the depths of the sea. He judges people, and He gives food in abundance. He covers His hands with lightning and tells it to strike its mark. Its noise declares His presence. My heart trembles at this. Listen closely to the thunder of His voice. Under the whole heaven He lets His lightning loose to the ends of the earth. He thunders with His majestic voice; He does great things that we cannot comprehend. He tells the snow to fall, and the rain to pour in a mighty storm. He stops the work of every man so that all men may know His work. The beast goes into his den and remains there out of the storm. From the breath of God ice is made; He loads the clouds with moisture, and disperses the cloud of His lightning. It changes direction at His command. Whatever it is, whether it is for correction, or for loving-kindness, He causes it to happen.

Listen, O Job. Do you know how God does all these things? Can you, with Him, spread out the sky? Teach us what we should say to God. We cannot draw up our case, because of our darkness. Shall I tell Him that I want to speak to Him? Would any man ask to be swallowed up? Man cannot look at the bright sun when the wind has cleared the clouds away, so how can we hope to look at God. Out of the north comes our God in golden splendor! Around our God is awesome majesty. We cannot find the Almighty, because He is exalted in power. He will not do violence to justice and righteousness. Therefore men fear Him; He is not awed by any man wise of heart.

The Lord speaks to Job out of the whirlwind (38:1-41:34):
Suddenly God Himself spoke to Job from a whirlwind.

And there follows one of the most beautiful, most majestic passages in the Bible. Job has been calling for God to answer him, to let him present his arguments before Him about why Job thinks God has been unjust. Now God speaks — and He invites Job to respond, to instruct God — but Job is overwhelmed at the greatness of God, and he places his hand over his mouth. It is impossible to do justice to this passage as we summarize it in prose. Read this passage aloud together in your class to see the power and greatness of Jehovah God. It will help us "put our hand over our mouths" as we stand humbly in His presence.

Notice that God does not even mention Job's suffering. He does not tell Job about Satan's challenge, or why any of it had happened. He just tells Job that he is in no position to argue with God, or to question His actions. Job, you are not wise enough!

Who is this who darkens counsel by words without knowledge? Stand up, Job, and face me like a man. I will ask you some questions, and you teach me! Where were you when I laid the foundations of the earth? Tell me, if you have so much understanding! Who placed the boundaries on the sea and bolted it shut with a door? Who told the sea, "Thus far shalt thou come, but no farther"?

Have you ever in your life commanded the morning to come? Have you ever walked in the deepest reaches of the ocean? Have you seen the gates of death? Have you understood the expanse of the earth? Tell me, if you know all this.

Where does light live? Do you know how to take the darkness to its home? Surely you know! You must have been born then because your years are so great! Have you visited the storehouses of the snow and hail? Who made a channel for the flood, or a path for the thunderbolt? Does rain have a father? Who gives birth to the ice?

Can you bind the chain of the Pleiades, or loose the cord of Orion *(constellations)*? Do you know the rules for the stars?

Can you call out to the clouds and tell them to rain upon you? Can you send forth lightning? Who put wisdom and understanding into the mind? Can you tip over the water jars of heaven and make it rain upon a dry ground?

Can you hunt prey for the wild animals, or provide food for the birds? Do you know when the mountain goats give birth? Who set the wild donkey free? He scorns the city and looks for his food in the mountains. Will the wild ox consent to serve you, to live in your barns, and to plow your fields? Do you think you could tame him enough to trust him to gather your grain?

The ostrich flaps her wings joyously, but she knows nothing about raising her young. She lays her eggs on the open earth, and leaves them to warm in the dust. She forgets that a foot might crush her egg; she does not worry if egg is destroyed and her effort has been in vain, because God did not give her wisdom. But when she lifts up herself to run, she can outrun the horse and its rider.

Did you give the horse its might? Did you make it unafraid to rush straight into battle? Is it by your understanding that the hawk can soar? Did you command the eagle to built its nest so high?

God said, "Will the fault-finder contend with the Almighty? Let the one who reproves God, now step forward and answer Him."

Job replied, "Behold, I am nothing! What can I say? I lay my hand upon my mouth. I spoke once, even twice, but I will say no more."

God continues: "Job, stand up like a man. I will ask you more questions, and you teach me! Would you discredit my justice? Will you condemn me in order to justify yourself? Do you have an arm like God? Can you thunder with a voice like His? If so, dress yourself with great honor and majesty. Pour out your wrath upon the wicked and proud. Then I will confess that you can save yourself by your own right hand."

But Job cannot answer, and God continues asking His questions. No one knows what animals God is describing when He speaks of Behemoth and Leviathan. There are no animals known today that exactly fits the descriptions. Do not stop to argue over which animal it might be; just look at the descriptions of these mighty creatures and marvel at the Creator who could make them. That is God's point.

Behold now, Behemoth, which I made as well as you. Look at his might, his strength, his power. Can anyone capture him when he is on watch? Can you catch Leviathan with a fishhook? Will he beg for your mercy? Could you tame him and make him a pet for your little girls? If you ever lay your hand upon him to try to take him, you will remember the experience and never try again. Could you make a creature like one of these? Could you control it?

Job replies in humility (42:1-6):

O God, I know that you can do all things. No plan of yours can be thwarted. You asked, "Who is this that obscures my counsel without knowledge?" Surely I spoke things too wonderful for me. I did not know what I was talking about. You said, "Listen and I will speak. I will ask you questions, and you instruct me." O God, I did not know you. I had heard of you with my ears, but now I have seen you with my eyes. Therefore I repent; I take back everything I said. I repent in dust and ashes.

Job is vindicated (42:7-17):

Then God spoke to Eliphaz, saying, "I am angry with you and your two friends, because you have not spoken the truth about me as my servant Job has. Now, therefore, take seven bulls and seven rams and go to my servant Job and ask him to offer them as a sacrifice for you. My servant Job will pray for you and I will accept a sacrifice from him, so that I will not repay you for your folly, for you have not spoken the truth about me as has my servant Job."

The three friends did as God had commanded, and Job offered a sacrifice in their behalf.

Did you notice that God calls Job His servant four times in this short statement? He says that the three friends were not right in what they had said. Though Job had no right to blame God for his affliction, and he had no right to demand an answer from God, he was right in saying he had not done some great sin that made him deserve his affliction. Did you also notice that God does not rebuke Elihu? The younger man showed more wisdom than the older men did.

The trials were over, and God restored the fortunes of Job by giving him twice the wealth he had before. His family and acquaintances came before him to show their respect as they had in times past. They consoled him and comforted him for all the trials that had come upon him. Job had seven more sons and three more daughters to take the place of those he had lost at the beginning. There were no women in all the land as beautiful as Job's daughters. Job lived 140 years after his trials and saw his children and grandchildren to the fourth generation.

The Psalms
The Jewish Hymnal

Psalms written by:
  David
  The sons of Korah
  Asaph
  Solomon
  Moses
  And others

Psalms:
  Tell history
  Praise God
  Confess guilt
  Call upon God for help
  Express thanks to God
  Predict the Messiah

Learn the Psalms. They teach us the most beautiful words to express every emotion we have.

Introduction:

As we said in our introduction to the Wisdom Literature, the book of Psalms was the Jewish hymnal. It is a collection of songs and poems that tell history, that praise God, that confess guilt, that call upon God for help in time of trial, that express thanksgiving to God, or teach some great lesson. No matter the style or subject matter of each, all are beautiful poetry. The word *psalm* comes from the Greek word *psalmos*, which was originally a song sung to the accompaniment of a lyre, or other stringed instrument.

The Psalms are divided into five groups or "Books:"

Book I - Psalms 1-41
Book II - Psalms 42-72
Book III - Psalms 73-89
Book IV - Psalms 90-106
Book V - Psalms 107-150

In addition to the divisions of the psalms into the five books, many of the psalms have titles that are of ancient origin. Even though these divisions of the songs are old, and the titles are old, they do not date back to the original writing of each psalm.

There is simply not space in this work to deal with each psalm individually, so we will look at different categories of them. We have already placed the psalms attributed to David by inscription in their historical setting in the narrative of his life. We will mention those only briefly in our classifications here. There will be overlapping of the classifications, because one psalm may be listed in connection with its author, and then again as its subject matter is described. Or, we may list a psalm in more than one category, because it fits under more than one subject heading. Our classification by subject matter is certainly not exhaustive. Let our classifications suggest one way to look at the psalms, and then do some classifying of your own, or some enlarging of our classifications, as you do your own study of the songs and poetry.

The psalms express every emotion experienced by man. They teach us the most beautiful words possible to help us express our emotions. Let us take advantage of the blessing God has given us by preserving these inspired songs for us.

Classification by Authors

The Psalms of David:

The largest group of psalms are those written by David, or at least attributed to him. The psalms having titles which indicate they were written by David are: 3-9, 11-32, 34-41, 51-65, 68-70, 86, 101, 103, 108, 109, 110, 122, 124, 131, 133, 138-145. In addition, Psalm 2 is attributed to David in Acts 4:25-26 by the apostles. Peter refers to the promise of God to David, using the wording found in Psalm 132 (Acts 2:30). Though Psalm 132 refers to the promise made to David, judging from the wording of the psalm, it was almost certainly written by someone after him.

Certain of the psalms of David have historical information, either in the title or in the psalm itself, by which a chronology can be determined. These are the ones we have included in the narrative section of David's life. Look back to his story and see how beautifully they fit the history. According to the notes found in the psalms, the earliest of his historical psalms is number 59, when Saul's spies watched David's house before he fled from Saul. Next is Psalm 52 which tells of evil Doeg who informed Saul that the priests of Nob had helped David, and then personally slew the priests for Saul. Psalm 56 tells about the Philistines seizing David in Gath. About that same time, Psalm 34 tells of David's being brought before Abimelech, king of Gath. David pretended to be insane and escaped. Psalm 54 tells that the Ziphites informed Saul where David was, and thus betrayed David. Psalm 142 tells about David hiding in a cave. Psalm 18 celebrates David's deliverance from Saul. Psalm 30 tells of the dedication of the house of David, either his palace, or, possibly, the house he built for the ark of the covenant. Psalm 60 celebrates his defeat of the men of Aram-naharaim, the Syrians that were beyond the River Euphrates. Psalm 51 tells of David's sin with Bathsheba after Nathan had come to reprove David. This psalm tells of David's deep penitence for his sin. Psalm 3 describes the rebellion of David's own son, Absalom. Finally, Psalm 7 tells of the mistreatment of David at the hands of Cush, whom we cannot identify.

Songs of the Sons of Korah:

The songs of the Sons of Korah form the next largest group of psalms (as classified by authors). They include Psalms 42, 44-49, 84, 85, 87, 88 (Heman is given as the author of this particular psalm), and 89 (Ethan wrote this psalm). The Sons of Korah were descendants of the Korah who died in the wilderness because of his rebellion against God's chosen leaders (Num. 16). His sons did not die with their father (Num. 26:11). They were also descendants of Kohath (Num. 16:1; 1 Chron. 6:37-38), who was one of the sons of Levi. Among them was Heman, seemingly the chief of three Levite song-leaders appointed by David. He is called "the king's seer" in 1 Chronicles 25:5. According to 1 Chronicles 6, he stood in the center to minister in song, with Asaph on his right (1 Chron. 6:39), and Ethan [also known as Jeduthun] on his left (1 Chron. 6:44). Psalm 39 is attributed to David, but written "for Jeduthun." Psalm 62, likewise, was written by David, but was "after the manner of Jeduthun." This Jeduthun is probably the same as Ethan in 1 Chronicles 6 and 16.

Psalms of Asaph:

Next are the psalms of Asaph. Psalms attributed to him include 50, 73-83. Asaph was one of the three directors who led the singers at the temple (1 Chron. 6:33, 39, 44). About the time David moved the ark into Jerusalem, he organized the Levites into various groups and assigned them certain tasks. Some were singers, some were door-keepers, etc. The arrangements made by David at this time reflect the presence of the ark in Jerusalem, while the tabernacle of Jehovah remained at Gibeon. Asaph and his brethren were to minister before the ark in Jerusalem continually (1 Chron. 16:37). Obed-edom, Hosah, and their brethren were to be door-keepers (guards) at the place where the ark was kept (1 Chron. 16:38). Zadok and his brethren the priests continued to serve at Gibeon before the tabernacle, because the altar of burnt offering was located there (1 Chron. 16:39-40), and with them were Heman and Jeduthun, who were "to give thanks to the Lord" (1 Chron. 16:41-42). After the temple was built, the priests and Levites, singers and all, served at the same place in Jerusalem. Since Heman, Ethan (Jeduthun), and Asaph were the three primary Levite directors of the singing of the congregation during times of service before Jehovah, it is not surprising to find them as composers of some of the songs. The sons of these men are said to "prophesy with harps, with psalteries, and with cymbals" (1 Chron. 25:1-6).

Psalms of Solomon: Solomon wrote Psalms 72 and 127.

Psalm of Moses: Moses wrote Psalm 90.

Classification by Style or Purpose

Songs of Ascent:

The second largest group of psalms consists of those called Songs of Ascent. These were probably songs sung as processions made their way up the mount to the temple during feast days, or on other times of special celebration before Jehovah. They are: Psalms 120-134. They include prayers requesting God's help and deliverance from enemies, and prayers for peace. They include songs of thanksgiving for His deliverance and for His protection of His people. Some of the songs express the basis for hope for God's help: that is, "Blessed is the one who fears the Lord, who walks in His ways..." (Ps. 128:1). As you can see, this group of songs and prayers were appropriate on many different kinds of occasions when the people approached the temple in worship.

Alphabetic Psalms:

One very interesting group of psalms is called the Alphabetic Psalms. In these psalms, each line begins with the succeeding letter in the Hebrew alphabet. The most famous of these is Psalm 119. Instead of each line beginning with the next letter in this psalm, there is a paragraph for each letter. In each paragraph, each line of the paragraph begins with the letter which stands at the head of that paragraph. Thus in verses 1-8, each line begins with the letter aleph in Hebrew; in verses 9-16, each line begins with the letter beth, etc. In addition, Psalms 25, 34, 37, 111, 112, 145 are alphabetic. In Psalm 37 every other line begins with a succeeding letter of the alphabet.

Hallel Psalms:

Several sections of the psalms are called Hallel songs, because at least some of the psalms in each section contain the expression "hallelu Jah," that is, "Praise Jehovah." Psalms 113-118 are called the Egyptian Hallel because they were chanted at the time when the Passover lamb was slain, a practice begun in Egypt. Psalms 118-136 are called the Great Hallel. These psalms were recited at the Passover Supper. Psalms 146-150 are called the Greek Hallel and are thought by some to have been chanted in the ritual of the temple rebuilt in the days of Haggai and Zechariah. All the psalms of the Greek Hallel begin and end with the expression, Hallelujah, which means, "Praise ye the Lord." Psalms 106, 113, 117, and 135 also begin and end with "Praise ye the Lord." Psalms 111 and 112 begin with "Praise ye the Lord," while Psalms 104 and 105 end with Hallelujah.

Classification by Subject Matter

Psalms that cry to God for help:

David wrote many types of psalms, but most of the ones we included in the narrative cycle of his life fall into the category of cries for help from Jehovah. It is easy to place these into the framework of his story, because the titles tell of some particular moment when he was in trouble and felt his need for God's help.

The psalms that cry for help fall into broad divisions as we look into their content. There are those like the ones we have analyzed from David's life that are a call from an individual who is facing a specific trial and he calls upon God for help. Psalms 3, 7, 34, 52, 54, 56, 59, 142, and others fall into this category. Then there are psalms asking for help for the nation when it was undergoing a specific trial. For example, Psalm 60 is a lament at a time when Israel was fighting the Syrians (Aramians) and Edomites and the struggle seemed to be going against them. Sometimes there is nothing in either the ancient title, or in the wording of the text, to let us see what the specific problem was, but the cry for help is still eloquent — whether it was for the nation, or for an individual.

The various types of prayers help us see that we have a right to call upon God under different circumstances. It is not a sign of weakness to call upon God for help — rather, it is a very responsible act of faith on our part when we cast our care upon Him, and call upon Him as the One who can truly help us in our times of trial (see 1 Pet. 5:7; Heb. 4:16).

Sometimes the cry for help includes a petition for forgiveness from sin so that the one praying will have a right to God's help. Look at an example of this type:

Psalm 25:

Unto thee, O Lord, do I lift up my soul. I am going to depend upon you, and no one who depends upon you will be put to shame. Show me your ways; teach me; guide me.

Lord, remember your mercy — not my sins. For your name's sake, O Lord, pardon my iniquity.

The friendship of the Lord is with them that fear Him. My eyes are ever looking toward the Lord.

Look upon my affliction and my pain; and forgive all my sins.

These prayers for help follow various patterns. For example, some begin with a direct cry for God's help, give a description of the present trouble the writer is facing, and then express praise and thanksgiving for His deliverance. Look at an example of this style:

Psalm 54:
Save me, O God, by thy name; hear my prayer.
For strangers rise up against me, and oppressors seek my soul.
Behold, God is my helper; He shall reward evil unto my enemies.
I will freely sacrifice unto thee; I will praise thy name.
For God has delivered me out of all my trouble.

Some of these prayers begin with an expression of thanksgiving for God's deliverance, and then give a description of the trouble that had come, and a description of God's deliverance. Look at an example of this style:

Psalm 18:
I will love thee, O Lord, my strength, my rock, my fortress.
I will call upon the Lord, who is worthy to be praised.
The sorrows of death compassed me, the floods of ungodly men made me afraid.
In my distress, I called upon the Lord.
He heard my prayer from His holy temple; then the earth shook and trembled, for He was angry... *(And there follows a very beautiful description of God's deliverance of David.)*

In some of these psalms, the Psalmist begins with an expression of complaint that God does not seem to be listening to him, that God has abandoned him. He then describes his troubles, as if he is asking God if He sees the trouble. But before the psalm ends, the writer speaks in assurance that God will indeed come to his aid, and he expresses his thanksgiving for God's help. Look at an example of this style:

Psalm 13:
   How long, O Jehovah? Will you forget me for ever? How long will you hide your face from me? How long shall I take counsel in my soul, having sorrow in my heart all the day? How long shall mine enemy be exalted over me? Please hear me, O God, lest I sleep the sleep of the dead, lest my enemy rejoice over me.
   I have trusted in thy mercy; I will sing unto the Lord, because He has dealt bountifully with me.

The most famous of the psalms that fit this last style is Psalm 22, which is the cry of the Savior for deliverance that was written by His ancestor David a thousand years before Jesus was on the cross and quoted the first verse of the beautiful prayer. The cry for help begins with the words: "My God, My God, why hast thou forsaken me?" Then the Psalmist develops this theme in verses 1-18. Things could not be much worse. God has completely abandoned him to his fate. But in verses 19-21, the Psalmist makes a heartfelt appeal to God not to be far off, to deliver his precious life from the power of the dog, to save him from the lion's mouth, and closes the section with the affirmation: "Yea, from the horns of the wild-oxen thou hast answered me" (22:21). Verses 22-31 are a song of praise for God, who has not forsaken the afflicted. When the Psalmist cried unto God, He heard and delivered.

In several psalms of this category, the language of the Psalmist seems harsh. Of the wicked he says, "Break their teeth, O God, in their mouth" (58:6). He says the righteous will "wash his feet in the blood of the wicked" (58:10). When the statements of the Psalmist have the nature of a curse upon the wicked, they are called *psalms of imprecation*, or *imprecatory psalms*. Many have puzzled over how to reconcile these psalms with the teaching of Jesus to love our enemies, and pray for those who persecute us (Matt. 5:44). Did Jesus teach a higher level of behavior than the Psalmist knew? How may we explain this problem?

In the first place, we must distinguish whether such sentiments as we see in Psalms 58 and 109 arise from a feeling of personal vengeance, or from a feeling of desire that the righteous be vindicated. Clearly, the answer is that these psalms express the desire of the righteous that they be vindicated, and that the way of the wicked be shown in its true light. Even in the New Testament, the souls of the beheaded cry out: "How long, O Master, the holy and true, dost thou not judge and avenge our blood on them that dwell on the earth?" (Rev. 6:10). In passages dealing with judgment, the wicked are dealt with harshly in the New Testament as well (Rev. 8; 9; 16; Matt. 22:7). "Behold then the goodness and severity of God: toward them that fell, severity; but toward thee, God's goodness, if thou continue in His goodness: otherwise thou also shall be cut off" (Rom. 11:22).

Sometimes the language is figurative, as in Psalm 58:6. There the wicked are compared to lions, who rend with their teeth, and the Psalmist asks the Lord to break their teeth. Note that the Psalmist calls upon the Lord, to whom all vengeance belongs (Deut. 32:35; Rom. 12:19; Heb. 10:30-31), to make things right, and to punish the wicked.

Finally, especially with such psalms written by David, those who fought and opposed David opposed the Lord's anointed. David's jealousy was not for himself, but for the Lord's anointed, the Lord's chosen one. Just as he himself respected Saul because he was the Lord's anointed, he expected others also to respect God's chosen leader (1 Sam. 24:6; 26:9-11).

As you look at the psalms that cry for help from Jehovah, be alert to the various forms they take. This is a very large category: Psalms 3, 4, 5, 6, 7, 10, 12, 13, 17, 20, 22, 25, 27, 28, 31, 35, 40, 41, 42, 43, 54, 55, 56, 57, 58, 59, 60, 61, 63, 64, 69, 70, 71, 74, 79, 80, 83, 88, 94, 102, 109, 120, 123, 129, 132, 140, 141, 142, 143, and 144.

Psalms of thanksgiving and praise for God's deliverance:

Psalms of thanksgiving are the logical ones to look at after the psalms that cry for help. The psalms that cry for help also include a section that give thanks to God for His deliverance. But then, there are some psalms that are more general expressions of thanksgiving. We do the same things in our prayers and expressions of thanksgiving. Sometimes we feel a deep need for God because of some specific problem; we cry to God for His help, and we express our thanksgiving that we can call upon Him for help and know that He will hear us. But then, there are times when we express our thanksgiving to God for all the blessings He has given us: whether it is for peace in our country, for our physical well-being, for help that He has given us throughout our lives, or for some other blessing we have before Him. We must never forget this category of prayer to God.

Psalms 9, 30, 116, 118, 126, and 138 are filled with expressions of thanksgiving. For example, Psalm 9 begins with an outpouring of thanks to the Lord: "I will give thanks to the Lord with all my heart; I will tell of all thy wonders..." and then it continues with an enumeration of all the ways God had delivered him from various trials, and an expression of praise for God's goodness.

There is a category of psalms that do not use the word thanksgiving so much, but fit into this same thought pattern. These are the psalms of praise to God for His deliverance. We have already mentioned Psalm 18 that is such a beautiful outpouring of praise for God's mighty power in deliverance. Look at Psalms 21, 27, 28, 31, 34, 40, 61, 77, 106, 107, 108, 112, 121, 124, and 144 as additional ones that praise God as our Deliverer.

Still closely related to this thought, there are psalms that express thanksgiving and praise to God as our Refuge. Not only does He deliver us when we are in the midst of trouble, He is the refuge where we can hide to avoid the troubles of life. Look at Psalms 11, 16, 46, and 62 that express this thought beautifully. There are so many beautiful expressions that describe God as our refuge, our stronghold, our place to hide while the trouble passes by. For example:

> The Lord is my rock, and my fortress, and my deliverer; my God, my strength, in whom I will trust; my buckler, and the horn of my salvation, and my high tower (Ps. 18:2).

> In the shadow of thy wings will I make my refuge, until these calamities be past over (Ps. 57:1).

Psalm 11:
> In the Lord I take refuge. How can you say to my soul, "Flee as a bird to your mountain, for the wicked are taking aim against you. What can the righteous do?"
>
> I can rely upon God, because the Lord is in His holy temple; the Lord's throne is in heaven. He tests both the righteous and the wicked. Upon the wicked He will rain snares, fire, brimstone, and burning wind. But the upright will see His face.

Psalms that praise God as the Creator and Sustainer:

Some of the most beautiful of the psalms praise God as our Creator: Psalms 8, 19, 29, 33, 65, 74, and 104.

Psalm 8:
> O Lord, our Lord, how excellent is thy name in all the earth!
>
> When I consider thy heavens, the work of thy fingers, the moon and the stars, which thou hast ordained, what is man, that thou art mindful of him? For you made him a little lower than the angels, and crowned him with glory and honor. You made him to have dominion over the works of thy hands, and have put all things under his feet.
>
> O Lord, our Lord, how excellent is thy name in all the earth!

Psalm 19:
> The heavens declare the glory of God; and the firmament showeth His handiwork. Day unto day uttereth speech, and night unto night showeth knowledge… There is no speech nor language, where their voice is not heard…

Not only did God create the universe, and all life upon the earth, He is the One who set in motion the laws of nature. He is the One who sustains those laws and makes them work from day to day. Our very existence depends upon Him every day.

Psalm 104:
> Bless the Lord, O my soul. O Lord my God, thou art very great!
>
> You dressed yourself with light as a garment. You stretched out the heavens like a curtain. The clouds are your chariot. You have made the wind your messengers, and flames of fire your servants. You laid the foundations of the earth, and covered it with the deep, as with a tunic. You rebuked the waters and they fled away; the mountains rose, the

valleys sank down to the place you prepared for them.

My God sends springs into the valleys, and waters the mountains from His chambers. He causes the grass to grow for cattle, and vegetables to grow for the use of man. The trees of the Lord are fruitful, where the birds make their nests.

He appointed the movements for the sun and moon. He made the dark, when all the beasts of the forest come forth. The sun rises, and they go home to their dens. Man goes forth to work until the evening.

O Lord, how manifold are your works. There is the sea, great and wide, full of all sorts of beasts, small and great. There go the ships. You have provided for them all.

Let the glory of the Lord endure forever. I will sing unto the Lord as long as I live. Let my meditation be sweet unto Him. Bless the Lord, O my soul. Praise ye the Lord.

Look at Psalms 23, 68, 87, 103, 131, 146, and 147 as examples of psalms that express general praise and thanksgiving for the blessings that God has bestowed upon us. "The Lord is my shepherd, I shall not want..." (Ps. 23:1). He is my Provider; my Caretaker. I can trust in Him the way a child can trust his mother (Ps. 131).

Psalms 122, 127, and 133 are interesting little psalms. They emphasize blessings that we sometimes forget to count as blessings. Each of these psalms has very well known verses in them. Psalm 122 begins with: "I was glad when they said to me, 'Let us go to the house of the Lord.'" It is a prayer for peace for Jerusalem as God's dwelling place, and an expression of praise for the place of worship to Jehovah.

Psalm 127 begins: "Unless the Lord builds the house, they labor in vain who build it; unless the Lord guards the city, the watchman keeps awake in vain." Without God's help, all our labor is empty; but with His help, our days can be a reasonable length, and we can enjoy our sleep. But then the writer focuses upon one of the very greatest blessings God has given to us: "Behold, children are a gift of the Lord. Like arrows in the hand of a warrior, so are the children of one's youth. How blessed is the man whose quiver is full of them."

Psalm 133 begins: "Behold, how good and how pleasant it is for brothers to dwell together in unity! It is as precious as oil upon the head, or as rain upon the mountains that are blessed of God."

Praise for God's mighty works for Israel:

There is a group of historical psalms that praise God for the mighty works that He did for Israel. One of the major faults of the Israelites was that they failed to convey the message from one generation to another concerning the great works which God had done for Israel. It was this failure that caused the generation that followed Joshua to be unfaithful (compare Judges 2:7, 10). We would do well to profit from their example. We must help our children to know from their earliest days what God has done. These historical psalms include 44, 66, 68, 77, 78, 79, 81, 83, 105, 106, 114, 135, and 136.

Psalm 78:

Listen, O people, to my instruction. I will tell of the things which we have heard and known, which our fathers told us. We will not conceal them from their children, but tell to the generations to come the praises of the Lord, and His strength and His wondrous works that He has done.

For He established a testimony in Jacob, and appointed a law in Israel, which He commanded our fathers that they should teach them to their children, that the generation to come might know, even the children yet to be born, that they may arise and tell them to their children, that they should put their confidence in God, and not forget the works of God, but keep His commandments…

Psalm 105:

O give thanks unto the Lord. Make known His doings among the people; glory in His holy name. O seed of Abraham, remember His marvelous works that He has done.

He has remembered His covenant forever, the one which He made with Abraham. He said, "Unto thee will I give the land of Canaan," when they were but few in number. They traveled from one nation to another, but God suffered no man to do them wrong. He said, "Touch not my anointed ones, and do my prophet no harm."

He called for a famine upon the land, and sent a man before them. Joseph was sold for a servant. The word of the Lord tried him. The king sent and loosed him. He made him lord of his house, and ruler of all his substance. Israel came into Egypt, and God increased His people greatly. He turned the hearts of the Egyptians to hate His people. He sent Moses His servant, and Aaron whom He had chosen. They showed the signs God had given: He sent the darkness upon Egypt; He turned their waters into blood; their land swarmed with frogs; He gave them hail for rain, and flaming fire in their land; He spoke and the locusts came; He smote their firstborn. He brought Israel forth with silver and gold. Egypt was glad when they departed. He spread a cloud for a covering and fire to give light in the night. He fed them with quails, and with the bread of heaven. He opened the rock and water gushed out. He remembered His holy word to Abraham, His servant. He brought forth His people with singing, and gave them the lands of the nations, that they might keep His statutes and observe His laws.

Praise ye the Lord.

Psalms that praise God for who He is:

Not only does God deserve our praise for what He has done for us, He deserves our praise for His character and nature. The little Psalm 117 expresses the thought this way: "O praise the Lord, all ye nations: praise Him, all ye people. For His merciful kindness is great toward us: and the truth of the Lord endureth forever. Praise ye the Lord."

Praise God for His mercy; praise Him for His loving-kindness; praise Him for His righteousness; praise Him for His justice. Praise Him for every characteristic of His nature and character (Ps. 36, 66, 67, 76, 92, 95, 96, 97, 98, 99, 100, 111, 117, 118, 134, 139, and 145). Praise Him as our King (24, 47, 48, and 93). Praise Him as our Judge (50). He is worthy of our praise, our worship, and our adoration (84, 148, 149, and 150).

Look at Psalm 115. It contrasts our Mighty God with the idols on every side of Israel. The idols are nothing; only Jehovah, the true God, can be relied upon.

Psalm 115:

Not unto us, O Lord, but unto your name give glory. For your loving-kindness and for your truth's sake.

Why should the nations say, "Where is their God?" Our God is in the heavens; He has done what He pleased. Their idols are silver and gold. They have mouths, but they cannot speak; eyes, but they do not see; ears, but they cannot hear; noses, but they cannot smell. They have hands, but they cannot handle anything; and feet, but they cannot walk. They that make them shall be like them.

O Israel, trust thou in the Lord. O house of Aaron, trust ye in the Lord. You that fear the Lord, trust in Him. The Lord will bless them that fear Him, both small and great. The Lord will bless you more and more. The heavens are the heavens of the Lord, but the earth He has given to the children of men. Those who are dead do not praise the Lord, but we will bless the Lord from now on.

Praise ye the Lord.

The Psalmist recognized the value of the words of the Lord. The words of the Lord reveal His mind, His character, and His will for us. To praise His word is another way of praising the Lord. Without any question, the greatest psalm praising God's word is Psalm 119. Several different words are used over and over again for the commandments of the Lord: ordinances, statutes, law, testimonies, and precepts. Let us summarize a shorter psalm as an example of this type poem:

Psalm 19:7-14:
The law of the Lord is perfect, restoring the soul.
The testimony of the Lord is sure, making wise the simple.
The precepts of the Lord are right, rejoicing the heart.
The commandment of the Lord is pure, enlightening the eyes.
The fear of the Lord is clean, enduring forever.
The ordinances of the Lord are true, and righteous altogether.
They are more to be desired than the finest gold; they are sweeter than honey.
By them, thy servant is warned.
Forgive me for my mistakes; and keep me from deliberate sins.
Do not let them rule over me. Then I shall be free from transgression.
Let the words of my mouth, and the meditation of my heart, be acceptable in thy sight,
O Lord, my Rock, and my Redeemer.

Contrast between the righteous and the wicked:
Sin is a common experience of men (Rom. 3:23). Many of the psalms touch on the subject in some way, but some deal with sin as their primary theme. There are psalms that describe the character of the upright and the wicked; and psalms that contrast their fate. The psalms describe the wickedness of men, grief for sin, judgment, and forgiveness. We will look at these psalms under their respective headings.

The wickedness of men:
There are two psalms that survey humanity, and the verdict is that humanity is full of sin (14 and 53). Paul quotes from these psalms to make the point that the Jews were sinners as surely as were the Gentiles (Rom. 3:10-12). The two psalms are almost parallel, so we will summarize only 14.

Psalm 14:
The fool has told himself that there is no God.
The Lord looked down from heaven upon men to see if there were any that were seeking after Him. They have all turned aside, and are become altogether filthy. There is none that do good.
Have the workers of iniquity no knowledge? Do they not understand? They were in

great fear when they saw that God is with the righteous in his activities.

Oh that the salvation of Israel were come out of Zion. When the Lord reverses the captivity of His people, then Jacob will rejoice, and Israel will be glad.

Two psalms describe those who have given themselves over to wickedness (36, 52). Psalm 36 describes the wickedness of men (36:1-4), and contrasts it with the mercy of God and His righteousness (36:5-12). Psalm 52 describes the vicious spirit of the wicked.

Psalm 52:

Why do you boast of your evil, O mighty man? Your tongue is like a sharp razor, working deceitfully. You would rather do evil than good. You love words that devour and destroy.

God will likewise destroy you. He will root you out of the land of the living.

The righteous will see it and will laugh. He will say, "This is the man that did not depend upon the Lord. But as for me, I am like a green olive-tree in the house of God. I will trust in God's mercy forever."

The character of the righteous:

Often the psalms contrast the character and/or destiny of the righteous and wicked (1, 37, 73). In Psalm 73 the writer says, "I had almost slipped. I thought: the wicked do not suffer for their wrongs. I see no difference between the fate of the wicked and that of the righteous. As I thought the matter over, it was too painful to think about — until I went to the sanctuary of God, and considered the ultimate end of the righteous and wicked. Then I realized the wicked is in a slippery place; he falls in a moment of time. My mind was in a ferment because I was thinking like a brute. But you, O God, are my portion. When all else fails, I can depend upon you."

Psalm 37 touches on the same idea, but it is a more general contrast between the righteous and the wicked. Let's summarize it:

Psalm 37:

Do not fret about the wicked, neither be envious of them, because they will soon be mowed down as the green grass. Trust in the Lord completely. Delight in the Lord; trust in Him, and He will grant your petitions. Wait upon the Lord. Envying the wicked leads only to evil-doing. They will be cut off, but they that wait for the Lord will inherit the land. After a while, you will look for the wicked, and will not be able to find him.

The meek will inherit the land. The wicked plots against the just, but the Lord will laugh at him. The wicked have drawn their sword and bent their bow to throw down the poor and needy and to slay the righteous. Their sword will enter their own heart, and their bows shall be broken.

The Lord upholds the righteous; they shall not be abandoned in the day of calamity, but the wicked shall perish. The wicked borrows and does not pay; the righteous deals generously and gives.

The righteous will have struggles, but the Lord will not abandon him. I have been young, and now I am old; but I have never seen the righteous forsaken, nor his seed begging bread. The Lord loves justice and will not abandon His saints, but the seed of the wicked shall be cut off.

I have seen the wicked in great power, spreading himself like a great tree, but one day I passed by, and the tree was gone, the wicked had disappeared. Note the perfect man, and consider the upright, because he has a future. As for transgressors, they shall be destroyed together, but the salvation of the righteous is from Jehovah.

There are many beautiful psalms that describe the character of the man God loves to bless (1, 15, 24:3-6; 26, 39, 91, 101, 112, 125, 128). The first psalm is considered by some to be a preface to the whole book of Psalms. Psalm 15 is a description of the citizen of Zion.

Psalm 15:
Lord, who will dwell in your tabernacle?
The one who is upright, and works righteousness, and speaks truth in his heart; he that does not slander with his tongue, nor does evil to his friend, nor helps to spread a reproach against his neighbor. In his eyes a reprobate is despised, but he honors them that fear the Lord. Even when he finds that he has sworn to something that will cost him, he does not change his word. He does not loan his money for interest, nor does he take a bribe for the innocent.
One who has this kind of behavior shall never be moved.

A similar question is asked in Psalm 24:3: "Who will ascend into the hill of the Lord, and who shall stand in His holy place?" The answer is: "He who has clean hands, and a pure heart, who has not given his soul to falsehood, and has not sworn falsely. He shall receive a blessing from the Lord, and righteousness from the God of his salvation." Psalm 101 is an interesting example, because in it we have the Psalmist expressing his intent to have the character of the righteous. One is not righteous by accident; it is something one *plans* to be. Psalm 128 describes the blessings of the upright that come in this life, to the person who walks in God's ways.

Nothing else really matters. One cannot trust in his riches, or in his long life, for his security. Let us look at two psalms emphasizing these thoughts:

Psalm 49: *This psalm describes the folly of trusting in riches.*
Why should I fear in the days of adversity, when the wicked rich surround me? They cannot buy my soul from God, for the redemption of my soul is costly.
The wise man and the senseless man all perish. They leave their wealth to others. They think their houses and their lands are theirs forever, and they name their lands after themselves, but their pomp will not endure. Death will be their shepherd. The upright shall rule over them, for God will redeem the upright.
Do not be afraid when a man becomes rich, because when he dies he will not succeed in taking any of it with him. A foolish man who boasts of his pomp is like a beast that perishes.

Psalm 90: *This psalm contrast the eternal nature of God with the brevity of men.*
Before the mountains were born, or the earth was created, thou art God, from everlasting to everlasting. Man returns to dust. A thousand years are as nothing in thy sight, when they have passed by. Man is no more long-lasting than a blade of grass that springs up in the morning, and then fades before evening.
So teach us to number our days, that we may present to thee a heart of wisdom. Show us your loving-kindness, that we may sing for joy and be glad all our days.

Kings and judges should rule righteously before God:
It is very important for the rulers of any country to realize that they, too, must determine to serve God as the foremost goal in their lives. Psalm 72 describes how a king should rule in

righteousness, and Psalm 82 describes how judges should rule with justice. In both instances, they should be careful how they rule or dispense justice, because they, in turn, stand before the greatest King and Judge of all.

Grief for sin:

When the righteous one sins, his heart is deeply grieved (Ps. 6, 38, 51). In our study of the life of David we looked at some of the psalms that deal with sin: the grief that comes, the penitence of the sinner, and the joy of forgiveness. Look back to the information about 2 Samuel 11 and 12. Psalm 51 reveals the grief of David over his sin, his grief at what sin cost him in terms of his relationship with God. The sixth Psalm is a prayer for mercy. David cries for mercy, saying: "I am weary with my groaning; every night I make my bed to swim in my tears." He renounces those that sin, and praises God who has heard his petition. Next to 51, Psalm 38 expresses the most intense grief and penitence for sin. David says, "O God, your arrows stick fast in me, and your hand presses me sore." He proceeds to describe the intense suffering he is enduring. His friends and family stand aloof from him. His enemies are after him. He says, "I will declare my iniquity, and I will be sorry for my sin." Even so, his enemies are busy and strong. His only hope is the Lord: "Forsake me not, O Lord; O my God, be not far from me."

Psalm 137 is one of the saddest of the psalms. It, too, is an expression of grief for sin, but it is the cry of grief from a whole company of people. The kingdom of Judah became very wicked, and finally God sent them into Babylonian captivity. There, in the land of Babylon, the people lifted up their cry to Jehovah in grief over their plight. Look at the psalm:

Psalm 137:

By the rivers of Babylon we sat down and wept when we remembered Zion. Upon the willows we hung our harps. Our captors demand that we sing songs of Zion, but how can we sing the Lord's song in a foreign land?

If I forget you, O Jerusalem, may my right hand forget her skill. May my tongue cleave to the roof of my mouth, if I do not remember and exalt Jerusalem above my chief joy.

Remember all that has happened to us, O Lord.

Forgiveness for sin:

The greatest blessing the child of God has is the opportunity to be forgiven of sin. Though many psalms touch on this idea, there are a few that emphasize it (25, 32, 85, 130). In the 25th Psalm we find the writer saying, "Remember your mercies, O Lord; do not remember the sins of my youth" (25:6-7). Later he says, "For your name's sake, O Lord, pardon my iniquity, because it is great" (25:11). "Consider my affliction and my travail, and forgive all my sins" (25:18).

We looked at Psalm 32 in connection with David's sin with Bathsheba. Paul quotes the first two verses in Romans 4:6-8 to show that David learned one of the greatest lessons a man can learn: it is the *forgiven* man who is blessed of God. None of us could hope to stand before God if He did not provide a way of forgiveness.

Judgment for sin:

Psalm 75: *In words reminiscent of the prophets, Psalm 75 sets forth the judgment of God against the wicked.*

We give thanks to thee, O God, for your reputation is known to us.

When I determine the time is right, I will judge uprightly. The earth and all its inhabitants shall be dissolved, for I set up the pillars of it.

I said to the wicked, "Do not be so proud. Do not speak with a stiff neck." There is no one to deliver you.

God is the judge. In His hand there is a cup, and the wine is strong. The wicked of the earth will drain the cup of its dregs and drink them. But I will tell it for ever; I will sing praises to the God of Jacob.

All the horns of the wicked I will cut off, but the horns of the righteous will be lifted up.

Messianic Psalms:

The psalms in this category deal with Messianic themes, or prophesy of the Messiah in some way. Our list does not claim to be exhaustive, but it does contain the chief Messianic Psalms. Included in this category are: 2, 22, 69, 89, 110 and 132:10-18. There are other psalms from which a verse is applied to the Messiah in the New Testament, and we will mention those, but these are the psalms which are predominantly Messianic.

It is very important to remember that these psalms were written a thousand years before the Messiah came. They therefore have the nature of prophecy. We can only stand in awe as we read these psalms and realize that, though they go into incredible detail about the Messiah's work, about His life, death, and resurrection, they were all written long before the fact. We will begin by looking at Psalm 2.

Psalm 2:

Why do the nations assemble with tumult, and the peoples plan a vain thing?

The kings of earth set themselves, and the rulers take counsel together against the Lord and against His Anointed. They say, "Let us break their bonds in two; let us cast away their cords from us."

He that sits in the heavens will laugh; He will view their efforts as ridiculous. He will speak in His wrath: "In spite of your efforts, I have set my King upon my holy hill of Zion."

I will tell of the decree He will make: The Lord said unto me, "Thou art my Son; today I have begotten thee. Ask me and I will give you the nations for your inheritance. You will break them with a rod of iron. You will dash them in pieces like a potter's vessel."

Therefore, be wise, O you kings. Serve the Lord with fear. Kiss the Son lest He be angry, and you perish, because His wrath will soon be kindled.

Blessed is everyone who takes refuge in Him.

There is a divine commentary on this psalm in Acts 4:25-28. In verses 27-28, the Lord's Anointed is identified as Jesus; Herod is representative of the kings of the earth; Pilate is representative of the rulers; the Romans are the nations (the heathen, or Gentiles); and the Jews are the people. As the apostles stated: O Lord, you, "by the Holy Spirit, by the mouth of our father David your servant, did say" these things. It is futile for man to try to keep God from accomplishing His will.

Paul quotes Psalm 2:7 in Acts 13:33 and applies the statement to the resurrection of Christ. It was at the resurrection of Jesus that God affirmed His Fatherhood of Jesus, and that is the meaning of the statement, "This day have I begotten thee."

Psalm 8 is not strictly a Messianic psalm. Jesus applied 8:2 to the praise the children were giving Him at the time of His triumphal entry (Matt. 21:16). It is uncertain whether Jesus regarded this statement ("Out of the mouths of babes and sucklings hast thou perfected praise") as prophecy, or whether He was saying that the words of the psalm appropriately described what the children were doing. Verses 4-6 are quoted in Hebrews 2:6-8 to make the point that the world was subjected, not to angels, but to men. Therefore Jesus came to help men, not angels, and in Him the promise of God is accomplished.

Psalm 16 is not chiefly a Messianic psalm, but it contains one of the most remarkable of the Messianic prophecies: that of the resurrection. Verses 8-11 are applied by Peter to the resurrection of the Christ (Acts 2:25-32). Most of the statements are applicable to David also, but verse 10 is not. "Neither wilt thou allow thy Holy One to see corruption [or decay]." Peter points out that David died, was buried, and his tomb was still with them. David's body saw physical decay. Therefore he did not speak of himself, but, being a prophet, and knowing that God had sworn with an oath to him that He would set a descendant of his upon his throne, he spoke of the resurrection of the Christ. The Christ was not left in Hades, nor did His flesh see decay (Acts 2:29-31).

Without a doubt, one of the most impressive of the psalms is 22. When we read it, so great is its detail, we have to stop and remind ourselves that it is not actually history; it is prophecy. Verses 1, 18, and 22 are quoted from this psalm in the New Testament. In addition, verse 8 tells almost the exact words the enemies of Jesus said as they taunted Him upon the cross (Matt. 27:43). The exact mode of His death is described in 22:16. Let us analyze this psalm. It has two parts: verses 1-21 constitute the complaint of the psalmist and his cry for help; verses 22-31 are praise for the deliverance the Lord has given. As we said as we described the psalms that cry for help, it follows the pattern of others that begin with a heart-felt cry to God, asking if He sees the Psalmist's great need: O God, where are you?

Psalm 22:
My God, My God, why hast thou forsaken me? I cry day and night, but you do not answer. But you are holy. Our fathers trusted in you, and you delivered them. They cried to you, and you saved them.

I am a worm, and not a man. I am despised by the people. Everyone who sees me laughs me to scorn. They stick out their tongues and say, "Commit yourself to the Lord; let Him deliver him. Let God rescue him, since He delights in him."

You are the One who took me from the womb; you are my God since my mother bare me. Do not be far away; there is no one else to help. I am surrounded by strong bulls of Bashan. I am poured out like water, and all my bones are out of joint. My strength is dried up like a broken piece of pottery, and my tongue sticks to the roof of my mouth. Dogs have surrounded me. They have pierced my hands and my feet. I may count all my bones. They look and stare at me. They part my garments among them, and for my tunic they cast lots.

Do not be far away. Rescue my precious life from the power of the dog. Save me from the lion's mouth. Yes, from the horns of the wild oxen you have answered me.

I will tell your name among my brethren. I will sing your praise in the midst of the assembly. All you that fear the Lord, praise Him. For He has not despised, nor abhorred the affliction of the afflicted. When the afflicted cried, God heard.

I will pay my vows before them that fear Him. The meek shall eat and be satisfied; they that seek the Lord shall praise Him. All the ends of the earth shall remember and turn to the Lord. For the kingdom is the Lord's, and He is the ruler over the nations. A seed shall serve Him. It shall be told of the Lord unto the next generation. They shall come and shall declare His righteousness to a people that shall be born, that He hath done it.

In Psalm 34:20, we have a prophecy quoted in John 19:36: "He keeps all His bones; not one of them is broken." When Pilate sent soldiers to break the legs of the men who had been crucified that day, the soldiers found Jesus dead already and therefore did not break His legs. Thus the prophecy was fulfilled.

The Hebrew writer quotes Psalm 40:6-8: "Sacrifice and offering thou wouldest not, but a body didst thou prepare for me. In whole burnt offerings and sacrifices for sin thou hadst no pleasure. Then said I, 'Lo, I am come (in the roll of the book it is written of me) to do thy will, O God'" (Heb. 10:5-7). The writer then gives an inspired commentary on the passage from the psalm. God was not primarily interested in receiving sacrifices and burnt offerings from men; He wanted their obedience. Jesus came to give that obedience, but He did so when He obeyed God to become the ultimate sacrifice through which our sins could be forgiven (Heb. 10:8-18). There is no hint of the teaching of the imputed righteousness of Christ in the passage. The emphasis of the Hebrew writer is on the obedience of Jesus in making His body an offering for sin, and this is how He saves us: through His sacrifice He made forgiveness possible for our sins (see also Heb. 9:26).

Psalm 45:6 is quoted in the letter to the Hebrews: "Thy throne, O God, is forever and ever, and the scepter of righteousness is the scepter of thy kingdom. Thou hast loved righteousness, and hated iniquity. Therefore God, thy God, hath anointed thee with the oil of gladness above thy fellows" (Heb. 1:8-9). The argument made is invincible. The words of the psalm are addressed to God, yet God, in some sense, has a God, because the writer tells the God whose throne is forever, that His God has anointed Him with the oil of gladness. The solution is simple, but profound. Jesus was fully divine, He was God; but He took upon Himself the human nature as well when He became man. As man, He was subject to God as all men must be. The Hebrew writer showed powerfully by this passage that Jesus was as far above the angels as God is above His creatures.

Paul quotes Psalm 68:18 and applies it to the return of Jesus to heaven in triumph over all His enemies: "When He ascended on high, He led captivity captive, and gave gifts unto men." Paul's inspired commentary follows: "Now this, 'He ascended.' What does this mean except that He also descended into the lower parts of the earth? He that descended is the same also that ascended far above all the heavens, that He might fill all things" (Eph. 4:8-10). It is the figure of a general who goes into battle, defeats his enemies, and leads them back to his capital in triumph. Jesus came, descended into the depths of the captivity of death, but returned in triumph, leading death and captivity as His captives.

Psalm 69 has more verses quoted in the New Testament than any other single psalm. Jesus quotes verse 4 and applies it to the hatred of those who opposed Him: "But this cometh to pass, that the word may be fulfilled that is written in their law, 'They hated me without a cause'" (John 15:25). Jesus came and gave His people a chance to believe, because He did His works before them. Therefore they were without excuse. They hated Him with no cause.

When Jesus cleansed the temple early in His ministry, His disciples remembered the words of 69:9: "Zeal for thy house shall eat me up" (John 2:17). Paul quotes the last half of 69:9 in Romans 15:3: "But as it is written, 'The reproaches of them that reproached thee fell on me.'"

Psalm 69:21 says, "They gave me gall for my food, and in my thirst they gave me vinegar to drink." This passage was fulfilled when Jesus was offered wine mingled with gall as He was on His way to the cross, and then when He was offered bitter wine just before He died (Matt. 27:34, 48). It may also be the passage John had in mind when he wrote: "After this Jesus, knowing that all things were now finished, that the scripture might be accomplished, saith, 'I thirst.' There was set there a vessel full of vinegar: so they put a sponge full of the vinegar upon hyssop, and brought it to His mouth" (John 19:28-29).

Verse 22 is quoted in Romans 11:9-10, as Paul is describing the way the Jews rejected Jesus, and were in turn, rejected by Him. Verse 25 is quoted in Acts 1:20 as Peter describes how Judas' place was left desolate, after he betrayed the Lord and then killed himself.

Matthew uses Psalm 78:2 to describe Jesus' use of parables: "I will open my mouth in a parable; I will utter dark sayings of old" (Matt. 13:35). Verse 24 of this psalm is quoted by Jesus: "And He rained down manna upon them to eat, and gave them bread from heaven" (John 6:31).

Psalm 89 and Psalm 132:10-18 are strongly Messianic. Both passages are talking about the promise God made to David concerning his throne and his kingdom. We dealt extensively with that promise, and with these psalms that speak of it, as we studied the narrative. Look back to the section describing that promise in 2 Samuel 7 for an analysis of these psalms and see how they fit with the information there.

Satan quoted a passage when he tempted Jesus by taking Him to the pinnacle of the temple and telling Him to jump down: "For He will give His angels charge over thee, to keep thee in all thy ways. They shall bear thee up in their hands, lest thou dash thy foot against a stone" (Ps. 91:11-12; Matt. 4:6). The passage is in a psalm that emphasizes the security of the one who trusts in Jehovah. It does not mean that we can do any foolish thing we think of, and the Lord will keep us from harm. Jesus replied to Satan by saying, "Again it is written, thou shalt not make trial of the Lord thy God" (Matt. 4:7; Deut. 6:16).

The Hebrew writer quotes Psalm 102:25-27 and applies the words to Jesus: "Of old didst thou lay the foundation of the earth, and the heavens are the work of thy hands. They shall perish, but thou shalt endure; yea, all of them shall wax old like a garment; as a vesture shalt thou change them, and they shall be changed. But thou art the same, and thy years shall have no end" (Heb. 1:10-12). The psalm is addressed to Jehovah (102:1). He is still the One addressed in verses 12, 24-25. The Hebrew writer, in order to show the superiority of Jesus to the angels, identifies Him as Jehovah in the Old Testament. No greater tribute to the deity of Jesus could be made than this.

The Hebrew writer also refers to Psalm 104:4: "Who maketh winds His messengers, flames of fire His ministers" (Heb. 1:7). The angels of God are servants, fleet as the wind, and capable of destroying like fire; but Jesus is God's Son, Deity itself, and therefore much higher than the angels who are only messengers.

Psalm 110 is a short psalm, but powerfully Messianic. The first verse says, "The Lord said unto my Lord, 'Sit thou at my right hand, until I make thine enemies thy footstool.'" This verse is quoted several times in the New Testament (Matt. 22:44; Mark 12:36; Luke 20:42, 43; Acts 2:34-35; Heb. 1:13). In the references in the gospel, Jesus used the verse to show that the reason the Jews could not explain how David's Son could be his Lord, was that they did not believe Jesus was divine. The Hebrew writer uses the verse to show that God gave Jesus a position of rulership and power, in contrast to the angels who are servants.

Psalm 110:4 is quoted several times in the Hebrew letter: "The Lord hath sworn, and will not repent: 'Thou art a priest for ever after the order of Melchizedek'" (Heb. 5:6, 10; 6:20; 7:17, 21). God had predicted that Jesus would be a priest different to the priests of the house of Aaron; He would be a priest comparable to Melchizedek. In chapter seven, the Hebrew writer argues that this promise in Psalm 110:4 clearly implied that the Law of Moses would be changed, since under it, only men of the tribe of Levi could be priests (Heb. 7:11-17).

In Psalm 118:22-23 we find these words: "The stone which the builders rejected is become the head of the corner. This is Jehovah's doing; it is marvelous in our eyes." This passage is quoted a number of times in the New Testament (Matt. 21:42; Mark 12:10-11; Luke 20:17; Acts 4:11; 1 Pet. 2:7, and alluded to in Ephesians 2:20). The Jews stumbled over, and rejected the stone that was right in front of their eyes. They crucified their Messiah, but that did not thwart God's plan — in fact, it fulfilled His plan! The rejected stone became the cornerstone of the building.

As you look at these psalms that are quoted in the New Testament, let it renew and strengthen your awareness of the foreknowledge of God. There were no surprises to God when the Jews rejected Christ; by crucifying Him, they made it possible for the sacrifice to be offered that fulfilled God's plan for the redemption of mankind from sin.

Proverbs
The Distilled Wisdom of the Ages

Introduction:

Like other wisdom literature, proverbs flourished in the days of the United Kingdom. The collection of proverbs found in the Bible was compiled from different sources. Most were written or collected by Solomon, but the complete book as we have it was not put together until at least two hundred years later, because it contains proverbs of Solomon which were copied by the men of King Hezekiah (see Prov. 25:1; 2 Kings 18:1).

All civilizations and all generations have had their own proverbs. A proverb is statement of condensed wisdom gleaned from years of experience. It is usually short, concise, and pithy in its form. For example, in Benjamin Franklin's day, one of his proverbs was: "Early to bed, early to rise, makes a man healthy, wealthy, and wise." In his rural society, the proverb was very fitting. Today, the wealthy man may work the night shift, although the diligence implied in the proverb is still necessary for success.

The difference between the typical proverbs of a generation and those found in the Bible is that the Holy Spirit guided the ones who collected and wrote these. This is the distilled wisdom of the ages; these are the gems of wisdom that fit every generation of men. First Kings 4:32 says that Solomon "spoke 3,000 proverbs." Those in the book of Proverbs are the ones the Holy Spirit guided men to write, or those He guided them to collect. The proverbs included here are inspired, whether the Spirit inspired the man to write it specifically at that moment, or to add an existing truth to the collection. These are the proverbs that have the fear of the Lord as their solid foundation.

A proverb is a short, pithy statement of wisdom gleaned from years of experience.

The proverbs of the Bible are the statements of wisdom that the Holy Spirit inspired the wise men to include for all men of all generations.

This is the distilled wisdom of the ages.

Let us learn the lessons from the Proverbs in order to avoid the pitfalls of life.

Outline of the book:
The book divides itself into a natural outline:

I. The fatherly instructor teaches his son wisdom, and urges him to seek after wisdom. (Chapters 1-9.)
II. The proverbs of Solomon. (Chapters 10-24.)
III. Proverbs of Solomon, copied by the men of King Hezekiah. (Chapters 25-29.)
IV. The words of Agur the son of Jakeh; the oracle. (Chapter 30.)
V. The words of King Lemuel; the oracle which his mother taught him. (Chapter 31.)

We are not allotting enough space in this book to make a thorough analysis of the Proverbs because the subjects discussed are too diverse. Instead, let us look at the purpose for the proverbs, and let us observe some of the interesting things about them. Then we will classify them into a few subject categories. Since some of the subjects are closely related, there will be some overlapping because we may list some verse in more than one category. We certainly do not claim that our list of subjects is exhaustive. This is merely a suggestion of a way to teach the book. Make your own analysis and add your own topics, or add some verse we have overlooked on a subject, as you study the book.

We are presenting the information in the book of Proverbs differently to the other books because of the diverse nature of the subjects. We are using more of an outline form than a narrative form.

Definition of terms:
Matthew 5:22 says, "Whosoever shall say, 'Thou fool,' shall be in danger of hell fire." Yet all of the Wisdom Literature uses the expression repeatedly. What is the explanation? Was it all right in God's sight to call one a fool under the Old Law, but not under the New? Or is the expression being used in two different senses? I think the latter explanation is the correct one. In Matthew 5, Jesus is condemning the use of such terms as oaths in which one calls upon God to condemn someone who has angered us. God is the Judge, and I have no right to call upon God to condemn anyone. He will take care of all judgment, and will show much more wisdom in doing so than any human being could show. Therefore, God's law forbids my using the expression "fool" (or any equivalent term) to express my condemnation of another.

In the Wisdom Literature, the word fool is a descriptive term. The writers use it to describe one who refuses to learn the lessons that are directly in front of him. He may be a fool simply because he is acting foolish by not recognizing pitfalls directly before him. He may make the same mistake over and over, and never learn the obvious lesson to avoid that path. Or, he may be a fool because he deliberately chooses to ignore the rebukes of the wise; he may deliberately choose to reject the way God has set before him. In that way, he is a fool because he has chosen to be one. The cry throughout the Wisdom Literature is to stay away from the path of the fool. If we are not careful, we may find ourselves in the path of the fool in some area of our life, even if we are showing wisdom in other areas. If so, let us follow the advice and turn away from the path of foolishness.

The book of Proverbs calls to the young man, to the "simple one." This is the person who has not learned the lessons of life. He is the ignorant one. He may be ignorant because he is young and has not yet had enough experiences to help him make wise decisions. The cry to him is to look at the experiences of others, and learn the lessons they have learned by hard experience. Do not make the mistakes that others have already made and suffered from. The simple one may be ignorant because he is not looking around him to see if there are pitfalls. The cry to him is to wake up; be alert to the evident lessons. The simple one is the naive one, that is, the one who is too trusting of others, or the one who is not looking to the end result of some action. Again, each of us has our areas of ignorance. Let us heed the cry to the simple one.

The wise man is the one who has learned the lessons of life. He has profited from mistakes he has made, and from the mistakes of others. He knows to avoid the paths of the foolish ones. He knows to be alert, and avoid the pitfalls the simple one may fall into. The truly wise man is the one who has learned the priorities of life and is basing his wisdom upon the solid foundation of the fear of the Lord (1:7).

The wisdom recommended in the book of Proverbs is the wisdom from above, the kind James in the New Testament recommends that we pray to God for (James 1:5). Wisdom that is merely the learning of information that men have discovered may or may not be of help in making our lives happier here, or in helping us go to heaven. But the wisdom that begins with the fear (reverence) of Jehovah (Prov. 1:7) sets our feet on the right path for true happiness here and in eternity.

Purpose for the Proverbs:

The first six verses of the book tell us what the proverbs are designed to do. Let us examine the points made. Some of the expressions are closely synonymous.

1. The first purpose is "to know wisdom and instruction" (1:2a). Wisdom is from the Hebrew word *hakam* (or *chakam*). It refers to the ability to see things as they really are, to sort out reality from fiction. Instruction refers to discipline, instruction which, in accord with wisdom, will enable one to control and conduct one's affairs in the best possible manner.

2. The second purpose is "to discern the words of understanding" (1:2b). The best translation of this is to understand the principles by which to examine information or a discussion, to see whether it is good or bad, true or false. Let me quote a summary of these thoughts from Delitzsch. Speaking of the proverbs generally in the light of 1:2, he says, "They seek on the one side to initiate the reader in wisdom and instruction, and on the other to guide him to the understanding of intelligent discourses, for they themselves contain such discourses in which there is a deep penetrating judgment, and they sharpen the understanding of him who engages his attention with them" (p. 415).

3. The third purpose is to receive instruction in the *whys and wherefores* of righteousness, justice, and integrity. The person who is guided by the proverbs will do these things, not by external constraint, or by custom, but by understanding the underlying principles of right and wrong.

4. The fourth purpose is to give prudence to the simple. The simple one here is the naive person, literally, the one who is open to various influences. The parallel says, "To the young man knowledge and discretion." The young man is he who, because of youth, is without experience. To him the inspired proverbs can give the knowledge of experience vicariously, and discretion, that is, the ability to comprehend the right purposes, to seize the right measures, to project the right plans. He can learn from the mistakes and wisdom gained from the experiences of others.

5. The fifth purpose is that the wise man may hear and increase in learning, and that the man of understanding, the one who is willing to be informed, the intelligent person, may gain sound rules of conduct or management. The word *tachebuloth*, according to Delitzsch, is from *chobel*, that is, a shipmaster, and refers to management, the skill to direct something. Thus the Proverbs can help one who is already wise and give him the ability to plan and direct both his own affairs and

the affairs of others wisely.

6. The Proverbs enable a person to comprehend a wise saying, to understand the words of the wise and their enigmas or puzzles.

The Fatherly Instructor
Chapters 1-9

The first nine chapters are written almost as if they were a letter of advice from a father to a son. The father advises his son on the most important principles of life, including his relationship with God. The information, of course, is applicable to all young people, whether sons or daughters. Also, the good advice is not limited to the young. It is for everyone who can use it, and any "son" will be wiser if he listens and heeds the advice given.

As you study these nine chapters, Fathers and Mothers, think about your responsibilities. The Proverbist calls upon the young man to listen to the advice of his parents; to seek for wisdom as he plans his life. But what if the parents are too caught up in their own affairs to take time to talk to their sons and daughters about wisdom? Then what do the sons and daughters have to guide their lives? Where will they find the wisdom they need? How can they listen, if nothing is being said? Parents have a grave responsibility to teach their children, and children have just as grave a responsibility to listen and give heed to the things taught.

I. Chapter 1:
   A. The purposes for the Proverbs (1:1-6).
   B. The fatherly instructor teaches how beautifully a son's obedience to his parents' training will adorn his life (1:7-9).
   C. Wisdom will keep one from suffering the fate of wicked, violent men (1:10-19).
   D. Wisdom is personified as a woman crying out loud in the street for someone to listen to her (1:20-23).
   E. The consequences of failure to listen to wisdom: in the day of calamity, she will not listen to you (1:24-33).

Proverbs are general principles of wisdom based upon experience, and are not without exception. Job and Ecclesiastes both teach, for example, that the same thing may happen to the good and to the wicked. Outward circumstances are not an infallible indicator of one's spiritual condition. But, as a rule, the principles of wisdom will deliver one from calamity. The wisdom recommended here is the wisdom based upon the fear of Jehovah (1:7). Therefore, the one who follows this wisdom will be living his life the way God says is best. He may have health problems, or other reversals in life as Job and Ecclesiastes teach, but he avoids all the pitfalls that sin and foolishness would bring to his life.

II. Chapter 2:
   A. The benefits of seeking and getting wisdom above all else (2:1-11).
   B. Wisdom will deliver you from evil men (2:12-15).
   C. It will deliver you from evil women (2:16-22).

The advantages of seeking the Lord are couched in spiritual terms in these verses. The one who finds this wisdom from above discovers the value of God's commandments. The one who has this kind of wisdom has God as his shield. What greater asset could he have? This kind of wisdom keeps the young man from falling to the appeals from his peers that will lead him into the pitfalls of the wicked. It gives him guidance for his life.

III. Chapter 3:
    A. The value of seeking the Lord (3:1-12).
    B. The value of wisdom is extolled: even the Lord used wisdom when He framed the worlds; wisdom gives comfort and security (3:13-26).
    C. Principles of wisdom: do not refuse to do good when the opportunity arises, and have nothing to do with the ways of the wicked (3:27-35).

Those who remember what they have been taught, and who continually seek the Lord, will also tend to be blessed physically and materially. Their adherence to the Lord's ways will be "health to the navel and marrow to the bones" (3:8). Honor the Lord with your substance, so shall your barns be filled to overflowing (3:9-10). Think of the passage in Malachi 3:10: "Bring ye all the tithes into the storehouse… and prove me now herewith, saith the Lord of hosts, if I will not open you the windows of heaven, and pour you out a blessing, that there shall not be room enough to receive it."

IV. Chapter 4:
    A. The fatherly instructor recalls the instructions of *his* father: make the getting of wisdom your chief aim, and she will reward you (4:1-9).
    B. Following after wisdom will give order to your life. Have nothing to do with the way of evil men (4:10-19).
    C. Pay attention to instruction; wisdom will guide ear, heart, mouth, eyes, and feet (4:20-27).

Young man, listen to the advice of your father. Let him tell you the advice his father taught him. Do not have to repeat the mistakes they made and learned to avoid. Listen! Pay attention! Their advice will give guidance to every aspect of your life.

V. Chapter 5:
    A. Let wisdom guide you in your relationship with women; beware the ways of the wicked woman (5:1-6).
    B. Do not waste your life and resources on the immoral woman; you will have nothing but ruin to show for it (5:7-14).
    C. Enjoy a relationship with your wife; enjoy the life you can build together; be carried away with your love and desire for her (5:15-20).
    D. Remember that Jehovah sees all; the wicked will not escape the consequences of his deeds (5:21-23).

The wise man repeatedly warns the young man against the wicked woman in these chapters that speak as father to son. He also warns against the path of the wicked man, but he returns to the warning against the siren call of the wicked woman because it is such a temptation to the young man. Do not destroy your life for a few minutes of pleasure with a wicked woman. Have your own wife and work together to build your future based upon this wisdom from God. Remember that God is seeing everything you do, and your time with the wicked woman will not escape unnoticed.

VI. Chapter 6:
    A. If you have made a bad deal, do everything you can to get yourself out of it (6:1-5).

B. Do not be lazy; idleness will rob you as surely as an armed man (6:6-11).
  C. The man who has a perverse mouth, shifty eyes, and shuffling feet is a worthless person; his calamity will come upon him suddenly (6:12-15).
  D. Six things the Lord hates; yea, seven things are an abomination to Him (6:16-19):
     1. An arrogant attitude.
     2. A lying tongue.
     3. Hands that shed innocent blood.
     4. A heart that plans wicked things.
     5. Feet that hurry to do harmful things.
     6. A false witness.
     7. One who sows discord among brothers.
  E. Remember the lessons of your father and mother; let them keep you from the harlot and the adulteress and the trouble they can get you into (6:20-35).

Be wise in your business dealings. Work diligently. Be cautious whom you choose as your business partner. Be alert to the signs the foolish, worthless man is showing, and do not choose him as the one you depend upon in a venture. If you find you have made an unwise business deal, be quick to withdraw from it. Learn the lessons from the experience.

Notice the strong words "hate" and "abomination." It has been drilled into the minds of our society that God is a loving God, One who loves us no matter how we behave. The Wisdom Literature uses such strong terms as these throughout the books. God hates wickedness; these things are an abomination to Him. Be alert to other strong terms the book of Proverbs uses to describe things God hates. Let us beware lest any of these characteristics are found in our lives. If it is something God hates, then He hates it in my life just as surely as He hates it in the most wicked person I know.

VII. Chapter 7:
  A. Keep in mind your father's words, to deliver you from the immoral woman. Do not be led by her as an ox to the slaughter; the ox does not even know he is about to be killed (7:1-23).
  B. Listen to your father: the immoral woman has slain a mighty army of men; do not think yourself in no danger from her (7:24-27).

In 1 Corinthians 6:18, Paul says, "Flee fornication." That is, run from it! In Proverbs 7, Solomon is sitting at his window and watching a naive young man fall into the snare of the wicked woman. The young man has made his way to her corner, the place where she lies in wait each evening. Solomon's cry to young men is, "Stay away from her corner. Avoid her! Stronger men than you have fallen victim to her trap of death and destruction. Do not think you can escape unharmed." Listen, young man of today! Learn the lesson! Fornication is not something to flirt with. A young man who is seeking to serve the Lord may deliberately go to the beach, or may deliberately date a girl with a bad reputation — because he wants a bit of thrill, with no intention of falling into the obvious trap. The wise man (along with Paul the apostle) cries out, "Run the other way. Don't stop to be tempted. Don't put yourself in that position."

VIII. Chapter 8:
  A. Wisdom calls to men and pleads with them to learn her value (8:1-11).
  B. Wisdom enumerates her gifts (8:12-21).
  C. Wisdom was God's helper in the creation of the world (8:22-31).
  D. Blessed is the man who hearkens to the cry of wisdom (8:32-36).

In contrast with the clamorous, wicked woman of chapter 7, wisdom calls men to come and learn her value. In every prominent place she stands and cries out. Her advice is good, not bad. It is worth more than silver and gold. Wisdom has an excellent history of accomplishment. By her princes and kings have ruled. She loves those who love her. She blesses those who pursue her by filling their treasuries. She gives them rewards even greater than silver and gold. The greatest recommendation of wisdom is that even God made use of her in the marvelous way He created and arranged the earth. How blessed is the one who watches and listens for wisdom daily.

IX. Chapter 9:
    A. Wisdom invites all to her feast (9:1-6).
    B. A man labels himself wise or foolish by the way he regards wisdom (9:7-12).
    C. Beware the invitation of the immoral woman (9:13-18).

Wisdom has prepared an elaborate house and a sumptuous feast. She is generous with her bounty. She sends her maidens to invite all to come. She beseeches the inexperienced and naive to forsake their ways and walk in understanding. A man tells whether he is a wise man or a scoffer by how he pays attention to instruction. A wise man will listen to instruction; the foolish man will learn nothing. The fear of the Lord is the beginning of wisdom. If a man is wise, he will profit from it; if he is foolish, he will pay the price.

Proverbs of Solomon
Chapters 10-29

Chapters 10-29 include two sections of proverbs (chapters 10-24 and 25-29), though all are called "Proverbs of Solomon." They are too diverse in subject matter to classify into paragraphs and analyze verse by verse, or chapter by chapter. Therefore we will place the verses into several categories, and we will summarize the lessons taught on the various subjects. Use our categories to suggest ways to teach the various topics discussed in Proverbs, and add categories of your own as you make your study. In our classification of verses in these two sections of the book, we remind you of similar passages in the first nine chapters, but we do not include every passage there in the subject where it might fit. Though chapters 30 and 31 fall into categories of their own, we include some passages from there that fit appropriately in some of these subject headings.

We call attention to several structured sections in chapters 10-29, but for convenience, we classify the verses in these sections as we classify the rest of chapters 10-29.

1. 22:17-21 is an appeal to heed the voice of wisdom, and the writer says, "Have not I written unto thee excellent things of counsels and knowledge?" (22:20).
2. In 23:1-8 there is a paragraph of instruction regarding one's conduct before a ruler.
3. In 23:15-24:22 the proverbs are presented as more advice from the fatherly instructor. Even in this section, however, the transition from one subject to the other is somewhat abrupt.
4. 23:26-28 is a warning against the immoral woman, similar to the warnings found often in the first nine chapters.
5. 23:29-35 is the most vivid and complete warning against drunkenness to be found in the whole Bible.
6. In 27:23-27 the writer urges us to be diligent, to see after our affairs. There must be balance in the affairs of life, but the Proverbs strongly encourage diligence in whatever we do.

The sluggard:

10:4-5, 26;	15:19;	21:25-26	26:13-16;
12:11, 24, 27;	18:9;	22:13;	28:19.
13:4;	19:15, 24;	23:21;	
14:23;	20:4, 13;	24:30-34;	

The sluggard is the person who is too lazy to work. He may combine his vice of laziness with another vice, such as drinking (23:20-21). He may be just lazy, or he may be always seeking the will o' the wisp (26:14-16). He may associate with vain companions, people who are up to no good. He may give reasons for doing nothing, but his reasons are merely excuses (26:13). If he did not have those reasons, he would invent others.

The sluggard may be the other side of the coin from the nagging wife. There are proverbs about the nagging wife, but the sluggard has no right to read the proverbs about the contentious woman to his wife, and blame her for his own negligence. He needs to read the ones that tell him to get up from his bed, or from his chair, and see to his business. Laziness will rob one of his possessions just as surely as an armed man (24:34). (Though the passages about the sluggard use the masculine pronouns, the principles apply the same way if it is the wife who is the sluggard. Then it might be the husband who is perceived as the nagging one when he tries to get his wife to do her work. Do not fail to see the lesson either way it fits.)

One may be classified as a sluggard according to the Proverbs even is he holds a good job and makes a good salary. What does he do with his salary? How does he care for his possessions when gets them? Does he buy things and then let them rot away from carelessness and neglect? Is his house and property a shame to the neighborhood? The Proverbist has no good word to say for the sluggard who allows his property to deteriorate through neglect, no matter what reason he gives for that neglect.

Contrast between the wise and the fool:

10:1, 8, 13, 14, 23;	15:2, 5, 7, 14, 20, 21;	21:11, 20;
11:12, 29;	16:22;	22:3;
12:1, 15, 16, 23;	17:10, 24;	27:12;
13:1, 16, 20;	19:25;	29:8, 9, 11.
14:1, 3, 6, 8, 9, 15, 16, 18, 24, 29, 33;		

In these listings, we contrast the wise man and the fool. Then we have separate listings for the wise man and for the fool. In this way one may make a study of either of these three topics, or a combination of all three. There is a good bit of overlapping, but there are also some differences in the lists. The main differences between the wise man and the fool are:

1. *The wise man is willing to listen; he profits from instruction. The fool is not only unwilling to listen, he cannot conceive of being taught how to do something.*
2. *The wise man plans his life and thinks about what he is doing. The fool is haphazard and has no plan. He just walks into the fan.*
3. *The wise man is careful about what he says, and he knows when to keep quiet. The fool opens wide his mouth and lets a torrent of foolishness come forth.*
4. *The wise man knows that actions and words have consequences, and he is careful to provoke by his words and actions the consequences that are desirable. It never dawns on the fool that something may be <u>his</u> fault, that something he did may have caused his misfortune, and he is doomed endlessly*

to make the same mistakes again and again.
5. *The wise man knows that the most important thing in life is to walk in God's ways. The fool may deceive himself into thinking there is no God (Ps. 14:1); or he may simply never bother to think about what life is all about.*

Description of a wise man:

10:1, 8, 13, 14, 19, 23, 31;	15:2, 5, 7, 14, 20, 21, 24, 31, 32;	20:5;
11:2, 12, 29, 30;	16:14, 21, 22, 23;	21:11, 20, 22;
12:1, 8, 15, 16, 18, 23;	17:10, 27, 28;	22:3;
13:1, 10, 14, 15, 16, 20;	18:15;	24:5-6;
14:1, 3, 6, 8, 15, 16, 18, 24, 29, 33, 35;	19:8, 11, 20, 25;	27:12; 29:8, 9, 11.

The characteristics of a wise man are:
1. *The wise man seeks to reverence God, believing that God's ways are best.*
2. *The wise man can be taught; he is quick to take instruction.*
3. *The wise man thinks how to express what he wishes to say.*
4. *The wise man plans what he wants to do.*
5. *The wise man is skillful in getting along with people.*
6. *The wise man does not hunt trouble.*

The wonderful thing about Proverbs is that the teaching of the book can help us learn to be wise. Surely we can see that being wise will help us have a better life now, and will give us a secure hope of life everlasting. Let us be busy gaining wisdom. There is no reasonable excuse to remain ignorant, or to remain in the path of the foolish.

Be very alert that the wisdom described is not the mere gaining of information. That kind of wisdom may help in climbing some corporate ladder, but the well-educated man may be a fool in the ways of God. The truly wise man is the one who bases his whole life upon the fear of the Lord. He may be rich or poor in material things, but he is the one highly blessed; he is the one who can enjoy life to its fullest.

Description of a Fool:

10:1, 8, 13, 14, 18, 21, 23;	16:22;	23:9;
11:12, 29;	17:10, 12, 16, 18, 24, 25;	24:7, 9, 30-34;
12:1, 15, 16, 23;	18:2, 6, 7, 13;	26:1, 3-12;
13:1, 16;	19:1, 3, 13a, 25, 29;	27:12, 22;
14:1, 3, 6, 7, 8, 9, 15, 16, 17, 18, 24, 29, 33;	20:3;	28:26;
15:2, 5, 7, 14, 20, 21;	21:11, 20; 22:3;	29:8, 9, 11.

The fool is, of course, the opposite of the wise man:
1. *He is haphazard in his life and plans nothing; or if he does plan, his planning is so scatterbrained it is of no value.*
2. *The fool does not seek God.*
3. *The fool will not listen and cannot be told anything.*
4. *The fool has convinced himself that he is earth's fountain of all wisdom.*
5. *The fool never realizes that he is his own worst enemy, and that his misfortunes are brought upon himself by his own words and deeds.*

6. The fool never thinks before he acts or speaks.

The sad thing is that the genuine fool could read these words, and they would make no impression upon him. Usually though, there is a little foolishness in all of us. If we see ourselves in one of the descriptions of the fool, let us be diligent to change our behavior, and deliver ourselves from the pitfalls that come upon him.

Children and parents:

10:1, 5;	19:13a, 18, 26;	28:7, 24;
13:1, 24;	20:11, 20;	29:3, 15, 17, 21;
15:5, 20;	22:6, 15;	30:11, 17.
17:2, 6, 21, 25;	23:13-14, 15, 19, 22, 24-26;	

Many people think that the only thing said about children in Proverbs is "Spare the rod and spoil the child." Actually, though the sentiment is found, the statement is not. There are several very important principles taught about the relationship between parents and children. Discipline, in the sense of punishment, is only one of the concepts. In reality, the word "discipline" is a broad term that includes all training, instruction, and guidance that a child needs. In that sense, it could cover the whole realm of the relationship between parents and children. For discipline and training to be effective, there are responsibilities on the part of both parties involved, and those are the points stressed in the book of Proverbs.

Remember all the passages in the first nine chapters that call upon the young man to remember and to heed the advice and teaching of his parents. Those passages fit very closely with this heading. In view of this subject heading, look at both sides of the picture. The wise man has called to the young man to listen to the advice of his parents; but, Parents, be sure you are giving the advice that your son needs. Do not forget to share your experiences and your wisdom with your children. If you fail to teach, then you share the blame if your child becomes the fool described in Proverbs.

There is a serious lack of natural affection in our day (see Rom. 1:31), both on the part of parents toward children, and children toward parents. Child abuse does occur. But making a child learn to mind is not child abuse. Spanking, as a part of a planned approach to discipline, serves an important role in training children. Countless millions of Americans have been reared by parents who sometimes paddled them. There was some abuse, but most of these people would say that they deeply appreciate what their parents did for them, and most of these people have been upstanding, law-abiding citizens. Spanking done out of love, with a desire to correct a child, still has a place in the discipline of children. It is by no means a cure-all, but neither can it be put off limits.

We can summarize the lessons from Proverbs about children and parents this way:

1. *Children are not born knowing how to behave. They do not have wisdom, judgment, or proper values. Children must be taught these lessons.*
2. *If a child is left to its own devices, it will be totally ruined, and will bring shame and grief to its parents. There is no greater pain parents can have than from children who bring them shame.*
3. *Discipline, while sometimes painful, will not kill the child; instead it will produce good results. It will deliver his soul from destruction.*
4. *One of the most valuable things a child can do for himself is to pay attention to what his parents have taught him. Of course, in the context of Proverbs, this means what <u>godly parents</u> have taught him.*
5. *One of the worst things a child can do is to show disrespect, to curse, or to afflict his parents.*

Fruits of wickedness and righteousness:

10:2, 3, 6, 7, 9, 11, 16, 20-21, 24, 25, 28, 29, 30, 31, 32;
11:3, 5-6, 7, 8, 9, 10-11, 17, 18, 19, 20, 21, 23, 27, 30, 31;
12:2, 3, 5-6, 7, 10, 12, 13, 21, 26, 28;
13:5, 6, 9, 15, 21, 22, 25;
14:2, 9, 11, 12, 14, 19, 22, 32, 34;
15:6, 8-9, 28, 29;
16:4, 12, 13, 17, 25;
17:13, 15;
18:10;
19:16;
20:7;
21:8, 12, 15, 18, 21, 26, 29;
22:4;
24:15-16, 19-20;
28:1, 10, 12, 18, 28;
29:2, 6-7, 16, 27.

Sometimes wickedness may seem to give one an advantage in a business deal. Therefore the righteous may find himself envying the wicked. The Proverbs teach over and over that we should never envy the wicked, because their "success" is very insecure, very short-lived, and not what it appears to be on the surface. The righteous will generally be blessed on this earth, and he will spend eternity in heaven because he seeks God. The wicked has nothing to hope for except judgment and calamity. He may have a little run of success, some sampling of pleasure, but he has nothing at all upon which he can depend for joy or security.

Some of the temporal rewards of righteousness depend upon the system working the way it is supposed to work. For example, if the land is fortunate enough to have a ruler who appreciates righteousness, then things will be good for the righteous; if not, then trials will come their way.

Some points about righteousness are:

1. *Righteousness delivers one from violence and calamity. We must remember that this is not always so. One cannot necessarily determine from one's prosperity or adversity whether he is righteous or not, but generally the principle is true: "Righteousness delivers from death" (10:2-3). Over and over this point is made (11:3-4, 6).*
2. *Righteousness has a secure reward (11:18). Even death does not rob the righteous of his reward.*
3. *The righteous man does righteous deeds (13:5).*
4. *Righteousness wins the love of good people.*

Warnings about business dealings:

10:4, 26;
11:1, 15, 24, 26;
13:7, 11;
14:4, 23;
15:22;
16:11;
17:18;
18:9;
20:10, 13, 14, 16, 23;
21:5;
22:26-27, 29;
23:10-11;
24:27;
27:23-27;
28:19;
29:24.

The Proverbs contain excellent and practical instructions for successful business dealings. They include the following:

1. *Do not be too quick to make a deal. Look carefully before you leap.*
2. *Be exceedingly cautious about standing good for another's debts (11:15).*
3. *If you find you have gotten yourself into a bad deal, do not rest until you have gotten yourself out of it (see 6:1-5).*
4. *Be scrupulously fair in your business dealings. You will give an account to God for the way you deal*

with others, even in business (11:1; 16:11).
5. *Work hard at your business. Show diligence. Keep up with things (10:4; 27:23-27).*
6. *Hire good help. To use sluggards will set your teeth on edge and will make your eyes water (10:26).*
7. *Be generous in your sowing, or you will get very little return (11:24).*

Materialism:

11:24, 25, 26, 28;	17:1;	22:1, 9, 16;
13:7, 11, 22, 25;	18:11;	23:4-5;
14:20, 21;	19:1, 4, 7, 17;	27:20;
15:6, 16-17, 27;	20:15, 17;	28:6, 8, 20, 22, 25, 27.
16:8, 16, 19, 26;	21:6, 17;	

There are many warnings and many principles taught about material things. One of the most common lessons taught is that joy does not come from one's possessions. It is better to have a little, with joy, than many riches in a house where there is contention and strife (15:16-17; 17:1). Be generous with your possessions. Do not trust in your riches; they could be taken away in a moment. Beware the evils of ill-gotten gain (15:6).

Value of a good wife:

12:4;	19:14;
18:22;	31:10-31.

Though there are only a few verses under this specific heading, their message is powerful. Proverbs 31:10-31 is devoted to the subject and beautifully describes the worthy woman and her value. Chapter 31 fits into a category of its own, but since its subject matter fits so well with this heading, we include it here.

The first three references given above stress that a worthy wife is a blessing from God. In Proverbs 31, her qualities are set forth. It seems strange to today's generation that there is no talk of how beautiful and sophisticated she is. The quality that makes a woman a good wife is that she is faithful, she is a worthy partner. Her husband does not have to worry about what his wife is doing, or with whom she is playing around. She is his partner in life, and together they are building a home and a worthwhile life (see 5:15-19). She is dependable; she is diligent. She works hard to keep the household in good condition. She enhances her husband's reputation by her conduct and by her wisdom.

This does not mean that there is no romantic side, no sexual side to consider in a marriage. Proverbs 3:15-20 makes it abundantly clear that there is a sexual side to the relationship of husband and wife. Proverbs, however, makes this side of much less importance than does modern America. Proverbs emphasizes that a husband and wife with the proper perspective do not count on the sexual relationship to hold their marriage together. It is only one of the aspects of marriage, and they are to take what they have and make it work, to be satisfied with it. When one nurtures a truly successful marriage, he finds that it is the practical, day by day things, such as consideration, true affection for one another, friendship, the ability to share one's deepest thoughts, dependability, and goodness that make a marriage the joy it can be.

The contentious, nagging woman:

19:13b;	27:15-16;
21:9, 19;	30:23.
25:24;	

The contentious woman is one with an abrasive personality. She is her own worst enemy. No one can get along with her. She is so negative in her outlook, she can see no good in anyone, especially in her husband. She has no wisdom in dealing with people. This type person not only deals misery to her husband, she deals misery to everyone who comes her way. And there is no relief from it. Day after day, she is the same, and her husband knows he faces the rest of his days dealing with her criticisms and complaints.

A woman who is married to a sluggard or a fool has a real problem. Her husband is too lazy to do what needs to be done, and she cannot do it all; or he is too foolish to heed instruction and is forever in trouble. Vainly she tries to get him to do what needs to be done. Not only does he refuse to see his own worthlessness, he accuses her of nagging, when she is only trying to get him to do the necessary work. The fool may not be a sluggard, but he does not have enough concern or sensitivity to listen to his wife's concerns, and rebuffs her efforts to express herself to him by accusing her of nagging. A woman in this circumstance needs to be careful that she does not nag, that she does not become contentious. If one of the couple has to be lost in eternity, let it not be her for nagging; let it be the husband for being a sluggard, and a fool.

Young people, look carefully at the one you are dating. Young man, do not choose a contentious, nagging woman as your lifelong companion. And, young woman, do not choose a sluggard or a fool as the head of your family. Bad characteristics a person has in youth tend to worsen through the years, not improve — unless the individual himself determines to change the characteristic. The marriage partner rarely succeeds in changing the other's personality. If you choose the wrong partner, you will spend every day of the rest of your life regretting it. But remember, if you have made a bad choice, and wish you could change your decision, that does not remove your responsibility to behave yourself as God has instructed you in your marriage relationship.

The immoral woman:
22:14;   29:3;
23:27-28;   30:20;
27:13;   31:3.

Remember the splendid passages on this subject in the first nine chapters of Proverbs: 2:16-19; 5:3-20; 6:24-35; 7:5-27; 9:13-18.

These warnings about the immoral woman are certainly appropriate for young women against immoral men also. They work basically the same way. The immoral woman may have different motives from the immoral man. She may not be led by her fleshly lusts so much as by her desire to be flattered, to get some advantage over another, or to obtain wealth. Whatever her motive, the young man must realize that she does not love him. He is only another beef going to slaughter. She will say the things he wants to hear, but she means none of it. She may be beautiful, and she may use the best perfumes, and her bed may be tastefully decorated, but it is a deathtrap. Do not be deceived. When a young man pursues immorality, whether it is with a particular promiscuous woman, or with harlots, he is building nothing. He is squandering his name, his resources, and his health. When it all comes to an end, he will have nothing to show for it but a ruined life of lost opportunities.

The young woman must realize that the smooth-talking immoral man is interested in only one thing, to get her in bed. She is a conquest; when he has conquered her he is through. Time to move on. Sometimes a man preys upon lonely women, widows, or those who have never married. He wants their money. His tactics are the same as those of the immoral woman. The same consequences follow the woman who listens to his flattery.

Fear of the Lord:

10:27;	16:6;	24:21;
13:13;	19:23;	31:30.
14:2, 26, 27;	22:4;	
15:16, 33;	23:17;	

The fear of the Lord is the main part, the foundation, of wisdom. The writer of Ecclesiastes says that the wisdom of this world is vanity, a mere grasping for the wind (Eccl. 2:12-17). If one does not reverence God, his wisdom will be to no avail. The fear of Lord leads us to walk uprightly; it is good for us; it protects us, and gives us refuge; it will give us great reward.

Remember also the excellent verses in chapters 1-9 on this subject: 1:7, 29; 2:5; 3:7; 8:13; 9:10.

The use of the tongue:

10:11, 13, 14, 18, 19, 20, 21, 31, 32;	16:1, 10, 13, 21, 23, 24, 27, 28;	24:2, 7, 24, 26, 28;
11:9, 11, 12, 13;	17:4, 7, 9, 14, 20, 27, 28;	25:11, 14, 15, 18, 23;
12:6, 13, 14, 17, 18, 19, 22, 25;	18:4, 6-7, 8, 13, 20, 21, 23;	26:4, 5, 7, 9, 20, 21, 22, 23, 24-25, 28;
13:2, 3;	19:1, 5, 9, 22, 28;	27:14;
14:3, 5, 7, 23, 25;	20:3, 15, 17, 19, 20, 25;	28:23;
15:1, 2, 4, 7, 14, 23, 26, 28;	21:6, 23;	29:5, 19, 20;
	22:10, 12, 14, 18;	30:8, 9, 10, 11;
	23:9, 16;	31:8, 9, 26.

As James teaches in the New Testament, the tongue is capable of many things, both good and bad. It is the hardest of all things to control (James 3:1-12). The Proverbs tell how the tongue can cut and wound, and how it can comfort and cheer others. With it we can lie, or we can tell the truth. The tongue can get us into immeasurable trouble very quickly. The Proverbist warns us to be sparing with our tongue. Take thought before you speak.

Be sure to consult the advice of the fatherly instructor in chapters 1-9 for additional information on the tongue.

Warnings against drunkenness:

20:1;
23:20, 21, 29-35;
31:4-7.

The Proverbs reflect that same split personality of the word "wine" that it has in the rest of the scriptures. It can be a blessing or a curse. Many would have us believe that the sole difference is the amount — that what is forbidden is drinking too much. Such a view is most popular with those who want to drink the table wines of today without criticism.

In both the Old and New Testaments, the word wine had a wide range of meaning. There were also two ways of handling it. The word can refer to fresh grape juice, or to grape juice that has been fermented to the maximum degree possible. When the fermented substance was used in that day, it could be drunk straight, as fermented as possible with a view to getting drunk; or it could be mixed with several parts of water to dilute the alcoholic content it had. Those who wanted to enjoy the blessings of "wine" would seek it as fresh as possible, and they would cut it with water to the degree it was needed. It is this sense in which "wine" is spoken of in various passages as a blessing (Ps. 104:15; Eccl. 9:7). Those who wanted the inebriating effects of "wine" would ferment it as much as possible, drink it straight, and drink it fast. It is in this sense "wine" is condemned, as in the passages above.

Do not stay so long on a discussion of the meaning of the word wine that you fail to get the impact of the warnings against drunkenness. The warnings are vivid, and they are needed in every generation.

Advice for kings:
14:28;
16:10, 12;
17:7;
20:8, 26, 28;

21:1;
25:2-5;
28:2, 15-16;

29:2, 4, 12, 14;
31:2-9.

Some of the passages above set forth principles regarding kings, such as, "In the multitude of people is the king's glory" (14:28). Most of the verses, however, advise the king to rule fairly and wisely. He has great power and needs to use that power for the good of his subjects. A country can be blessed or ruined depending upon the character and nature of its ruler. This subject heading fits very closely with the next one on our responsibilities as we deal with kings or other men in positions of power.

Warnings about dealing with men of power:
14:35;
16:13, 14, 15;
18:16;
19:12;

20:2;
22:11;
23:1-8;
24:21-22;

25:6-7, 15;
27:18;
29:26.

Solomon warns us that men of power can be capricious, and very arbitrary in their judgments. If we anger them, they have the ability to do great harm. When a man deals with those of great power, he must realize just how slippery his position may be. Do not presume too much, or you may find you have been demoted, or in some societies, beheaded!

Many of the passages deal with the ideal situation in which a ruler appreciates truth and goodness. Under such circumstances men need to be sure to tell the truth and to do what is right. Woe to a country, though, when the rulers are crooked and corrupt. It is then very difficult for scrupulous men of principle to deal with such rulers.

Miscellaneous principles of living and conduct:
10:12, 17, 18, 19, 22, 27;
11:2, 3, 4, 13, 14, 16, 17, 22, 24-26, 27, 28, 29, 30, 31;
12:1, 8, 9, 11, 14, 17-19, 20, 22, 25, 28;
13:2-3, 7, 8, 9, 10, 12, 13, 14, 15, 17, 18, 19, 20, 23;
14:5, 6, 10, 12, 13, 14, 17, 20, 21, 22, 25, 26, 27, 28, 29, 30, 31, 34;
15:1, 3, 4, 10, 11, 12, 13, 15, 18, 22, 23, 25, 26, 30, 31, 32, 33;
16:1, 2, 3, 4, 5, 6, 7, 9, 10,

16:16, 17, 18, 20-24, 25, 26, 27-30, 31, 32, 33;
17:2, 3, 4, 5, 6, 7, 8, 9, 11, 12, 13, 14, 15, 16, 17, 19, 20, 22, 23, 26;
18:1, 3, 4, 5, 8, 9, 10, 11-12, 14, 15, 16, 17, 18, 19, 20, 21, 23, 24;
19:2, 4, 5, 6-7, 9, 10, 16, 17, 19, 20, 21, 22, 23, 27, 28;
20:6, 7, 8, 9, 11, 12, 15, 17, 18, 19, 21, 22, 24, 25, 27, 29, 30;

21:2, 3, 4, 5, 6, 7, 10, 12, 13, 14, 15, 16, 21, 22, 23, 24, 27, 28, 30, 31;
22:2, 4, 5, 7, 8, 10, 11, 12, 17-21, 22-23, 24-25, 28;
23:9, 10-11, 12, 16, 17-18, 20-21, 23;
24:1-2, 3-4, 8, 9, 10, 11, 12, 13-14, 17-18, 19-20, 21-22, 23-25, 26, 28, 29;
25:8-10, 11-14, 16-17, 18, 19, 20, 21, 22, 23, 25, 26, 27, 28;
26:2, 17, 18-19, 20-21, 22-28;

190

27:1-2, 3, 4, 5, 6, 7, 8, 9, 10, 11, 14, 17, 19, 20, 21;

28:2, 3, 4, 5, 9, 10, 11, 13, 14, 17, 19, 21, 23, 25, 28;

29:1, 5, 9, 10, 13, 18, 19, 20, 21, 22, 23, 24, 25, 26, 27.

As you can tell by looking at the sheer number of passages above, the principles of living and conduct are numerous in the book of Proverbs. They include such things as:

1. *Practice honesty.*
2. *Seek to be healthy emotionally.*
3. *Learn to follow advice.*
4. *Beware of pride and over-confidence.*
5. *The way we treat others will determine how we are treated.*
6. *Do not talk too much.*
7. *Be diligent in your activities.*
8. *The most important thing in life is to fear God and to walk in His ways.*

There is a good bit of over-lapping between this heading and other topics. We have designed these listings so that any one of the topics will have the particular verses that pertain to it. In this way a complete study can be made of a particular subject without having to look under all the other categories. Or, this broader heading can be studied as an overview of wise principles of living.

The Words of Agur and King Lemuel
Chapters 30-31

We come now to the last two chapters of Proverbs. They actually form appendices to the proverbs of Solomon. Notice that Solomon is not the author of these two chapters. The first, 30:1-33, are the words of Agur, son of Jakeh. The second, 31:1-31, are the words of King Lemuel which his mother taught him. No additional information is given about the identity of Agur or Lemuel.

The observations in chapter 30 are diverse, but they consist of brief discussions on various topics, rather than the short proverbs we have seen in chapters 10-29. The warnings from Lemuel's mother are about the dangers and temptations a king faces, and she tells him the value of a worthy woman. Think about it: what warnings, what messages would you want to tell your son if he were about to be king? After thinking what you might say to your son, look at what Lemuel's mother said to her son.

I. The words of Agur the son of Jakeh (30:1-33):
   A. Introduction (30:1).
   B. Agur affirms that he knows nothing of that which can be known of the Holy One; it is too high for him (30:2-4).
   C. Every word of God is carefully tested and proven; do not presume to add to His words, lest you be found a liar (30:5-6).
   D. Agur prays for two things (30:7-9):
     1. Remove lies and falsehoods far away from me;
     2. Keep me from poverty lest I steal, and from riches lest I forget my need for Jehovah.
   E. A proverb: Slander not a servant to his master, lest he curse you, and you be held guilty (30:10).
   F. Description of a wicked generation (30:11-14):
     1. They curse their parents;

       2. They do not recognize their own depravity;
       3. They are selfish and arrogant.
   G. There are four things that are never satisfied (30:15-16):
       1. Sheol (the realm of the dead),
       2. The barren womb,
       3. Fields that are never satisfied with water,
       4. Fire that never says, "Enough."
   H. A proverb: The eye that mocks his father and refuses to obey his mother, the birds of the heavens will pluck it out (30:17).
   I. There are four things which leave no immediate trace (30:18-19):
       1. An eagle flying through the air,
       2. A serpent crawling over rock,
       3. A ship moving through the water,
       4. A man who has been with a maid (sexually).
          Verse 20 may have been added as a illustration. The adulterous woman engages in her sexual immorality and then wipes her mouth and says, "I have done no wickedness." The point is that one may commit fornication with a woman without immediate consequences, but that does not mean no evil has been done.
   J. There are four very unfortunate situations that occur from time to time (30:21-23):
       1. For a servant to be a king,
       2. For a fool to be filled with food,
       3. For an odious woman to be married,
       4. For a handmaid to inherit her mistress' position.
   K. There are four things that are little upon the earth, but who are exceedingly wise (30:24-28):
       1. Ants that provide their food in summer;
       2. Coneys (animals like the marmot) that make their houses in the rocks;
       3. Locusts that have no king, yet they go forth in bands;
       4. The lizard that one can seize with the hands, yet she roams kings' palaces.
   L. There are four things that are stately in their march (30:29-31):
       1. The lion, which is mightiest among the beasts and does not turn aside for any;
       2. The greyhound;
       3. The he-goat (as he leads the flock);
       4. The king who leads his army forth.
   M. If you have foolishly gotten into situations in which you had no business, or have thought evil, lay your hand upon your mouth (be cautious what you say), because, as the churning of milk brings forth butter, and the pressing of the nose brings forth blood, so the stirring of anger produces strife (30:32-33).

II. The words of king Lemuel, the message which his mother taught him (31:1-31):
    A. Introduction (31:1).
    B. Warnings from a mother to her son, the king (31:2-9):
       1. What shall I tell thee, O son that I have brought forth? (31:2).
       2. Do not dissipate your energies and plans with women, and have nothing to do with anything that destroys kings (31:3).
       3. It is not for kings and princes to drink, O Lemuel, lest they drink and forget the law and pervert justice (31:4-5).
       4. Give drink to the one ready to perish, to the bitter of soul. Let him drink and forget his poverty and his misery (31:6-7).

5. Defend those unable to speak for themselves, and administer justice to the poor and needy (31:8-9).
C. Lemuel's mother describes for him the worthy woman (31:10-31):
1. A worthy woman is rare, and her price is far above rubies (31:10).
2. Her husband trusts in her and shall profit from her; she shall do him good and not evil as long as she lives (31:11-12).
3. She is industrious and works diligently to provide for those who depend upon her and to meet her responsibilities (31:13-22).
4. Her husband's reputation in the city is enhanced by his wife (31:23).
5. She produces income for the home (31:24).
6. She is clothed with strength and dignity and does not fear the days to come (31:25).
7. Her mouth is full of wisdom and kindness (31:26).
8. She looks well to the operation of the household and does not eat the bread of idleness (31:27).
9. Her children grow up to call her blessed, and her husband praises her saying, "Many daughters have done well, but you excel them all" (31:28-29).
10. Physical appearance and beauty are deceitful and vain, but the woman who fears the Lord shall be praised. Let her enjoy the fruit of her hands, and let her works praise her in the gates (31:30-31).

Ecclesiastes
Life Under the Sun

What gives life under the sun its value? Where is the profit?

Life *without* God is vanity.

But there is an alternative. Live the way God has planned. It is God who gives us the ability to enjoy the good things of life.

A fulfilling life is the one that seeks a relationship with God.

"Fear God, and keep His commandments; for this is the whole of man."

The word *Ecclesiastes* is from a Hebrew word *koheleth*, which is commonly rendered *preacher*, the one who addresses the congregation. Some say the koheleth was the one who called the assembly together. In Ecclesiastes, it is the koheleth, the preacher, who addresses us. He is identified in 1:1 as "the son of David, king in Jerusalem." He furthermore says, "I the Preacher was king over Israel in Jerusalem" (1:12). He said, "Lo, I have gotten me wisdom above all that were before me in Jerusalem" (1:16). There can be no doubt that the writer was identifying himself as Solomon. Nevertheless, there is serious dispute among scholars about the identity of the writer. First we will list the arguments *against* Solomon's authorship, and then the arguments *for* Solomonic authorship.

Arguments against Solomon as the author:

The reasons for a post-Solomonic authorship are weighty, and many conservative scholars hold such a position. These are the chief reasons they give.

1. It is difficult to know when Solomon would have written such a book. It is written from the standpoint of a man who has tried everything and seen everything — not a young man. Yet the text of 1 Kings indicates that Solomon died without repenting of the idolatry that his wives led him into. God's last words about him are thoroughly critical (1 Kings 11:31-33, 40).

2. The language, it is argued, fits that of the fifth century B.C. (500-400 B.C.), rather than the tenth century when Solomon lived. This view is held by such conservative scholars as E. W. Hengstenberg, Edward J. Young, Franz Delitszch, and Leupold.

3. Solomon does not write simply as himself, but as "the preacher." If the book were literally written by Solomon, then it would bear his name, not just hints that this was Solomon. When the writer tells us that he is

the koheleth of the congregation, this is his way of telling us he is speaking with the persona of Solomon. In other words, they say it was written by someone else (identity unknown), but writing as if he were seeing things through the eyes of the wise man Solomon.

Arguments for Solomon as the author:

1. Those who champion Solomon's authorship say that he must have repented at the very end of his life, when there was no time left to right all the wrongs he had done, but there was time to write this book for the benefit of others. It is in keeping with the psychology of the book for it to have been written by a man who realizes a truth with blinding clarity, but too late for his own profit.

2. There is a strong correlation between numerous things in Solomon's life and points made in Ecclesiastes. For example:

   a. In Ecclesiastes 1:16, Solomon refers to the surpassing wisdom he was given from God. Compare that statement with 1 Kings 3:12 where God promised to give Solomon greater wisdom than anyone before or after him.
   b. The general description of Solomon's greatness in Ecclesiastes 2:4-10 is clearly borne out in 1 Kings 4:20-34.
   c. In Ecclesiastes 2:7 the writer mentions the servants he freely accumulated. Compare with 1 Kings 9:20-23 where the description is given of how nearly everyone in the kingdom served the king in some way.
   d. In Ecclesiastes 2:4-6 the writer describes his building projects. In addition to the temple of the Lord, and Solomon's own elaborate palace (1 Kings 6-7), many other extensive building projects and enterprises are described in 1 Kings 9:15-19, 26-28.
   e. Compare the writer's statement in Ecclesiastes 7:20 ("Surely there is not a righteous man upon earth, that doeth good, and sinneth not") with 1 Kings 8:46 ("For there is no man that sinneth not").
   f. Ecclesiastes 12:9 says that the writer "pondered, and sought out, and set in order many proverbs," while 1 Kings 4:32 says that Solomon "spake three thousand proverbs; and his songs were a thousand and five."

3. There are many thoughts and expressions in Ecclesiastes that are also found in other books of the Wisdom Literature. We feel that these similarities are evidence that Ecclesiastes was written in the same era as the other books of Wisdom Literature. For example, the point made in Ecclesiastes 5:15 is also found in Job 1:21; the thought in Ecclesiastes 4:5 is found in Proverbs 6:10 and 24:33. Note also the many proverbs found in Ecclesiastes: 4:5, 6; 7:1-9, and other passages. The similarities abound.

4. Though it is true that a majority of conservative scholars believe the Hebrew of Ecclesiastes is late, the verdict is by no means unanimous. There is also evidence that the language is old. We feel that no conclusive argument can be based on the age of the language of the book. Certainly, linguistic arguments are not conclusive enough to offset the other arguments that can be made for Solomonic authorship.

5. The most powerful argument for Solomon's authorship, though, is that the writer himself is emphatic that he was better qualified than anyone else to speak of these matters simply because

he was Solomon, with all his gifts (1:12-17; 2:1-9; 12:9-10). If, however, the writer were *not* Solomon, then his argument is for nought. Why should we have any more confidence in his thoughts than anyone else's if he is not Solomon? If it is answered that "he was inspired," then we would have to accept the following conclusions: God inspired a man to write as if he were Solomon. He inspired him to make arguments on how his being Solomon qualified him in a unique way to deal with this subject, while all the time he was not Solomon at all.

6. Those who defend Solomon as the author have more to go on than those who champion someone else. No one has even a clue who the writer might have been, if not Solomon.

We will not argue the question in more detail here. We will proceed with the belief that Ecclesiastes was written by Solomon. While we freely acknowledge that there are some difficulties in such a view, we believe that there are more serious difficulties with the other view.

Outline of Ecclesiastes:

Some divide the book into two sections of six chapters each (some four chapters and eight chapters). Others prefer three sections of four chapters each. We believe the best division of the book is into the following four sections:

I. Discourse 1— (1:2-2:6):
  A. There is nothing in life on the earth that can be depended upon for joy and fulfillment.
  B. The ability to enjoy life is a gift from God.
II. Discourse 2 — (3:1-5:20):
  A. God has a vast plan into which man must fit. It is a plan with a purpose.
  B. Man can understand the plan enough to see that God is in charge, but he can never understand it all, so that in the end he must depend upon God.
III. Discourse 3 — (6:1-8:15):
  A. Solomon defends his conclusions that God is in control, and that only He can give meaning to our lives.
  B. Often, when men see the inequalities of life, and the seemingly unfair variations in divine providence, they say, "How can there be a God?" Solomon deals effectively with these objections.
IV. Discourse 4 — (8:16-12:14):
  No new material is introduced in this last section. Solomon ties up the loose ends and draws his grand conclusion.
  A. No matter how wise we get, or how much we learn about life, there are still mysteries we cannot fathom. Do not allow these mysteries to dampen our spirits, or to diminish our enthusiasm for life.
  B. Live life fervently in view of the fact that death will come one day, and that we will give God an account of the deeds we have done.
  C. Hear the conclusion of the whole matter: Fear God, and keep His commandments; for this is the whole of man.

The most helpful book I have ever read on Ecclesiastes is the excellent little book by Walter Kaiser: *Ecclesiastes: Total Life*. I have relied on it a great deal and would like to acknowledge that fact.

Basic message of the book:

One of the most common remarks made about Ecclesiastes is that it is a very depressing book. This comment is interesting, because, apparently, many today consider life itself depressing. American society has become very humanistic and materialistic. Depression and suicide are common. People are trying to live without God, and life just is not always very rewarding and joyful. Almost anyone has some good times, some good moments, but, overall, they do not balance out the bad parts. Life without God is depressing, and many apparently do not consider it worth living.

Many people think that the writer of Ecclesiastes is agreeing with that pessimistic outlook on life. They think that all through the book he is saying that life is worthless, vain, empty, hopeless. There is a tidbit of pleasure here, a little wisdom there, but it is all worthless. Then at the very end of the book, he drops us a rope of hope and says, "Fear God and keep His commandments; for this is the whole duty of man." If that is the message, then its view of life is depressing.

But look at the message in its entirety. The writer of Ecclesiastes affirms the pointlessness of life, the vanity of life without God, *but he does not recommend life without God. There is an alternative to the vanity of life.* His conclusion is, "Fear God and keep His commandments, for this is the whole of man" (12:13). The *whole book* is an argument that it is God who gives us the ability to enjoy life, and that *apart from Him* life is empty and meaningless. All of life is therefore summed up in the responsibility to seek a relationship with God and to live life His way. The following passages show that throughout the book the writer is dealing with the difference God makes in the meaning of life: 2:24-26; 3:13, 17-18; 5:1-7, 8, 18-20; 8:12-13; 9:7-10; 11:5, 9-10; 12:1-7, 13-14. The mistake that men make about life on earth is expecting more from it than there is. If we see ourselves from a divine perspective, then earthly life occupies its proper place in our existence.

One of the points made in the book is that life is arranged so that, even though most of us have ideas of just what we would like from our life here on earth, we cannot count on achieving our earthly goals (1:2-11; 9:11). Even those who do obtain most of what life on earth offers (such as Solomon) find it unfulfilling by itself (2:1, 25, 18-23). Likewise, the book teaches this corresponding principle: *There is good in our life here upon the earth.* We should consider that good a blessing from God. The enjoyment of one's work (3:22), the enjoyment of food and drink (5:18-20), and the enjoyment of youth (11:9-10) are all gifts from God, *but remember that these things are not what life is really all about.* Life is about having a relationship with God (12:13), and He will "bring every work into judgment, with every hidden thing, whether it be good, or whether it be evil" (12:14).

The Old Testament reveals very little of what lies beyond this life. In Ecclesiastes men are taught to rely upon God for the future. There are many inequities in life; there are situations beyond our power to change. We must trust in God to deal with such things. The implication is clear that there will be a future time when God will right all wrongs, even if not in this life. In a way the message of Ecclesiastes can be summed up in the words of Jesus: "Seek ye first the kingdom of God and His righteousness, and all these things shall be added unto you" (Matt. 6:33).

Definition of terms as used in the book:

Solomon uses some expressions over and over in the book that we need to analyze to help us understand the points he is making when he uses them.

1. **Under the sun:** At least thirty-four times, the writer uses the expression "under the sun," or similar expressions such as "under heaven," or "on earth." Solomon is by no means denying that there will be life after death, and he emphasizes that God will hold us accountable in that life

for the way we have lived life under the sun. But life after death is not the emphasis of Solomon's study in this little book. What makes life of value here on this earth? Why am I here? What should I pursue as my primary goal? Solomon had the wealth to allow him to indulge every whim, and he had the wisdom to observe the outcome of his experiment. He makes his search, and he says that if one relies only upon the things found in this life for its meaning, then it is all worthless. There is no profit. The only way man can be happy *upon this earth, in his daily life,* is to choose to live as God prescribes.

What a valuable lesson for modern man! The saint who serves God today has the hope of eternity with God in heaven, but he also has the very best this life has to offer, because he is letting God plan his life.

2. **Vanity:** The word is used in several different senses in Ecclesiastes. It can mean sorry, empty, worthless, fleeting. Remember that Solomon's study is to find out what makes life valuable *under the sun.* There is nothing I can do, nothing I can pursue as my life-long goal that has any lasting meaning apart from God. Just as regularly as the writer declares that "all is vanity," he also says that there is some pleasure in nearly every endeavor. He says enjoy the pleasure, but realize it is only fleeting. When earthly life is over, there is nothing left to say this was worth living for; this earthly pursuit made my life complete.

3. **Profit:** What can I hold in my hand as lasting value from any endeavor in life? What profit do I show? Will it follow me beyond the grave? Can I eat more meals than the poor man, can I wear two sets of clothes at once? When the end comes, what will I have to show for my time here on earth? Even more than the word *vanity,* this word *profit* reaches the heart of the book's message.

4. **Wisdom:** The book of Proverbs cries out to the young man to seek for wisdom, that it will be his greatest asset. Yet here in Ecclesiastes wisdom is called vanity. It only increases man's awareness of the inequities of life. Is there a contradiction? No, the wisdom praised in Proverbs is the wisdom that has the fear of Jehovah as its firm foundation (Prov. 1:7). The wisdom that is called vanity in Ecclesiastes is worldly wisdom — that gained from learning more and more information that some man has discovered. Solomon declares that wisdom (even this earthly wisdom) is better than folly, because it lets you see where you are heading and helps you avoid some of the pitfalls of life, but in the end the wise man dies and is buried just the same way the ignorant man dies and is buried. So, what is the lasting profit?

5. **The wise man:** In most of the Wisdom Literature, and particularly in Proverbs, the wise man is the one who has looked at his own experiences, and has looked at the experiences of others, and he has learned the lessons of life. He learns early to avoid the pitfalls of the wicked, to follow the ways prescribed by Jehovah. He is wise in the truest sense of the word. In nearly every incident where the expression is used in Ecclesiastes, the wise man is merely the one who has learned much information (what we would call the "well-educated"). This use of the term fits with the rest of the book, because Solomon's study was about life under the sun. Is the gaining of an education (wisdom) the end-all purpose in life? Can the well-educated man depend upon his education to bring him happiness and fulfillment in life? And the answer is no, it is only a grasping after the wind.

6. **The fool:** Throughout the Wisdom Literature, the expression "the fool" is used to describe the one who refuses to learn from his own experiences, or from those of others. He is the one who

has chosen to reject God's ways. He does not listen to rebukes from the wise, nor does he turn toward God even when his way leads him to calamity. Some contexts emphasize the idea that the fool brings hardships upon himself because he is deaf and blind to advice. Other contexts emphasize that the fool is one who has shown himself to be condemned before God by his conduct (see Psa. 14:1 for example).

7. **The young man:** This is the one called "the simple one" in the book of Proverbs. In Ecclesiastes he is referred to as the young man — the one who has not yet experienced the ups and downs of life. He does not know what path to choose, because he is inexperienced. In Proverbs, the term carries with it a degree of naivete', possibly one who is older but who is not watching and learning the lessons before him. The cry in Ecclesiastes is to this young man, the one who has not yet chosen the wrong path: "Look around you. Choose the right paths. Enjoy your blessings, and realize how blessed you are while you are experiencing them." The point is summed up most beautifully in Ecclesiastes 12:1-8: "Remember now thy Creator in the days of thy youth...," before it is too late.

Summary of Ecclesiastes

The words of Koheleth, the son of David, king in Jerusalem.

Discourse 1 — 1:2-2:26:

In this section Solomon argues that there is nothing in life on the earth that can be depended upon for joy and fulfillment. The ability to enjoy life is a gift from God.

Life is the greatest of vanities. Everything is empty and without profit. What is the point of all that a man does under the sun? Generations come and go. The sun rises and sets, and the wind blows in a circle. The rivers run into the sea, but the sea is not full. That which has been is what will be. If anyone says, "This is new," why, it is not new at all. It happened long ago in ages past. There is no memory of past generations, and in time to come, this generation will be forgotten also. (1:2-11.)

Remember that it is not merely life Solomon speaks of, but life <u>without God</u>, life for itself. The various activities of life give man no profit, nothing he can take with him when it is all over. One of the most important concepts of Ecclesiastes is this idea of "profit." What do we have to show for having lived?

It is ironic that the features of the world that do not have life are the ones that endure, while men, made in the image of God, are here today and gone tomorrow. Compared to the rivers and mountains, we humans are ephemeral — a mere mist that appears for a little time and then drifts away (see James 4:14). How soon we are forgotten. Certainly the meaning of life for man cannot be discerned from the world.

I, Koheleth, was king over Israel, and I decided to seek to know, to find out by wisdom, the meaning of earthly activity. I concluded that it is a grievous task that God has given men.

There are so many things that seem pointless and unfair, and the inequities of life are numberless. So I consulted with myself and said: Look, I have gotten wisdom greater than all before me. I also have had much experience in matters of wisdom and knowledge. Therefore I decided to explore wisdom and madness and folly.

My impression was that to gain profit from wisdom and knowledge was like trying to grab the wind, because there is much grief in wisdom, and he who increases his knowledge also increases his sorrow. Therefore any profit is balanced out by the disadvantages. (1:12-18.)

Kaiser expresses the point this way: "Man is trapped by the difficulty of the problem and his own divinely implanted hunger to know" (p. 54). Of all creatures, man is the one who asks, "Why?" and who searches for meaning in life. It is God who has planted in us this desire to know.

The wisdom here is not the wisdom that has the fear of God as its foundation. It is worldly wisdom, wisdom under the sun. The more wisdom and knowledge one has, the greater his awareness of the inequities of life, and the greater his frustration at his inability to understand all he sees around him.

I tried mirth, thinking that perhaps I could find good there. It was empty. Laughter is crazy, and mirth, what does it accomplish? I continued my search, how to cheer myself with wine, to make sense of folly, until I could see what men should be doing under the heavens during their lives.

I built buildings, planted vineyards, prepared gardens and parks. I bought men-servants and maid-servants and acquired great possessions above all that were before me, but I did not lose sight of what I was doing; my wisdom remained with me. I withheld nothing from myself. Whatever I wanted, I got, and I enjoyed certain results of my labors, but this was all my labor was good for. From the standpoint of giving meaning to my life, when I looked at all I had done, it was empty, and a grasping after wind. There was no profit under the sun. (2:1-11.)

Solomon learned that such things do not have the power by themselves to bring joy and satisfaction. He does not deny that there can be momentary joy from such things, but the point Solomon argues is that such joy cannot be <u>depended</u> upon, and, as he proceeds, he shows why (2:18-23 for example). Compare this passage with Jesus' story of the rich man in Luke 12:13-21.

I compared wisdom, and madness, and folly. I saw that wisdom excels folly as much as light excels darkness. Yet wisdom does not guarantee blessings, because what happens to the fool can happen to the wise man. Therefore, why is wisdom better? I saw then that wisdom is also vanity. How frustrating, that the wise man must die as the fool. So I hated life, because there was no satisfaction in anything I did. (2:12-17.)

Again, we must remember that this wisdom is wisdom under the sun, not the wisdom which is from above that is based upon the fear of God.

I hated my work also, because I can only leave it to the man who follows me. Who knows whether he will be wise or a fool? So what is the point of all my labor? One man with great skill and effort builds a great estate or kingdom, and he leaves it to someone who does not know what to do with it. (2:18-23.)

Here Solomon shows why one cannot count on joy, as he plans his life, by saying, "I will find fulfillment in the works I accomplish."

So far as his work is concerned, there is no guarantee that a man will be able to eat and drink and enjoy the good things his labor brings him. This is a gift God gives. Who can eat or enjoy any blessing apart from God? To the man who pleases Him, God gives true wisdom and knowledge; but to the sinner He gives hard labor, to gather and heap up wealth that it may be given to the one who pleases God. (2:24-26.)

I believe that our paraphrase of 2:24-26 reflects the correct translation of these verses. This and similar passages are not teaching that you must enjoy whatever task you have. They are teaching that man cannot assure himself of good, or joy, from what he does. These are gifts from God. As James puts it in the New Testament: "Every good gift and every perfect gift is from above, coming down from the Father of lights" (James. 1:17).

Discourse 2 — 3:1-5:20:

God has a vast plan into which man must fit. That plan has a purpose, and we can understand enough of it to see that God is in charge. But we can never understand it all, so that in the end we must depend upon Him.

What we do in life is to a great degree determined by circumstances. For everything there is a time and season. The circumstances of life determine what is appropriate. To a great extent, therefore, it is not we who determine what we do, but life, as God has appointed it. It is a difficult task God has given men to live upon the earth. He has made everything beautiful, or appropriate, in its time. He has also set eternity in men's heart, yet so that they cannot fully comprehend the work God has done from the beginning even to the end. (3:1-11.)

God's plan covers all of life and every facet of existence. This is not a plan in which God has predetermined every thing that happens. Rather, it is a plan in which God has taken into account everything that life holds. Life is not the paradise that it was before the fall in the garden, but God is in control, and all things are in His hands. The thought is much the same as that expressed by Habakkuk: "The Lord is in His holy temple; let all the earth keep silence before Him" (Hab. 2:20).

God has given men a difficult situation to handle. In His all-embracing plan, God has accounted for evil and for good, for war and for peace, for birth and death. He has also set in man a desire to know and to understand the real purpose of existence. Yet man is unable to fathom all the facets of life and to understand how all things fit into God's plan. Of all creatures, man is the only one that seeks answers to his questions. He is made in the image of God, and even if he does not acknowledge that fact, he manifests that it is true because he is driven to find purpose in existence.

I know that there is nothing better for men than to rejoice and to do good so long as they live. It is God's gift to men that they should eat and drink and enjoy good things from their labor. Nevertheless God is in charge, and whatever He does it is for ever. The system we live under is one which He has ordained, and He has done it that we might fear before Him. That which is was planned long ago, and God is able to relate the past to the future. (3:12-15.)

If God can give men the good things of life, and the ability to enjoy those gifts, and if He gives some knowledge of His all-encompassing plan, why does He allow men to live in a system where there are many inequities and unanswered questions? It is so that we might fear before Him. As we pointed out earlier, throughout the book of Ecclesiastes, not just at the end, the writer stresses the importance of man's relationship with God. Regarding the fear of 3:14, let me quote the words of Kaiser: "The one who fears God dreads nothing more than God's disfavor. Such a worshiper wants nothing more than to know the living God intimately and submit to His will. And God Himself wants to be known and obeyed by man; accordingly, He has shut man up to the enigma of life, yet given him an unquenchable hunger to know how it all, from the simplest to the most profound, fits with everything else" (p. 68).

In the section 3:16-4:16, Solomon looks at many of the things in life that are apparent contradictions to the idea that God is in charge, that He is in His holy temple.

One of the things I noticed in life is that, where justice should be, wickedness resided. I said to myself, God will judge the righteous and the wicked. (3:16-17.)

One of the inequities of life is that so often, where justice should be, wickedness is found. Men have had frequent opportunity to know that often the legal system is the last place they can hope to find justice, and that, more often than not, judges seem to have the least judgment of all. Nevertheless, this problem need not upset us because God will judge the righteous and the wicked.

I reasoned within myself that God tries the sons of men, that they may see that [*without Him*] they are but beasts. In many ways men appear to be but beasts. What happens to animals happens to men. One dies as the other dies. They all have one breath. Man without God is no better than the beast. Everything that dies returns to the dust. The spirit of man goes upward, but the spirit of the animal goes downward when they die. (3:18-21.)

God points out to man his frailty in order that he may seek God and that he might receive from His hand the gifts of life and the ability to enjoy them.

So I saw that a man should rejoice in the doing of what he does; that is his portion. For who will bring him back to see the results of his work after him? (3:22.)

Solomon was not encouraging a Pollyanna approach to life in which we try to find good where there is no good. Nevertheless, some people never derive satisfaction from anything. To what extent they can, they should enjoy what they do, because when they are done with earthly life, there will be no coming back to savor it. Contentment is largely a state of mind in which one determines to be at peace in whatsoever state he is (Phil. 4:11). God's portion for man is to give him joy in his activities. To enjoy properly what life has to offer, man must seek God and fear Him. The point is not that the God-fearer will never have any hard times, but that he will recognize the blessings of God and will rejoice in them. He will rejoice that even in the chaotic, upsetting times of life, God is in control.

I pondered on other inequities of life. I looked at the oppression around me. So many things are unfair. Then I praised the dead that have been dead a long time. How much better off they are than the living. Yes, even better is the one who has never been born, because he has never seen all the evil things that are done under the sun. (4:1-3.)

Oppression is one of the horrible experiences of life. We see the tyranny of men over their fellows, and we ask: How can these things happen in a world ruled by God? The Psalmist had a similar question in Psalm 73. He confessed that he had almost been overcome by this problem, because he saw the prosperity of the wicked (73:3). The question continued to plague him until he "went into the sanctuary of God, and considered the latter end of the wicked" (73:17). God is the judge; He does not ignore nor forget the wickedness of men. Ecclesiastes itself emphasizes that "God will bring every work into judgment, with every hidden thing, whether it be good, or whether it be evil" (12:14). As men of this world wrestle with these inequities of life, often they take the solution mentioned above: life is not worth living; they wish they had never been born; it is better to be dead, and many commit suicide. But throughout the book, the writer shows that there is an alternative: live one's life for God. Rely upon Him to right the wrongs that exist.

So much of what men do is motivated by rivalry with one another. This is also pointless, a grasping for the wind. In thinking about this, one may be foolish and decide not to try, not work. Just sit with folded hands — and eat his own flesh. A far better solution is to be moderate in one's desires. It is far better to eat a handful in peace than two handfuls with hassle and strife. (4:4-6.)

It is discouraging when one tries his best only to be envied and resented for it. Sometimes one is tempted simply to give up and do nothing. A generation of Americans decided to "leave the rat race;" they became beatniks, and later, hippies. They wound up "eating their own flesh." We cannot act the part of a fool and a sluggard without consuming our own flesh. We cannot be intimidated by the jealousy of others so that we do nothing. We do not need to worry about the envy of others as we prosper, but we also need to be moderate in our desires so that it is possible for us to be satisfied.

Another sad situation I saw was when a man is alone. He has neither son nor brother. Nevertheless, he is not satisfied, but works on accumulating, though he may ask himself, "For whom am I working and slaving and doing without?"
It is much better not to be alone. If one falls, the other can pick him up. If two lie together, they will have warmth. Likewise, if a man overcomes one man by himself, he will not be able to overcome two. A cord made of three strands is not easily broken. (4:7-12.)

Loneliness is one of the things that may keep us from enjoying our work or possessions. Solomon is still dealing with arguments showing that earthly things cannot be counted on for joy and satisfaction in living.

Popularity is fickle and fleeting. There may be an old king who does not know how to listen to advice anymore. A young man comes from nowhere and is made king. Everyone is enthusiastic about their new, young king. The time will come, however, when his subjects will become unhappy with him. (4:13-16.)

Because of these inequities in life, many would question whether there is a God, and whether He has a plan for men. In 5:1-17 Solomon raises cautions about such reasoning and gives explanations for some of the moral and ethical imbalances of life. Some men are quick to reject God and to embrace unbelief. Solomon shows that such an alternative is completely unacceptable.

Be very careful when you go to the house of God. It is far better to go planning to listen and to profit than to go through the motions of offering a sacrifice. The fool who does things like that does not even know he is doing evil. Do not be rash in what you say. Do not impulsively say things in God's presence, because He is in heaven, and you are on earth, so let your words be few.

When you make a vow to the Lord, do not put off paying it. He has no pleasure in fools. Pay what you vow. It is much better not to vow at all then to vow and not do what you say. Do not let your mouth cause you to sin. Do not say before the magistrate that it was a mistake. Why would you want God to destroy you? Fear God. (5:1-7.)

In this passage, once again, we see that Solomon does not wait until the end of the book to draw his conclusion that men should fear God and serve Him. He makes a powerful argument to that effect here in the middle of the book.

If you see the oppression of the poor, and justice and righteousness denied in a state, do not wonder at such a thing. Neither be dismayed. One higher than the high sees what is done and will deal with it. It is a wonderful blessing when a king understands that he will prosper as his land prospers and rules accordingly. (5:8-9.)

If one loves silver, he cannot be satisfied with it. When one gains more than he can use, what can he do with it except look at it? A man who works hard sleeps well at night, but the wealthy man cannot sleep because of worrying about his possessions.

One of the greatest ironies I have seen in life is that a man will love silver and accumulate it to his destruction. Through ill fortune it can be lost. Has he not noticed that, if he has begotten a son, when he was born he had nothing in his hand? As a man was born with nothing, so he shall die, and will take nothing from his labor which he can carry in his hand. So what is the point of all his travail and striving? Just a grasping for the wind. Nevertheless, there are men who will spend their days bearing heavy burdens, and feeling very distressed, for just such empty goals as this. (5:10-17.)

Look, what I have seen to be good and of benefit for a person is to eat and to drink and to enjoy good in all one's labor as long as he lives. This is God's gift. To every man to whom God has given riches and wealth and the ability to enjoy it, this is the gift of God. (5:18-20.)

This argument of the writer takes us back to the question of what <u>profit</u> is there in labor and wealth? We have here a conclusion similar to the one in 2:24-26. Nothing this life has to offer can guarantee joy and fulfillment to men. Only God can do that. And, as the writer pointed out in 2:26, God gives that blessing to the one who pleases Him. Therefore, enjoy the benefits, the pleasures that come from the work or the possessions you have, but do not place your dependence upon them.

Discourse 3 — 6:1-8:15:

What Solomon does in this section is to take his conclusions that God is in control, and He alone can give meaning to our lives, and he defends those conclusions. Often, when men see the inequalities of life and the seemingly unfair variations in divine providence, they say, "How can there be a God?" How often people of the world, who do not know God at all, follow this line of reasoning. Solomon deals effectively with these objections.

In the first section of this discourse, the writer shows that apparent inequalities are often not what they seem. A close look behind a man's outward prosperity may help to explain the apparent inequalities of divine providence. (6:1-7:14.)

One of the bad things I have seen is for God to give a man riches and wealth and honor, and then not give him the ability to enjoy his blessings. The quality of life is certainly not in the length of days. A miscarried child is better than one who may live a thousand years twice told and yet enjoy no good. (6:1-6.)

All a man's labor is to fill his mouth, and yet the appetite is never satisfied. It is better to enjoy what one has than to be constantly wishing for what he does not have. (6:7-9.)

Prosperity may not always be what it appears to be. It is not the possessions that one has, but the ability to enjoy them, that counts. If prosperity satisfies, why can those who clamor for material things never have enough?

Whatever has been, it was named long ago, and it is known what man is, neither can he contend with Him that is mightier than he. When men talk endlessly about life, and what they think should be done, do they improve the situation? Because who [*among men*] knows what is good for man? (6:10-12.)

God knows us far better than we know ourselves. He knows what is truly best for men. Prosperity is not necessarily a blessing. We need to accept God's blessings as He gives them and not be forever clamoring for more.

Having raised the question, "What is good for man?" Solomon proceeds to tell us through a series of parables about some "good" things that are better than prosperity. (7:1-14.)

A good reputation is better than precious oil, and the day of death is better than the day of one's birth.

Most men do not see it this way, but though one does not have the finer things of life, if he has a good reputation, he is more blessed than if he were wealthy. Men generally consider the day of death to be a tragedy, but then the race is over, the toil is done, and the influence of a good life can linger on as the aroma of precious perfume.

It is better to go to the house of mourning than to the house of feasting. The wise will profit from the house of mourning, but the fool likes to frequent the house of mirth.

Once again, most would consider it far better to go to a party than to a funeral, but adversity is superior to pleasure because of the benefit it confers upon men who meditate upon it.

It is better to hear the rebuke of the wise than to hear the singing of fools. The laughter of fools lasts no longer than the crackling of thorns under a pot.

Which is better, to be rebuked, or to have friends laugh and sing with one? The world would say, without question, to have friends laugh and sing with one. But the situation is not what it appears on the surface. The reality is that the rebuke of the wise is better because of the profit it brings.

Wisdom is as good as an inheritance, even better, for the man who still lives. Wisdom is a defence even as money is, but wisdom can preserve the life of the one who has it.

Think about the work of God. Who can straighten what He has made crooked? It is impossible to predict prosperity and adversity. So, enjoy prosperity, and in time of adversity, profit from the experience. God has made such times to be unpredictable so that man cannot always figure out why they come.

In some ways, this passage is worth the writing of the book: Enjoy prosperity, and in times of adversity, consider. In the New Testament, the apostle Paul had learned in whatsoever state he was to be contented (Phil. 4:11). He had learned to treasure even the bad times, because it was then he depended upon Jesus. When he was weak, he became strong, because then he depended upon the strength of Jesus instead of his own powers (2 Cor. 12:9-10).

In the following verses, Solomon shows that many times, an accurate assessment of a man's character and life will explain apparent inequalities in divine providence. (7:15-29.)

Let me tell you what I have seen in my fleeting life. Here is a righteous man who perishes in his righteousness, and here is a wicked man who prolongs his life even in the midst of his wickedness. Do not go to extraordinary lengths to establish your own righteousness, neither attempt to be too smart. On the other hand, do not abandon yourself to wickedness, nor be foolish. Why would you bring your life to a premature end? You should pay attention to this point: it is the one who fears God who will come through everything. Wisdom is a strength to the wise man more than ten rulers of a city. [*Wisdom serves as a counsellor to the wise man, and the fear of God is the true wisdom*]. (7:15-19.)

Solomon is not saying that one can be too righteous in the sense of pleasing God and actually doing His will. He is referring to the efforts some make to go beyond what is required. They invent their own rules for obtaining holiness and righteousness. They become guilty of will-worship, and appoint all sorts of ordinances, which may make quite an impression on their observers, but which have little value in guarding against the indulgence of the flesh (see Col. 2:20-23).

Nobody is perfectly sinless. Do not expect too much of others. If you listen too carefully to what others are saying, you may hear your servants curse you, but then you may have cursed someone else in your own heart. (7:20-22.)

Guided by the principles of wisdom, I set out to be wise, but it was an impossible task. To understand the workings of life is far off and very deep. Who can fathom it? I set myself to explore thoroughly for wisdom, to understand things, and to know the wickedness of folly and the foolishness of madness. (7:23-25.)

This passage could be rendered, "I had set myself to explore..." The writer keeps before us his objective in this essay. Remember that the writer has already told us a great deal about how life can have meaning through trust in God and in the fear of Him. He continues here his refrain that the world gives us no answers about the meaning of life. Indeed, the world has no answers!

I find more bitter than death the woman whose heart sets snares and nets, and whose hands are handcuffs. The one who seeks to please God will escape her, but the sinner will be captured by her. This is what I have found: weighing one thing against another to find the meaning of life, for which I am still looking, one man in a thousand have I found, but a woman among all these I have not found. What I have discovered is that God made men upright, but they have hunted for new ways to do wrong. (7:26-29.)

As in Proverbs, Solomon warns against the immoral woman. The general point he makes seems to be that people are given to wickedness, and this causes many of their problems. In fact, among men he has found very few who are genuinely worthy, upright men, but among women, not one among a thousand. Why did Solomon say this? Does it reflect the prevailing condition of things? Solomon spoke of his experience. Therefore he spoke of what he had found in his circles. I would think that a harem of seven hundred pagan wives, and three hundred concubines, would not be the best place to look for a worthy woman. My experience has been that among the saints of God, there are as many, if not more, worthy women, than men. There are other explanations I have read of this point, but they seem very speculative and far-fetched.

God has designed that a large part of the apparent inequalities of divine providence are alleviated through righteous government. How often the troubles of a nation are brought upon it by a corrupt government, and how often a corrupt government arises from a corrupt people. (8:1-14.)

Who is the wise man, and who knows how to interpret a thing? One can see the wisdom of a man upon his face; it makes a difference in his countenance.

Keep the king's command in view of your responsibility to God. Do not be hasty to go out of the king's presence. Do not persist in an evil thing, because the king does what he pleases. The king's word has power, and no one says to him: "What is this you are doing?" He who obeys the king will stay out of trouble with him, and a wise man can tell when the time is right to say or to do a thing. For every matter there is a time to bring it up, a time to make a decision on it. The misery of man is that it is often difficult to know what to do or to say because he cannot know the future, and no one can tell him. He just has to do the best he can.

Nobody has power over his spirit to keep his spirit. In other words, no one has power to keep himself from dying when death comes, just as no one can get a furlough while the battle rages. Neither shall wickedness deliver the one who is given to it. (8:1-8.)

The first verse of chapter 8 goes with the subject in 7:19-29. It also is appropriate to include it in 8:1-8 because of the emphasis upon wisdom in verse 5.

How often men complain today over the injustice in the world, and how seldom they realize that men are responsible.

Life and death are in the hands of God. This too is frustrating to man. The remedy is to place oneself in the care of God, and trust Him to make all things turn out well.

In my research many times I have seen these situations: There are occasions when one man has power over another to do him harm. I have seen the wicked buried, when they had come and gone from the holy place, and they were forgotten in the city where they had done their evil. Just because sentence is not executed quickly upon the wrong doer, do not assume that he will escape judgment. Sometimes men see that punishment is postponed and decide they can give themselves wholly to evil. But no matter how long a sinner lives, and how much he seems to prosper, I know that it shall be well with them who fear God and who conduct their affairs in fear before Him. It shall not be well with the wicked, neither shall he be able to prolong his days, which are like a shadow, because he does not fear God. (8:9-13.)

The questions that inevitably come to mind about why God allows injustices to occur are answered here. Men are free moral agents. God allows them space to make their choices, good and bad, and to see the consequences of their decisions. Nevertheless, He observes, and without fail the wicked will be judged, and the righteous will be rewarded.

A senseless thing that I have seen is that things happen to the righteous man as if he were wicked, and there are wicked men to whom things happen as if they were righteous. (8:14.)
Then I recommended mirth, because a man has nothing better to expect under the sun than to eat, and to drink, and to be joyful, and that this should accompany him as long as God gives him to live. (8:15.)

Solomon says that the child of God can acknowledge therefore that there are things he does not understand about the way things work. But he is given enough insight about the workings of God to believe that God knows what he is doing. In view of this, he can commit his life to the Lord, and enjoy the pleasures this life affords, realizing that his blessings come from God.

Discourse 4 — 8:16-12:14:

In this last section, Solomon does not introduce new material. He ties up the loose ends and draws his grand conclusion. He acknowledges that no matter how wise we get, or how much we learn about life, there are still mysteries we cannot fathom. He strongly urges that we not allow these mysteries to dampen our spirits, or to diminish our enthusiasm for life. We must live life fervently in view of the fact that death will come one day, and that we will give God an account of the deeds we have done.

Solomon's first point is that though much remains that we do not know about life and how it works, we must not allow the mysteries of life to rob us of the joy we can have from God. (8:16-9:9.)

When I studied to know wisdom and to see the travail that goes on upon the earth (for there are those that labor night and day) I beheld the arrangement of God, that man cannot understand all that God does. No matter how much he seeks to know, he will not be able to understand it all. In spite of all this, I set my heart to study this point: the wise and their works are in the hand of God. Whether it be love or hatred, man does not know. All is before them. (8:16-9:1.)

It is important to see that God, even in His inspired scriptures, does not tell us everything about how He works. One cannot always tell by the outward circumstances of a thing whether it is an object of God's love, or of His hatred. We can come to a greater understanding of life, but we can never know it all, because God will never reveal it all in this life. Many times, our frustrations and questions do not come from what we do not know and cannot explain about life; they come from our unwillingness to trust in God, to place our affairs in His hands.

So often the same event will happen to the righteous and to the wicked, to the one who sacrifices and to the one who does not sacrifice. This is a bad thing, and it is also bad that the disposition of men is to do evil, and they behave irrationally, and then they die. For the one who is still alive there is hope, because a living dog is better than a dead lion. The living face death constantly, but the dead are gone; they face nothing anymore [*The time of trial is over for them. The text does not say that the dead are conscious of nothing anywhere. It says that they do not have any more portion in life under the sun - v.6.*] (9:2-6.)

Go on, therefore, with your activities. Eat your food with joy, and drink your wine with a merry heart. Let your garments always be white, and put the finest oil upon your head. Enjoy life with your wife whom you love all the days of your fleeting life, the life which God has given you. That is your portion of life, and of your labor. (9:7-9.)

What a wonderful, cheering message for earth dwellers. So you don't know everything. So things do not always work out right. Go ahead and enjoy the pleasures God gives us. The message is this: do not make the obtaining of pleasure the end-all of your existence, but wholeheartedly enjoy, without guilt, the good things of life that come your way.

A second point the writer makes in this final section is that we must not allow the mysteries of life to paralyze us into inactivity. (9:10-11:6.)

Whatever your hand finds to do, do it with your might, because there is no work, nor planning, no exercise of knowledge, or of wisdom in Sheol where you are going. (9:10.)

Again, the point is not that there is no existence after death. The context all the way through the book is life under the sun. All earth-type planning and working will be over.

I resumed my observations and saw that the race is not to the swift, nor bread to the wise, nor yet riches to men of understanding, nor yet favor to men of skill; time and chance happens to them all. Man is not able to take into account all the factors involved in an endeavor. As fish caught in a cruel net, or birds taken in the snare, so men are often caught by a bad time and are taken by surprise. (9:11-12.)

Though the world is arranged so that most often the battle is won by the strong and the shrewd, and the race is most often won by the swift, God has ordained things so that it is not always so. It is impossible to take into account all factors. The purpose of this arrangement is that men may learn to depend upon God for success. We have a proverb which expresses the thought: the best laid plans of mice and men often go astray. To put it another way: men cannot guarantee themselves success.
If we wait to plow, or to build, or to invest, until we know the future, and can take into account every factor that may affect our effort, we will never do anything. Be as wise as possible, but the time comes to act.

I have seen this example of wisdom under the sun, and it greatly impressed me. There was a city, with only a few men to defend it against the enemy. A great king came against the city, and besieged it. Now in this city there was a poor wise man, and by his wisdom he delivered the city, yet no one noted or remembered that it was the poor man that saved the city.
I observed from this that wisdom is superior to strength, nevertheless wisdom is often set at nought, and a wise man's words are not heeded. The words of the wise heard in quietness is better than the shout of one that rules among fools. Wisdom is better than weapons of war, but

one sinner destroys much good. (9:13-18.)

Wisdom is the highest of earthly qualities, and the least appreciated. Wisdom may be extremely effective and yet little noticed or rewarded. In chapter ten, Solomon gives us a Proverbs-like sample of this wisdom. Wisdom is far preferable to foolishness

In the same way that dead flies cause the perfumed oil to smell bad, so a little foolishness will spoil a great deal of wisdom and honor. A wise man keeps his wisdom handy and ready to use. The fool keeps his heart on his left, awkward and unhandy to use. When a fool walks along, his heart forsakes him, and he says to everyone that he is a fool. (10:1-3.)

If the spirit of the ruler rise up against you, do not leave your place, because a soft response will prevent great offenses. One bad thing that I have seen in this life has to do with rulers: a very foolish, unworthy person is set in a high place, and the rich sit in a low place. I have seen servants upon horses and princes walking like servants upon the earth. (10:4-7.)

Be careful not to provoke the ruler lest he retaliate against you. Rulers are themselves often foolish and self-serving, in that they appoint their favorites to high posts of honor, not the best people for the jobs.

When one undertakes any endeavor, there are dangers that are inherent in the effort. If a man digs a pit, let him be careful not to fall into it. If a man breaks down a wall, let him be careful lest a serpent bite him. Whoever moves stones will get hurt in the process if he is not careful. One who splits wood is in danger. If one's axe is dull, it requires more strength to do the job, but wisdom is profitable to direct any undertaking. If the serpent bite before it is charmed, then there is not much need to call the charmer. (10:8-11.)

In any kind of task there are risks and dangers possible. Wisdom advises to take precautions when you do a job, and take them before the job, not afterward, when it is too late.

A wise man's words are gracious, but a fool will stick his foot into his mouth. From beginning to end, his speech is foolishness. He will multiply his words, yet he does not know what he is talking about. Any fool's labor tires him out because he does not even know how to go to town. [*We would say he does not even know to come in out of the rain.*] (10:12-15.)

Woe to a nation when its king acts like a child, and the princes begin feasting early in the morning. Happy is a nation when its king is a noble man. Laziness will cause the roof to leak. It is very bad when all rulers are concerned with is partying and drinking, and when they think that money solves all problems. Do not revile the king even in your thoughts, and do not speak evil of the rich in your bedroom, for a bird will tell him what you said. (10:16-20.)

Many ills are brought to a nation by selfish, inept rulers. Even so, be careful what you say about such rulers, because he may have ways of knowing what you said, which you did not realize.

Cast your bread upon the waters, and after many days, you will find it again. Be liberal with your possessions because you never know when bad times may come upon you. One who spends all his time observing the wind will never sow, and he who worries about the clouds overmuch will never reap. Just as you do not know the way of the wind, or how the bones grow in the womb of a mother-to-be, so you will never know all the work of God, who does everything. In the morning sow your seed, and in the evening, do not hold back, because you cannot know what will prosper. You must do the best you can. (11:1-6.)

What great advice! We simply can not foresee all the ripples an action may cause in the sea of life. Work hard, try different things, be generous to others. It will come back to you. As we pointed out earlier, one who would accomplish things cannot forever be waiting to see what the wind is going to do, to see if it will rain. Sometimes, even with the best effort to take into account the various factors that may affect a given enterprise, we will fail, but we must go ahead and try again. Eventually we will succeed.

The last point before Solomon's final conclusion is that the knowledge that death will surely come, and that judgment is certain, should influence everything we do in life — our work, our family life, our worship, our play — everything we do. (11:7-12:8.)

Truly the light of day is sweet, and a pleasant thing to behold. Yes, and if a man lives many years, let him enjoy them all, but remember that the days of darkness will come, and they shall be many. (11:7-8.)

Live life with zest, but remember that it will all end, and there will be a reckoning.

Rejoice, O young man, in your youth, and be cheerful, and live your life as you think best, but know this: in connection with all you do, God will bring you into judgment. Therefore do not provoke Him and do not engage in sins of the flesh. Your youth will be gone before you know it. (11:9-12:7).

Young man, enjoy the days of your youth, but remember two things: One, you will be judged for everything you do, even for things you do when you are young, even for your "wild oats." Two, youth will not last long; enjoy it while it is possible.

Remember your Creator in the days of your youth, before the decline of your body and mind, when you no longer enjoy the things of this life, before your body returns to the dust, and your spirit goes back to God who gave it. (12:1-7.)

In 12:1-7, Solomon uses a series of figures, such as the sun, and the light of the moon and stars being darkened, and the doors shut, and the golden bowl broken, to represent the shutting down of the systems of the body and the failure of its members. His point is clear: do not wait until life is over, and you have nothing left with which to serve God, to remember your Creator. Young man, learn the lessons now! Do not wait until your life is over and wasted to see how you should have lived.

Final conclusion - 12:8-14:

Vanity of vanities, says Koheleth; all is vanity. (12:8.)

By repeating the statement made in 1:2, Koheleth lets us know he has written his essay and *is ready to draw his conclusion. It is that life is empty and meaningless — <u>without God</u>.*

Because Koheleth was wise, he continually taught the people knowledge. He listened for and searched out many proverbs. He also tried to find excellent messages that would convey truth. (12:9-10.)

Solomon was certainly one of that fraternity known as the wise, or the sages, and he excelled them all (1 Kings 4:31). According to 1 Kings 4:32, Solomon spoke three thousand proverbs, and his songs were one thousand and five.

The words of the wise are as goads to move men to action; they are as nails, well fastened, which can be depended upon. Furthermore, my son, be advised: there is no end to the making of books, and much study is tiring to the body. (12:11-12.)

Surely Solomon's point is that men may write their books and make their studies, and little will be accomplished except to tire themselves and their readers, but the words of God through His inspired men are those things to which we should give heed. They contain those thoughts that we shall truly find to be profitable.

The conclusion of the matter is this: Fear God and keep His commandments, for in this the whole of man's existence is summed up. Because God will bring every work into judgment, with every hidden thing, whether it be good or whether it be evil. (12:13-14.)

All of our life is encompassed by the great plan of God. The child of God has a world view from God. He knows what life is all about. He does not understand everything about life, but he knows where he comes from and where he is going. He knows that life has a purpose, and that the backdrop of life is the divine plan. He also realizes that man is a responsible being who lives his life before the eyes of God, and that one day he must give an account for the work he did, the pleasures he sought, the attitudes he had, and the way he treated others. To him there is a goal for which he strives, an end for which he longs: to be with God eternally, and to share life with Him forever.

Song of Solomon
A Love Song

The Song of Solomon is a love poem that is nearly 3,000 years old.

There are two possible settings for the love poem:

1. **It may be Solomon and his new bride as they seek to resolve their differences and come to a loving relationship.**

2. **It may be Solomon trying to win the love of a maiden who loves an humble shepherd.**

We take the second of these two settings as our basis for interpreting the book.

Interpretations of the book:

Opinions concerning this work have varied through the centuries. Almost all scholars confess the difficulty of interpreting the book. No one has advanced an interpretation and then successfully fitted in all the details from the text. The casual reader finds it perplexing, and comes away wondering who was speaking, and what it was all about. We join with others in admitting the difficulty of interpreting the book's message, but we think there was a reason why the Holy Spirit inspired someone to write it, and there was a reason why it is included in the Bible. We do not take a dogmatic view about its interpretation, but we offer reasons why we think one of the prevalent views seems to fit the text best, and then we analyze the book on that basis.

There is no serious objection to Solomon's authorship. Even some who argue most convincingly against Solomon's authorship of Ecclesiastes say that the evidence is strong that Solomon wrote the Song of Solomon. Therefore we will proceed on the basis that Solomon is the author. First Kings 4:32 says that Solomon wrote a thousand and five songs, but the Bible includes only this one.

Through the years there have been two primary interpretations given for the book, with the second primary one broken down into two different views. Let us look at each interpretation, and give reasons for and against each one.

1. In the early church, and until the Protestant Reformation, the most popular view was that the Song of Solomon was an *allegory* of Christ and the church. That view said there was no real love story at all, no real people under consideration. Instead, it was all a story written to describe Christ and His church.

    Even later scholars have had a tendency to cling to such interpretations, claiming that the story of Solomon and Shulammith is *typical* of Christ and the church. That is, they say that it was a story about Solomon and a Shulammite maiden, but that Solomon typifies Christ in the story, and that the maiden is His bride, the church.

We flatly reject the allegorical view; neither do we accept the view that it is a type of Christ and the church. The major argument advocated for the typical view is that the Song of Solomon would not have been included in the canon of scripture unless it had a religious, spiritual lesson; therefore it cannot be merely a love poem. This argument assumes that love (whether married love or mating love) is not a proper spiritual subject. Yet God ordained marriage and all the aspects of love that accompany it. Marriage and the family are dealt with at length in the scriptures.

No quotation is made in the New Testament from the Song of Solomon. There is never any application of the book to Christ and the church. What a chance Paul missed to use the Song of Solomon in Ephesians 5, when he compared Christ's relationship with the church to the husband/wife relationship — if that is indeed the message of the Song of Solomon. We cannot use assumptions to argue that the Song of Solomon is not what it claims to be.

2. The book is a poem of love. But among those who take the position that this work is a love poem, and not a love poem describing Christ and the church, there are still two positions. One is that the groom in the story is Solomon, who in fancy talks of himself as a shepherd wooing his rural bride. The other is that there are three main characters: Solomon the king, who seeks to win the heart of the Shulammite maiden, and a shepherd from her home to whom she has given her heart. There are good arguments made for each of these positions. Let us examine each view:

A. Married love. Love between Solomon and his bride:

If the poem is describing married love, it is that between a new bride and groom, because he is still wooing her. It simply does not fit the long-established love between two partners who have welded a good marriage. It is a description of two young lovers seeking to resolve their differences, and to come to the pleasant, loving relationship of newlyweds.

Those who argue for this position say there are only two lovers: Solomon and his bride, the Shulammite maiden (called Shulammith for convenience). As they describe each other, and as they woo each other, and respond to each other, Solomon sometimes speaks as a king with all the pomp of royalty and majesty around him, and at other times as a rural shepherd seeking to win her with an humble love. She, in turn, imagines her royal lover as an humble shepherd, one whom she can describe in terms of the beauties of nature.

But this view seems a strained interpretation. When Saul was anointed king, there had never been a king in Israel before him, and he returned to farming in uncertainty about his duties (see 1 Sam. 10:26; 11:5). David was brought from the field, where he was watching sheep, to Samuel, who waited in Bethlehem to anoint him king (1 Sam. 16:1-13). David kept his love for sheep throughout his lifetime (see 2 Sam. 12:1-6; Psalm 23). Either of those kings could have described the beauties of nature vividly; he could have in fantasy sought to woo a maiden in terms of a shepherd or a farmer. But Solomon was born and reared in a palace in a city. He never, so far as the record goes, spent any time as a shepherd or farmer. He would have no reason to fantasize himself as someone else. He had wealth and power, everything he needed to woo a maiden. And why would a maiden who had agreed to marry a king want to describe him as a shepherd? Most young women fantasize up from their station of life, not down. It seems logical to assume that any maiden who accepted a king's proposal would want the pomp and ceremony that would come to the wife of a wealthy king. Why would she fantasize him in any other way? It seems that if it is a poem describing a bride and groom and their first efforts at solving their differences and winning each other's love, then they had major problems. Each is fantasizing, and neither is loving the other for what they really are.

- B. Mating love. A courtship as Solomon tries to win a young maiden:

    According to this view, Solomon saw a young maiden and had her brought to the royal residence and put her in the care of the court ladies. He tries to persuade her to marry him by offering her elaborate compliments and by displaying all his wealth and pomp. She, however, is in love with an humble man from "back home." She dreams of him and longs for him, even while she is in the beautiful surroundings of the king's harem. If this is the interpretation, Solomon fails to win her love, and she returns to her shepherd lover in the last chapter.

    Those who object to this view say that if the song is about two lovers — Solomon and a shepherd, each wanting to win the young lady's heart — the book is not very flattering to Solomon. It tells of his failure to win a beautiful young wife, while a simple shepherd holds her heart. If that is the situation, why would Solomon want to write of his failure for all generations after him to see?

    In reply to that objection, the story itself is beautiful. From a purely literary standpoint it is worthy of the interest of Solomon. There is no reason to think that the story, written in the form of a play, could not have been based upon an incident in the life of Solomon. He saw a beautiful maiden and sought to make her another of his wives. He wooed her and impressed her with his wealth and royalty, but she was already in love with someone else. She was devoted to her true love, and her heart was not for sale. She would not trade her genuine love for an humble man for all the riches laid up for a wife in the king's harem. Solomon was a wise and good man for many years. Surely such a plot would have intrigued him; the Spirit could have used Solomon's inclination to write this account and have guided him in writing this touching story of commitment and true love.

    We feel that the book is a song of mating love, of the love that moves a man and woman to desire marriage and to get married. If this book describes courtship, and the strength of true love and commitment, then the Bible deals with all aspects of life. If it describes married love, then the Bible never deals with the subject of mating love. Yet, since God ordained marriage, and the leaving of parents to be joined to a marriage partner is part of God's pattern, then God's plan includes the proper wooing and winning of a mate. We feel that the book is included in the canon of scripture because it does deal with mating love. No spiritualizing of the book is necessary to justify its inclusion in the Bible.

The poem is written in the form of a play. It is in conversation style, with very little description of its setting. Dialogue is easy to understand if we know who the speakers are, but, unfortunately, the little book does not tell who is speaking in each verse, or paragraph. That makes it very hard to interpret. It is impossible to be certain who is speaking at some points, and sometimes we cannot be sure of the meaning of individual verses and passages. The different speakers can be determined to some degree from the pronouns used in the original Hebrew; for example, it is possible to tell whether it is a man or woman speaking, or whether it is an individual or a chorus, but beyond that no one can be certain about who says each line. Therefore we cannot be dogmatic in our treatment of the song.

Another thing that adds to the difficulty in understanding the book is that it is a love poem that is nearly 3,000 years old. Therefore the compliments seem strange to us. We cannot visualize the scenes they are describing, nor can we see beauty in things our lives have never touched. A girl of today reads the poem and thinks that she would not like those compliments, or a young man reads it and feels ridiculous using those phrases to describe the girl he loves. So, we read the little book and wonder if we are interpreting it correctly as a poem of love. Maybe it has some vague, allegorical application after all! No, it is obvious that it was written as love poetry, but we have to accept it in its own setting of time and place.

Let us learn a very important lesson from this little book. Love can be pure and chaste; it can be steadfast and loyal; it can withstand the lures of riches and pomp and not be willing to sell itself to the highest bidder; and it can see the beauty of true love from an humble person. Do not let us become so preoccupied with sex that we superimpose the morals of our century upon a beautiful poem of love from many years ago. Rather let us look at the message of the book and lift our own attitudes above those portrayed by Hollywood.

Let us stroll through the book, as it were, and look at this play and try to see the story before us. We will be taking the position there are two men trying to win the heart of the Shulammite maiden. With that in mind, let us begin by listing the possible actors in this play:

Solomon:
He is the mighty king who has great riches to offer a young maiden. He can give her everything money can provide. He can give her a life of luxury. He describes her with elaborate compliments.

The Shulammite maiden (Shulammith):
She has grown up working in the fields and vineyards. Solomon has seen her, has brought her to his court, and is trying to win her love.

The Shepherd:
He is a young man from the Shulammite's home town. He is not present in the court of the king, but he is very much present in the young maiden's heart. Shulammith longs for him, dreams of him, and searches for him. When he speaks in the first chapters, it is only in her mind as she remembers their conversations, or as she daydreams about him.

The ladies of the court (the chorus):
These are the ladies of the harem. These are either the maids who take care of all the wives, or the wives themselves. Since they show no jealousy of this pretty young maiden the king is wooing, then it seems they were not the other wives. These ladies of the court cannot understand how any girl could turn down the opportunity to be a wife of the king. They cannot understand her longing for her shepherd.

Narrator:
There are spots in the poem that seem to be explanations. If so, then those words are spoken by a narrator who is supplying information for the reader.

The Shulammite's brothers:
Her brothers speak in the last chapter.

The Song of Songs which is Solomon's
1:1

Shulammith: May he kiss me with the kisses of his mouth! (*Then speaking in her heart to her beloved*) for your love is better than wine; your oils are pleasant; your name is like the purest oil. Therefore the maidens love you. Draw me near you (1:2-4a).

Chorus: Let us run after you! (1:4b).

Shulammith: The king has brought me into his chambers (1:4c).

Chorus: We will be glad and rejoice in you; we will praise your love more than wine. Rightly do they love you (1:4d).

Clearly the Shulammite maiden desire's her lover's kisses (1:2a), but that raises a question already: Is she wanting kisses from Solomon her groom, or from someone else whom she loves? Those who argue the two-party position say that everything that follows is Solomon and his bride working out their difficulties and enjoying getting acquainted. We will see.

In verse 2b, the speaker addresses someone in the second person, and the use of the second person continues through verse 3. The possessive pronouns show that the Shulammite is addressing her lover.

From the statement, "The king has brought me into his chambers" (1:4c), it seems evident that Solomon has found the Shulammite maiden and has brought her to his palace to woo her and wed her.

This passage is one of the more difficult to sort out, but we believe that this analysis of the dialogue is best.

Shulammith: Do not look down on me, O you daughters of Jerusalem, because I am burned black by the sun. I am black, but beautiful. My mother's sons were angry with me and made me work in the vineyards, but my own vineyard I have not kept (1:5-6).

Tell me, O thou whom I love, where do you feed your flock? For why should I come looking for you as if I were a stranger? (1:7)

Chorus: If you do not know where your lover is, O you fairest among women, go follow the trail of the flock and feed your kids beside the shepherds' tents (1:8).

We begin to see a distinct difference between the Shulammite maiden in the chambers of Solomon attended by her chorus of maidens, and the location of her shepherd lover. She does not know where he is at the moment, but Solomon is relatively nearby — and he is not feeding his sheep.

Solomon: I have compared you, O my love, to a beautiful mare among Pharaoh's chariots... (1:9-10).

This passionate outburst is from an individual, and the language is much more what we would expect from Solomon, a king, with its comparisons to a horse among Pharaoh's chariots, and jewelry, rather than from a shepherd lover.

Chorus: We will make for you chains of gold and beads of silver (1:11).

The switch from "I" to "we" sounds as if the chorus joins in with the praise from Solomon to Shulammith.

Shulammith: While the king sat at his table, I could smell the fragrance of my perfume. My beloved is to me like a sachet of perfume sending forth its pleasant smell. My beloved is like a bouquet of henna blossoms in the vineyards of Engedi (1:12-14).

These are the thoughts of the Shulammite. It sounds as if they were perhaps at a meal: "The king sat at his table," but the maiden is not speaking to the king. She is thinking, not of "you," but of her beloved. She says he is like a bundle of myrrh, a small pouch of myrrh that lies between her breasts. The point is not the intimacy, but the pleasant smell that would come forth from a sachet so placed; so the memory of her beloved is pleasant. It seems that this thought of her lover takes her into a reverie that lasts through 2:7.

Shepherd: How beautiful you are, my love, how beautiful! Your eyes are like doves (1:15).

This is either the voice of Solomon or the shepherd. The imagery is from nature and does not fit with the highly polished compliments that we find another actor in this play giving the Shulammite. This voice is that of the shepherd. Remember that he is not actually present in the company of the king, but she is remembering how he would speak to her.

Shulammith: How handsome you are, my love, how charming. Our couch is green. The beams of our house are cedars, and our rafters are firs (1:16-17).

The Shulammite returns her lover's compliment and, in her thoughts, is with him in the forest, away from the splendid palace of Solomon.

I am just one of the flowers that grow in Sharon. *(She minimizes herself.)*

Shepherd: As a lily among thorns, so is my love among the daughters. *(Her shepherd lover will not accept her disparagement of herself. She stands out above other women as a lily stands out among thorns.)*

Shulammith: As the apple-tree among the trees of the woods, so is my beloved among the young men. In his shadow I sat down with great delight. His fruit was sweet to my taste *(continuing the figure of the apple tree)*. He brought me to the banqueting house, and his banner over me was love. Sustain me with raisin cakes, refresh me with apples, because I am faint from love. His left hand is under my head, and his right hand holds me. I adjure you, O daughters of Jerusalem, by the gazelles, or by the deer of the fields, that you disturb not, nor interrupt love until it pleases (2:2-7).

There are a couple of questions in this section that make it difficult. Is Shulammith sick from love in the sense that she is deprived of her sweetheart's company, and she pines for him, or is she faint from the ecstasy and joy of being with her lover? Perhaps the latter fits the language better. The second question concerns 2:7, which appears to be a refrain. It appears again in 3:5 and in 8:4. Is the Shulammite telling the maidens not to interrupt her time with her beloved, or is she asking them not to prompt him to come to her? Probably the former.

Shulammith: Listen! My beloved! Look, he is coming, leaping as a deer upon the mountains. Look, he is standing behind our wall. He looks in the windows and glances through the lattice. My beloved spoke, and said to me:

> Rise up, my love, my dear, and come away. The winter is past; the rain is over and gone. The flowers are springing up, and the birds are singing. The fig-tree is ripening her green figs, and the vines are in blossom. Come, my love, my dear, come away with me. O my dove, let me see your face, let me hear your voice, because your voice is sweet, and your face is beautiful.

Capture the foxes that spoil the vineyards, because our vineyards are in blossom. My beloved is mine, and I am his. He feeds his flock among the flowers. Do the things you have to do until the day cools, and evening comes (2:8-17).

The section 2:7-3:5 expresses the daydreams of Shulammith. The Shulammite hears the voice of her beloved. He was not with her as Solomon was; her beloved is coming from afar. The context makes it clear he is not really there, so the maiden must be dreaming or imagining his coming for her. When he comes, the Shulammite's sweetheart speaks to her, asking her to come away with him. It is spring, and the earth is putting forth. He tenderly calls her his love, his fair one, his dove.

In verse 15 the Shulammite is thinking of her rural surroundings, of the vineyards where she worked, where she came to know and to love her shepherd. She says, "Let us capture the foxes that spoil the vineyard." Then she professes her love for her sweetheart and thinks of him feeding his flock among the flowers. She closes her reverie wishing he would come to her.

Shulammith: At night, as I lay on my bed, I sought the one I love from the depths of my heart, but he was not there. I said, I will arise, and go about the city, and look for my sweetheart. I looked all over for him, but I did not find him. I asked the watchmen that patrol the city if they had seen him. It was just after I left them that I found him, the one I love so much. I held him and would not let him go, until I brought him to my mother's house. I adjure you, O daughters of Jerusalem, that you not interrupt love until it pleases (3:1-5).

The maiden is dreaming, and in her dream, she rises to find her lover. She goes out into the streets of the city, not the rural setting she speaks of so fondly, to search for him. It is highly unlikely that a young woman under the care of the Jerusalem's daughters would actually have done such a thing. Also, if it were Solomon she was seeking, she looked for him in a strange place — go out and look for the king, who lives in the palace, in the streets?

Narrator: Who is this that comes up from the wilderness like pillars of smoke, perfumed with myrrh and frankincense? Look, it is the litter of Solomon. Sixty mighty men of Israel are his bodyguards, everyone an expert in battle. Solomon made himself a palanquin with pillars of silver, the base of it gold, and the seat covered with purple. Go forth you daughters of Jerusalem and behold king Solomon, wearing the crown wherewith his mother crowned him on his wedding day (3:6-11).

From the wilderness Solomon comes in stately procession. Does he come to the maiden's home? There is nothing to indicate this. Instead the daughters of Jerusalem are told to go out and behold King Solomon with the crown his mother has given him for his wedding. If there are only two main characters in the play, this might be when Solomon brought the Shulammite to become his wife. Is it a flashback to 1:4, when Solomon brought the Shulammite to his chambers? Or has there been some time, and now Solomon has fetched her to marry him? The word "espousal" is best translated "wedding," or "betrothal." There is no mention whatever of his bride to be. The attention is wholly upon the king. Perhaps it is best to think that he has been gone and has returned, thinking to make the Shulammite his bride. Some would argue that this would explain the Shulammite's lonesomeness and longing for her lover. The only problem is that the imagery she uses to express her longings does not fit Solomon at all. This scene simply plays up the tension that builds as Shulammith is pressured to become one of Solomon's wives, while her shepherd remains her true love.

Solomon: How beautiful you are, my dear, how beautiful. Your eyes are as doves behind your veil... (4:1-5).

Solomon praises Shulammith's beauty, her teeth, her lips, her mouth, her neck, and her breasts. He compares her neck to the tower of David. In this chapter there are two passages praising the Shulammite's beauty: verses 1-5, and verses 7-15. Does all this praise come from Solomon, or from the shepherd, or does part of it come from one and part from the other? Note there is no direct response from the Shulammite to the praise in verses 1-5. Compare her statement in verse 6 with her reply to the praise in verses 7-15. One must believe that she does not care for the praise of the first lover. The figures in verses 1-5 contain a mixture of some agricultural features, but there is also the reference to the tower of David, upon which there hang a thousand bucklers. This imagery sounds much more as if it comes from Solomon.

Shulammith: I will get myself to the mountain of myrrh and to the hill of frankincense until the evening (4:6).

These words probably belong to the Shulammite, although some make it Solomon, with heavy sexual overtones.

Shepherd: You are altogether beautiful, my love. Come with me from Lebanon, my bride. You have carried my heart away captive with just a glance. How wonderful is your love, my bride. Your lips are as sweet as honey; the smell of your garments is as fresh as Lebanon. My sweetheart is an enclosed garden with all sorts of precious fruit and spices (4:7-15).

These words are much more consistent with a shepherd's background than verses 1-5 were. Note the response of Shulammith to these words.

Shulammith: Awake, O north wind, and blow south. Blow upon my garden, that the spices of it may flow out. Let my beloved come into his garden and eat his precious fruits (4:16).

Shulammith responds intensely and passionately to the words of her shepherd lover. This passage furnishes a good opportunity to make this point. Some interpretations of the Song of

Songs turn it into a marriage manual. Many of the expressions are exaggerated to make them sexually explicit in content. Such an approach is a distortion of the book. The jaded, sensual views of modern America are injected into a love song written 3,000 years ago.

There is nothing shameful about the sexual relationship. In its place it is wonderful, but it is not nearly everything in a relationship. When a couple is very much in love, and planning marriage, they are conscious of the sexual attraction they have for one another. They anticipate the sexual aspect of marriage, but that is not all there is for a young man to enjoy about his sweetheart, or for a young woman to enjoy about her loved one. There is no need therefore to make 4:7-16 exclusively a sexual passage. The anticipation of marriage includes the contemplation of the sexual relationship, but it includes everything else that a couple loves about one another as well.

Shepherd: I have come into my garden, my sister, my bride. I have gathered my myrrh with my spice; I have eaten your honeycomb with my honey; I have drunk my wine with my milk. Eat, O friends; drink deeply, O loved ones (5:1).

Shulammith imagines the consummation of their marriage. She and her sweetheart are married. In her thoughts they are together, and they have each other. The shepherd bids those who are in attendance at the marriage feast to join in their celebration. Some think that these last words are the chorus saying to the couple, "Eat, O friends; drink deeply of love," but the term translated love or beloved is plural. If it is the chorus, they are including the shepherd with the Shulammite as the "loved ones."

Shulammith: I was asleep, but my heart waked. I thought to myself: It is the voice of my loved one who knocks, saying, "Open to me, my sister, my love" (5:2-8).

The Shulammite dreams of her lover, but he is not there. She hears his voice. The description is exactly that of a dream. She thinks of the inconvenience of getting up. Everything seems real, but when she gets up, filled with ecstasy at the thought of seeing her loved one, there is no one. Some have this lover to be Solomon. He comes asking to be let into his bride's bedroom, but when she does not readily open to him, he leaves. The course of true love is not running smoothly. But this interpretation just does not seem to fit. She goes out searching the streets — for Solomon? She asks the watchmen if they have seen — Solomon? The watchmen slap her, apparently having no idea that she has any connection with Solomon. They take her mantle from her, cruelly teasing her, but she does not find her lover. The refrain of 5:8 is a little different this time. This time she adjures the daughters of Jerusalem that if they find her beloved to tell him that she is faint from love. The context here demands the idea that she loves him very much, but she cannot express her love to him, she cannot enjoy the love she has for him. She is lovesick.

Chorus: What is so great about your beloved, most beautiful of women? What is your beloved more than any other beloved? (5:9).

The chorus of maidens is intrigued. They want to know what is so special about her loved one? They do not understand why the Shulammite cannot be satisfied with anyone but her shepherd lover.

Shulammith: My loved one is the handsomest of ten thousand. He has a finely shaped head, with thick, black hair (5:10-16).

Through the eyes of love, the Shulammite tells about her lover, how handsome he is, how wonderful he is.

Chorus: Where has your beloved gone, so we will know where to seek him with you? (6:1).

It is almost amusing that when the daughters of Jerusalem hear the description of Shulammith's loved one, they are ready to help her look for him. It would indeed be a tragedy to lose such a one. But their response does not fit the idea that Solomon is Shulammith's love, because they already knew him quite well.

Shulammith: My loved one is gone down to his garden, to the beds of spices (6:2-3).

The word "garden" is the same one as in the expression, "Garden of Eden." Shulammith's beloved has a garden in which spices and flowers grow. Once again she professes her love for him. Her sweetheart feeds his flock among the lilies. Solomon might pretend to be a shepherd, but I seriously doubt that he fed his flock.

Solomon: You are as beautiful as Tirzah, my love, as lovely as Jerusalem, as awesome as an army with banners (6:4-9).

Even though some of the references in this section sound like the shepherd (for example, the pastoral references in verses 5b-6, and the reference to "my dove"), the speaker in this passage is probably Solomon. Some of the expressions match those in 4:1-5. The terms in verses 4-5a, and the references to the queens and concubines would point to Solomon. He would be the one to know the reaction of these women to the Shulammite maiden, not the shepherd. Solomon wants her to become another of his wives — one among many, even though he says she stands unique among them. With her shepherd, she will be his, and he will be hers.

Narrator: Who is she that looks forth as the morning, fair as the moon, clear as the sun, awesome as an army with banners? (6:10).

If verses 4-9 are Solomon's words, verse 10 is not. These words belong either to the chorus or to the narrator. It seems to fit a narrator, because by this time, the chorus of maidens knows Shulammith and would not ask this question.

Shulammith: I went down into the nut garden to see the green plants of the valley, to see whether the vine budded, and the pomegranates were in flower (6:11-12).

These words belong to the Shulammite. Is this a flashback to when she was first found and taken by Solomon, or is this after she has left to go back home, and he comes to try to persuade her again? Perhaps the answer is found in 6:13a.

Chorus: Return, return, O Shulammith. Return that we may look upon you (6:13a).

Shulammith: Why will you look upon the Shulammite? (6:13b).

There are different ways to analyze this passage. Both 6:13b and 6:13c may be the voice of the Narrator, but most likely this the modest Shulammite wondering why they would wish to look upon her.

Chorus: It is as looking upon the dance of Mahanaim (6:13c).

The chorus praises the dancing of Shulammith, saying it is like the dancing of Mahanaim. The reference is to some common festival held at Mahanaim, at which excellent dancing was beheld, or the reference may be a way of saying that the maiden's dancing was like that of angels, since Mahanaim was associated with the hosts of angels (Gen. 32:1-2). The Shulammite proceeds to dance, and the daughters of Jerusalem praise her beauty.

How beautiful are your feet in sandals, O prince's daughter! (7:1-5).

It is the chorus of ladies who praise the maiden's physical beauty, displayed as she dances. In verse 5 they speak of the beauty of her ebony black hair by which the king is held captive. The words that follow are Solomon's.

Solomon: How attractive and how pleasant you are, O my love. Your stature is like a palm tree, and your breasts are like its clusters (7:5-9a).

The speaker here is seeking to claim the Shulammite for his own. It seems, as he does, that the maiden thinks of her sweetheart in terms of what Solomon has been saying and completes his thought in 7:9b, but applies it to her shepherd sweetheart. Solomon says, "Your mouth is like the best wine," and she finishes the thought:

Shulammith: That goes down smoothly for my beloved! *(The Shulammite's words are very decisive:)* I am my beloved's, and he wants me. Come, my beloved, let us go into the field; we will lodge in the village; we will go down to the vineyard. There I will give you my love. (7:9b-13).
   Oh that you were as my brother. When I should find you outside, I would kiss you, and no one would think anything about it (8:1-4).

The Shulammite longs for the kisses of her sweetheart. She wishes he were her brother so that when she met him, she could kiss him freely, and none would think anything about it. Together they could love one another. Note the refrain: Do not disturb or interrupt her.

Narrator: Who is this coming up from the wilderness, leaning on her beloved? (8:5a).

What a contrast between Solomon's coming up from the wilderness with all his wealth and pomp (3:6-11), and these two sweethearts coming up together.

Shulammith: Under the apple tree I awakened you. There your mother was in travail with you (8:5b-7).

The personal pronouns make it clear that the speaker is addressing a male. We believe the male is the shepherd. Perhaps the best interpretation to make of the shepherd's mother being in travail beneath the apple tree is that his mother was very troubled about her son, wanting him to be happy, but not knowing how to insure that he would be. The Shulammite goes on to speak of the power of love, of the cruelty of jealousy, but she pledges her undying love to her shepherd.

Her brothers: We have a little sister. How can we make her appeal to someone? (8:8-9)

Shulammith's brothers seem typical of brothers. They wonder how they can make their little sister appeal to someone enough to make him want to marry her. If she were a wall, they could decorate her battlements with silver, but what can they do to make a little sister pretty?

Shulammith: I am a wall, and my breasts like the towers of it (8:10).

The maiden has grown up. She has become beautiful. No one has to do anything to help her attract a suitor. She has found him.

Shepherd: Solomon had a vineyard at Baalhamon... My vineyard, which is mine, is before me (8:11-12).

It seems that here the shepherd is speaking of one of the vineyards of Solomon, which he leases, but the shepherd has his own vineyard, the Shulammite, which is sufficient for him.

You who dwell in the gardens, the companions listen for your voice. Cause me to hear it.

As indicated, we believe this is the shepherd' voice. He is speaking to the maiden. Her companions, the daughters of Jerusalem, listen for her voice, but he is the one who will hear her words now.

Shulammith: Make haste, my loved one.

The maiden calls for her sweetheart to hurry to her.

Bibliography

Aharoni, Yohanan, and Avi-Yonah, Michael. *Macmillan Bible Atlas*. Revised ed. New York: Macmillan Publishing Company, 1977.

Biblia Hebraica Stuttgartensia. Edited by Karl Elliger and Wilhelm Rudolph. Stuttgart: Deutsche Bibelgesellschaft, 1983.

Eerdman's Handbook of the Bible. Edited by David Alexander and Pat Alexander. Grand Rapids: William B. Eerdmans Publishing Company, 1973.

Hailey, Homer. Syllabus on *The Psalms*. n.d.

Crockett, William Day. *A Harmony of the Books of Samuel, Kings, and Chronicles*. Grand Rapids: Baker Book House, 1966.

Keil, Carl and Delitzsch, Franz. *Biblical Commentary on the Old Testament*, 6 vols. AP&A edition in six vols. (Vols. 2, 3, 4). Reprint. Grand Rapids: Associated Publishers and Authors, Inc., n.d.

Kaiser, Jr., Walter C. *Ecclesiastes: Total Life*. Chicago: Moody Press, 1979.

Waldron, Robert E. and Sandra L. *In the Days of the Judges*. Waldron Publications, 1992.

_____. *History and Geography of the Bible Story*. Fairmount, Indiana: Guardian of Truth, 1984.